D0160414

In Your Eyes
a Sandstorm

The publisher gratefully acknowledges the generous support of the Humanities Endowment Fund of the University of California Press Foundation.

In Your Eyes a Sandstorm

WAYS OF BEING PALESTINIAN

ARTHUR NESLEN

 University of California Press Berkeley Los Angeles London

University of California Press, one of the most
distinguished university presses in the United States,
enriches lives around the world by advancing scholarship
in the humanities, social sciences, and natural sciences.
Its activities are supported by the UC Press Foundation
and by philanthropic contributions from individuals and
institutions. For more information, visit www.ucpress.edu.

University of California Press
Berkeley and Los Angeles, California

University of California Press, Ltd.
London, England

Library of Congress Cataloging-in-Publication Data

Neslen, Arthur.
    In your eyes a sandstorm : ways of being Palestinian /
Arthur Neslen.
        p.   cm.
    Includes bibliographical references.
    ISBN 978-0-520-26427-4 (cloth : alk. paper)
    1. Palestinian Arabs—West Bank.   2. Palestinian
Arabs—Gaza Strip.   I. Title.
    DS110.W47N47   2011
    305.892′74—dc22   2011012388

Manufactured in the United States of America

20   19   18   17   16   15   14   13   12   11
10   9   8   7   6   5   4   3   2   1

For Chris Mooney,
fighter, dancer, friend, inspiration

In Lidda, in Ramla, in the Galilee, we shall remain like a wall upon your chest, and in your throat like a shard of glass, a cactus thorn, and in your eyes a sandstorm.

Tawfiq Ziad

CONTENTS

ACKNOWLEDGMENTS

So many people helped in the writing of this book that I have never known all their names. Inevitably, I will have forgotten some of those who went an extra mile for me, misplaced the business cards of others who should have been mentioned, and lacked the space to fit in everyone who contributed. But an imperfect list of credits is better than none. Any kudos for this book should be shared, even if the mistakes are mine alone.

My most profound thanks must go to Bilal Abu Ajua and the Hamas policemen in Gaza City who protected me when I could not protect myself. Without their urgent intervention, there might have been no book. I am also indebted to the Sarraj family, and to Sara and Daragh for their kindness, comfort, and care in the days that followed.

My literary agent, Sam Stoloff, practically initiated this project, added clarity and direction to it, and worked steadfastly to bring it to fruition. Niels Hooper, my editor, fought in my corner and made sure I was well advised when advice was needed. Eric Schmidt, Sheila Berg, Kate Warne, and the UCP production team were as thorough, skilled, and committed as I could possibly have wished.

Every interview in this book has a story behind it, and many of them involved the painstaking work of a translator or fixer. Bekriah Mawasi in Jerusalem was a stalwart and resourceful aide throughout my time in Palestine, and Rami al-Bali in Jenin was tireless, generous, and professional. The following people also helped to set up or translate interviews: Ahmad Abu Zubeyda, Grietje Baars, Khulood Badawi, Emmanuelle Bennani, Celine, Hillel Cohen, Uri Davis, Khalil Fawadleh, Ingrid Jaradat Gassner, Asmaa al-Goule, Angela Godfrey-Goldstein, Tom Greenwood, Koen de Groof, Abd al-Hafez, Wisam al-Haj, Gazi Hamad, Reem el-Hamed, Samir al-Harb, Hassan at the TRC, Amira Hass, Samar Hawash, Brigitte

Herremans, Haifa Jamal, Amal Ka'awash, Liad Kantorowicz, Adam Keller, Vivienne Korsten, Maan News Agency staff, Mahmoud, Mahmoun, Nur Masalha, Rory McCarthy, Ayman Nijim, Sonia Nimr, Dotan Olivier, Rosemary Sayigh, Charmaine Seitz, Omar Shaban, Reem Shadid, Samira in Tel Aviv-Jaffa, and Lisa Taraki. I am also deeply grateful to the interviewees who shared their stories with me; I regret that I am able to include only about half of their accounts here.

Special thanks are due to the friends whose encouragement and solidarity helped me through a sometimes difficult four years, in particular, Ilona Aronofsky, Duncan Cohen, Armen Georgian, Kim Linekin, Jessica McCallin, Russell Miller, Jesse Rosenfeld, Joel Schalit, Rachel Shabi, Leslie Taylor, Matthew Tempest, Martin Todd, Dave Watson, and Ian Wright.

Agnes Bertrand pushed me to write the book, and her warmth, wise counsel, and belief in the project enabled me to finish it. My family—Chaim, Diana, Esther, and Asher Neslen and John Cresswell—provided all the inspiration and unstinting support that I could have asked for.

My final appreciation is reserved for the Palestinians, the most hospitable people on earth, still denied a land of their own. This book is also dedicated to them. May their voices be heard outside the battlefields.

INTRODUCTION

The Palestinian people have captured news headlines for over forty years, but the world has heard surprisingly few of their voices. Mainstream politicians, shell-shocked victims, and fiery guerrillas have occupied the limelight, but even their words have been shoehorned into predictable story lines. We hear almost nothing from ordinary Palestinians, and as a result we know almost nothing about their lives, times, and beliefs. Bad PR and a creaky national consensus share some responsibility for this, but it is first a measure of how dominant the Israeli perspective has become. From many experiences as a journalist, I can give two small examples of how Palestinian views were suppressed and the attendant consequences.

In August 2001 I was working in the BBC radio newsroom when Abu Ali Mustapha, leader of the Popular Front for the Liberation of Palestine (PFLP), was killed at his Ramallah desk by rockets fired from an Israeli helicopter. The PFLP put out a statement vowing revenge, but a high-ranking Israeli official called to ask us not to air it, in case it contained a coded cue for retaliation. The acting editor decided not to broadcast, in apparent deference. Three weeks later the PFLP assassinated the Israeli tourism minister, Rehavam Ze'evi. Their forewarning was not heard by listeners to BBC radio news bulletins.

By contrast, Palestinians who phoned in to complain of bias were often treated with disdain. After one such call, an editor on shift with me slammed down his phone, exclaiming, "If I get one more phone call from a moaning Arab . . . ," to general office mirth. Palestinian complainants tended to come from lower down the ranks of officialdom, and this one had no implied "terror collusion" threat to back up his sally in the media war. News writing sometimes suffered as a result.

But the BBC was far from being the most unfair broadcaster of Middle

East news. There are structural reasons for the unequal treatment applied to Israelis and Palestinians across the international media as a whole—racist assumptions, Holocaust guilt, the fear of lobbyists, the relative power of their "terror" and "occupation" narratives, the ability to impose meaningful economic and political sanctions. These all have particular trajectories and effects, but their net result is the same: It is the cadence of the Israeli story we hear, while authentic and representative Palestinian voices are muted. This book is intended to help redress that imbalance.

I grew up the child of left-wing and anti-Zionist Jewish parents in London. The first encounter I had with the Palestinian issue was when I spoke in a school debate against Israel's first Lebanon War in 1982. But even then the concept of the Palestinians as a people was fuzzy to me. Probably it was best informed by the music of the Clash—who I loved—but whose awareness of Palestinian politics in songs such as "Tommy Gun" did not seem to go much beyond the murderous Abu Nidal group. Adorned in the checked kaffiyeh of the West Bank peasantry, the guerrillas of the Palestinian national cause appeared glamorous and uncompromising, a little bit country and a little bit rock and roll.

I did not meet any real Palestinians until I went to Manchester University, which then had the largest Jewish and leftist populations of any British college. As the First Intifada raged, I took courses on its background and became embroiled in the interminable campus slugfests that still rage over the issue. I began writing about Palestine in the 1990s for the now-defunct *City Limits* magazine and then *Red Pepper* (where I worked as international editor). I first visited the region during the Second Intifada.

Between 2002 and 2009 I reported on the conflict for the websites of the *Economist* and Al-Jazeera, and for the Jane's group of publications. I also contributed articles, op-eds, and analyses about "Israel-Palestine" to the *Guardian*'s "Comment Is Free," the BBC, the *Observer, Haaretz, Private Eye, Jewish News,* and others.

I based myself in Tel Aviv in 2004 while I wrote my first book, *Occupied Minds,* about Israeli Jewish identity. Its aim was to tell a story about the country's psyche in as unmediated a way as possible, using the words of Israelis themselves. This book was conceived of as a companion piece. It proved a more complicated proposition.

Working in Israel, a society I understood far more intuitively, had been straightforward. Interviewees were easy to contact and usually happy to share their views with a Diaspora Jew they naturally assumed was sympathetic. In the occupied territories, however, interviews often could not be agreed on or fell through at the last minute. Sources were harder to find, fewer people spoke English, and I had to travel widely while negotiating checkpoints, closures, bureaucratic restrictions, and the caprices of the Israeli army. In Israel I had found the soldiers friendly and good-humored, even to Westerners they imagined as naive or unwitting agents of terror. In the occupied territories they were mostly nervous and frightened, sometimes paranoid, and always inclined to assume hostile intent.

Among the Palestinians I spoke to, trust was often difficult to establish. Conversations were either conducted in English—which posed challenges for interviewees—or translated—which posed challenges for me. Interpreters diligently plucked at clouds of words, only for their meanings to sometimes become lost in the ensuing rains. Interviews were canceled for reasons of travel, ill health, injury, or arrest. Different conventions sometimes applied in setting them up and conducting them. Israeli officials declined to forward media requests. Soldiers refused to accept my international press credentials, and many people I hoped to interview could not be found or were simply too scared to talk. It was an exhausting process but also a hugely rewarding one.

The recurring themes that emerged from my research were of land, exile, resistance, and trauma, perhaps the most irreducible (if not necessarily unique) denominators of Palestinian identity. All Palestinians trace their origins to the land of Palestine, although most were displaced from their homes in 1948. The varying forms of resistance mounted to that displacement have stamped their collective view of themselves—whether or not they participated in, supported, or even knew about them. Most Palestinian families have members who have suffered some degree of trauma as a result of their dispossession, the repression that followed resistance, the divisions that grew between Palestinians, or a combination of these. Other identity motifs depended on location and circumstance: the desire for return, relief, protection, and a normal life; the need for a homeland; the terror that conflict brings; the divisive influence of factions; the weakening of traditional gender-based family roles; the restrictive impact of religious and cultural mores; and the identity contradictions that especially afflict Palestinians living close to Israeli Jews.

More than fifty Palestinians talk about these issues in this book. They form an unrepresentative but enlightening sample of Palestinian society. Some were people or "types" that I had long wanted to talk to. Others I found through contacts, nongovernmental organizations (NGOs), or chance conversations. Interviewee selection is usually more of an art than a science. But my criterion was always the same: to find compelling accounts that shed new light on the Palestinian experience, which had not been fully explored elsewhere. Some of the voices here are famous. Others will probably never be interviewed again; they are farmers and fighters, models and musicians, drug dealers and policemen, their stories containing the fragments of a collective national journey.

I have chosen to structure the journey by beginning with the youngest of my subjects and gradually moving backward through the generations. For that reason, the book opens with Bisan and Abud, two traumatized teenagers in today's Jenin refugee camp, and ends with two veterans of the 1936 Revolt. They are refugees from (and to) the villages that Bisan and Abud were named after. Along the way a history of hope, struggle, and injury unfolds that makes some sense of Abud's wish to be a *shahid* (martyr) and Bisan's impoverished dream of a Palestine in which all the Jews have left and are dying.

The book is organized into chapters that loosely represent the generations shaped by the key events of Palestinian history, from 1936 to the present. This categorization is not perfect, partly because "generation" is such a loose category. But this method of proceeding is a way to peel back the many layers of Palestinian experience.

I have left historical exposition to the chapter introductions. But the markers chosen—the Great Revolt, the Nakba, the 1967 war, the Palestinian revolution, the First Intifada, the Oslo Accords, the Second Intifada, and the disengagement endgame—have had the greatest influence on today's Palestinian consciousness. They also mark distinct periods of the nation's social history and, therefore, individual perceptions.

I recorded most of the conversations between November 2007 and June 2009 in the West Bank, where I was based, and in Gaza, Israel, Jordan, and Lebanon. I interviewed more than one hundred fascinating individuals from all walks of Palestinian life, some three or more times. Space constraints prevent me from using all their accounts here. But their wisdom, grace, and dignity informed my understanding of Palestinian identity and taught me how little I had previously known.

Before I moved to Ramallah, I had been concerned that my ethnicity and religion might put off interviewees and in a worst-case scenario make me a target for attack. Anyone with access to the Internet could learn that I was Jewish, and many did. But to the best of my knowledge this did not affect their candor, bearing, or hospitality.

Some readers may feel uncomfortable with the anger—sometimes rage— that some Palestinians express toward Israeli Jews. Sometimes this may appear to be misdirected at all Jews. The colloquial use of "Yahud" to describe

Israelis common in Palestinian street discourse is explained in the interview with Bisan and Abud. Grating as it is, I do not believe that it evinces anti-Jewish racism per se, certainly not of the genocidal European variety. Racism depends on power relations more than prejudice.

When the balance of power was different in Palestine, Muslims and Jews lived as peaceful neighbors. They fought side by side against European crusaders, and when Jews faced trial and mass murder during the Spanish Inquisition, thousands were welcomed into Palestine as refugees. The roots of today's seemingly age-old antipathies in fact date back relatively recently, to the mass arrival of European Zionist Jews in the late nineteenth century.

In his pioneering work, *The Arabs and the Holocaust,* Gilbert Achcar recounts the story of Shaykh Rashid Rida, an influential cleric of this time. Rida's adoption of ideas from Wahhabism and the Protocols of the Elders of Zion set the tone for later anti-Semitic positioning by Haj Amin al-Husseini, the Muslim Brotherhood, and Hamas. Yet Rida had defended Jews during the Dreyfus Affair in France as descendants of the prophets of God facing persecution from a secular and Christian West. It was not until the late 1920s that he embraced the Muslim (and, paradoxically, Christian) traditions most hostile to Jews, and then because he realized that the new settlers would not compromise on their intent to take over Palestine.

The source of the animus, though, was the practice of Zionism rather than anything inherent to the Jewish religion, culture, or peoples. The complicating factor was that Zionists, then as now, claimed to act in the name of the Jewish religion, culture, and people. Many Palestinians are aware of the difference between Jews and Israelis but cannot be bothered to make what seem like fine distinctions when a privileged Jewish Diaspora rarely does so, nor seems at all interested in Palestinian suffering, which it is arguably benefiting from and often contributing to.

Materially, as Palestinians see it, Jewish settlers forced families from their land and homes in 1948 under a Star of David flag. They confined them to wretched, diseased, and poverty-stricken refugee camps, mostly outside Israel. They instituted a "Jewish state" in which any Jew could claim citizenship but to which no Palestinian could return. In 1967 they occupied what little land they had not seized the first time around and began moving in settlers who believed that God had given it to them. And from within and without Israel, Jewish leaders often labeled criticism of this state of affairs anti-Semitic.

In such circumstances, the biggest surprise for me was that Palestinian "hatred" toward Jews was not greater. In my experience, any Diaspora Jew—or invited Israeli—who disassociated himself or herself from the occupation and behaved respectfully was welcomed as a guest. Even the worst-case scenarios may not always be what they seem.

In May 2009 I was taking photographs outside the United Nations Relief and Works Agency (UNRWA) Gaza City compound when a young man in a red bandanna tapped me on the back. He had a short-trimmed beard and was smiling luminously. He looked so pleased to see me that I automatically smiled back and greeted him with the traditional sobriquet "Ahlan wa Sahlan."

But the man seemed in a trance and, still smiling, held out a long red-and-white-handled dagger in a sheath in front of him. Then he unsheathed the blade with his left hand, raised it above his head, and plunged it toward my chest. I swiveled with a jolt and sprinted down the street fast as I could, shouting for help, mostly in English. Palestinians are notoriously friendly to foreign visitors, sometimes embarrassingly so. But this time, as if in a nightmare, everyone I passed on the street just seemed to ripple toward the walls around the Islamic University, which were high and had no doors.

After about two hundred yards I reached a road junction, out of breath and screaming for my life. There, another bearded man peeped out from behind a metal doorway and frantically ushered me into the courtyard of a security compound. From within, a Hamas policeman in a black uniform barged past me. The door clanged shut behind him, and two AK-47 gunshots exploded deafeningly on the street outside. More Hamas officers poured out onto the street after him, one offering me his pistol as he went. I declined. My attacker was overpowered and arrested in seconds.

At a nearby police station I gave a statement and went to identify the man. He sat with his arms handcuffed behind a chair, his head lolling from side to side, looking bedraggled and pathetic. I asked the policeman with me to tell him that I did not consider him my enemy. The officer did this and asked him why he attacked me. The man just mumbled, softly repeating after the policeman, "You are not my enemy."

The officer said my attacker told him that he thought I was a Yahud who had come to steal Palestinian land. I found out later that the man's name was Mohammed Mustafa Ahmed; he was twenty-seven and had a history of mental illness. According to a statement he gave to the Al-Mezan human rights organization, during Israel's invasion of Gaza he had gone to the az-Zaytoun area to watch the fighting and tell the Israelis not to kill so many civilians. The Israeli soldiers there fired shots at him and then detained him for four days. During this time, he said, the soldiers stripped him naked, blindfolded and bound him, spat on him, beat him severely and repeatedly, and cut his right hand "with a sharp tool." Then they used him as a human shield, standing him in the open windows of buildings they were working in, to deter sniper attacks. After this, he was chained with his arms around a concrete pillar for a twenty-four-hour period, during which he was denied food and water. He was then driven in a tank to an Israeli jail where he was imprisoned for two months. Finally he was taken to the Erez checkpoint and released back into Gaza.

The title of this book refers to a line from a poem by Tawfiq Ziad that uses a powerful image of Palestine's disturbed land. Every spring there is a fifty-day period across the southern Mediterranean called the *khamsin,* when sandstorms suck up silt from the Sahara before randomly—and suddenly—depositing it over large areas. At its peak, buildings, streets, and cars from Gaza to the Galilee become coated in sand overnight. Dust particles swirl in the air, stick to your skin, and make going out painful to the eyes, nose, and throat. The Nakba began at this time of year.

"In your eyes a sandstorm" can simultaneously be read as a threat, a curse on settlers, and a description of how Palestinians are often perceived. A tendency to revel in the amorphous but existential fear that resistance provokes among Israeli Jews has not helped the Palestinian cause. But it is at least understandable in the anguished and powerless context of Ziad's poem. Sandstorms also obscure a clear line of sight, protecting the hunted and disadvantaging the hunter. They distort the view that those within it have of each other. They are a fitful phenomenon of the region's landscape.

Unlike Jewish identity, Palestinian identity has always been based on earth. Its loss was associated with a loss of self-image. As the Palestinian writer Fawas Turki put it, "Among Palestinians when you want to ask for the whereabouts of a certain person—'Where is Mohammed nowadays?'—you say, 'Mohammed, wein ardu filhall ayyam?'—'Where is Mohammed's land nowadays?'" Similarly, the most awesome challenge, or abuse, you can direct at a Palestinian is "Biddi ahrek ardak!" "I shall burn down your land!" In the 1920s the stock Palestinian response to demands from the British mandate authorities to see identity cards was often "Ardi hiya hawiyati," "My land is my identity."

Palestine's terrain ranges from fertile coastal plains to forests, mountains, and deserts. Arguably, Palestinians have a "being culture" like the Chinese—in which identity is defined by who one is—rather than a "doing culture" like that of America—in which it is defined by what one does. But the core elements of their identity are rooted in the region's turf: Arab nationalism; Palestinian nationalism; Islam; strong family, tribe, and clan affiliations; and codes of behavior passed down from one generation to the next.

Arab nationalism (or pan-Arabism) began in the early twentieth century as a secular movement for an independent Middle East comprising all the region's peoples and religions. Its premise was that from Morocco to Iraq, the Arab world constituted one nation united by a shared language, culture, and history. It had a right to self-government free from exploitation by the West. By the 1920s this idea was morphing into a specifically Palestinian movement. The first Palestinian newspaper had been published in 1908 with the aim of fighting land transfers from poor Arabs to rich Jews, and in 1911 several journals were circulating.

But Palestinian nationalists, most notably the Palestine Liberation Organization (PLO), failed to create a homeland in the twentieth century and Political Islam grew more powerful. As hopes of rescue by secular Arab regimes faded, groups from Hamas to Israel's Islamic Movement turned to the Qur'an as a model for Arabic legal, business, and political systems.

The presence of Jerusalem—the Muslim world's third most holy site—had anyway guaranteed religion a major economic and cultural role in Palestine. But even without it, the mosque was the place for Palestinians to meet friends and neighbors, to escape the pressures of family and home, to pray, to demonstrate, and to reaffirm community ties.

According to a poll taken in 1992, the ultimate loyalties of a group of 2,500 Palestinians in the occupied territories were to their families, the Palestinian people, the Islamic nation, and the Arab nation—in that order. Family in Palestine, as elsewhere, comes first. Palestinian society itself is a potpourri of clans, notable families, and Bedouin tribes. A clan usually consists of several extended families with a shared paternal line. The structure began as a way to organize shared agricultural land. But in the absence of a strong state system, clans offered security to the powerless, financial assistance to the needy, and, most important, a source of spouses in a society where 48 percent of all marriages are to cousins, according to the Palestinian Central Bureau of Statistics.

Clans may be in long-term decline, but they were deliberately fostered by the PLO leader Yasser Arafat in the 1990s to prevent the emergence of challenges to his authority. Corruption grew. When Israel later destroyed Palestinian security, government, and court infrastructure in the Second Intifada, clans often tried to fill the breach. They provided communities with armed defenders, social care, and a deeply ingrained *sulha* (mediation and reconciliation) system for resolving disputes.

Political leadership in Palestine society has historically come from notable families. Under the Ottomans, they formed a privileged leadership caste, and their services were used during the British occupation. Religious, business, and military figures were played off against each other in the familiar colonial game of divide and rule.

Israel nurtured these notables until the 1970s, when land confiscations for settlement building began to undercut their power base and nudged them toward the PLO. In the 1980s a newly educated but often unemployed middle class seized the gauntlet, moving politics onto the streets. Yet to this day the notables are a fixture in Palestinian society, most of them supportive of the Oslo Accords. Their primary interest lies in stability and a strong state that allows them to maximize the relative life advantages they were born with.

Palestine's other clanlike grouping, the Bedouins, descend from a nomadic tribe whose presence in the country some date to the fourth century B.C.E. Very few Bedouins live even seminomadic lifestyles today. Encroaching modernity and Israel's land seizures and restrictions on free movement have decimated their traditional way of life. Still, they retain a strong group identity based on culture, economic deprivation, and patterns of marriage.

Palestine has many other linguistic and religious minorities, from the Druze of the Galilee to the Samaritans of Nablus. The most important are the Christians, who make up less than 10 percent of the population but play a central role in the life of cities such as Jerusalem, Bethlehem, and Nazareth.

Whatever their social standing, all Palestinians absorb cultural norms, such as the *mithaq al-sharaf,* or code of honor, which ties male clan members to their extended families. An attack on one is an attack on all. Vendettas, revenge attacks, or honor killings can automatically result. Violating the *mithaq* can bring dishonor and shame on individuals and whole families. Honor has traditionally been redeemed by sacrifice.

The very name of the original Palestinian resistance in 1936, *al-Fedayeen,* means "those who sacrifice themselves." But the ultimate sacrifice—and the uses to which it can be put—is often viewed more ambiguously. In cities like Nablus or Jenin, *shahid* kitsch can be found on posters, videos, DVDs, key rings, and T-shirts. Yet Palestinians often write and talk about the phenomenon with black humor, even if they would balk if Westerners did the same.

Suicide bombing began in Shi'ite Iran, but today even the atheist militias of the PFLP and the Democratic Front for the Liberation of Palestine (DFLP) have their *shahids.* These dead "Fedays" are honored as soldiers in any country are, regardless of how they lost their lives. That their victims may have been civilians is no more relevant here than in Israel, where accused war criminals are routinely awarded medals and top jobs. But the lives of young Palestinian fighters can be taken more cheaply. Because of this, remembrance is a form of resistance and identity.

Crucially for wider Palestinian society, religious significance is attached to martyrdom. Thus a martyr's death is honored not by mourning but by putting up a tent and receiving congratulatory visits from neighbors, family, and friends. The phenomenon is closer to what Emile Durkheim called "altruistic suicide" than the carnival of hate many suppose.

Perhaps the most central concept in modern Palestinian identity is *sumud,* or steadfastness. This ethos is about remaining rooted to the land, like an olive tree or (as often depicted in paintings) a peasant mother, pregnant with a child. *Sumud* first emerged after the 1967 war. It highlights the fear that another Nakba-style flight of refugees could permanently consolidate the ethnic cleansing of Palestine. At its simplest, *sumud* is about holding your ground.

The descendants of those who were expelled or fled in 1948 are the world's largest refugee population today, estimated at between 7.0 million and 10.9 million. Most refugees live in the neighboring countries of Jordan, Syria, and Lebanon where decent health care, housing, education, travel, and employment are rare. Every Palestinian you meet in the camps seems to long for a return to his or her homeland, though few believe it likely.

In *sumud,* the spirit of the nonviolent but stubborn fellah who refuses to leave his land is just as important as armed resistance. On its own, some feared that this "static *sumud*" could degenerate into resignation, passivity, and self-pity. So in the 1980s it was transformed by the Intifada into "resistance *sumud,*" a panoply of industrial walkouts, tax strikes, activism, and mass demonstrations.

As Yasser Arafat described it in 1985, "The most important element in the Palestinian program is holding on to the land and not warfare alone. Warfare comes at a different level. If you only fight, that is a tragedy. If you fight and emigrate, that is a tragedy. The basis is that you hold on [to the land] and fight." The other side of *sumud* is an unremitting saga of victimization and suffering, which has become institutionalized, ritualized, and, often, ignored.

Taken together, these three normative values—*sumud,* honor, and sacrifice—have sustained successive generations of the Palestinian self-image. To some extent they correlate with the facts of land, resistance, and trauma. But boundaries naturally overlap in Israel-Palestine and are routinely changed by force. Land can equate to honor. Trauma may be steadfast. Resistance tends to the sacrificial. Exile shades them all.

Many Palestinians idealize "Palestine"—sometimes dangerously—as a place of security and transcendence, an Ithaca that may never be reached. Yet it is also a byword for home and selfhood. In the West, too, Palestine has been a symbol—of envy, empire, conflict, and unacknowledged guilt. The baggage from centuries of interference, as well as misplaced atonement for the Holocaust, can all too easily funnel sympathy toward today's oppressor.

It is my hope that the journey for readers of this book will be fourfold: to discern the faces behind the kaffiyeh, veil, or flag; to realize their human qualities separate from the oppression and resistance dynamics that have shrouded them; to recognize something of the history that they have made, and which has been imposed on them; and to disentangle all these from their own preconceptions. If nothing else, I hope that it will help to remove some sand from the eyes.

The
Disengaged
Generation

Most Palestinians today are under the age of seventeen. There are several reasons for the population bulge: the political optimism of the Oslo days, the economic facts of life under occupation, even the dawn-to-dusk curfews of the Second Intifada. But one result is that this generation may not be as amenable to peace processes as previous ones. Fewer of them speak Hebrew, know Israel, or have met friendly Jews. Many of those who can will use international contacts to emigrate. The people interviewed in this chapter are mostly just above this age group, but they share a separation from Israeli Jews and the Oslo dream, as well as a weakening of bonds to Palestinian national parties, institutions, and traditions.

If the West Bank Wall and disengagement from Gaza marked an Israeli shift to unilateral separation from all things Arab, the lack of a coherent national response inspired a different kind of detachment among young Palestinians. By early 2011 the Palestinian Authority (PA) had come to be seen largely as a bureaucratic source of largesse (at best) and Gaza's government as a religious police state. Families and clans were traumatized and impoverished, while paternal authority had been severely undermined by national failure, military humiliation, and the encroaching cultures of individualism and DIY buddy capitalism. A minority of Palestinians reacted, according to Eyad Sarraj, by "identifying with the aggressor." The West Bank factions that spearheaded the resistance were mostly languishing, smashed on the rocks of espionage, repression, and their own fatalistic heroism. Public support for them had also fallen off due to their perceived military naïveté and economic gangsterism.

The continued humiliations of occupation had ensured a steady stream of young recruits. But the Gaza blockade attested to a powerlessness that Hamas—the last redoubt of armed resistance—shared with Fatah. As the onetime Fedayeen of the PLO governed the West Bank, the Israeli wall—and Jewish settlements—expanded. When the thirteen-year-old son of a Palestinian friend told us that he loved an especially violent video game because it allowed him to "break the arms" of other characters, his mother winced at me. "Break their arms" was Yitzhak Rabin's famous instruction to his troops during the First Intifada. When young Palestinians look westward, they inevitably pick up on echoes of their own oppression.

Since the international community transformed its aid to Palestinians into a mechanism of "divide and rule," it had become linked in the popular imagination with Fatah cronyism. This had been a matter of national disgust ever since former Prime Minister Ahmed Qureia's family company was found to have shipped cement used in building the separation wall from Israel in 2004. Young Palestinians felt badly let down by the "Tunis generation," just as young Algerians felt let down by their secular nationalist parents in the early 1990s. They had watched the international community reward Fatah with the equivalent of ceremonial feathers—and Israel with grotesquely generous trade and aid packages. They had seen their brethren in Gaza punished with ever more debilitating sanctions. Many had experienced war trauma, and some might yet bite the Western hand that has fed them, if nothing more.

In Gaza, Israel's "disengagement"—that is, withdrawal of settlements—from the Strip in 2005 was followed by several shocks: an election that Hamas won, a bout of fratricidal fighting that banished Fatah as a military force, a grievous blockade that reduced daily life to a bare minimum, and, finally, a war waged by an advanced army against the Gazan people as a whole. At the time of writing, more than half of Gazans were unemployed, 70 percent lived on less than $1 a day, and 80 percent depended on UNRWA for food. This had combined with a lack of existential security in disastrous ways. The American academic Sara Roy, who lived in Gaza for many years, wrote in her book *Failing Peace:*

> Thirty 15-year-old boys were asked, "What does authority mean?" All answered that "Authority means the enemy." When told, "But authority could mean your teacher as well," several of them replied, "You mean our teacher is a collaborator?" "Do you have authority at home?" was another question. "Yes," they replied, "the authorities have entered our homes many times." Children in the Gaza Strip are increasingly incapable of conceptualizing authority in traditional terms since parents and teachers, unable to protect the young from constant abuse and threat, have ceased to exist as authority figures. Authority is now the enemy and it is inherently evil.

Studies in Gaza indicate that 85 percent of children have seen their homes raided by the Israeli army, 42 percent have been beaten, and 55 percent have witnessed their fathers being beaten. A twenty-four-year-old friend on the Strip had experienced all three. He described a beating by soldiers in which two teeth were broken and a humiliation in which soldiers forced his father to clean feces off a jeep as "incidents that make me laugh."

The inability of family and clan networks to shield their young from Israeli army attacks led many of Gaza's children to seek protection in factions and militias before 2000. Hamas's failure to shelter civilians during Israel's last invasion led to trauma on a frightening scale. According to a Gaza Community Mental Health Program study, in 2009 more than 60 percent of Gaza's children were suffering severe to very severe posttraumatic stress reactions, and 30 percent were experiencing moderate posttraumatic stress. This generation does not have the emotional space to process its war wounds, its siege pains, or the more general despair that being a teenager in a walled camp engenders.

By dint of their numbers, intense suffering, and forced absence from the world's eyes, young Gazans may well come to define what it means to be Palestinian in the future. The raw and pained power of the "Gaza Youth Break Out" statement in early 2011—"There is a revolution growing inside us, an immense dissatisfaction and frustration that will destroy us"—may retrospectively appear an unheeded wakeup call.

Israel's own Palestinian minority underwent contradictory experiences in the late 2000s. As the Second Intifada waned, Islamist ideas grew, and secular young Arabs tried to somehow fashion more personal life narratives. How to keep true to valued traditions while "becoming someone" in your own right was a typical preoccupation. Palestinian Israelis are wealthier than their cousins in the occupied territories, can travel, and have a growing sophistication, worldliness, and self-confidence that has so far not been reflected in Israel's political scene. They also understand Israeli Jews far better than their contemporaries in the occupied territories and, as a fruit of struggles over many years, expect equal citizenship rights in a way that their parents did not. But they have been deliberately isolated from Palestinians in the occupied territories.

Laws prevent contact with "enemy" Arabs, travel beyond much of the Green Line, and even, since 2003, living in Israel with spouses from the West Bank and Gaza. One Palestinian in Bethlehem complained to me that he could not even travel in a car with his Jerusalem-born wife. "We were so lucky to find a small rented house in a zone where I can reach her. We live together now, but nobody knows about it," he said. "It's not right."

Refugees have had to watch such developments from afar. In Lebanon, discrimination, insecurity, and war trauma sometimes compared to the norm in Gaza. But elsewhere, the primary travails were poverty, neglect, and abandonment, exacerbated by the incremental death of any hope for change or meaningful national relief. Talk on Palestinian street corners still gravitated toward a third Intifada, but it was unclear whether Palestinian society had the emotional strength, political strategy, or military ability to mount another revolt. The end result was a degree of wariness among the young, a trend to individualist and sometimes globalized solutions (complicated by ambivalent feelings toward the West), and an unhooking from established political parties and processes.

Previous Palestinian generations inherited vibrant liberation movements and international initiatives. Even after the Nakba, the hope of return remained. The coming generation seems to have been bequeathed a compromised political horizon, a divided polity, and two mirror image failed police states, neither of which can realize their aspirations or protect them from an aggressive neighbor that appears to wish their disappearance. One poll in 2009 indicated that 40 percent of Gazans and 25 percent of West Bankers wanted to escape from their homeland. In 2010 Palestinian youth workers reported up to 80 percent of some classes wishing to emigrate. But the drift to personal rather than national life narratives reflected a global trend as well as a weakening of traditional national identities.

The meaning of loaded concepts such as resistance, liberation, and identity continues to evolve in circumstances that do not favor universalistic conclusions. The disengaged generation has been let down by its political leaders and military factions. Clan networks and families have been unable to substitute for them, and the Western and Arab worlds have substantially betrayed them. New social, cultural, and political formulations, perhaps with deeper roots among Palestinian-Israelis, could blossom one day. But for now an old order atrophies while a new one cannot be born. If it ever arrives, it will have to chew its way through a formidable umbilical cord linking the apparatuses of Fatah and Hamas, the occupation, a traditional land-and-family-based self-image that can no longer sustain itself, and a national fragmentation, the healing of which may prove akin to piecing back together the shell of a shattered egg.

Abud, 15, and
Bisan Abdul Khadr Fihad, 12

Students

JENIN CAMP, WEST BANK

A bird flying over Palestine   In a small house crunched into the maze of Jenin's refugee camp, Bisan and Abud lived with their parents and one younger brother. Sitting in the family's salon with their mother and a translator, Bisan said that she rarely saw Abud these days. He changed after the Israeli army's invasion of the camp in 2002 and was now always on the streets. During that invasion, at least fifty-two Palestinians were killed and the old refugee camp was demolished.

Bisan was named after the family's hometown, which now lies within Israel. In 1948, the Palmach, a standing army of Jewish troops, captured it and expelled its Arab residents, renaming the town Beth She'an as they went. The Fihad family were among those displaced.

Abud said he visited the town of Bisan once for a wedding and found it "a beautiful village, more beautiful than the Jenin camp." He would have liked to live there, he said, but could not "because of the occupation." Beth She'an is now a Jewish town in Israel, and no Arabs remain. Bisan has visited Jericho, Jerusalem, and Haifa only once, on a school excursion. "I prefer Jerusalem because of the holy places," she said. "It keeps me in contact with our Islamic origins. I love my religion, and *insha'allah* I will go to Mecca." Both children prayed regularly in order to satisfy God and so that they might reach heaven one day. "It's a way of feeling okay," Bisan explained. Her smile was often bright and precocious, but in a moment it could turn pale and expressionless. Abud was more fixedly hunched and sullen.

When I asked the children what their favorite lessons were at school, Bisan piped up, "I love English!" with a grin. Abud said nothing. Bisan told me that they played Intifada games in the Jenin camp by dividing themselves into two groups—Jews who shot, and Palestinians who threw stones. The Palestinians always won.

What do you want to be when you grow up, I asked Abud. "It's difficult to say," he replied. "I can't say." My translator suggested that Abud felt inhibited by his mother's presence in the room, and we asked her to leave. Finally Abud muttered that he was afraid. "I want to be a fighter," he said quietly. "I don't want to be with any political parties, just to be a fighter. I saw many people dying in the camp, and because of that I want to fight and die a *shahid*. I saw Abu Janda and Fady in my neighborhood killed and Mohammed Delal when he was a child. Mahmoud Afif, Abas Damaji . . . " He reeled off the names as though pointing out graves. How did they die, I asked? "The Jews killed them," he said. The room felt very empty.

Ordinary Palestinians often refer to Israelis as Jews, and interpreters usually translate this back as "Israelis" or "Zionists." Some would call this anti-Semitism. Sometimes it is. But as far as it goes, it is usually accurate. Among older Palestinians, use of the word *Yahud* is sometimes associated with a reaction against the old Fatah saw, Sahiouni (Zionist). It denotes a certain kind of defiance, informality, rejection of accommodation with Israeli Jews, and religious affiliation. In Abud's case it is automatic, the language of the street he lives on and which lives in him.

"About three months ago I saw a guy who the Israeli soldiers had killed," he said, stuttering, "and his brain was outside his head. I was at the edge of the street, and I saw the jeeps stop. I heard the guns shoot, and then when they left, I went and saw the bodies. When the soldiers came to take them, one collapsed on the floor when he saw the guy's brains. I just ran away and told some friends and the fighters about it. I couldn't sleep that night."

But he did not pray either. "I was confused," he said. "I just walked around the neighborhood and returned to the house. I always have nightmares with people dying or silhouettes passing by my face quickly, one by one. You can only see their bodies. I'm scared of them. When it happens, I wake up and then cover myself with a blanket."

"One child died when I was with him. We saw some tanks, so we said to each other, 'Let's go and throw stones at them!' My friend Mohammed ran ahead about a hundred meters and started throwing stones. Then we heard shooting and I saw him collapse in the street. He was shot in the head. We went and looked at his body. I cried a lot." Mohammed was twelve years old, and his death left Abud with a kind of survivor guilt—the feeling of culpability for having survived that is common to Holocaust survivors and

Palestinians alike. "I still feel guilty because we were all telling each other to go and throw stones," he affirmed.

The psychotherapist Abud saw did not help at all. "I just want to be a *shahid*," he said. "I want to die, because so many other people have died. I don't have a future. A group of children in my neighborhood have decided that we will all become fighters." A Gaza Mental Health Community Center study found that more than a third of Palestinian boys between the ages of eight and twelve wished to die in attacks on the Israeli army.

"I also saw many dead people in the camp!" Bisan chimed in, listing her roll call of local *shahids*. "I keep having flashbacks and feeling sad and afraid but also appreciating them because they died protecting the camp. I also saw some children whom the Jews killed in the streets." Unlike her brother, Bisan's experience of the occupation had left her hopeful for the future—she now wanted to open a pharmacy—but the route to her decision had been unconventional.

"We went to my grandmother's house when the invasion started," she remembered, "four families all living in one room. We just sat in the salon, staring at the tanks shooting and the rockets from the helicopters. When they were fired, the sky would light up. After a minute we'd hear a strong explosion, the house would start shaking, and then I'd hear a deafening sound in my ears."

"During the night we tried to sleep, but I couldn't because of the explosions. Then my cousin tried to wake me, but I couldn't. When my mother looked at my face she couldn't recognize me in the dark. My mouth and eyes were open wide and my heart was not beating. My body was cold. She started screaming, 'My daughter is dead!' My uncles and aunts came in from the other room to see what was happening . . . "

While she was talking, Abud had started to cry. "I went to the corner of the room and started praying to God, 'Don't take my sister,'" he said. "She was lying there, and I went to touch her, but then I got scared. I started screaming and went back to the corner to pray again." Bisan continued, "My uncle ran over quickly and started giving me resuscitation—beating me on the chest and breathing into my mouth. Suddenly, I felt my body shaking and my heart beating first slowly, then fast. When I woke up I didn't know what had happened. Because my uncle helped me I decided to become a doctor so that maybe in the future I can help someone."

Abud thought that the Israelis treated Palestinians badly "because they want to kick us out of our land, like they did in '48." Bisan reasoned, "They are angry because we have fighters who want to protect us. They want to kill them, destroy the Al Aqsa Mosque, and then take our houses." The only Israelis either had ever met wore uniforms.

"I was always scared of soldiers," Bisan said. "Whenever I saw one, I got paralyzed and had to sit down. Once I was playing outside my grandmother's house with my brothers and cousins when tanks suddenly attacked the area. We tried to run back to the house, but a tank was quicker. We froze in the street and started crying. The soldiers appeared from the tank and started screaming at us. The tank pointed its guns at us too, but then our uncles ran out and brought us inside."

Abud also did not talk to soldiers. "Even if they came to me out of uniform, I would be too scared," he said. "The only time I've talked to Jews was when me and my father were interrogated at a checkpoint." Their prospects were bleaker than most children in Israel could possibly imagine, but Abud believed that—*insha'allah*—Palestine would one day be free.

Bisan was hopeful too. "I imagine myself as a bird flying over Palestine," she enthused. "I travel from city to city and see the children playing safely in peace and freedom, and the Jews are dying and not one of them is living here in Palestine." "And I hope that Al Quds will be free soon," she added conscientiously. Abud just stared at the ground or occasionally straight ahead, resolutely.

Sharif al-Basyuni, 21

Unemployed

BEIT HANUN, GAZA

The next step   Sharif was slightly cross-eyed, with an intent but glazed stare that slipped easily into the middle distance. His fondest memories were of playing football at school. Barcelona fans, Sharif and his friends used to kick a ball around the dusty potholed streets of Beit Hanun in the old days. "We didn't really have positions," he recalled. "I'd play everywhere. I used to be good—we even had a team—but when the Second Intifada began things changed. The other guys started to play with stones instead."

Beit Hanun is the closest major population center to Gaza's border with Israel. The Israeli town of Sderot, which has borne the brunt of Hamas's rocket campaign, is only four miles away, and Sharif said that his town had suffered more Israeli military invasions than any other part of Gaza. "The Israelis demolish infrastructure, uproot trees, and arrest people whenever they come in," he said. "It creates terror among the people."

Sharif was just sixteen on January 24, 2003, when the Israeli army invaded Beit Hanun unannounced in an attack they called Operation Prolonged Effort. "It was a Friday at midday, and I was playing football in the middle of the street, close to [a neighbor's] front door. People don't usually expect tanks and bulldozers at that time. But they closed all the passages to Beit Hanun and started shooting randomly. I was shot here," he said and motioned toward his hip. Sharif and his father both swore that no Palestinians in Beit Hanun had fired at Israeli soldiers before, during, or after the incident. The dumdum bullet that cut down Sharif severed his spinal cord and caused massive internal injuries.

"It was like a fire in my body," he said matter-of-factly. "I was crying and waiting for someone to help me because I couldn't get up. But the other kids who were playing football panicked and started running around. When one tried to pull me out, the Jews would shoot at him. I was down for about fifteen or twenty minutes. Because the gunfire was preventing the *shebab* [street youths] from rescuing me, they threw a rope from a house across the street. I hung onto it, and they pulled me. It was tiring, painful, and actually made my condition worse because when you're shot, you should stay still until you're put into the ambulance."

Sharif lost a lot of blood but managed to somehow prevent himself from going into shock. "It was very scary. I was injured and I could see death coming," he said. "The main thing I was thinking was that I was going to die. I kept crying, looking at the people around me, wondering what's going to happen to them after [I've gone]. There was an ambulance nearby, but the Jews shot at it whenever it tried to get close. It took them ten or fifteen minutes to get to me and half an hour to get me into the ambulance after being shot. First they took me to the Al Quds hospital, and then the Shifa hospital in Gaza. After that I fell into a coma. The next thing I knew I was being woken up at the Tel Hashomer hospital in Tel Aviv."

The family was never given a military explanation for Sharif's shooting, but the army's invasion was nominally a response to the firing of five Qassam rockets at Sderot the night before. The military occupation of the town that followed lasted forty-seven days, and when it ended the army had destroyed all of Beit Hanun's bridges and many of its streets. Sharif heard about it in his Israeli hospital bed. "They treated me like a normal patient there, but no one from Gaza could get out to visit me. For the first fifteen days I was alone. After that, my mum stayed with me for about a month, but then her permit ended, and for the rest of my time there I was alone again," he told me.

This could not have been easy for someone who spoke little Hebrew and had never even talked to a Jew before. But Sharif managed to strike up conversations with other patients and hospital staff. "Many of them were actually shocked that the Jewish army could do such a thing," he said. "A lot of peace camp people—Arabs, Jews, and other foreigners—came to visit me. The Jews organized it, and it made me feel a little better because [it meant] somebody cared."

"Before I was shot I thought they were occupiers, and afterward that feeling got stronger actually. I felt more hatred toward them." But Sharif distinguished between the peace camp and soldiers. "There were doctors and nurses in the hospital who refused to go to the army," he said. Even so, the time spent there was "much harder than the injury itself," he maintained. "The injury took months to recover from, but my suffering will be for the rest of my life. They used a 250mm bullet that exploded inside my body and destroyed the entire lower part of my spine."

Since 2003 Sharif had been doing regular physical therapy, but his rehabilitation had been set back by the Israeli army's refusal to allow him through the Erez checkpoint to get the metal leg braces that his doctors at the Tel Hashomer hospital prescribed for him. "I'm stopped from being helped because no one can go out to get the braces. They've been ordered by the Israeli hospital. But the borders are closed, and they refuse to open them." Sharif said that this secondary punishment made him feel like "a collapsed person." "Every time I want to take the next step I'm forced back. The physical therapy I've been doing is for nothing because I need the instrument to move."

The Israeli peace camp people lost interest in Sharif's case after he was sent back to Gaza. "I think they forgot about me," he said. "Since I got back, my life has been totally different. I either sit in front of the computer or take care of the flowers and vegetables in my garden. Maybe once or twice a week, I get flashbacks to the moment that I was injured, or think about myself in the hospital. Then I get depressed and scared again." Sharif had received no psychotherapy. The biggest struggle he faced was boredom. He felt nothing in common with Israelis who had been paralyzed in rocket attacks. "We are different because the Jews have more [military] equipment and can do more damage," he said. "They also prevent people from continuing their lives after they've injured them."

"I can't predict what tomorrow is going to bring. It is mysterious—all of our futures are. We are like robots controlled by the Jews. Palestinians have control of about 10 percent of their lives. The Jews control us by locking us in near the border. We can't even control the products that go in and out." Sharif said that he would never forgive the soldier who shot him. "If you want to kill the resistance groups, you can go to their places. You don't have to destroy the whole town." Do you support the resistance groups? I asked. "Yes, I do," he replied.

On January 25, 2003, Brigadier General Gadi Shamni commended the soldiers from the Givati brigade who participated in Operation Prolonged Effort in Beit Hanun. He said it had been intended to stop Qassam rocket fire, not to punish the innocent Palestinian population. "[But] we are willing to go even further to combat terror," he added. "The terrorists must not be allowed to recover and must always be [kept] in a defensive state." Shamni went on to enjoy a glittering military career and at the time of writing was serving as Israel's military attaché in Washington, D.C.

Amira al-Hayb, 24

Soldier

WADI AL-HAMAM, ISRAEL

How to think the right way   The Israeli army press office sat on my request for an interview with Amira al-Hayb for three weeks before refusing it on national security grounds. Setting up an interview in Haifa eventually involved numerous calls to the mayor's office in Amira's village and then several more to her brothers and to her, most by my translator, Bekriah.

In 2003 Amira became the first Bedouin woman to serve in the Israeli army, but she didn't seek publicity. In 2005 her eldest brother, Taysir, was sentenced to eight years in prison for killing the twenty-two-year-old British photographer and anti-occupation activist Tom Hurndall in Gaza. Five years later, he was released. Witnesses said that Hurndall had been attempting to shield children from Israeli gunfire when he was shot in the head.

The al-Hayb clan is well known in the Galilee for its fighting prowess. Amira's hometown of Tuba az-Zanghariyya was partly named after her family. Some Bedouins in the town helped protect Jews during the 1936 revolt, and in 1948 they formed the Pal-Hayb unit of the Haganah to defend Jewish settlements. The rewards they accrued for such loyalty to their neighbors are debatable.

Amira's first words to me were spoken with roll-call disinterest: "I'm not comfortable talking about the origins of my family. I'm from Wadi al-Hamam, my mother's village near Tiberius. I have five brothers, and my father is from Tuba. He told me stories about it, but I was never curious about the clan's history. It could be something interesting, but I never wanted to know. It's not in my nature. That's just how I am."

The al-Haybs "have always had *asabiya* [loyalty] for the Israeli state and army," Amira said. "They've been volunteering as officers and fighters for a long time." But they never shared their Nakba stories with her, and she preferred it that way. "I'm an Arab Israeli," she explained. "I wasn't born in Palestine. Our parents did not educate us to say we were Palestinians. They told us we were born here in Israel." Being an Israeli for Amira was about "nationality." "I don't have a homeland," she told me. It seemed a strange thing for a Palestinian to say.

There is actually no such thing as Israeli nationality. In 1972, when Professor Georges Tamarin petitioned to be declared an "Israeli" rather than a "Jew," Israel's Supreme Court ruled against him, arguing that "there is no Israeli nation apart from the Jewish people." This is the nature of the Jewish state and the reason Arab refugees may not return to it. I asked Amira how she felt when she heard "Ha Tikva," Israel's national anthem, being played. "I didn't even know it until my commander taught it to me," she giggled. "But in the army, it was a beautiful thing to sing. It is kind of a good prayer. I didn't feel that I was a Jew when I sang it." Even though the words are all about Jews? "We were taught it as a way to express our love for the country," she replied, "and to prove the Jewish existence in Israel."

When she was growing up, both of her parents were unemployed. Still, she remembered a happy childhood. Wadi al-Hamam was "calm, sweet, and *hilwe* [nice]," she said. "We had a house, but in 2005 my father knocked it down and built a cabin next to it. It was illegal to build. It was demolished. My father was upset, and that was it." Didn't you spend the first years of your life living in temporary structures? I nudged. "My father and brothers prefer Bedouin tents with sheep and goats to regular houses," she replied. "Life wasn't that difficult." But as a teenager wasn't your house destroyed by the authorities? I pressed. "Yes, it was destroyed more than once," she said finally. So how did you feel about that? Amira shrugged. "I didn't really pay it much attention."

This was odd because, despite her coquettishness, Amira always saw herself as a fighter. "Since I was a kid I dreamed of being a soldier in a Magav fighting unit," she said. "I saw myself as a famous person doing something complicated. It is something I was born with inside me." As a child she played war games and sometimes fought—and beat up—boys at school. "I was strong then, and I'm still strong," she said. "But now I follow the law more."

"My father's family tried to stop me from joining the army. It's allowed for guys, but I am a woman, and they didn't want me to meet guys from other religions. My mother was the only one who supported me. The community and neighbors were unhappy because I am a girl. They blamed my mother." Amira's neighbors even threw stones at her house in what she said was a personal dispute. "They attacked me verbally, but they didn't use violence. They tried to break me down with their words, saying that girls went to the army to have sex, which is untrue. But they would be scared to do anything to the house of a soldier!"

Amira did not have many boyfriends before the army, but, she added, "I'd rather have a Jewish boyfriend than an Arab, because Arab guys have the wrong image of Arab girls. Society limits them to families, kids, diseases, no school. Women don't go places or see the world, and they accept this."

Amira's brother Taysir supported her decision to join the army. But she did not want to talk about him and missed a beat when I asked if the authorities prosecuted him only because he was an Arab accused of killing a white European. "It was difficult for him to accept being jailed," she said tentatively. "Everyone was against him—Israel, Britain, and the international community. He did something wrong, and he was punished." She thought that Taysir might have been a scapegoat.

In the army Amira learned Hebrew—"the writing, how to talk, and how to think the right way"—and afterward she felt "a lot" more part of Israeli society. But the unit she served in, the Magav border police, has an especially bad reputation among Palestinians for violence, racism, and brutality. Many of its soldiers are Ethiopian and Russian Jews, Druze, and Bedouins. Amira served in "a fighting position but didn't fight," and she saw no misbehavior. She did not feel she was policing her own people. "It's my job," she said simply. "We do what they tell us."

Her senior officer told the *Maariv* newspaper that if he had more girls like her, "95 percent of problems at checkpoints would disappear." Amira agreed. "He would like to use us because we know the language and make things easier." Aren't you being used cheaply? I suggested. "Not necessarily," she countered. "You can start working on the checkpoints and get a higher position." But you were protecting settlements. "So what? It needs to be done. There have to be borders to control things and prevent chaos. Our work is not just protecting settlements. It could also be protecting myself."

"The Jews go to the army. They study. They get more help from the government because they contribute to the country. My parents didn't go to the army, so I can't ask for the same kind of life. To get my rights, to prove

I exist here, I have to do more work." How does it feel when you're wearing an army uniform? I asked. "I feel like a sun that the whole universe can see," Amira replied, a smile breaking out across her face. "I feel that all eyes are on me because I am a Bedouin." Such attention, though, had a downside. As I was preparing to leave, Amira blurted out, "I'm afraid that one day I will break down. Despite the fact that I am a strong person, I am a human being. I prefer to suffer silently because I don't like people to know what is inside of Amira. I don't trust everyone."

Three years before, Amram Mitzna, a former Israeli commander and Labor Party leader, told me he had been raised with a similar idea: "Don't trust anyone. Do it yourself. Initiate. Don't expect the outside world to help you. Understand that the world is full of interests and fight for yours." But it felt as though Amira was fighting for someone else's. Her dream was to live in the Golan Heights.

Although her situation was different, it reminded me of Ghassan Khanafani's seminal short story, "Return to Haifa." In it, two refugees called Khalid and Safiyya return to their former house to find that the son they had to abandon in 1948 has been adopted and raised as a Jew. He is now an Israeli soldier. In the denouement, Khalid asks Saffiya, "What is a homeland?" His wife responds by weeping. "The homeland," Khalid says, "is the place where none of this can happen."

Niral Karantaji, 22

Model

HAIFA, ISRAEL

The war in our minds   Ethnic minorities in Western countries often complain that they confront a glass ceiling preventing them from getting on. For Arab citizens of Israel, it sometimes feels more like a locked submarine hatch. Although they constitute 20 percent of Israel's population, 53 percent of Israel's impoverished families are Arab, thirty-six of the forty towns with the highest unemployment rates are Arab, and Arab workers are paid some 29 percent less than the equivalent Jewish worker's salary. Their average household income is only 57 percent of that of a Jewish household. Compared to incomes in Gaza, these are still wages of the rich. But they are not experienced that way.

Only 40 percent of men—and less than 20 percent of women—officially participate in the workforce. Meanwhile, the Israeli government spends $1,100 per year on each Jewish student, compared to $192 for each Arab student. Pleasant Arab neighborhoods are under constant threat of demolition or a gentrification process that always seems to exclude Arabs. The police cede ghettos to criminal gangs. Arabs are as absent from Israeli television shows as they are from most academic posts, and they frequently feel as though they were born to fail. This makes the exceptions to the rule that much more remarkable and celebrated. Niral was both.

A twenty-two-year-old self-declared "Arabic-Palestinian-Turkish-Muslim-Israeli," Niral soared to stardom when she won the Israeli reality TV show, *The Models*. But accusations of racist bullying and discriminatory treatment marred the competition's afterglow. Eating in her beloved Haifa restaurant,

Faces, Niral was restless bordering on manic, alternately burying her face in a menu and anxiously scanning the patio for suspect stares or people.

On a train once, a religious Jew screamed "Arab whore" at her, and Niral had to call security. But many Arabs also resented the way she allowed herself to be depicted on television. "I eat shit from both sides," she said insouciantly. She told me she only slept three hours a night, and then sat bolt upright.

"Because I've come here today, everyone will talk tomorrow," she said, rattling out the words like maraca shakes. "You don't have privacy when you're famous. Everyone knows all the small things you do. If I go to the mall, I'm not body-searched. All the girls follow me, and the cameras are like this," she explained, acting out a cameraman taking a close-up. "At first it was very nice, but now I feel like my life is destroyed. I'm starting from zero."

Niral grew up in Haifa's poor and largely Arab Hadar district. It lies at the bottom of Mount Carmel, upon which Haifa's Jewish society arranges itself in a hierarchy of wealth. "It's downstairs," she laughed with her mouth wide open. Niral and her four siblings were raised in a liberal environment by her father, a chef in a Chinese restaurant, and her Balad-voting mother, a caregiver to the elderly.

Their life was not easy. "I always took the bus to school and looked at the rich families coming in their cars," Niral remembered, "and my family didn't have a car, you know? It made me like, 'Why can't my mummy and daddy take me in a car?' I cannot tell you I had the good clothes, the good life, the daddy and mummy environment, because I didn't. My parents had to run and run and work to live. If you're Jewish, it's easier."

Before becoming a model, Niral worked as a waitress in a restaurant, on shop floors, and with children in summer camps. But, she said, "I always wanted to change the world, to change everything. I don't want to live this fucking life. I want to be somebody else."

From a young age, she wanted to be a model. "I like to be photographed, I like the clothes, and I wanted to do something special with my life," she explained. Although she faced a problem—"They prefer blonde-haired girls here"—Niral turned her "exotic" looks to her advantage and was accepted on *The Models*. A lot of baggage came with the "exotic" tag, though.

"When I entered the room [at the audition], everyone was strange to me, you know? They were talking about me like, 'Oh, she's an Arab among us, what's she fucking doing here?' All the girls wanted to kick me out. They were mostly from rich families in Tel Aviv and Herzliya. In Israel you have two worlds, and their life is not our life. 'Why does she walk like this, talk like this?' Sorry, but it's because I am like this." "I stayed there on my arse because I believe in myself," she said, lighting a cigarette. "I believe in myself," she repeated and put the cigarette out.

Once Liat Feldman, the program manager at Channel 10, which produced *The Models,* denied that Niral had been picked to spice up the show with racial tension. "We didn't play on it," she said. "But that is not to say that we didn't enjoy it." Niral's take was different. "They chose me because they thought I'd give them good ratings. They used me like a gimmick. One Arab girl and fourteen Jewish girls on a reality show. It will be interesting," she laughed.

"I didn't know what I was getting into. It was nasty. The other girls never accepted me. They kept choosing me to go to the judges [for a removal vote]. Why? Because I'm Arab, I'm bad. They always invented stories to kick me out. But I was smart. I understood this. One girl didn't even want me to sit on her bed. Off camera, she called me a terrorist." This girl, an Ethiopian Jew named Mimi Tedessa, became Niral's nemesis on the show, although their relationship developed into something more complex and nuanced afterward. When I suggested that race might have been a factor in Mimi's reactions, Niral went into a tailspin. "I don't know," she said three times. "I don't want to say that it's political."

Niral did not like politics, and she berated me for asking political questions. "Listen," she said, "in the end I'm a person. I don't want to speak for Muslim opinion. I just want to live my life. Palestinians have very difficult lives because of the war. The Arabs of Israel have a different war, a special war of how you live every day. We've got the war in our minds."

War is life in the Middle East, but politics in Niral's world are something that television people do. Even *The Models'* editing was contentious. "They always showed me fighting," she grumbled, taking a sip of wine. "Thirty percent of the editing was just lies. If I talked about a girl they made it seem like I was talking about someone different. They wanted me to seem angry and aggressive when I was only protecting myself, you know?"

Ironically, it was Niral's irrepressible street sassiness that encouraged so many people to vote for her. Her stock response to the Jewish girls' bitchy comments, "I'm scared of Arabs" and "She makes me feel frightened," was *"Ani lo frierit habibti!"* a Hebrew-Arabic mix that means "I'm no sucker, honey." It became a popular catchphrase.

This was also ironic because in the view of many Palestinian Israelis Niral was unforgivably suckered by the program makers, twice. When I asked her why she agreed to appear topless on television, with only her hands covering her breasts, she inhaled sharply and giggled. "I'm sorry I can't sit still," she said skittishly. "I'm hyperactive. You know, if a contestant is chosen [for a removal vote] more than four times, she goes home without being judged. It was the fourth time that I had to go topless. They told me that if I didn't, I'd have to go home."

Why didn't you just say, "To hell with it, good-bye?" "I didn't want to put my hands like this," she cried, raising her arms. "But I will never do it again," she added, repeating "Ne-ver" for emphasis. "I felt pressure and a lot of conflict in my head, but I had to pay a very high price. The Arabs in Haifa and the villages wanted to kick me."

Appearing topless is an offense to religious sensibilities. But the prize photoshoot for an underwear company's ad campaign that she won equally offended nationalist sentiment. In it, Niral appeared wearing a gilt necklace bearing the Star of David, Israel's national symbol. "You know, I was on the set like this," she said, striking a pose, "and I didn't see what the stylist put on me, but the cameramen started looking at me weirdly, and I was like, 'What's happening?' Then I saw what they'd done."

"I said, 'Why did you put that on me? Take it away.' The stylist said, 'No, it's in fashion, it's the mode.' I told her, 'Give me a break and stop lying, okay? So put this on the Christians and tell them it's for fashion.' It wasn't me who wore this." Niral reportedly continued to be photographed wearing the necklace but took it off immediately afterward.

Many Arabs concluded that Niral had had to be Judaized because, as an Israeli women's magazine put it, she was "not one of us." Palestinian-Israelis had seen this fashion shoot before. In 1999, Niral's longtime friend Rana Raslan, an Arab-Israeli, also from Haifa, was adorned in a white dress with a large blue Star of David on it when she won the Miss Israel contest. However, Niral was never paid for her winning photoshoot and claimed she had not received her promised modeling trips either. "They lied and lied and lied to me," she said sadly. "They gave me crumbs. They used me and threw me away."

It must have been a huge shock after the euphoria of winning the show. "I felt like I was on top of the world," Niral recalled. "It was peace now, and I was on the top. I wish I could feel that every day because it was an amazing feeling. But for a few months after, I was very down. I sat for one year in my home doing nothing, and I'm famous! There is no justice."

Although she learned from the experience, Niral said she would not go on *The Models* again. She had not been able to find work as a model since winning the show and now planned to go back to college to study communications, get married, or emigrate as Rana Raslan did, to find modeling work abroad. Ori Saly, head of programming at Israel's entertainment channel, summarized Nidal's predicament brutally: "I don't see any big Israeli fashion label taking Niral as their big face for a campaign because she's Arab. Let's not mince words."

In Arabic, her name means "optimism," but Niral said she was only feeling "fifty-fifty" optimistic. She leaned forward and spread her arms across the table, then rubbed her nose absent-mindedly, hiding a beauty spot. "Since I was young I wanted to run away from the facts of how we live," she said. "I thought *The Models* would be better for me, but it wasn't, and I'd prefer to go back to how I was before, to my real life. Sometimes I don't know if people like me for who I am or because I'm Niral, you know?" For all her fame and designer clothes, Niral had not yet attained the good life she wished for. As she waited for her taxi home, she fretted about how she had come across in the interview. She had to be up early the next day for a new job, she said, answering telephones at a Tel Aviv car lot.

Doha Jabr, 23

Dancer

RAMALLAH, WEST BANK

When you celebrate, you resist! A bass-heavy dabke with insistent tabla beats boomed around the gym club hall in Ramallah's al-Bire outskirts. Inside it, young Palestinians in tracksuits and Nike T-shirts were running, skipping, crouching, and clapping in sweeping compasslike circles. Darting under their arms to shape and reshape the kaleidoscopic pattern, Doha looked diminutive and pretty in her pink tracksuit, almost like a manga cartoon heroine. But the overall scene as the as-Sayel troupe rehearsed for an upcoming Egyptian tour bore closer resemblance to the U.S. TV series *Fame*.

Like many Palestinians, Doha described herself as being from Jaffa rather than Ramallah where she had lived for over twenty years. "Of course, I know my family history!" she chided me. "I'm very proud of it." Her grandfather, a war hero, was shot in the leg during the Nakba and escaped to Nablus on a horse. Doha was born in the city's Balata refugee camp to a liberal father who worked as a teacher, writer, and actor. "He grew up in a camp, but his mind is open and free," she said confidently. Her mother, now a school headmistress, was unable to work in Israel for fourteen years while Doha was growing up. She was convicted of working with the DFLP and spent three years in jail.

The occupation crumpled Doha's life in many ways. "I very much wanted to be a ballet dancer when I was a child," she said, "but we didn't have ballet shoes. We didn't even have ballet schools." Instead, the ten-year-old Doha joined a club to learn dabke, a traditional music and dance form popular in Palestine, Lebanon, Syria, and Jordan. The word literally means "stomping" and despite regional differences is associated with feelings of solidarity and nationhood everywhere.

"Dabke is born with us," Doha enthused. "It's our identity from the very beginning. That's why we don't have any party, wedding, or celebration without it. For me, it's about action. The beat is hard and fast and Palestinian. When you're dancing you forget the words, the stress, everything. You just go with the mood, the music, and your partners."

Dabke songs often evoke specific places—the Ramallah, Nablus, or Hebron of old—and so do its costumes. Doha gingerly showed me her stage dress with lace to represent Ramallah, stripes for Hebron, and an open sleeve for the north. "We collect all the cities of Palestine in dresses and change them onstage," she said.

"We do dabke that represents the Intifada and occupation. We have drama—throwing stones or someone being killed on stage. It's not just celebration—or maybe celebrating means not being depressed and abandoning your traditions. When you celebrate, you resist!"

As-Sayel began in 1994 and grew quickly as young Palestinians recruited their friends and family as dancers. Today it is one of the best-known Palestinian troupes, supported by the PA's Culture Ministry and regularly touring the festival circuits in Yemen, Jordan, Algeria, and Morocco. All dabke troupes share a noncompetitive patriotism, Doha said. But then she added, "We jump higher, go lower on the floor, and kind of fly. In other countries they're just a line moving in circles."

In Lebanon dabke often has a techno beat, but Doha felt that the music "is old and should be old. If you add a rap it won't be dabke anymore." Traditional dabke is hypnotic enough, with mesmerizing tabla rhythms, bagpipe-like wailing noises, and ouds. A band director signals the tempo with claps, shouts, or a stomp of the foot (emphasizing his treelike connection to the land), and the dancers always lead with the left foot.

"Dabke relates to the land, and we stomp on it because we want to grow from it, not be forced from it," Doha sighed. "Do you know there's an Israeli dabke troupe? They stole our traditions, our food, and our costumes. But in every step of life, you should say, 'I'm Palestinian, this dabke is for us—not them!'" Of course, she added, she would never perform in Israel.

As a mixed-gender troupe, as-Sayel might also be banned from performing in Gaza today. "Hamas say it's *haram* [forbidden]," Doha remarked, chewing on a stick of gum. "This hall belongs to the [municipal] council, and because Hamas controls it, they decided to stop us from training here. But we have our relations in Ramallah, and we forced them to back down."

"Being a Palestinian shouldn't be related to Fatah or Hamas," she stressed. But her lean was against Hamas. "Their ideas are wrong," she said. "I'm a Muslim, but this is my own thing, between me and God. I don't wear a hijab, but I pray. I fast on Ramadan. I do this stuff. So you can't tell me that I have no right to go to Paradise because I don't wear the hijab."

For Hamas, though, mixed dance troupes simply facilitate sexual partnerships before marriage. "That's why they forbid boys and girls from dancing together," Doha said. "It's not right. Our troupe is like brothers and sisters, a family. Our problems are the same; our celebrations are together. We grew up together, and we're connected. We all love each other and look out for each other. I don't have a problem with hugging and kissing my brother, and he doesn't have any desires toward me. *Khallas!*"

But sexual relationships have been forged in as-Sayel, so maybe Hamas was right. "It's not wrong!" Doha almost yelled. "You know, when we travel, we're together for twenty-four hours a day, so we become closer." She herself had not met any boyfriends through dabke.

"Men have the right to do whatever they want, especially in our Arab world, but for a woman to be in a dabke troupe is not easy. We have periods when we don't have three girls because their fathers won't allow it. It's *haram,* not allowed, not good for you, not suitable to touch a boy, or even travel with boys. To be a woman in a dabke troupe means your family is very liberal and free."

"The girls in this troupe are mainly sixteen- and seventeen-year-olds living in Ramallah," Doha continued, "but most of the boys are in their twenties and come from the villages. Dabke is more popular there since villagers are more connected to the land because they live and work on it. But they're more traditional, and their minds are more closed."

I jotted a note that with her floppy hair and sneakers Doha could pass as a poster girl for the Westernized Palestinian. She revered her traditions greatly, preferring the music of Fairuz and Shaykh Imam to rap and techno. But she also had a soft spot for Celine Dion, and the wedding shop she had cofounded would not look out of place on a British high street.

"I studied English literature at Bir Zeit University," she said, "but I always liked weddings and celebrations—any kind of party or happiness—so when I graduated, my sister and I decided to open the shop. We sell flowers, wedding cards, invitations, the lights, the purple, the snow machines. We've only been going for a month and a half, but the idea is very new in Palestine and we're struggling." Celebration and struggle are close relations in Palestine, but they are not always seen together.

"I remember the demonstrations in the First Intifada," Doha said, "the Jews coming to our street and killing people, the checkpoints, the breaking of boys' arms. One time the Jews chased a boy past our house. His head was bleeding from where they'd hit him, and our neighbor, an old woman, said, "He's my son and I want him back!" They just hit her and threw her to the floor. Then they started beating the boy despite his injuries and arrested him. I had bad dreams for years after that."

"In the Second Intifada, a friend of mine was throwing stones at Beit Il, a settlement near the city. They shot him in the head. Now he's dead in the earth so I can't . . . " her voice trailed off. "He was fourteen. I was sixteen. This memory will stay with me." As she recovered her composure, Doha's tone solidified. "I want a beautiful day," she said. "I don't just want to be like the people who lose their families or sons."

Doha wanted to live in Palestine forever but could not even visit Jerusalem legally because she did not have a blue ID card. Three months before our interview she went anyway, for the first time in ten years. "I took my friend's ID," she explained. "It was risky, because if they'd caught me, I'd have been sent to jail. I started crying when I passed the Hizme checkpoint because this is my land, you know? When you get there, you're in a new world, not like the old days. Jerusalem used to be crowded and busy. Now it's like visiting a dead person."

Hizme is known in Ramallah as a settler checkpoint with relatively slack protocols. Jerusalem is only a fifteen-minute drive, but because of the checkpoints it can take over an hour to reach. "Imagine being prevented from entering your house," Doha said. "How would you feel? That's how I feel. Checkpoints humiliate people. They tell us, 'You're nothing. We control you. Your life is in our hands.'"

When her grandfather in Nablus died at the beginning of the Intifada, Israeli checkpoints prevented Doha and her family from reaching the funeral. As a result, she rejects peaceful coexistence in one state. "They hate us, and we hate them," she said. "It would have to be two states, but they shouldn't live here because I can't forgive them for taking my land and killing my friend. I just can't." This seemed a good place to end the interview.

But a few months after we said good-bye, a funny thing happened. Doha's face began appearing on billboards all over the West Bank. After a chance conversation with a friend, she had been invited to model for a rice company. "Modeling was never my hope or dream," she told me in an email. "But seeing myself on a billboard and being famous gave me a crazy nice feeling." She seemed to have taken the attention, chaos, fanfare, and jealousy of public recognition in stride. "Many people said bad things about it, but that didn't mean anything to me," she wrote. "I have self-confidence, and I don't think that this is my career."

In spring 2010 Doha's day job was as youth coordinator for a USAID-funded project, Ruwwad, giving leadership training and team-building sessions to young Palestinians. Her wedding shop had long since closed. She was engaged to be married in the fall. "My passion is still ballet dancing," she said.

Abdul Rahman Katanani, 25

Artist

SHATILA CAMP,
BEIRUT, LEBANON

We are zinc plates   The Shatila camp at midday was bleaching under a vindictive Lebanese sun. It had been a few days since Samir Quntar, four Hezbollah militants, and more than two hundred bodies were released in a swap with Israel for the bodies of two soldiers. Across the camp, poorly adhered posters of the men fluttered raggedly in the breeze.

It was desperately poor and dirty. Gaunt, shoddy buildings stood pocked with bullet holes that had spread across the camp like measles. Around them, spaghetti tangles of illegal electric cables threatened to electrocute passersby. There was little water—or space—and on the way up the stairs of the dark and decrepit tenement block that Abdul lived in with his family, a child raced past me carrying a bowl of feces.

Shatila felt like a cross between Dickens and an Arabic version of the 1970s Bronx. Subway-style graffiti adorned the camp's streets, much of it drawn by Abdul Katanani, a Palestinian artist who, if you caught him at the right angle, resembled a young Malcolm X. His signature was a door key, the most potent symbol for Palestinian refugees whose forebears often fled their homes in 1948 carrying little else.

Abdul's family hailed from the Jaffan village of Yazur, which was leveled and cleared of Palestinians in 1948. He was religious and prayed every day, but, unusually for a Shatila resident, Abdul had a degree in sociology and economics and a diploma in fine art and was studying for a master's degree. His artwork had been showcased in over thirty exhibitions, including three one-man shows. Yet Beirut's American University declined to accept him as a student on the grounds that his scholarship came from an organization with links to terrorism.

"I was surprised," Abdul told me, deadpan, "because I'm not a terrorist." He was reluctant to try the Lebanese University because of the control that militias such as Amal and Hezbollah allegedly held over admissions but nonetheless scored the third highest grade in entrance exams. He said he was the only Palestinian among more than a thousand students at the university.

"Most students are in Hezbollah, so we have good interactions. They respect me, and my cause," he said nonchalantly. Every day something happens in the camp. They'll say, 'Abdul, it was you! You did that!' It's so funny." According to Abdul, few Palestinians had converted to Shi'a Islam, but 90 percent of refugees supported Hezbollah against Israel, and Hassan Nasrallah was the most popular politician in the camp.

"Abu Mazen?" he repeated incredulously, when I asked what people thought of him. "We have to cut his head off! He's so bad that even Fatah here doesn't like him. He is a traitor. Dahlan, Rijoub, what kind of people are these? Marwan Barghouthi is the best." Barghouthi, a younger, more articulate, and more radical Fatah leader, was jailed in 2001 on terror charges. Most Palestinians believe that these were trumped up or that they were not offenses.

But Abdul was not a natural politico. An admirer of classical art and the work of the seminal Palestinian street artist Naji al-Ali, Abdul made his art from the environment in which he lived. "I get random shapes in the camp made from the clothes that hang on our buildings, the zinc [corrugated iron] plates, wood, tubes, pipes, electrical wires; my paintings contain all these. When the clothes are stuck together it symbolizes many people in the camp."

Abdul showed me a picture of a flaglike person painted without color. "He turned into zinc plates because it's a symbol of waiting," he expounded. "We are not human anymore. We are zinc plates." The camp makes the man? "Yes, inside the camp, you just see these materials. Everything is moving, but the humans are frozen on the balconies or streets. So is the man wooden or human? My painting carries the message that we are not treated like men. They treat us like material, but we have to live, breathe, make something." But the man is also the cause? "I am Palestinian. I am the cause. When I die, the cause goes to my children and to the children of my children. That's the meaning."

In addition to fine art, Abdul drew political cartoons aimed at the Arab authorities, Israel, America, and collaborators—"but also against us Palestinians," he pointed out. "I believe in self-criticism, because to improve ourselves, we have to learn from our mistakes." Abdul has received threats from political organizations offended by his cartoons, but he would not say which ones. "Every time I paint, they tell me, 'Ah, you are with Fatah, and this is not good.' Then they tell me, 'Yes, you are with Hamas!'" Abdul stopped himself, laughing. "I told them, 'I'm in a straight line, and the organizations are moving like this.'" He made a snakelike movement with his hand.

We were sitting on the fifth-floor walkway-turned-balcony of the Gaza Building tenement block where Abdul lived and was born, in 1983, when it was still a PLO hospital. He spent his formative years moving from one refugee camp to another. Fifty-six percent of Palestinian refugees in Lebanon were jobless. Two-thirds existed on less than US$6 a day. Approximately one-third of refugees were estimated by UNRWA to have a chronic illness and the same number to be suffering from malnourishment.

"Conditions here are a catastrophe," Abdul said. "If we continue inside this cage, something very dangerous will happen when you open the doors because we are dying here slowly. You can't imagine how people live on top of each other. Each family has between four and eight people, and there are four hundred families living in the four buildings that make up the block. Some families live eight people to one room, but we have eight people in two rooms, four in each." Abdul's room was about four meters long by five meters wide.

The result was claustrophobia for the 17,000 people who lived in what was once a purely Palestinian camp. Around 20 percent of Shatila was Palestinian now. Other residents were Lebanese, gypsies, or immigrants from countries such as Syria and Bangladesh. "People have a lot of problems between each other," Abdul said. "The immigrants don't care about cleanliness or health."

"The electricity is not sufficient for the whole camp. Some immigrants steal it by cutting cables from outside the camps, but they are protected by the political organizations. At best some of us sometimes get electricity for six hours a day, but sometimes we go two or three days without."

"Water is also not available every day. We don't get portable drinking water—we have to buy it in gallons. One water pipe that comes over the street leaks onto the electric cables. It's so dangerous." Abdul punctuated the sentence with a swig of bottled water, poured into his mouth refugee-style, so that the plastic did not touch his lips. He seemed relaxed, assured, and absent the defensive caution so common among his West Bank peers. But his life was far from stress-free.

"To live everyday in Lebanon is a problem," he said, momentarily alarmed. "To eat is a problem. To drink is a problem. Alcohol, hashish, and opium are big problems. Everything is a problem! We can't work in Lebanon. I couldn't even get a job as the caretaker of my building or a trash collector." A law passed by Lebanon's parliament in August 2010 eased this position slightly, allowing Palestinians to apply for private sector work permits. But some thirty professions in the public sector—including medicine, law, and engineering—remained off-limits to them. They could not even buy property.

Despite obstacles like these, Abdul was by nature an optimist. "If we act positively, we can find something positive from each other," he said. "If I have a bad day and my friend has a beautiful day, we can handle it if we cooperate and talk."

Shatila's worst day was still talked about. On September 16, 1982, Phalangist Christian militias, backed up by Israeli soldiers, massacred between 800 and 3,000 people in the camp. There is no official death toll because so many bodies were buried in unmarked graves. "Two of my aunts lost their husbands in the massacre," Abdul said. "They still don't know what happened to the bodies, and a lot of my family's friends were also killed."

Provisional conclusions drawn rapidly in the massacre's aftermath remain set today. Abdul believed that Shatila was targeted because some of the Palestinian guerrillas who "took part in the Munich operation in 1973" came from there. He still saw Lebanese Christians en masse as a selfish and self-centered people "who deal with the Israelis." He had also inferred that demands by Washington and Tel Aviv for Palestinian disarmament could be precursors to acts of genocide.

"Israel and the Americans want to smash us by diplomatic or military means. They always say that the camp army has to leave, but the Lebanese didn't protect us before, so how can we give them our guns? There is a problem with guns in the camp around how we behave toward each other. Fatah, Hamas, and the other militias have conflicts and each organization has its families so political problems turn into bigger family conflicts. But even the Lebanese who fought each other recently didn't disarm, so how can we?" he asked.

Repression, disenfranchisement, poverty, and a perceived need for armed protection help to unite refugees in Lebanon with their relatives in the occupied territories. "We fear when they close Gaza or put West Bank people in prison," Abdul said. "We feel very happy when the resistance organizations"—he made a *wheeew* sound—"get rockets or bang [kill] some soldiers. When Fatah and Hamas fight each other, it's a disaster. We are always thinking of them. We all want the right of return."

Until that happened, Abdul believed that anyone with one Palestinian grandparent should have the right to vote in PA elections and "of course" on a final-status peace deal. "You are Palestinians!" he shouted rhetorically. "The Palestinians who live in America and Europe are the most important because they've got good educations and economic situations. We lose more than them if we neglect them."

As we finished the interview, a crack of automatic gunfire echoed around the concrete walls and thin streets of the camp. Students were celebrating their exam results, Abdul told me. Are you sure that they weren't shooting their teachers? I joked. Abdul laughed. "All I see is that we are still waiting in the camp to go back to Palestine," he reiterated.

"Nabil," 25

Student

RAMALLAH, WEST BANK

A gay man's blood is for everyone Western visitors to the occupied territories are often surprised by how gentle Palestinian society still is. It is difficult for many to reconcile this tenderness with the masked avenger iconography favored by TV news bulletins and Palestinian wall art alike. The awesome cloak of *shahada* (martyrdom) is one dissonant jolt, but there are others. Traditional masculine identities in Palestine have been undermined by factors ranging from intense exposure to Western culture and the decline of pastoral life to checkpoint humiliations and brutality. Those Palestinians who do not conform to time-worn gender identities have often borne the brunt of wounded male reactions.

"Nabil," who asked that his real name not be used, was a pale and well-groomed twentysomething who had lived in Ramallah all his life. He dressed stylishly and moved lightly, with a calm demeanor he ascribed to a bone ailment that incapacitated him for years as a child. For reasons of privacy, we agreed to meet in a sparse but noisy restaurant. Every few minutes Nabil swiveled around in his seat to check the positioning of the waiters and clock the newly arrived diners.

For its long-term residents, Ramallah feels very much like a village. "Everyone knows each other," Nabil whispered. "They're related to each other, so it's very restricted. You can't do what you want because people will know. But more foreigners and Palestinians are coming from other areas now. I like that. It makes the city more alive and free."

Nabil came from a large middle-class Christian family that was displaced from the Jaffa area during the Nakba. He warmly remembered fun picnics with his extended family in Israel during the early 1990s. "My family gave me everything I wanted," he said. But their embrace was also "restricting," a word Nabil used often. He was twelve years old when he began a personal Intifada. "Boys start thinking about girls at that age, but I started thinking the other way," he said, "the men's way. I didn't tell anyone because I knew it was a problem. I felt like I was the only gay person in the world."

"There was no one I could talk to because I was very shy, so I tried to look like other people in my class. It was very hard pretending all the time. I lied when my friends talked about girls because if I came out, I would have lost some friends and others would have spread it around that I was gay. It wouldn't have been good for me. I don't want to be known."

A high profile can be very dangerous for gay men in straight Palestinian society. "They hate us," Nabil said, leaning back. "Most of them think that homosexuality doesn't exist in our society. It's only with the Europeans and open societies, and it's very bad. It's like a matter of honor to kill someone in your family if he's gay. I've heard about it happening."

"When my father figured out that I was hanging out with gay men he was so shocked that he hit me. But after that he became afraid for my safety, and he wouldn't let me go out. He'd say, 'This is a disease. Those people will infect you, so don't see them, don't speak to them, and you will be okay.'" He laughed softly as he finished the sentence.

Nabil's first sexual experience arrived in 2006 via an Internet chat room. "I found a lot of websites, but when I tried to chat with people, they were very sexual and dirty. I didn't like it. I don't care about sex so much as the feeling of freedom. By chance I found a guy from Ramallah, and he became my first date. When we met I wasn't feeling secure because I'd spoken to so many bad people on-line. One straight guy tried to find out which people were gay to attack them. I was scared and didn't trust anyone, so meeting this guy was very hard for me—but he turned out to be very nice."

"He introduced me to a group of his friends who all knew each other. I was so happy when I met them because I could just be myself and act the way I am. I didn't have to lie. They took me to Jerusalem for a party and that was . . ." Nabil started to snicker. "That was my first sex, my first time." Since then he had begun a relationship with another member of the group.

Ramallah had little infrastructure for young gay men. Nabil explained, "I heard that there are some underground parties, but I never go to them because they're invitation only. I used to go to gay bars and private parties in Tel Aviv. You get a lot of Israelis and some Arabs there, and no one knows each other."

"At the Arab parties, it is always the same people, the same scene. A man there will drink too much and act bad—sexually—and he will not remember you the next day. I think most Palestinian men are ashamed of their sexuality. In the Israeli parties people drink, but no one comes to tell me, 'I want to . . .'" Nabil bashfully refrained from finishing the sentence.

The music on the Palestinian gay party scene blended traditional Fairuz classics with American pop and the occasional drag act. Respectable married men mixed with Palestinian lesbians and the occasional she-male from Jerusalem. But gay Palestinians had other, subtler ways of recognizing each other. "I believe there's a sixth sense," Nabil said, "a gay sense, because I can feel by looking whether a man is gay or not. There are also words we use in my group. Like if some handsome guy came in here, we'd say he was 'hakim.' We know it means 'sexy,' but the others don't. Gay men used to wear their hair long and their shirt out, but it's become fashionable now, even for straights."

Although homosexuality is proscribed in most Islamic societies, gay scenes flourished in Beirut and other cities. In Palestine, though, the occupation had complicated matters. "The wall closed all the doors, and I can't go to Israel to meet Israeli men now," Nabil said gloomily before recounting a list of checkpoint travails. More grievously, the tendency of the Israeli army to blackmail gay men into becoming informers has led to their being viewed as a fifth column in Palestine.

"From the moment I'd get on the bus to Israel until the door of the party or gay beach, I'd be afraid," Nabil remembered. "My father feared that people would think I was a traitor—and that soldiers would put pressure on me to collaborate by threatening to tell everyone I'm gay." When I asked if that had happened to any of Nabil's acquaintances, he paused before answering. "I don't know for sure," he said, "but a friend I had a relationship with told me that soldiers had taken him and asked these things." He did not want to elaborate.

The consequences for an outed gay man in Ramallah could be severe. "A father absolutely might kill his son for being gay and then say he was a traitor," Nabil said. "To tell others that your son was gay would bring shame on all the family." But would having a son who collaborated bring less shame? "Yes," Nabil answered, "and if you killed a son who collaborated, it would be more of an honor because you killed him for love of your country. Gay or collaborator, both ways he will be killed. It comes to the same."

Nabil believed the problem lay in Islamic mores. "In Christian families, the worst thing that happens is separation and the son goes to another country—'We don't know you,' you know? But Hamas and Islamic Jihad say that a gay man's blood is for everyone; anyone can kill him without questions asked. I think Fatah is also not good, but it's the best worst thing we have."

The interface with the state locally is not always pleasant for vulnerable groups. "Some of the PA police are good, but they're from the community, and most of them have got girls . . . ," Nabil began, before thinking better of it. "If you're protected by someone in power, no one will touch you. He will protect you. Most people with a powerful backer become more aggressive."

"I'm starting to think that everyone has a relationship like this, because every day I hear about someone getting a job this way." Do you have someone to protect you too? I asked. Nabil chortled. "I don't like to use it, but, you know, yeah." Protection was a necessity in Ramallah. Many of Nabil's friends who came out were forced to leave the city by the factions. "They phoned one friend and said, 'We will fight you until you are better, or you leave,'" Nabil said. "So he chose to leave for Europe. I don't know if they would have killed him, but they can, they easily can, and he was scared for his life."

"There is no law practiced here. You can't take someone to court and prove he was a collaborator, so they kill him instead. In 2001 I saw someone killed in al-Manarah [Ramallah's town center]. A car stopped in the middle of the square, and two people were brought out from the back of the car covered in hoods. And they shot them. Then they started hitting their bodies, and some of the passersby joined in. It's easy to kill people and find out afterward that they weren't collaborators."

For anyone living in a community that could kill as easily as protect them, loyalties must become strained. It is easy to imagine a situation in which being gay could make one feel less Palestinian or in which by siding with the Palestinian cause a person might have to appear less gay. The $64,000 question—for a Westerner—is whether that leads to a greater affinity with gay Israelis or straight Palestinians? Nabil chewed my question for a heart-beat before firing back, "Straight Palestinians, for sure. There's also a close relationship with gay Israelis, but I am a Palestinian; it's my identity."

It was the soldiers of the occupation who arrested Nabil's father for taking part in a tax strike when he was a child, the checkpoints that went on to prevent his movement as a young man, and the military's tactics for recruiting collaborators that continued to endanger his life. Nabil blamed "the Israeli government and Fatah" for the present situation. He expected to leave Ramallah for Europe soon but was not sure when. "I've never thought much about the future," he said. "It was never in my hands to decide."

The
Second Intifada
Generation

The Second Intifada struck Palestine like a bolt of lightning from a sky that had been clouding over for years. After accepting a Jewish state on 78 percent of their original country, Palestinians had expected the Oslo process to offer them a sovereign state on what was left. Instead, the settler population in Gaza and the West Bank more than doubled, major travel arteries were blockaded, passage into Israel became obstructed, and corruption and political repression took hold, all while an interminable carousel of negotiations dragged on. Palestinians in the occupied territories were faced with an emotional-political choice: fight or flight.

By the time Ariel Sharon staked Israel's claim to the Al Aqsa Mosque with a visit in September 1999, it did not seem much of a choice. The PA's five-year interim mandate had already ended without the final-status negotiations delivering anything but a deepened sense of grievance. The *shebab* of Jerusalem had seen Lebanon's Hezbollah militia force the Israeli army from its eighteen-year occupation of South Lebanon with armed resistance. They had also seen older siblings, cousins, and parents rise up during the First Intifada—and many were scythed down. To honor them if nothing else, the Second Intifada's only articulated demand was that Israel make good on the concession—statehood—that Palestinians believed had ended that revolt. The problem was that Israel had never made such a concession.

Within five days of the rioting that broke out in Jerusalem, forty-seven Palestinians had been shot dead and almost thirty times as many were injured. Amos Malka, Israel's then-director of Military Intelligence later said that his forces had fired 1.3 million bullets within the first month of the uprising. This had the effect of militarizing the conflict as the *shebab*'s stones were discarded for faction guns, women were increasingly forced back into the family home, and Political Islam came to function as the revolt's metier.

There were far more weapons in Palestinian homes than were ever used, but the armed young men of the militias still came to symbolize the resistance.

The Second Intifada played to Israel's military and political strengths. Yasser Arafat found himself trapped between a wave of popular anger that he tried to surf and international demands that the violence be stopped to allow more negotiations. But street sentiment by now viewed the Oslo process as a pretext for establishing "facts on the ground" that would prejudge any negotiated outcome. Palestinians were trapped between two tactics, one in which the leadership followed, dragged by its feet, the other in which factions tried to lead without the means or strategy to succeed.

The result was that the new uprising, quickly rebranded the Al Aqsa Intifada, became an epic "one last heave" moment. It was simultaneously cruel, spontaneous, exhilarating, and tragic, with a tempo dictated by the Israeli army. As Israel assassinated more assumed Palestinian fighters and leaders, Hamas sent more *shahids* careering into Israel, Fatah was forced to compete, and the Al Aqsa Martyrs Brigade was born. Political activists were marginalized in favor of a new generation of military leaders who were cut down almost as quickly as they rose up. The cult of *shahada* offered some emotional compensation but no way forward. From 2000 to late 2002 the uprising was on the offensive, but a strategic inability by the militias to protect the civilian populations they purported to represent—or even their own fighters—led to stagnation from 2003 onward and, ultimately, military defeat.

Yasser Arafat's death in November 2004 and Mahmoud Abbas's Western-backed rise to power a few months later marked the Intifada's end for many. But there was no final crescendo, and Gaza's physical separation from the West Bank in 2005 or the Hamas takeover there in 2006 could also be read as denouements. While some resistance continued, the statistics of the second part of the decade tell their own story.

Between 2000 and 2004, 949 Israelis were killed, compared to 3,523 Palestinians, a ratio that could suggest an unequal war. However, in the period from Abbas's declaration of an end to violent resistance in December 2004 to Israel's withdrawal from Gaza in January 2009, 117 Israelis were killed, compared to 3,111 Palestinians. The clear majority of Palestinian dead in both periods were civilians. At the same time, the economy tanked, national trauma overflowed, and hostility between Fatah and Hamas almost ended in civil war. The resistance maintained pride, honor, and negotiating leverage—but it also enabled a turkey shoot in Gaza. *Sumud,* the quality that sustained generations of Palestinians, began to come under intense stress as the strong family and clan ties that facilitated it were steadily undermined.

The killing of some thirteen Palestinian Israelis by Israeli policemen and soldiers in October 2000—the so-called October events—prevented the Intifada from spreading into Israel. But it also radicalized Arab citizens. It offered some cover for a raft of racist and authoritarian provisions, ranging from a ban on marriages involving Palestinians in the occupied territories to the disqualification of anti-Zionist political parties from running for office. Asmi Bishara's *Vision* document was perhaps the one clarion call to emerge during this period. Its argument for "a state for all its citizens" resonated among Arabs in Israel and stirred the embers of the PLO's old dream of one democratic secular state. However, for resurrecting the ghost, Asmi Bishara was, in Palestinian eyes, punished with trumped-up charges and exile.

Palestine's most disadvantaged constituency, the refugees, had mostly again to watch events unfold as spectators from afar, often in Arab countries that seemed to value friendship with Israel more than their continued presence. In Lebanon at least, the unilateral withdrawal of Israeli troops in 2000 and the rise of Hezbollah allowed Palestinians some breathing space. The exiled political leadership of Hamas was less fortunate, being forced to move from one country to another, ending up in Syria in a burgeoning alliance with Iran. The international solidarity movements meanwhile became increasingly central to the identities of Palestinians in the Diaspora.

The Second Intifada forced the Palestinians back onto the world's agenda and won formal recognition of their demand for a state. But internally it allowed the PA and militias to complete the destruction of the street democratic mechanisms of the First Intifada (and what was left of Palestinian civil rights) in pursuit of a struggle that would advantage their members in an imagined future Palestine. Ultimately, their failure to reach it diminished all the militias and poisoned civil society.

The Al Aqsa uprising ended with the Palestinian leadership in perhaps their most divided and defensive state since the Nakba, glowering menacingly at each other from symmetrically deformed substatelets. At the grassroots level, resistance remained as popular as ever. But it increasingly wobbled on a tightrope between nihilism and careerism, from which Palestinian women were once again mostly excluded.

**Firaz Turkman, 26, and
Alla Subharin, 31**

Islamic Jihad

JENIN, WEST BANK

Do you hear the voice of Haifa? Firaz and Alla made an odd couple. Firaz was physically imposing, gruff, and taciturn in a deliberate sort of way. Alla was deft, intellectual, and restless. Firaz's father sold vegetables in Jenin City; Alla's was an unemployed farmer who once worked in Israel. Both men joined Islamic Jihad in their teens and by the time we were first introduced in the Jenin refugee camp in March 2007, seemed up to their necks in it.

Setting up the meeting required several street conversations with intermediaries, a twilight rendezvous at a third party's house, and a dash through the camp's byzantine back alleys to a concrete shed, around which local children kept watch. They had the air then of fugitives living on borrowed time.

Alla was a spokesman for the group and Firaz a camp fighter. In those days, the faction was divided into political activists who worked by day and fighters who ghosted through the deserted streets at night "defending" the camp. In practice, the fighters spent much of their time evading undercover Israeli soldiers who ruthlessly hunted them down.

"At night we put fighters around the camp and lay mines," Firaz said. "We remove them [mines] again during the day to protect people. But if the occupation tries to enter the camp, we fight them. When our camp leader called me to say that the occupation had killed his son, we planned a funeral and a revenge attack." Jenin has an unusually high percentage of Afro-Palestinians, but Firaz would only say that his name "goes back to the time when Turks came here with Muslim soldiers." Many Afro-Palestinians arrived as slaves during the Ottoman era, and discrimination continues today. Firaz threatened to walk out of the interview when I asked about his experiences of racism.

At school he got into "lots of fights," he said, but could not remember if he was defending himself, or who won. Soldiers bullied and humiliated him too, but Firaz could not recall whether they singled him out because of his color. The one fighting memory that remained—vividly—was his decision to join Islamic Jihad.

"In 2002 I reached a point where I could no longer endure the occupation," he said. "One of my friends was killed in fighting in the camp just after September 11. He was nineteen years old. It was the first time Israeli tanks attacked the camp. I decided then that I had to stand up and fight. My friends were in Islamic Jihad, and I liked the way they understood the Palestinian issue, so I asked to become a fighter with them. Palestine is an Islamic land for all Muslims, but Fatah and Hamas would build a country on a small part of it. Islamic Jihad would not."

Firaz was arrested in 2003 after an all-night house-to-house chase. "Finally they surrounded me and sent their dogs in. One bit my hand like this," he said, baring his teeth. "I was in prison for three years after that." During this time, like most prisoners, Firaz claims that he was tortured. "Sometimes they left me in isolation for twenty or thirty days—except for interrogations. They'd threaten to destroy my house or arrest my father, and they made me sit in stress positions on a chair for several hours at a time. It was the most miserable period of my life."

Alla was imprisoned at around the same time, but his journey to Islamic Jihad was smoother. Religion had been central to his childhood—"like my strategy in life," he said. At the age of fifteen, he joined Islamic Jihad because they offered "a balanced resistance," he said. "The occupation enters the West Bank and kills our people, so we go there and kill theirs. We have no tanks or machine guns. We aren't equal. We know we can't defeat them militarily, but still we will not give up."

"If somebody took your house, kicked you out, and you had no law to turn to, what would you do?" If he had more weapons I might look to a political way forward, I replied. But Alla was convinced that Israel would be defeated—because it was written in the Qur'an—and Western incomprehension of a strategy of using *shahids* was irrelevant. "Europeans kill themselves because they split up with their girlfriends or got depressed because they were unemployed or their parents left them," he reflected. "These are weak reasons. We believe in the justice of our cause and the need to protect ourselves from occupation. Palestinian people have strong reasons to kill themselves."

In Alla's vision of a future Palestinian state, Jews would not be allowed to live as equal citizens because they refused to live as equals today. "We know that the Nazis killed them, but how can we treat the Jews well when they occupy us?" Curiously, though, he did not object to having Jewish friends. "It's something normal and natural," he said. "If there was no occupation why would I refuse Jewish friends? The Jewish people are rich, and they control many banks in Europe, but they're just front-line troops fighting Arabs to protect America's interests in the Middle East." Alla talked about forcing Russian Zionists to return to their lands, but family tradition seemed to be his primary motivation. "I respect the old people because they have a memory of our land," he explained. "They are the Palestinian culture, and we have to protect them because Israel tries to erase their experience." Like most people in the Jenin camp, Alla's family was expelled from the Haifa region in 1948.

"In the 1980s my grandfather took me to his old village," Alla said. "As he showed me the destroyed houses and told me the stories, I felt strange, like there was something I had to keep deep inside and remember. Then he fell to the ground and started crying." The young Alla had to take him back to Jenin in an ambulance. "That generation worked the land. Now they work for a pittance just to stay alive. We must pass on their message because the Israelis want our children to forget their traditions and embrace a new culture. If they do, this generation will be lost. Haifa is like a woman in pain, crying out. Do you hear the sadness in the voice of Haifa? She asks you when freedom will come. One day we will answer her call."

Firaz and Alla had not experienced the shame that some of their parents' generation felt during the Nakba, but it was still a bone that could not quite be swallowed. "Sometimes I feel angry about it," Firaz admitted, "but I don't blame our grandparents because they had no guns. They were simple farmers. They couldn't do anything, as I know from my experience here. We had a few guns in 2002, but after ten days of resistance, the occupation destroyed our camp. Still we fought in order not to leave and repeat their mistake."

The motto that it is better to die on your feet than to live on your knees could have been written for the Jenin camp. Its architectural density and political intensity made it the nerve center of the West Bank's Intifada until Israel demolished it in 2002. But the clock in Israel and Palestine often seems to run at a faster tempo than elsewhere, and by the time I returned to meet Firaz and Alla a year later, the camp militias had been all but smashed. Other "resistance" was tapering off into destructive local power plays, such as a religious campaign against the *al-Hurriye* Freedom Theatre, then the West Bank's only community drama resource. As we waited for Firaz and Alla outside a barbershop, my translator—who had aligned himself with Islamic Jihad in prison for reasons of safety—amused himself by pointing out the current status of the various boys modeling haircuts in the shop's posters. "Jail, prison," he began, "dead, dead, prisoner . . . "

Firaz and Alla were no longer in hiding. In fact, we met in a beautiful villa owned by Firaz's father just outside the camp. When I asked a much more relaxed-looking Alla about his involvement with Islamic Jihad, he even allowed himself a joke. "I sold my soul," he smiled. "But I'm still carrying their ideas. Islamic Jihad has almost stopped in the camp because of Israel's killings. Most of the leaders have died or run away, scared. Gaza also affected things. Before, the political parties' purpose was to fight the Jews, but afterward everything changed. People stopped trusting the parties."

Since our last interview, Alla had gotten a scholarship to study law and now wanted to work for a human rights group. He was sanguine about his years with the Jenin resistance. "A few times we were successful in protecting the camp," he said, "and sometimes we injured soldiers. But then the Jews would destroy hundreds of houses or kill or arrest people. They have the power, the tanks and helicopters. They have everything." Firaz had also moved away from his old life. "After Gaza, I felt depressed because all the parties were fighting each other, so I stopped and decided to get married," he said.

Both men appeared to be settling down after completing a form of national service. But that was not easy. "I can't work because of my situation," Firaz said. "I can't leave the camp or travel either because the Israelis would arrest me if they found me. I'll wake up at 9:00 or 10:00 A.M.—I don't sleep well—and ask my wife what I can get for her. Then I'll collect wood to make a fire because of the cold, and go to smoke *nargila* and talk about political things."

An amnesty that Israel offered to fighters in the Al Aqsa Martyrs Brigade who turned in their guns had also changed the camp atmospherics. "We can't understand how they accepted that," Alla sniped. "They are fighters, and the Jews are the enemy. If they were waiting for forgiveness from the Jews, why did they fight them in the first place? The Jews always try to trick us. People look at the Al Aqsa Martyrs differently now."

Firaz and Alla expected an eventual Hamas takeover of the West Bank. According to Firaz, "Many individuals in Islamic Jihad have started carrying Al Qaida thoughts." But a rather alarmed Alla interjected, "There are no schools or political parties teaching their way of thought. They don't exist here. The Jews just claim that as an excuse to kill our fighters. Al Qaida is a terrorist party." At that, the two Jihadists began an impassioned debate. But the times in Jenin were clearly changing.

When I asked Alla if he now watched any Western TV shows, he sheepishly admitted to a fondness for *The Bold and the Beautiful*. "I like those kinds of romantic shows," he said. Kitsch can be seen as a reaction to trauma anywhere. Firaz harrumphed, "I just watch Al-Jazeera." Alla was still unwed then, unlike Firaz. But both men looked relieved when the conversation steered back to politics.

**Ayman Nahas, 32,
and Hanna Shamas, 36**

Comedians

HAIFA, ISRAEL

On both sides   Within a few decades of Israel's founding, many Arabs living within it had been paralyzed by identity crisis. Unaccepted by an Israeli state that had expelled their families, they still benefited economically from their new citizenship compared to their brethren in the occupied territories.

Ayman and Hanna grew up in a schizophrenic world of unmentionables that advantaged humor as a form of truth-telling. When they were teenagers, Oslo, globalization, and the West's "humanitarian" interventions had suggested an inexorable trend toward Palestinian statehood and civic equality. Yet Israel retrenched and expanded, feeding a resentment that exploded in October 2000. Afterward, as in the old Soviet bloc, it proved safer to register resistance through the arts.

The *Washington Post* dubbed Ayman and Hanna "the Arab version of Laurel and Hardy," but to their fans they were simply Shamas-Nahas, the most popular Arab comedians in Israel. Ayman—the thinner, wild-looking funny guy—was a village boy from Tashiha in the Galilee who experienced a "traumatic" move to Haifa when he was eleven. He quickly became the class joker. Hanna, the straight man, was assured, mature, and a little reserved, smiling to himself for long minutes at a time, as though privately reviewing a shaggy dog story.

"We actually met on November 4, 2001, at an open mic night," Hanna said. This was also the sixth anniversary of Yitzhak Rabin's assassination, a national memorial day, but he did not mention it. "Somebody asked me if we wanted to try something together. I said, 'No, leave me alone.'"

"We both did different monologues," Ayman jumped in. "Mine was a kind of stand-up tragedy, just improv. He was doing a voiceover with some actress. But it was a nice energy. He was working here in this restaurant, *Fatoush*—or he told me he was—so I hung around in the kitchen and we wrote material by the back door. We started performing monthly sketches in a pub and then moved to a theatre." The pair's reputation spread by word of mouth, and they quickly moved up to top billing.

Unlike Laurel and Hardy, though, they performed in Arabic and in a political tinderbox. According to Ayman, the two red lines they crossed at their peril were "the Jews thing and connecting racism with the Holocaust." Still he said, "We don't want to be the funny Arabs doing it for the Jews." Their roleplaying, which morphed into satire, exaggerated the dark kookiness of everyday Palestinian life—checkpoint etiquette, witnessing bus bombings, Arab male chauvinists in the kitchen, and so on.

"It would be boring if we just tried to explain the history of the Palestinian situation," said Hanna, who now had a gig on children's TV. "It's not our way to say this is the truth, this is the soldier, and we should go on the streets to burn, destroy, and fuck the government." One "brain mechanic" skit they performed involved Ayman being offered a new identity trade-in at the garage. "My existence is broken," he outlined. "It's like the people that walk near the wall saying, 'God protect me.' We call it the '67 identity because our parents are like this." The skit ended with the man qualifying for a new confident, patriotic identity.

But neither comedian grew up feeling very confident or patriotic. Ayman was politicized by racism. "At eighteen you look for a job and it's like, 'Why aren't you in the army?'" he said. "'I don't have to, I'm Arab.' 'Ah we see.'" When he went to Eilat to try to meet girls, Ayman used to call himself "Rami," a name popular with Israeli Jews, or he would speak with a French accent and call himself "Louis." "It was an experience of being 'not me,'" he said, "of acting. If I told a girl that I was an Arab, nothing would happen. I tried this." The issue of Arab Muslim men pretending to be Jews in order to bed Israeli Jewish women is political nitroglycerin in Israel.

When he spoke Arabic in the street, Ayman was stared at. When he spoke it at his first job—as a delivery boy—he was admonished by his Jewish co-workers. "They'd be like, 'It's amazing that you're an Arab! Your skin is so light, and you speak Hebrew so well. You don't pronounce the *d,* you pronounce the *p.* You don't look Arabic. You're different from the others. You are a good Arab.' Sometimes I'd even say, 'I'm not Arab, I'm a Christian Israeli.'"

"Until I was nineteen, I thought *Palestinian* was a bad word, kind of a curse. There was a period of believing that I was an Israeli Arab, but something always felt wrong inside. What is an Israeli Arab? It's nothing. During the Second Intifada, I started to look at life as a Palestinian. It was a relief. I felt safe and secure after so long trying to deny it. This is what I am, what I was looking for, where I belong. The first stamp in erasing our identity was the term *Israeli Arab*. It's a border, a limit, a frame that you're born into without seeing what's behind it. You don't even see yourself in it. This is the identity crisis."

The Nakba had not been talked about in either comic's home. The response was "nothing, just silence," whenever Ayman raised it. "I started talking to my grandparents a few years ago. They were like, 'Leave those things alone!' My grandfather said, 'We had the Turkish and the British, now we have the Israelis. It's the same. I will live with what comes.' My grandmother told me, 'Be grateful that you are living every day with enough food and air to breathe!' They always tried to keep a low profile."

Hanna's family came from Lebanon and Haifa, the city where he was born and now lives with his wife, two daughters, Nefas the dog, and a bird called Fufu. His family is split between several countries. He did not meet many Jews as a child, although when one called him a "dirty Arab" at school, he remembered that they were both punished. His father's best friend was imprisoned for Fatah activities, and politics were rarely discussed.

One of his strongest memories dated to the late 1980s. "All the Israelis were flying their flag for a national holiday," he said, knitting his fingers tightly together. "I wanted to put something on the balcony too, so I took a picture of a sexy woman from my mother's magazine. My father was like, 'What are you doing? It's not our day.' After that I understood. Years later I tried to remember the moments that we spent together, because there weren't a lot. I asked myself why we didn't talk more, and then I started crying. If he was still alive, I think we would talk about this."

Ayman's father was a bus driver for Egged, the Israeli national bus company, and so were his grandfather and uncle. He grew up around Jews and, after narrowly missing a suicide bomber in a Haifa restaurant, had mixed feelings about armed resistance. "I have my fear," he said. "During the Second Intifada, every time a bus was bombed, my family was shaking. It's like you're on both sides. We are part of Israel, but inside we are *there*. During the Lebanon war it was really difficult being between the two sides and feeling part of both. In my village three people were killed by a Katyusha, but when Nasrallah told the Arabs of Haifa to leave the city there was pride also because the world began to know about us as Palestinians. It was the first time an Arab leader had recognized us as part of this conflict."

The '48 Palestinians are citizens of Israel just as the '67 Palestinians live in the West Bank and Gaza. Ayman said he used to envy the '67 Palestinians, despite the far worse oppression they suffer because "at least they know their occupier." "They don't see Israelis in civilian clothes. They deal with the soldier. Here the occupier is part of you—your neighbor, your friend, and also a human being. I don't want to hate him because then I will lose my humanity. But he has a clear identity, and I don't. He's gaining because I'm losing. He's building because I'm being destroyed."

"It takes two parts to coexist," he continued edgily. "But I don't exist here. I believe in communism, but I'm becoming very nationalistic. I can't be a universal part of this big world while I don't feel part of my own nation." In Ayman's view the "October days" improved relations with the West Bank, but Hanna hedged with the observation that many Palestinians in the occupied territories would disagree. "They can feel real pressure and a real army, but we're dealing with the same issues and conflict," he said. "I don't think that Ayman or I ever feel that we are the same—because we live in Israel—but we were born here, and this is all Palestine. You might have a discussion with someone from Ramallah about who is more Palestinian. But I am a real Palestinian. I don't need to prove that."

In Ramallah and the Daheisha refugee camp near Bethlehem, Ayman now led acting workshops. In Israel he was most angered by passivity in his community. "It's about being unaware of danger, ignoring reality, and being afraid. They say, 'We don't care.' I say, 'Be someone and do something, and if not, this is your choice. Don't be a wall blocking people who want to move.' As a community from 1948 to October 2000, we were very passive. Over the past ten years, we started to get into something. I don't know if it's good or bad, but I feel good, and so do people in the streets. More people are saying we are Palestinians now. Even if they're saying it just to be 'in,' it's something."

The night before, Ayman had had a dream that the Shabbak, Israel's internal security service, was trying to recruit him as an informer. He linked it to doubts about why the authorities had not cracked down on Shammas-Nahas yet, but "the Shabbak agent" could symbolize a range of inner voices or feelings. For minorities portrayed as a fifth column, oppression is rarely just an external experience.

Asmaa al-Goule, 27
Journalist
GAZA CITY

The enemy is inside us Asmaa had a lot on her mind and few people to share
it with. An award-winning short story writer and journalist, she was born in
Rafah's refugee camp but later moved to Gaza City. During most of Asmaa's
childhood, her father worked as an engineer in Dubai, and she grew up in
what became a renowned Hamas family. But her uncles beat and disavowed
her at a young age because she sang the muezzin's call to prayer, *"Allahu
Akhbar,"* and wore dresses. Now she was a secular single parent who read
Henry Miller, shunned head coverings, and delighted in her independence.
As we sipped coffee among Rimal's heeled and headscarfed café society, consciously or not, Asmaa presented herself as the last sane person in the asylum.
Maybe she saw herself that way, or perhaps she just understood my need for
a narrative. I was, after all, a fellow journalist, and she was doing me a favor.

"Journalism here is stupid," she confided. "We have news by numbers, with
no stories or culture. You never read about poetry, books, or movies in Gaza.
We talk about blood and martyrs. It's stupid, and I'm against it. We have a
culture of death, *shahada* and heaven, even in our pictures. As a Palestinian,
it makes me sad. People want peace. The parties want to fight. I just want
to drink a cup of coffee. This is my dream. But journalists here prefer to be
Palestinian first. It's the problem. Even me during the war, I couldn't write
things."

"Before one interview I was conducting for Palmedia [a Palestinian TV
company], a doctor told me that seventy people who died in an area were
fighters, not civilians. I asked him if he would say it in front of the camera.
He said, 'No, no, we will say it was civilians.' I saw people praying for the

fighters when the fighters had come to fight between their houses. I wrote this in my newspaper *al-Ayam*—and prayed that nobody from Hamas would read it. Everybody then was saying, 'Look to the Hamas leaders,' but they didn't help us. They all hid underground. We heard that Fawsi Barhoum was seen in the delivery section of al-Shifa Hospital. If our leaders are underground and the victims are under the planes, what is this government for?"

On one occasion during the war, Asmaa said, the same Hamas spokesman, Fawsi Barhoum, turned up at the Palmedia offices unannounced to request the use of their studio for a press conference. "We were up on the fourteenth floor," Asmaa recalled, "when I looked out the window and saw Israeli warplanes circling the building. The sound grew louder, and I saw that Fawsi was afraid. His face turned yellow." It was the first time the Hamas leadership had been humanized for her.

"Before he went on air I told him, 'Don't worry, we will all die together,' and I still feel that we shared that human moment of fear together, as Palestinians. But I also felt like, we have guns, why are you acting like a scared child? Or, if that's the situation, why are you on Al-Jazeera saying, 'We will win the war.' At that moment, though, I also felt that I had to support them. I would have died trying to protect them, because in the end they were our war leaders and so they were more important for the people than I am."

After the press conference Fawsi appeared shell-shocked. He complained that the Egyptian government wouldn't even answer phone calls from Hamas's leadership and said that on December 26, the night before Israel's attack, the Egyptian government had called Hamas to tell them that Israel would not attack the Strip for another two days. This would, of course, have been disinformation. But that story has already been told.

Asmaa characterized Hamas's evolution under blockade in surprisingly feline terms: "You take this Islamic cat, put it in a room, close the windows and doors, and it becomes a tiger. This is Hamas—or how they started to think of themselves anyway—but compared to Israel, they were not. Nobody knew."

All the same, her articles elicited threats from Hamas, and her newspaper refused to print some of her stories for fear that the government would close their offices. When I asked her what kind of threats she was talking about, Asmaa put her face in her hands and sighed. "Divorced woman, free woman, different woman, what do you think they would say?" I don't know, I replied. What did they say? "It's a prostitution issue," she looked down and laughed faintly. "Yeah, they said, 'Nobody will sue us.' There are three accusations here: prostitution, drugs, and spying. A friend of mine had already been framed, imprisoned, and beaten. So I stayed home for three months, just thinking about it. Eventually, the PFLP helped me rent another house when Hamas came into my area asking questions about me."

Asmaa drew Hamas's ire by focusing on subjects the government preferred swept under the carpet. She wrote about honor crimes, how women were told to return to violent husbands by Hamas officials, the way unemployment was forcing young men to work for the Hamas police, and how poverty and corruption remained unchanged under the new government. "The only difference is that Fatah made its corruption in ten years, Hamas did it in three," she quipped. "One person I asked for an opinion said a funny thing: 'I want to kill Gaza.' But Hamas didn't want me to write anything bad about the Gaza Strip. I sent a lawyer to talk to them, and he helped a lot."

Surprisingly perhaps, Asmaa saw Fatah's violations of civil liberties in the West Bank as "crazy" and "even worse" than Hamas's in Gaza. "At least here we have a voice and can talk," she noted. Our interview was taking place well below the ambient level of café noise, but I understood what she meant. "Fatah was better for me as a secular person when it was in power, but it put Islamic writers and journalists in jail just the same. Fatah threatened and beat them too. There was no difference. But I can talk with Hamas about it. They couldn't do that with the Fatah big people."

Of Mohammed Dahlan, the former Fatah leader of Gaza, Asmaa declared, "I can't say that he's a Palestinian. Businessmen don't have a homeland." But when asked what "homeland" meant to her, she became ambivalent. "I don't know if the homeland means where you were born or if it's my son in Gaza or a dream in my mind or a country that I visit, like America. But when I'm outside, I can be myself. Like in a train or a subway, I'm quiet. I'm nobody. Here everybody knows me. I prefer being anonymous, so nobody judges you. You don't have to be what other people want all the time."

But if anonymity offered a home in the Gaza hothouse, it was one that Asmaa could not afford. "Journalism protects me," she said, "because everybody knows who I am—and who my uncle is. I wrote an article titled, 'My Dear Uncle, Is This the Homeland We Want?' It became very famous and he threatened to kill me, but because I was a journalist I could write about it and he couldn't do anything. I don't care. I'm not frightened of death. I'm frightened of what will happen to my son if something happens to me. If my uncle can kill Fatah people—and he has—he can kill anyone. He has a lot of guns in the house. He even used our house in Rafah to jail people. It is shameful, but he can do anything."

As such, the drive for protection through publicity had its limits. "You must write things your way and try to tell your story because this gives you power," Asmaa said. "But it's not simple. This is a hell house." The oft-cited figures of Gaza's decay—95 percent of private industry mothballed, 65 percent of people unemployed, and so on—fail to capture the way that crisscrossing loyalties of family and faction have become poisonously barbed.

"We Palestinians don't like each other a lot," Asmaa mused. "We have such bad images of each other. We're in the same place under the same blockade, with the same ideas from the same books in the same schools, with the same people, and there are no new experiences. We just eat each other. That's why I don't have friends here. I can't trust anybody. I only talk superficially with people in the shop—and even my friends—because everyone here judges you all the time, even if they do it silently. If you were an outsider you'd say, 'There's a lot of suffering, and the enemy is Israel.' But it's not true, the enemy is inside us."

A few weeks after our interview, Asmaa was detained on a Gazan beach by a local Hamas security force, the Committee for the Propagation of Virtue and Prevention of Vice. She was accused of not wearing a headscarf or having a male escort and of "laughing out loud" with male friends. Her passport was confiscated, her friends were beaten in police custody, and she subsequently received death threats by email. A few weeks after that, citing political pressure, she quit her reporting job on *al-Ayam*.

Neriman al-Jabari, 26

Widow

JENIN CAMP, WEST BANK

Happiest days The widows of martyrs hold a double-edged status in Palestinian society. They are revered for their sacrifice and admired for their steadfastness. But they also often go financially unsupported and are expected to preserve their loved one's memory by not remarrying. This worsens their economic position. Between September 2000 and June 2008 Israel extrajudicially killed 348 suspected Palestinian fighters, mostly in street ambushes, without a trial.

Neriman al-Jabari comes from one of Hebron's most important clans—the Hebron governor was also a Jabari—but few notable families lived as she did. In her striped headscarf, long black *jalbab,* and frumpy brown cardigan, Neriman looked older than her years. She lived with five children in a tiny dwelling that was poor even by the Jenin camp's dismal standards. Her husband, an Islamic Jihad leader, was assassinated by Israeli forces in 2004.

She agreed to talk to me about him with her father-in-law, five children, an Islamic Jihad official, and friends all present in her tiny front bedroom. The company inhibited her answers—especially where criticism of Islamic Jihad was concerned—and added a degree of performance. But Mohammed's death was a collective loss to Jenin, and the interview was multifaceted too.

"I'm a Palestinian, and we don't have any happiest days," Neriman chastised me when I asked an ill-judged opening question about her childhood memories. "I grew up in the First Intifada so I didn't have a normal childhood. I was scared of the occupation from the day that my brother was shot in the arm for throwing stones."

Four days before, Neriman's mother had died from cancer. Her sisters had taken care of her in her last days, and, painful as the loss was, "it didn't affect me as much as my husband's death," she said. "That was the most horrible thing for me. It changed my life." Religion must have been a solace, but her father-in-law, Mohammed, answered when I asked about it. "It's not just Neriman's religion. We all respect Islam. It's our way of life."

"It gives me comfort and rest," Neriman interjected. "When I read the Qur'an I feel safety. I support Islamic Jihad . . . ," she started, but someone else immediately chimed in, "because of her husband!" Neriman was not confident about speaking above others' voices. "I'm not educated, and I can't get a good job," she murmured when the hubbub had died down.

"My husband used to work for the city council before he became a fighter. After he died they gave me 1,000 shekels a month. It's nothing," she said with a mixture of sardonic resignation and disgust, again interrupted. But as she told me the story of her husband, who shared the same name as his father, she visibly relaxed.

"I didn't know Mohammed before we got married. My uncle brought him to my house and introduced us in 1998, and I just liked everything about him. He had a sense of humor. I loved him for that." Mohammed the elder took his cue. "I used to work in a store selling cups of tea," he said, "and in the mornings Mohammed would come and say, 'My father, give me one shekel.' I'd ask why. He'd say, 'Just give it to me,' and so I would. Then he'd go to the next store, to ask the same thing as a tease. But he always returned in the evening and gave me 100 shekels."

The young Mohammed came to see Neriman every two or three days, and after two weeks he proposed to her. The marriage improved with time. "Every year that passed was happier than the one before," Neriman said. "Obviously I loved him, but I'm too shy to talk about it. Mohammed was a fan of Fatah, but my brothers persuaded him to join Islamic Jihad."

"During the First Intifada, he was arrested and spent thirty-three months in jail," Mohammed's father continued. "When he was let out in a prisoner release, he tried his best to get a job, but Fatah wouldn't help him at all. He felt sad and started with Islamic Jihad."

"Our life completely changed for the worse," Neriman said, picking up the thread. "Mohammed became wanted, and he started to sleep outside the house. If we were eating, he'd get a phone call and have to run away. One morning, as I was preparing breakfast for the children, I heard that there were soldiers in the camp. I tried to call Mohammed, but his phone was off. It was the first time that had happened, and I felt a strange new feeling. I went to see my mother, and she said he was near the hospital. The night before, Mohammed had told me he would sleep around the hospital."

"So I went out onto the street and heard some women talking about the invasion, saying that people had been killed. Many women came to my house, just looking at me. They knew that my husband had died. One came and hugged me. I asked her why. She said, 'Oh, it's nothing.' Then her cousin hugged me and started crying. That's when my cousin called her husband, and he told her that Mohammed had died. I started screaming and crying. After that I don't remember anything. At some point I woke up and started screaming my husband's name. Then I just collapsed again."

"On February 28, 2004, Mohammed came to visit me at six o'clock in the morning," Mohammed the elder continued. "He said, 'Father, give me one shekel.' The same joke. He said he wanted to visit a friend and I told him, 'Don't go, I heard that there are soldiers in the city.' He said, 'Okay, just for five minutes, and then I'll turn back . . . ' He went to the camp."

"Later, someone passed by my store and started talking to someone about Mohammed—he didn't realize that I was his father. The other guy said, 'Don't speak loudly, his father is here.' But I overheard and told them to tell me what happened. They'd heard that Special Forces had killed Mohammed and two other Islamic Jihad leaders, Ashraf and Alla. The Special Forces had followed their car, but they didn't have their guns so they tried to escape. Their car hit a wall, and the Special Forces got out and shot at their heads and bodies for ten minutes."

"When they finished telling the story, I collapsed. I went to the hospital with Mohammed's daughter, but we couldn't get in, and after a couple of hours they brought the body to my house. Two thousand people came to his funeral." Mohammed looked lifeless and proud as his frail yet commanding voice subsided. "I felt hopeless," Neriman added. "I stopped working in my house. I couldn't take care of the children. For months, I'd wake up in the morning and sit in front of the house for hours. I felt that I had nothing, and was nothing, without my husband. My life was completely negative."

Eventually, Neriman's responsibility to her children snapped her out of mourning. "I tried to get back to our old life, to fill the vacuum that Mohammed had left in their lives by doing things he used to—like the shopping. My family offered to look for another husband for me, but I refused and told them it was none of their business. I don't want to get married again. No one can replace Mohammed."

Did she see the wives of *shahids* as having particular responsibilities? "I try to keep my good reputation so that people won't forget Mohammed," Neriman said. "I try to feel proud when I walk the street because my husband died defending the camp, and I try to deal with his friends and family so people will remember that I am the wife of a *shahid*. You have to live with that."

Neriman's mornings were difficult now but not as tough as the Eid holiday. "The night before Eid, Mohammed used to take us to the city to buy clothes," she recalled flatly, "and we enjoyed ourselves, joking together until midnight. Every year now, I feel sad when I remember." Palestine is awash with such reminiscences, and those with the most painful memories are often doubly burdened with their safekeeping. Neriman said she spent as much time as she could tending to a special guest room where Mohammed sat for hours every day. "It was always special to him. He'd close the door and just sit there, with his friends or alone," she said.

When I asked if the wives of *shahids* had special needs that should be more recognized in Palestinian society, a spat involving Mohammed and the Islamic Jihad official threatened to derail the interview. Finally the noise receded, and Neriman ventured, "The most difficult thing for me was that Mohammed borrowed money from many people. They want it back, and it's difficult for me to pay them. I must—it's my responsibility—but I have no support from society, just from our friends who come to visit us. None of the political parties look after us at all." The Islamic Jihad representative explained that there were so many wives of *shahids* now that his group could not afford to give them money anymore.

As we finished, Neriman invited me to see Mohammed's old guest room. It was a large, modern, furnished apartment, decorated in martyr kitsch.

Photos of Mohammed adorned the walls, cut into heart shapes, some framed with AK-47 shapes. Neriman pointed out a portrait of Mohammed near some teddy bears and a doll in a hijab. In it, he was standing with one leg crossed in front of the other, wearing a guerrilla cap and striped sweater. A rifle sloped off his shoulder. His beard lent him an aura of tree-chopping strength and generosity rather than anything pious. Neriman looked warmed beneath his image as Mohammed stood there, smiling benevolently down at his wife and children forever.

Tamer Nafar, 29

Rapper

LYD, ISRAEL

The only one who actually lived   Tamer Nafar was nineteen when he formed DAM—Da Arabian MCs—in 1998 with his brother Suhell and friend Mahmoud Jreri. In Hebrew, their name means "blood"; in Arabic, "eternity." DAM was the first Palestinian rap act, and before the group was offered a record contract—by a British label—its debut single "Meen Irhabi?" (Who's the Terrorist?) had already been downloaded more than a million times from its website.

Most of Tamer's family were musicians. His father played guitar and drums and also decorated Arabic musical instruments. But he was unable to interest the boys in learning to play. "We just write lyrics," Tamer shrugged. "We don't know shit about music." His bedroom was bedecked with posters of Tupac Shakur and other musical and political icons. They did not look out of place in the dilapidated housing project Tamer shared with his extended family on the outskirts of Lyd (Lod in Hebrew).

"Lyd was one of the last cities to fall during the Nakba," he said augustly. "The kibbutzim and *moshavs* kept being defeated here because the population fought bravely until they ran out of ammunition." At the city's Dahmash mosque, 176 fighters were massacred after they had turned in their old rifles. In all, 426 men, women, and children were killed after the Fedayeen surrendered.

Tamer's family was originally from Jaffa but arrived in Lyd in 1948 after stopping to rest on the way from Ashkelon to Amman. "My father's family in Jaffa was pushed into the sea," he explained. "A psychological war was going on back then. All it needed was for soldiers to come with weapons, and people got scared. They told my family to return after a few weeks, but when they came back, a settlement had been built. 'This is not your house anymore.' They'd lived in Jaffa for as long as anyone could remember."

"They've knocked the house down, but you can still see my grandfather's store. It's empty. The problem is that Israelis can't admit they did something wrong. A solution will start only with an admission of what happened in 1948, the same as with slavery or the Holocaust. There has to be an apology, and then Israelis have to stop treating us arrogantly. After that, I suggest we follow Martin Luther King. He said, 'When you see your enemy is beaten, reach out your hand.' Don't knock him down."

You don't prefer Malcolm X? I asked, surprised. "I'm closer to Malcolm, but I believe in both of them. Let's say one person shakes the tree and someone else collects the fruit. Tupac is another inspiration. I haven't learned as much from him as from our heroes or Che Guevara, but he was born in prison, the son of a Black Panther. He grew up in the ghetto as a thug. He didn't write intellectually; he came strictly from the street and educated himself. He made something out of nothing, and that's the spark."

Tupac and Che of course were both assassinated, but Tamer also revered Palestinian literary figures like Mahmoud Darwish, Tawfiq Ziad, and Ibrahim Tukan. "Our basic inspiration is this window," he said, pointing, "and our main problem is identity. At school you study lies about Zionists as heroes, even if they kicked the shit out of the losers, our grandfathers. You're put in the worst class with no decent books, no air-conditioning, and you grow up with low self-esteem. You don't even know where you're coming from, or going to. You study poems in Hebrew and learn about European culture, never your own. You have no role models, nothing, and you start to think, 'Why the hell was I born Arab?'"

"I just felt weak. You see that all you're about is putting humus on the table or selling drugs. It stings when you grow up and listen to Tupac talk about

Malcolm X. You say, 'Man, we need heroes like that in our community.' Then you meet intellectuals who say, 'Why go so far? You have people like this here.' And why the hell did nobody tell me? Why did the Israeli government deny me this knowledge? You have to go back to the east through the west, and that shows how occupied we are. It makes you thirsty. Suddenly, there are no books here, and you want to read everything. You start liking documentaries more than Hollywood films. You go deep. You start to feel stronger."

"The '48 generation had awareness but no power. The next generation just wanted to survive—I don't blame them because if they hadn't we wouldn't be here—but now you have a generation that's aware and unafraid. It's like there was a monster near the fountain and we were thirsty but too scared to drink. Today, we just step in."

Tamer's lyrics have struck a chord in the occupied territories, where they are sometimes chanted at demonstrations. In conversation, though, he could be difficult to understand and was wary of being misunderstood. At school, he found interaction with Jews difficult. "They used to do coexistence meetings where you'd meet the Jews and all these kinds of . . . left-wing tricks," he said. "We'd talk, but we knew nothing. They'd say, 'We came from this, and we have Israel and the Holocaust,' and all we knew is, 'We see you killing Arabs on TV. We see you kill Palestinians, not us.' We didn't know where we came from. And they came ready, you know? Strong. Aware."

The young Tamer must have uncompromisingly turned his ambitions inward. "There's a story by Khalil Gibran," he said, "about a knee-high flower that asks God to make him grow. He gets to the same height as the cat, and the cat tells him, 'Enough, accept what you have,' and he's like, 'No, I want to grow taller.' So he grows higher and meets a tree that tells him the same. Then he meets some birds, and the birds say, '*Khallas*' but, *yani,* 'I want more.' Finally, when he reaches the sky, a wind chops him in two, and they all tell him, 'You see, you should have stopped there!' And he replies, 'Well, maybe I died before you, but I'm the only one who actually lived.' It's hope. I read that they teach the same story in rabbinic schools, except they stop where he gets split in two. What do you learn from that? Accept what you have."

In Lyd that wasn't very much. Palestinians only met Jews in the neighborhood for soccer games and then would be subjected to taunts of "*Aravim masriach*" (dirty Arabs) or "neighborhood barbarians." "They ruled the country, we ruled the streets," said Tamer plaintively. "We're already 25 percent of the population, but they're trying to change that by kicking us out. They don't give us permission to build, and they demolish our houses. The Russian neighborhood they built helped win this round of the demographic problem for Zionism. It delayed the solution—that we all have one enemy. We fight the Russians and the Russians fight us and we both suffer from the same people. But while they suffer, we really suffer."

Lyd's municipal planners still reputedly try to maintain a 20 percent cap on Arab housing by withholding building permits. But there is also what Tamer calls a "gray area" between the ethnically "pure" neighborhoods. "If you buy a map of Lyd you won't find the Arabic neighborhoods on it," he said. "There are cops here all the time. You have no street lights, unemployment, drugs, and a five-meter-high separation wall between Arab and Jewish areas. You know when somebody does something very ugly, and he doesn't want to look in the mirror? That's the wall."

The taxi driver on the way to this district told me the town's old Palestinian buildings were still being knocked down to build new Jewish housing blocks. "They're trying to bury the Arabic culture!" Tamer said. "To bury the Arabic stone. One hundred years from now, it'll all be Western, as if there were no Arabs here. I heard that when they build, Israelis throw shekels on the foundations so that future archaeologists will find them and think it was Jewish land."

Some activists have campaigned for Arabic street names, a cause Tamer is ambivalent about. "We want our streets to have Arabic names because we're Arabs. But if my ghetto looks like shit, I don't want it called Mahmoud Darwish. I want to call it something Zionist, like Balfour," he said.

Why do you sometimes rap in Hebrew? I wondered out loud. "Language is a bridge, and I have stuff to say," he responded. "When I rap to Palestinians in Arabic, I talk about different things like women's rights, educating ourselves, or the lies we learned at school. I don't think we have a big Jewish audience, just the left—or extreme left—crowd. A couple of Israeli radio stations play us, and one project asked us to do a song about coexistence. I did the part in Arabic and the Jews did the bit in Hebrew, but it didn't get played on the radio until they produced a wholly Hebrew version. Even in that song we didn't have an existence. The Arabic audience makes us feel warmer. We sparked the whole rap scene in Gaza, and it's getting big. But when we perform 'Stranger in My Own Country,' which is about being a Palestinian in Israel, you have to explain it to them."

The tipping point for the way Palestinian-Israelis were seen by others—and the way they saw themselves—was in October 2000 when thirteen people were shot dead in Israel's north while protesting in support of the Intifada.

"It made us start talking politics," Tamer said. "As kids, we'd seen them shoot Palestinians in the First Intifada, and suddenly they were shooting us. It meant that we were Palestinians. The complication is that people also have a different war here: drugs. This is the Middle East's drug center. There's a big market for crack and heavy drugs, and it's only in the Arab ghettos."

Growing up, Tamer dreamed of becoming a football player "because it's the only field where you hear Arabic names." Increasingly music came to seem like a path out of the ghetto, albeit one DAM had to pioneer. But for someone raised to fail, performance had its compensations. "It feeds your ego," Tamer said. "Every time we play in Ramallah or Bethlehem, the place is packed. People know our songs and how old we are, the personal stuff about us. We're superstars."

But stars can disappear, and many are snuffed out. The death-or-glory rap motif has a particular resonance for many young Palestinian men, tied to martyrdom and honor. "I'm doing political hip-hop, and if I fight, it's because I believe there's something worth fighting for," Tamer insisted. "I want to live." What frightens you most about becoming famous? I asked. "Nothing, except that it's taking too much time," he replied and then hunched over, concentrating. "This is what I want," he said in an eerily quiet tone. "I want power. I want fame." The words were hyperbolic, but Tamer looked dead serious when he said them. Above him, Tupac stared defiantly at the wall.

Abu Abed, 26

Tunnel Engineer

RAFAH, GAZA

The air that Gaza breathes The hot air in the tunnel was sticky and thick. It made your breath raspy and short if you moved too quickly. This, apparently, is why tunnel workers breathe through their noses. The floor was slippery, and the clay ocher-brown walls moist and smoothed over. There was nothing to hang on to if you fell except some weathered cables and pipes that had been nailed into the ceiling. The "ceiling" was little more than a meter high.

In summer 2009 there were hundreds of tunnels linking Rafah City in Gaza to Rafah town in Egypt, maybe more than a thousand. But to move along this particular concertinaed stretch, Abu Abed had to double himself over at an almost 90-degree angle and scuttle like a mole. He still advanced with grace and speed, no doubt aided by the pall of claustrophobia and inert danger that settle when you stop moving.

Several workers and my translator had helped lower us into the burrow hole by a cable that dangled into the tunnel's rickety wooden shaft. By the time we exited, though, they had already run for cover to the shell-like ruins of a nearby concrete structure. Overhead, Israeli F-16s had appeared, creating deafening sonic booms that shatter your thoughts but are inaudible underground. It is the usual prelude to a bombing raid.

That morning leaflets had been dropped on Gaza City warning people to stay away from the border region, but Abu Abed worked on as usual. Not just anyone can be a tunnel engineer, he said. "It needs someone with a brave heart who doesn't care about life or death." Once, a new worker started crying when he saw the tunnel: "No! I want to see my son! I don't want to die." "This is weak," Abu Abed chided, as he absently twirled his phone. "He couldn't work here."

Because of the international blockade, Gaza's private industry had effectively shut down and exports had ground to a halt. Without them, Gaza's tunnels provided a customs frontier, goods entry point, and link to the outside world. They were tolerated, according to local people, because Israeli planners knew that without them living standards in Gaza would slip below the minimum thresholds the international community would tolerate. Embassy cables published by Wikileaks in early 2011 confirmed that U.S. diplomats were told by Israeli officials that the siege was intended to bring Gaza to "the brink of collapse" without actually precipitating a humanitarian crisis. The goods that did make it through might have been expensive and unsuited to local needs, but even if they just stacked shelves with counterfeit pasta and tins past their sell-by date, they kept shops open—and allowed a percentage of Gazans to participate in the world's free market. Abu Abed was one of them.

When Israel occupied Gaza in 1967, his family was cut off on the Egyptian side of Rafah. In 1991, toward the end of the First Intifada, they moved to the Palestinian side, and he changed schools, eventually studying administration at college for two years. Although his brothers were achievers—two studied medicine in Germany, and one worked with UNRWA in Gaza—Abu Abed skipped class and walked out of a job with UNRWA after just three months, much to his father's displeasure. U.N. posts are like gold dust in Gaza, but Abu Abed did not fit into the world of academe and official jobs. "I was always different," he explained. "I liked challenges more than my brothers did."

Outside of the tunnel, he ambled slowly and despite his uniform jeans and baseball cap, looked haggard. The way he told it, his journey underground started with Hamas's takeover of Gaza. "A new period of history began in 2007," he said. "Everything closed, and there were no jobs. The only solution for men like me was to work in the tunnels." As a middle-class Gazan with an escape route to Egypt, though, Abu Abed must always have had choices.

Around the time of the 2008–9 war, he went into business with three partners, bringing food and clothes into the Gaza Strip. "That's why I don't have money yet," he smiled. "I'm a new partner. I borrowed from here and there and put all my money—$30,000—into the tunnel. Now I have a 20 percent stake. Do you want to be the fourth partner?" I politely declined. Abu Abed shrugged and grinned.

Many investors in Gaza's tunnel industry have become millionaires. But many more have been ripped off in Ponzi-type scams. The tunnels have spawned a nouveau riche class that Gazans admire, envy, or distrust, depending on the circumstances. Workers like Abu Abed argue that they are providing a wartime service to the resistance. "Tunneling means breaking the blockade," he said. "The tunnels are like the air that Gaza breathes. They are Gaza's underground border now." Around him, his coworkers were cooking tea over an open fire. They were paid $100 a day, he said, a king's ransom in Gaza.

Yet the people of Rafah looked kindly on the tunnel workers, according to Abu Abed, "because without tunnels there wouldn't be food or water. The tunnels make diesel very cheap." He fumbled for his cell phone to prove the point and started playing a tinny dabke pop tune by Abu Ayash. The words were translated to me as, "Let's go to the tunnels to say hello to the workers. We appreciate the workers here and on the Egyptian side. If there are more border closures, seven workers will be there to help us. The F-16s [Israeli warplanes] and Apaches [helicopters] come, and the workers don't care." It seemed absurdly optimistic.

Abu Abed actually sat out most of Israel's military offensive in his house, only venturing outside twice a day to check the tunnel's state from a safe distance. "Every day they attacked the tunnels four or five times," he said. "Many were so damaged that it took months to fix them, but we worked hard and repaired ours in ten days." If there was another war, he vowed that he would continue tunneling: "Even if they bomb them every day we won't stop. They'll only destroy one percent of them."

In Palestine as elsewhere, bravado confers status on young men. But the abject lack of self-esteem inflicted by the blockade had raised the stakes uniquely in Gaza and might even have helped recruit new tunnel workers. The sandy earth around Rafah is prone to collapse, and this had led to the deaths of more than one hundred people since June 2007. Abu Abed said he always felt in danger underground—the tunnel drops to 28 meters at its deepest—and he had seen a friend trapped there for a week. The man was kept alive with water and milk he received through the tunnel's oxygen pipe until he was rescued on the Egyptian side. Luckily, he was not caught in the 900 meters of the tunnel that lack pipes.

Sometimes, when Israeli planes are about to attack, Abu Abed said, the Egyptian police "run away and call the Palestinian soldiers here, and they tell the workers to evacuate." The workers still underground are alerted and told to move to the Egyptian side until the attacks have finished. They are less likely to be bombed there, and bigger tunnel openings in Egypt make it easier to breathe. The tunnels for food and goods were broadly tolerated in Egypt, Abu Abed believed.

"The Egyptian security police are more active in western Rafah because the [Fawsi] Barhoum family is involved there, so they think Hamas might be moving guns," he said. "Here we only move food and clothes. We support the fighters, but moving weapons would scare our Egyptian contacts because the security police would find out. There's a special tunnel for those things."

Abu Abed's tunnel did not transport heavy drugs either, due to a Hamas prohibition. "They will break the body of anyone who brings in drugs," he said dispassionately. "But at the same time a lot of hashish and pills come in, even with Hamas's eyes." Moreover, "a lot" of Russian brides were smuggled in from Egypt, until they were banned when Cairo accused Hezbollah of smuggling weapons and operatives through the tunnels. Big "P" politics seemed to seep underground from every angle. "If Hamas said to close the tunnels we would do it," Abu Abed said hawkishly at one point, "but only on the condition that the border was opened and food and goods were allowed in again." He was not a Hamas supporter. "They're just the government, police, law, and authority. We hate them like cow offal."

Even so, I could not help wondering why he chose to work under their authority, not to mention the risk posed by Israeli warplanes and the vicarious protection of Egypt's security police. "I didn't choose anything," he retorted. "Palestine chose me. My life is here, even though I have relatives in Egypt. I'm proud of my nationality and also of my Gazan identity. It's special because of this big jail we live in. We're fighters in a jail unlike any other people. We don't have big possessions, and I've never even seen a bridge. If there was a border we would go outside to work in Europe, but I'd miss life in Gaza."

From the road beyond our concrete cave, some workers on a passing lorry threw Abu Abed a pack of Marlboro cigarettes. It took everyone but him by surprise. "The next time you come, you'll see me in a nice suit with a big car," he said grandly. "This will be a five-star tunnel, and you'll be able to walk through it without bending over." Already he claimed to be turning over $10,000 a day, although he was vague as to whether this represented profits, the volume of trade, or just surety for his workers. "If I'd put my money under the pillow I'd take everything, but now that I've put it into the tunnel I will maybe win more," he said airily. As the interview ended, he motioned me to follow him outside. Uncertainly, I followed in his tracks. Abu Abed offered me a rose from his rubble-strewn garden.

"Omar," 32

Drug Dealer

EAST JERUSALEM, WEST BANK

The way of the people who run The *hashishin* (hashish users) have a long history in Arabic and Persian culture. The word *assassin* derives from a medieval sect that reputedly killed while under the drug's influence. Until the Six Day War, hashish cafés were common in West Bank cities. Their demise after 1967 coincided with the opening of a Palestinian market to Israeli manufacturers of other mind-altering substances. In spring 2010 PA police said they had seized $1 million worth of ecstasy pills in Hebron. One young artist in Ramallah told me that he and his friends liked to take the stimulant before joining riots at the start of the Second Intifada. Jerusalem's proximity to Israel, access routes to Lebanon and Egypt, and front-line location on the world's east-west axis made it the hub of the West Bank's drug economy.

"Omar," a dealer in his early thirties, knew its grooves better than most. He was a resourceful font of local history, a blithe raconteur with a colorful story up his sleeve, and a habitué of the Old City's streets. He could not walk ten yards down an Old City alley without a barrage of greetings from *shebab*, friends, comrades, and family. Omar's unglued life story mirrored the tumult of a proletarian home city he loved and hated in equal measure, and which he had seen slip away from him.

The air in Omar's six-hundred-year-old stone terrace was wispy with cannabis smoke during our three interviews, and we talked over the gurgle of his TV set, which was tuned permanently to Hezbollah's al-Manar station. Every so often, friends would stroll in through the courtyard for a smoke. The Old City where Omar lived was the sclerotic heart of Arab East Jerusalem. The Al Aqsa Mosque may be the third holiest site to Muslims, but, since 1967, a war of attrition waged by settlers—with military support—had effectively annexed growing pockets of the Casbah. Daily life was a drama.

"Whatever makes me a living and gives me an okay life, I'll do it," Omar said, gulping hard. "I started buying and selling hashish seven or eight years ago because I need to make my smoke." Omar went through around $200 of hashish a week, and to fund this, he hustled in Jerusalem's tourist economy, arranging everything from trips to Nazareth to trips at parties. "I'm a good tour guide, and sometimes I change money," he said. "A couple of restaurants like me to work for them [bringing customers in off the street]. If I'm outside you will find me dealing. You can judge me for it, but to survive here you must be strong."

Omar regularly traveled north to pick up his hash—"from the Palestinian-Israeli side," he qualified. "I don't trust Israelis." This was just as well because Omar was convinced that "the best hash comes from Hezbollah," with Israeli connivance. "Ninety percent of it comes through Ghajar and Majdal Shams [in the Golan Heights]. *Habibi,* you have a lot of black things going on, on the Israeli side. Always the Israeli generals get involved with drugs, and a good lawyer knows the judge or the policemen who come to court. They make a deal and *khallas, yani.*"

According to Omar, the hashish economy in the Old City was encouraged by Israeli (and Palestinian) authorities so long as the dealing was hidden, and no Israeli Jews were involved. "The biggest Jerusalem dealers are in the Mount of Olives," he said. "But if one Israeli scored there, the Mount would be closed and the dealers jailed. They have spiders [spies] everywhere. The Israelis don't crack down because drugs make you forget about things and that's what they want. I've talked to Israel's 'Palestinian' soldiers in the city, and they told me they let drugs in to keep people quiet. They help to send them. They found that they could make us druggers easily."

There is a thin line between using drugs to celebrate life or to escape from it. In Omar's case, the fight or flight pattern was established early. He had his first joint when he was sent to jail for forty-five days, at twelve. "It helped me to stop giving a shit about the people around me," he said. Omar spent most of his teenage years in jail after he followed his older brother into the PFLP's youth wing during the First Intifada. "The first four or five days inside are always the worst because of the questioning. I was beaten all over, denied sleep. And I had to spend days alone in a small room. They'd play music and throw stuff at you—stones, humus, every night something—but after that it was like a normal jail," he said.

On his thirteenth birthday he was arrested again and sentenced to fifteen months for throwing a bicycle at a soldier. "You have to survive it," he said with ursine resolve. "You have to respect yourself, *yani,* but you also need to be in a faction because they protect you and manage the jails inside." Protection outside was another matter.

"I felt shit when I was released," Omar said. "Oslo was the shittiest thing. We could drive to Israel before, but the Israelis put checkpoints everywhere. My way of thinking changed too, but I wasn't aware of how. At first you get more respect, but then everybody in my time went to prison. If you didn't, people looked at you like you did something wrong. To be killed was something special. A lot of my friends were killed, some of them around me." Omar was released two months before the end of the school year, feeling "too smart for school." Six months later, he was sent back to jail for another two years. Denied avenues to formal social status, he found respect on the streets—and returned it too.

"We used to have a nice relationship between Christians and Muslims," he said. "To me, we are all Arabs. Of course the Christians don't feel the same way about us. Since the First Intifada they've been trying to be on the Israeli side. When I was sent to jail, we had four or five Christians here in the PFLP. Now there are none." Some family stories suggested Omar had Yemeni-Jewish ancestry, but he maintained, "We are Bedouin, *habibi,* 100 percent." Like other Jerusalemites, Omar's family was only mildly affected by the Nakba and the Six Day War. He did not carry that fact lightly. "My grandfather ran away to Jordan, but what the fuck?" he said. "There wasn't much fighting. I don't want the refugees who left to come back, *yani.* The Israelis have more right to the land than these Palestinians because they fight hard while these people ran away."

When I countered that the refugees were powerless and scared for their lives, Omar exploded: "So we have to live in shit because they were scared? *Khallas,* you destroyed this area by running. You left your villages and your brothers and sons. This is the way of the people who run. If you left it, you left it. Why do you need to come back? You didn't fight for it. You didn't live the shit that we lived—even if you lived an even shittier life. Sorry, but we lived under the occupation all our lives and still fight the Israelis." Omar had little sympathy for people who ran.

"Mama mia, *habibi*! They really fucked us with the wall," he exhaled after one tightly packed bong hit, before slouching back into the sofa. "All our lives used to be among the West Bank people, and they don't come now. Ninety percent of business is down because Old City people returned to the West Bank or lost their ID cards." And as Palestinians were forced out, new arrivals took their place.

"We never had so many settlers in the city before," Omar said. "Every week they demonstrate now. They never used to close my street for the Israelis. Now thousands of them march by shouting, 'Fuck Arabs! *Am Yisroel Chai!*' Nobody fights them anymore. This is Fatah's fault. They taught people that we could have a good relationship with the Israelis when it wasn't true."

In Omar's view, Hamas had made Palestinians in Jerusalem more powerful. Fatah people voted for them now, and so did he. "I never believed in Hamas. We've just seen too much shit from Fatah," he said. "They only respect people because of their fathers. But who deals cocaine? Fatah. Who deals guns? Fatah. Who are the thieves? Fatah. All black market under-the-table stuff is Fatah. They're trying to move the economy toward Israel because they can't live without the Tel Aviv people."

"Look how much security we have for the settlers in the city!" he thundered. "In the last twenty years, they've bought a house on every corner and always they take the rooftops. They have all the big houses, and they could live over there," he pointed westward, "unlike us." It must have made it difficult to see them as noncombatants, I said. "I started to hate Jews," Omar replied bitterly, "to hate the meaning of the Jews. The Israelis showed us that their right to be here comes from the Bible."

"They are the cheapest community in the world," he winced. "You can easily buy the Jewish man with money or drugs and the Israeli woman we know very well, *yani*. We always say that the fathers of these Israeli guys are Palestinians because the Israeli men are shit. Go and ask on the Israeli side why all these Jewish girls come around the Palestinians. For all our problems, we know how to respect women." What about honor killings? I asked. "*Habibi*," Omar momentarily lowered his voice an octave, a hint of hostility playing around his lips, "you have shit everywhere."

It was impossible to quantify how much of Omar's anger was reaction, exhibition, or stance. I knew he had Jewish friends, had driven miles to give a Jewish soldier he felt sorry for some hash, and even had an Israeli Jewish girlfriend once, although he talked about her with macho brusqueness. "We had a nice relationship for six months," he shrugged, "a good bed life, *yani*, but talk about politics, and it'll never work. Her family didn't know about me." Omar's family knew about her, though. "They know I like to fuck around," he said, recovering some pride.

Omar had never had a Palestinian girlfriend. "I was always afraid of community life. A lot of Arab women try hard to talk to me, but I don't know how to talk to them. I'm too good with the internationals," he said. "I used to be the Casanova of the city." Once, Israel's Shin Bet security police tried to blackmail him into becoming an informer by luring him into a honey trap with a local woman, he claimed. Certainly, the Israeli authorities in East Jerusalem are an unavoidable presence, and Omar had relations "even with the spiders." A prominent restaurant near the Old City's Jaffa Gate was, he said, run by an informer who was also a cousin. I asked how he could trust spies enough to have relations with them, but his cell phone interrupted. A Hassan Nasrallah ringtone screeched "*Meen inte?*" across the room. "Who are you?"

"A lot of people have problems in life," Omar said, relighting his bong once the call was done, "or problems in the head. They don't feel really human. Since '93, I haven't trusted anyone in this city, but it's more and more in the West Bank too. Palestinians get killed by spiders there for small change." Still, he accepted the need to work with Israelis, if only to get drinks in West Jerusalem. "But I won't spy for them," he cautioned. "Jerusalem people have a 'fuck you' attitude, but then it's like, 'Hello Israelis busing by the Wailing Wall. What can we do for you?'" Yet in the space of a few sentences, Omar could insist with equal passion that if Israeli soldiers respected the Old City *shebab,* "we will respect them and live in peace." Dignity seemed a more valuable commodity to him than land.

In 2002 Omar was nearly killed when he was shot in a West Jerusalem district where there had been several suicide attacks. "I was leaving a bar at 3:30 A.M. when three Israeli guys approached me and one of them asked for a cigarette," he recounted quickly. "He was drunk and said, 'What's an Arab like you doing here?' I said, 'What are you doing here?' and we started fighting. I started to run when he shot the first bullet at me. I ran to the hospital because I thought they'd help me there, but he shot me the second time in the hospital doorway." Omar was wounded in the foot, back, stomach, and hand.

There was a trial but, according to Omar, no justice. "This guy was a soldier, so of course he was only imprisoned for two days," he said. He still has nightmares about the incident: "I feel it when I take a shower. You always have this wound. The first time I went back to the area by car after the attack, really, I was too stoned. I just opened the car door, jumped out, and ran down the street. I freaked out and forgot myself. All I did was run like crazy all the way back. I was just out of my mind."

Omar has also stood and fought, many times. On the day after Ariel

Sharon visited the Al Aqsa Mosque, Omar was arrested in the riot that began the Second Intifada. "The soldiers had all kinds of weapons, and we just had our shoes," he remembered. "They started kicking us, and we had to fight because a guy inside the mosque had been killed and all the guys were angry and had come outside. Fuck them! But it was a hand fight. I was arrested and brought to court for throwing stones. I said, 'Sorry, Judge, look at the TV pictures'—because they showed me throwing my shoes at a soldier."

"The street mood was great. We'd taken a lot of shit from the Israelis. People had stopped believing that they'd give us Jerusalem back, and when Sharon visited the mosque everyone was like, *khallas*. We had to show them that we didn't care if we were killed. We thought the rioting would only last for two or three days. We never thought it would start another Intifada. The time of the Aqsa tunnel, when the Israelis killed sixty Palestinians, was much harder. This was only like a couple of hours. We were fighting for the respect of the mosque, and that's it. *Yani*, 90 percent of the guys were stoned and drunk, including me. Really, I don't give a shit about Islam."

In the future Omar expects an upsurge of violence. "The Israelis closed us in like animals, tighter and tighter," he said. "I don't believe in weapons and destruction, but the next generation will fight the Israelis in really crazy ways, all kinds of fighting." Omar's generation fought old school. "It was a good feeling with the fighters because the PFLP had a good name," he said, "the best. Wherever we went, we had respect." Omar started to slip into a stoned and oddly nostalgic reverie. "Yes, we used to have all the respect from the other groups," he said, putting down his bong and furrowing his brow as though a butterfly chasing an elusive thought. "We'll never have the freedom that we dream of, just a new dream every night."

The Oslo
Generation

"Nothing happens unless first we dream," the American writer Carl Sandburg said. With the Oslo Accords, though, first the Palestinians dreamed and then nothing happened. At the start of the 1990s, the Palestinian streets of the West Bank and Gaza had been ground down by four years of fighting. Equally, their official leadership was becoming increasingly desperate to end its exile in the Maghreb. Some optimism had attached to Iraq in the run up to the 1990 Gulf War. To this day Saddam Hussein remains a popular figure for his perceived steadfast support of the Palestinian cause. One refugee camp leader described him to me as "my number one most admired political figure, a real Arab leader who wanted to unify the Arabs and found one Arab country."

Nonetheless, Yasser Arafat made a strategic blunder by supporting Iraq in the Gulf War. Short of international allies as the USSR imploded, he was eager to use the Intifada's capital—and the PLO's new American contacts—as a springboard to a 1967 borders state. In November 1991 an international conference was convened in Madrid attended by Israel and the PLO. One of the Palestinian negotiators there, Hanan Ashrawi, talked to me at length about it (see chapter 6). This was followed by initially secret talks between the two sides in Oslo, culminating in an accord that was signed by Arafat and Israeli Prime Minister Yitzhak Rabin on the White House lawn in September 1993.

The Oslo negotiations were harshly reviewed by many Palestinian intellectuals. The legendary Palestinian academic Edward Said said they were conducted in a "state of supine abjectness." One of the PLO's Oslo advisers, Rashid Khalidi, called the organization's planning for negotiations and eventual statehood "virtually worthless." In the accord that Oslo produced, the Palestinian National Authority (PNA, or PA) was created to last for five years while a permanent agreement was thrashed out. Israel was supposed to progressively withdraw its forces from parts of the occupied territories, allowing the PA to begin governing in an embryonic Palestinian state. The Tunis exiles and their families came home. As the Cold War ended and Western ideologues predicted "the end of history," it seemed for a moment as if peace might be in sight. But the agreement deliberately avoided the contentious issues of the new state's borders, the status of Jerusalem, refugees, and settlements, and over the course of the 1990s, it unraveled.

The assassination of Yitzhak Rabin was retrospectively seen by many as its swan song. But Palestinians were badly hit by decisions that he had not objected to—such as closing Israel to Palestinian workers, curtailing free movement in the West Bank and Gaza, and the hyper-acceleration of settlement growth. Roads, walls, fences, tunnels, and checkpoints began to carve up the West Bank, connecting meager Jewish settlements in a grid matrix, even as they isolated and strangled once-bustling Palestinian cities. The Israeli army oversaw the process, while Israeli governments dragged their feet on implementing even the limited concessions agreed to in Norway. Tensions rose. In 1994 twenty-nine Palestinians were killed when a Jewish settler opened fire on worshipers in a Hebron mosque. The riots that followed claimed twenty-five Palestinian and five Israeli lives. In 1996 fighting broke out in Jerusalem over a controversial archaeological dig under the Al Aqsa Mosque. Fifteen Israeli soldiers and sixty-one Palestinians were killed.

Hamas grew easily in this period, its steadfast reputation enhanced by a principled rejection of Oslo. Israel's expulsion of four hundred of its activists to a no-man's-land on the Lebanese border turned the organization's new leadership into heroes. As corruption and repression increased in the occupied territories, thousands of Palestinians looked to Islamist groups that had not been incorporated by the PA or Fatah for an alternative. When, in 1996, the head of a senior Hamas bomb maker, Yahya Ayyash, was blown off by a booby-trapped cell phone, Hamas launched a wave of suicide bombs in Israel, killing over sixty people. That offensive almost certainly helped to oust the pro-Oslo Israeli prime minister, Shimon Peres, in favor of Benjamin Netanyahu.

More than Hamas, though, the "Tunis generation" was the indisputable beneficiary of the Oslo period, as were some sections of the Palestinian middle class in Israel who (arguably) enjoyed some peace dividend. In the occupied territories, Palestinian professionals also benefited to an extent as over a thousand Palestinian NGOs flourished and tourists flocked to what was fast becoming a remotely administered aid economy. But the combination of rising Palestinian hopes, worsening conditions on the ground, Islamist growth, and disaffection with the peace process would have foreseeable consequences in 1999.

The Oslo generation lived through a time of negotiation—and became skilled at horse trading. After the Intifada, Palestinians felt less fear of Israeli Jews. They learned to haggle with soldiers at checkpoints and bureaucrats in offices for visas, ID cards, building permits, and the means of transit. Within the developing PA economy, they bargained with NGOs and foreign government funders as other sources of finance dried up. Most strikingly, they bargained with each other as the PA's experiment in self-government divided Palestinian society and opened up new possibilities for largesse and self-advancement.

During the First Intifada, popular committees and grassroots organizations had disbursed funding that arrived through the various factions in the PLO. Corruption was deterred by a local democratic accountability inherent in the community-based popular resistance model of organizing. In 1994 Palestinian groups reportedly provided 60 percent of primary health care services, 50 percent of secondary and tertiary care, and 100 percent of all disabled services and preschool education. By 1995 U.S. and European Union (EU) aid agencies were funding the majority of these projects through Oslo-generated schemes. USAID alone sprinkled $1 billion across the occupied territories between 1992 and 2003. By the end of the 2000s, the EU was providing the PA with over €500 million a year.

Politically, as the international NGOs and the PA shifted the Palestinian narrative away from resistance to state-building, repression increased on West Bank streets. Hamas in particular was targeted, but civil society activists across the spectrum found themselves jailed for human rights or opposition work. All the while, the PA's real authority decreased with each new story of corruption. To many, the international community seemed to be effectively creating another weak, nepotistic Arab police state. But it did at least ensure that many Palestinians who came of age in this era would have a globally oriented outlook, albeit bitterly so.

In the Diaspora, dreams soared to the sky. Palestinians from across the world returned to the occupied territories in anticipation of statehood and peace. Not all of them stayed. For refugees in the Arab world, the 1990s were another period of waiting for the curtain to lift, punctuated by piercing screams from the stage behind. In Lebanon even as Israel wound down its occupation of the country's south, its army and air force bombed a U.N.

refugee center in Qana in 1996, killing 106 people. Somehow hopes of return remained high.

But Oslo's blurry promise would be realized "tomorrow in the apricot"— probably never—as the local Arabic saying has it. An Israel unable or unwilling to give up its territorial ambitions or meaningfully recognize an equal Palestinian people thought Oslo meant an autonomy deal with more or less trappings. Palestinians thought it meant a sovereign state on every inch of the occupied territories and an honorable return for refugees. This gap could not be papered over. Oslo was a beautiful dream, but for Palestinians the light of day was harsh indeed.

Diana Buttu, 37

Lawyer

RAMALLAH, WEST BANK

An exotic bird "This was never an issue in the past eight years," Diana Buttu groaned, "but in the last week it's happened to me three times already." A beggar had just approached us for money on the patio of the Café de la Paix, a boutiquey hangout for Ramallah's well-to-do. It was June 2008, and Ramallah was suffused with batteries of Western consultants—and a conveyor belt of donor dollars. Chichi bars and restaurants opened like Klondike guest houses—often closing just as quickly—while rents and food prices soared to match the inflated salaries of the "internationals" in Palestine's de facto capital. The Western-backed NGOs that employed them picked up the tab that Israel, as an occupying power, should have paid but did not. Diana believed that the NGOs also obstructed the development of an independent economy and funneled the best and brightest away from any form of resistance to occupation.

A former legal adviser to the PA, she was a litigant at The Hague court hearing that declared Israel's West Bank Wall illegal. But her early life was far from politicized. Born in Canada to secular working-class parents, the past was rarely talked about. "We didn't even speak Arabic at home," she said, "and I never once heard the word Palestine mentioned in our house. I think my parents made a conscious decision to try to start a new life."

Diana's family hails from Nazareth. They moved there from surrounding villages during the Nakba. In 1965 her paternal uncle was killed by a Jewish drunk driver during a religious holiday. "It sent my father into a tailspin," Diana said. "He felt that he wasn't part of this country and would never be treated as an equal. The police gave them all the excuses—'Ah, it was Purim, it was this, it was that'—and no political motive was ever attributed to the lack of prosecution. It was like the big family secret. I didn't find out about it until I was in my twenties." The incident prompted her father to move to Canada.

Racism was a given in the lower-middle-class district of Mississauga where Diana grew up. She feared being associated with an Indian family on her street because of the enormous discrimination they suffered. "I didn't question the injustice," she said. "I just didn't want to be in their shoes. I remember going to school with a *zatar* and *zeit* (thyme and olive) sandwich and my classmate going, 'Ewww, she's eating a dirt sandwich!' I definitely didn't have a Palestinian identity. I was very ignorant."

Now, she identified as a Palestinian at every opportunity. But the young Diana Buttu was conservative and against abortion. "I liked Michael Jackson," she giggled, embarrassed, "and Dépêche Mode, Wham, and George Michael. I thought Arabic music sounded like a dying cat. I love it now but at the time . . . " She rolled her eyes. It was a seventeenth birthday trip to Nazareth on the first day of the First Intifada that changed how she viewed herself—and the world.

"I kept seeing powerful, troubling images of protests on TV," she recalled. "When my cousins explained the injustice of the situation to me, I decided to become a lawyer—and a Palestinian. I didn't know what a Palestinian was before that. I felt Canadian but different. You didn't think about life there, you just lived. Here, you had deep and moving conversations. We never talked about the future of the Canadian people." She suppressed a laugh.

Coincidentally, Diana returned to work as a legal adviser with the PA's Negotiations Support Unit (NSU) on the first day of the Second Intifada in 2000. "My experience of being Palestinian is centered around Intifadas," she smiled. But she had initially seen her NSU appointment as a year out, and the upsurge of violence forced a bout of soul-searching. "I was staying at the Best Eastern hotel in Ramallah, and the Israelis would fire flarelike things that fell behind it. A couple of them actually hit the radio station nearby, and that freaked me out. I just thought, 'Why is this happening?'"

Ramallah had been seen as a party town, but by September 2000 "it was chaos," Diana recalled. "Anyone with a foreign passport was leaving, especially the ones who came during the Oslo years with dreams. Most internationals stayed at the American Colony hotel in Jerusalem, and they wouldn't come to Ramallah. Many international organizations were unprepared for the uprising and frightened by the violence, although it was actually contained to Fridays, at a certain place. But there were occasional bombings, and people didn't know how long the Intifada would last or how bad it would get. They started to return in late 2003. But I really felt a strong attachment here." Diana stayed.

Ramallah is a friendly town, but she found that one of its biggest divides was between people born in the territories and those from abroad. "There's a level of resentment, maybe anger, toward the people who seem to be reaping the benefits of returning, as opposed to those who really suffered under military rule," she said. "I don't get upset about it. I understand it." Diana did not think that Diaspora Palestinians romanticized the country. "But then I'm what my friend calls an 'exotic bird' because my family are Israeli citizens," she said in a here-we-go voice, as though the anecdote was recurrent. "People impute a cultural difference, but I don't really see it. My family will say—they're snobby—'We're just not like people in the West Bank or Gaza,' only to realize that they're exactly like them and Israel views them that way too. Palestinians here think they're more nationalistic than people inside Israel, and that's accepted," she said.

Although she found it "good fun," going to work for the NSU must have been a brave step for someone who "wasn't so wedded to the idea of negotiations," as she puts it. "I didn't and don't think they'll yield anything for the Palestinians, but I felt that was the vehicle that I could best help Palestine with," she said. "I was torn between the end and the means." The NSU was formed with British support in 1998 to provide Palestinian negotiators with positions and advice in the legal, policy, and communications fields. It also participated in negotiations. Four other European governments got on board and the Adam Smith Institute (ASI), a right-wing think tank, administered the project—and tens of millions of pounds from Britain's aid budget.

According to Diana, "The ASI makes money by charging donors a higher fee for their working papers than they pay out. So you were constantly encouraged to get more and more experts. But their roster was weak, and very skewed toward Conservative politics. They weren't really of much use to the Palestinian negotiators or positions. Here's an example: the Palestinian refugee experience is almost unique because they want to go back to their homes, not to be resettled. Yet almost all the papers and experts they brought in would only focus on how to resettle them in third countries."

"Money would get allocated to the PA and accounted against the Palestinian people, who never saw a dime. It went to expensive salaries, lavish expense accounts, foreign travel, cars, and providing people with a very comfortable lifestyle. Projects overlapped and got repeated, and only the internationals benefited." The ASI also, in her view, provides a mechanism for external influence. When the Second Intifada began, Diana and her friend Michael Tarazzi, a PLO legal analyst, were seen as media-savvy rising young stars at the BBC, where I then worked. Yet both seemed to disappear.

"They made us disappear!" Diana exclaimed on the hop. "By early 2004 a backlash had started against us within pro-Israel circles like Labour Friends of Israel in the United Kingdom. They would send over delegations, ask us a million questions, and then splice it as 'PLO spokesperson said blah blah: I support terrorists killing settlers,' even though we weren't spokespeople. Thankfully, I recorded all of my speeches, and there's a British Hansard [recorded parliamentary] debate of my [key] response—that the jury is out in terms of international law because Israel puts settlements in, claims that they're military bases, and therefore the people there cannot be civilians. Do I support it? No. Is it a good strategy? No. That was exactly my answer. They took that as 'Ms. Buttu supports terrorism' and started pressuring Hilary Benn, the development minister, saying that DFID [Department for International Development] was funding spokespeople, not legal advisers."

"Hilary Benn in turn put pressure on the ASI, adding to the pressure coming down on us. They agreed to a review of the NSU's activities in October 2004. At the same time, Michael had written a perhaps poorly timed op-ed calling for the one state solution. That was seen as renegade. It sent the lobbies and Hilary Benn into a frenzy and increased the pressure." The British investigators reported back that Diana and Michael Tarazzi were damaging the Palestinian cause but failed to mention that, in each case, they were proceeding with oversight.

"Every op-ed," Diana said, "every everything, had to be signed off by the NSU and Saeb [Erekat, the PLO's then-chief negotiator] himself. He was always looking to appease somebody. Rather than stand up when he knew we were doing things correctly, he capitulated. So we ended up being the fall guys. They recommended that our activities be curtailed so that we were no longer allowed to speak to journalists or write op-eds. The donors then put more pressure on the ASI, and in July 2005, a few months later, we were told, 'Thank you very much for your services, but it's time for you to go.'"

Diana does not think she was seen as being too radical. "I think it was because we were effective. It was the first time the Israelis had had to spar with Palestinians, so they had a very difficult time," she said. "Also, there were a lot of internal problems in the NSU. Mahmoud Abbas's daughter-in-law was working there and people viewed it as an elite and out-of-touch body. That rubbed off on us somehow. Other people saw us as a threat because we were gaining popularity and taking away the spotlight."

During her involvement in talks with Israel, Diana's view that the Palestinians would never get anything through such processes was reinforced. "It was like negotiating over a kilo of tomatoes," she said. "There was no debate. We had no leverage. It was very frustrating. I remember at one session in Taba, we said to Gilead Sher [then Israel's co-chief negotiator], 'On what legal basis do you want a concession for such-and-such an issue?' He turned to me and said, 'Look, we will respect the law when we're forced to respect the law, and until that time, it's just me and you in a room.' It was clear. You have the power. I do not. It means that we're never going to have free and fair negotiations."

"The most offensive thing for me was when they gave you an analysis of your political situation. They'd say, 'Look'—dropping the 'Look' bomb— 'Look, I know more than you do. This is how things are. You're going to have a difficult time, and if I were in your position, I'd take this.'" She remembers one Israeli official telling Palestinian negotiators in 2005, "'Look, you're going to have to kill a few of these Hamas people, and it's going to be painful, but you're just going to have to do it.'"

Palestinians abroad often complain that the PA ditched an "international law–based" approach for negotiations based on extant power relations that privileged Israel. Diana agreed but saw the problem as systemic. "It doesn't benefit the Authority if it focuses on international law," she reasoned. "They have to accept that they've been defeated—and that's a hard pill to swallow. They're not prepared to admit that Fatah is a dead organization, and they've failed. They won't move toward international law because it means bringing other powers into the room."

"It takes away from their image of power. How do you convince a leader that he's useless?" The question rolled off her tongue like dice. "Abu Mazen needs a permit to go from Ramallah to Jerusalem. How much more useless can you get? Yet he won't admit that he's the leader of an occupied people and act accordingly."

"Useless" was a word that Diana also employed to characterize her former boss, the chief Palestinian negotiator, Saeb Erekat. "He lost sight of the fact that his purpose was over in the 1990s, so he latched on to anybody, whether it was Abu Mazen or Arafat," she said. "He was really lacking in personality and always tries to shows that he's the 'good Palestinian.' I don't have a lot of respect for him."

The PA itself "was put together in a very hasty manner," she thought. "It was like, 'slap two pieces of bread together and call it a sandwich.' They didn't go through the process of defining corruption. They were so hush-hush about the side investments that their politicians had, and that created a lack of confidence. People would bring furniture into an office, and the next thing you knew, it was gone. I saw this. One of the ministers would take it to his house. It's petty, stupid things that could have been addressed but that the PA never turned its eyes toward."

A big question for Palestinians is how much of the blame for such failures to lay at the door of Yasser Arafat. Diana's perspective was that the structures he put in place made him "impossible" to work with. "A very paranoid atmosphere was created, and a lot of energy was focused on preserving his position—which wasn't under threat—in the most destructive ways. It was like a bicycle wheel with a central hub and all the little spokes around it. He was the hub, and everyone else was a spoke, and nobody talked to each other except through the center. He would throw things down to this one or that one, and they were always fighting so you never really knew what the system was. There was always a big fog around Arafat, but personally I found him very nice, very warm. I was the 'exotic bird' to him. He thought I was Pakistani because my last name is Buttu." Diana chuckled.

She believed that in the period after September 11 Arafat recognized the world had changed but didn't know how to respond to it. "His only strategy became personal survival because that had worked for so long and ensured the survival of the Palestinian cause." Like most Palestinians, she suspected that his death, ostensibly from a rare blood disease, was actually an Israeli assassination. "When it comes to Arafat, you can't think otherwise. I kept saying, 'This is exactly like superman—only kryptonite can kill him,'" she said. "In the lead-up to his death, Saeb Erekat had traveled to London in March 2004 and come back saying he'd had a terrible meeting with the Brits. They'd told us that if Arafat did not make changes before Ireland's presidency of the EU [ended], I think at the end of June, the United States would not block any measures to go after Arafat." She found it "pretty creepy" that by November Arafat was dead.

With hindsight, she agreed that signing the Oslo Accords had been a mistake, even if Arafat was in a "damned if you do, damned if you don't" position. "Oslo was a disaster," she said, "but at that time Arafat realized that he'd lost a lot by supporting Saddam [in the first Gulf War] and it became another personal survival strategy." The problem is what happens when you die, I said. "Precisely," she agreed. "There were no institutions created. Fatah became the PA, and the PA became Fatah." Within the PA, this may have contributed to the lingering of old prejudices. While Diana was warmly welcomed by some, she was also excluded from involvement by one senior Palestinian leader—"because she's an Israeli"—and at other times was "treated as a sort of secretary because I was the woman."

Diana happily quotes her friend Amira Hass as saying that the Palestinian-Israeli conflict is really about "whose is bigger." But "masculinity does have an impact," she continued, "especially when men are humiliated by younger female soldiers. It's very difficult for this society to deal with." It fueled violent reprisals, she argued, as a way to regain masculinity. "Nonviolent resistance is often seen as being weak. In Gaza, even if men didn't have money, they'd buy guns to show they had the ability to protect someone. That was sad."

The cult of *shahada* was also "a huge problem," in Diana's view. "I don't want to be part of a society that views our heroes as martyrs. It's their way of dealing with senseless and unexplained loss. I understand that. But I want a live hero who's done something great for our society, like Edward Said. When he died, they called him 'the *shahid* Edward Said.' He was great, so he must be a *shahid*." One alternative strategy—a return to the grassroots committees of the First Intifada—"has already gone," she believed. "We've moved from a collective society based on struggle to a society of individuals, and the individuals are all *shahids*. This is the time of the Islamic religious movements. I understand that. Wearing a veil is a means of holding on to one's honor. People can't control their lives under occupation, but they can control their relationship to God." In Gaza, where she worked as a legal consultant in 2005 and 2006, Diana felt pressured to wear a veil, but she refused. Like Asmaa al-Goule, her life experiences seemed to have taught her the value of visibility.

"Israelis don't see Palestinians anymore," she concluded. "In '87 the Intifada brought them into the Israeli living room. It was earth-changing for a lot of Israelis. With the Wall and this Intifada, Palestinians have been pushed away again. No one thinks about Gaza anymore. The settlements have become acceptable. We need to bring Palestinians back into Israeli homes through peaceful protest and boycott, divestment or sanctions. I'm not hopeful that things will change, but this is an incredibly powerful people. Maybe it's out of pure stubbornness, but they keep going." So does she, sometimes inspirationally, but there is of course a cost.

Haifa Dwaikat, 33

Student

NABLUS, WEST BANK

Uprooted Haifa had a reedy voice. The first thing she said to me was, "I might be giving birth any time, anyhow." The second was, "My mother is a martyr, and my father died two weeks ago." Perhaps she feared that I was a hostile journalist. She probably had not met many. In the pastoral villages of the West Bank, worldliness is limited, and patriarchal traditions continued during the Oslo period, even as women's expectations of life increased. Haifa was a child bride who had realized her dream of going to university too late, she felt. She was now studying Arabic literature at An-Najah University, close to her village, Rajub. Her male heirs had been village mukhtars "until this thing ended," she said pointedly. Haifa's traditions had been eroded from within and without Palestine.

During the "period of chaos" in Nablus that spanned much of the mid-2000s, her family's cars were set ablaze by arsonists. So on January 15, 2006, Haifa's twenty-year-old brother, Fawsi, decided to stand guard with a rifle. He was sighted by an Israeli army patrol that apparently believed it had discovered a militant hideout. "My brother was shot by the Israelis at the window," Haifa said calmly. "When my mother went to see what was happening, she was shot too. There were twenty bullets in her body. My father and four of my older brothers were also injured." One brother still has the scars from where a bullet exited his back. "I don't have the words to express anything," Haifa said. "I feel extremely paralyzed."

Were your brothers fighters? I asked. "Neither my father nor any of my brothers was ever arrested. My father was a driver from Amman to the West Bank. We never had any problems with the occupation. We always had permits." Haifa said that the army apologized for shooting her brother. It had been a mistake. What about your mother? I inquired. "They apologized for that too." Do you accept their apologies? "I don't, but, *khallas,* everything is with them—the law, the power, the world. My father wanted to sue the soldiers, but the occupation said he should pay 3,000 [Jordanian] dinars to have the case heard in court. He couldn't because he was bankrupt. He'd already had to pay out of his own pocket for the treatment of my injured brothers."

Haifa's mother had mostly taken care of the large family as only one of her sons had married. "It felt as though our home had been demolished," she said. "Our mother looked after everything. The others were really young, so they needed someone to take care of them." Just going on with life felt "sort of like a dream," she said. "We all know that it's God's will in the end, despite all the catastrophes. Patience is what keeps us going—and those who are still alive. My injured brother had two young daughters. That's why we have to live." Haifa's early life had not given her much to hope for.

"I got married at fourteen," she said coldly. "I got divorced at fifteen. My husband was eighteen. It's sort of usual. My grandfather's mentality was really conservative. He didn't want me to continue my education. He just thought a woman should get married, and that's it." But Haifa found that her husband's mother was an "executive manager" in the relationship, forbidding visits to Haifa's parents and even choosing her clothes. "She used to tell him what to do all the time," Haifa said. "She managed my life, not him. She was my husband, not him. I had to obey her every word. She told me whether I could go out or not and what I could buy. She was really forceful because he was her only son—after twenty years of marriage." Almost two decades later, Haifa had not forgiven her.

"She didn't want me to laugh because she wanted me to get pregnant," Haifa said, a smirk intruding on her otherwise expressionless face. "She used to say that if I became pregnant I mustn't laugh or else I would abort the baby." Less amusingly, her husband sometimes kicked her—and tried to hit her on several occasions. "He never did, though, because he feared my parents," she said, straightening her back. "Whenever we had any 'hot discussions'—he used to scream and curse me with bad words—I went to my parents' house." But most of Haifa's complaints centered on his inability to stand up to his mother. "He never defended me when she forced me to cook for her and her daughters, even though that wasn't one of my responsibilities as a wife."

The couple were far too young to have gotten married. But the first time they talked—on their wedding day—Haifa "felt safe" with her prospective husband, she said, "because he told me that he loved me and that he'd sent his mother to get me engaged. I thought my parents were fine with it, so I said that I had no problems. He was nice." The wedding, though, "was a mess." Haifa explained, "I was told that I would wear a white dress, and I asked my brother to get me an ice cream. I was happier about the ice cream than the dress. My main concern was whether I would miss the cartoons on TV. I spent the day crying because I was leaving my brothers, sisters, and parents. I felt uprooted, and I didn't know where I was going or what marriage meant." She did not know what divorce meant either. But when she thought that was what all her family—apart from her grandfather—wanted, she sued for one. "I usually stood aside and let them manage things in one way or another," she said. "But the truth was that I couldn't continue."

In court, Haifa's family asked for their daughter to be awarded a separate house. When that was denied, the marriage was annulled. "Usually it's really hard for a woman to get divorced," Haifa reflected, "and we get fewer marriage opportunities a second time. People don't want 'experienced' women for their sons." Her husband had no such problems.

Shortly before the divorce, Haifa's mother-in-law had started looking for another wife for her son. "He got married immediately afterward," Haifa said sharply, "and I got a shock at the beginning of my life. To this day I hate men. They are irresponsible and can't make their own decisions. I was the one who paid the price for this."

Even so, Haifa's parents supported her going back to school, and through them she met her forty-four-year-old second husband. "He's a widower who wanted to marry," she explained. "People told him about me. We talked together and decided to marry. We've been married for nearly one year. He's okay, but I married him because my mother died and I couldn't be alone. And then my father died. If I could turn back time to before my first experience I'd have married someone else. They tell me that I'll be happy when I give birth to my baby, but I still feel totally destroyed inside."

Haifa's advice to young girls today: "Try to make their own decisions." But even if she could go back in time, she admitted, she would not have acted differently. "I got engaged at an early age, but in the end I knew that I had a mother who cared for me," she said. "My little sister's life is much harder than mine was."

What sort of woman was your mother? I probed. "She had a leadership personality," Haifa replied, her pale face softening. "I always thought that she should be a leader of something. She planned our lives perfectly. She married at fifteen but she was really happy with my father. They made a very nice environment for a family. But she's dead." Haifa looked around the Women's Center. Unbidden, she abruptly signaled that she had something else to say. "I'd like to add that my grandfather didn't want my father to interact with any political movements because he was his only son." I did not probe any further.

Hala Salem, 32
NGO Director
AMMAN, JORDAN

You must let your hair fly in the wind The first time I visited Amman, in September 2002, I met a twenty-three-year-old West Banker who was "on holiday" while his workplace, Ramallah's Muqata compound, was besieged by Israeli tanks. He was desperate to return. "It must seem strange to you that I want to go back to a prison," he said. "Please understand that staying here is just what the Israelis would like us to do, and it is also a prison."

Nearly three million Palestinians live in Jordan, more than half the country's population and twice the number of Palestinians in Gaza. The largest number arrived in 1948 as refugees, but another 300,000 or so "displaced persons" fled the 1967 war, sometimes after their villages were destroyed. Other Palestinians found themselves in Jordan as a result of the collateral damage of occupation, such as deportation, revocation of residency rights, or denial of family reunification.

Most of those who arrived in 1948 and 1967 were granted citizenship rights. Without these they would be unable to, for example, buy land. But even Palestinians with Jordanian citizenship suffer harsh discrimination in government employment—they are blackballed from working for the police or joining the army—and have restricted access to university education. This is keenly felt as the average Palestinian in Jordan is eighteen years old and has migrated at least once in his or her life.

Disadvantaged as they are, Palestinians form one of Jordan's most entrepreneurial communities. Parts of some urban camps are indistinguishable from the middle-class neighborhoods that have grown up around them. Hala Salem lived and worked in one such district, Jabal al-Hussein in Amman. Her family arrived in Amman from Ramle in Israel. She was born in Jordan's Souf camp along the way in June 1976. It was not the sort of place that teachers like her parents would have chosen to bring up a child. Their two-bedroom apartment already housed Hala's large extended family, and water had to be transported there from wells on a person's head or on a donkey.

Souf was low-class. "It's dirty," Hala said, wrinkling her nose, "and the people there are dumb. Petty crime is a way of life and there are so many social problems. The camp people are conservative and old-fashioned. Most of them treat women badly—sometimes violently—and it's not even acceptable for girls to wear long sleeves. They need permission from a husband, brother, or father to go outside the camp or visit friends. It's not like the city."

The family moved to Riyadh, which was also "behind civilization," Hala said. "It was just a desert with Bedouins who looked at us in a very strange way. There was nothing there, no paved roads, electricity, or air-conditioning, and it was very hot. The homes were made of clay, and we got bush snakes and scorpions in ours. Once, when I was seven years old, I was watching television with my hand against the wall when I felt a big scorpion crawl over it!" Her jaw dropped open in dismay.

Palestinian alienation was compounded by Wahabism, an extreme state-sanctioned form of Islam. Hala was just ten when a government edict ordered girls to wear the veil in class. "I didn't accept that," she said, rolling up her sleeves. "I fought with my mother, and when I left school I'd take it off. I felt like I'd become an old woman. It worried me. It's very hot, and you can't see anything clearly in it, you know? You must let your hair fly in the wind to feel free."

"We had to pray three times a day in school. I don't like to pray. In Riyadh, if you are not a believer, there's no freedom." Older Palestinians accepted this as the price of residency but not the younger generation. "We made a community among ourselves and expressed our culture there," she told me. "Most Saudis don't respect other cultures because they consider them less religious. They are so conservative and fanatical—and they get better salaries and legal treatment. The environment forces you to imitate their culture because they treat you like a stranger. They imposed Wahabism on us."

"Singing is *haram* there. We couldn't even do our national dances or wear our beautiful national dresses. I was veiled, and the men—including my father—had to wear this *dishdasha* [ankle-length garment]. It's very strange." Hala paused to chuckle at the thought. "My family wanted a better living standard than the camp, but all we got from Saudi Arabia was a home. You're just a Muslim, and there's no difference between Muslims anywhere." Other cultures "melted" in this environment, she stated.

But in some ways Hala saw the situation in Jordan as worse. "This is Wahabism," she said, lifting her headscarf: "If you are with us, you are loyal. If not, be a Jordanian or whatever. But they won't ask you to delete your national identity. Here, they do. They tell us that if we express our national culture, the Palestinian identity would revert, and there would be no Jordanian identity."

In 1995 Hala returned to Amman to study politics with a view to a career in diplomacy—"because I can talk well and I look good," she said, accurately. But she was soon disillusioned. At the university, Palestinian students had to wear a red Jordanian kaffiyeh rather than the black and white Palestinian one. "You couldn't even hear Palestinian songs on the radio," she said, "only Bedouin songs. The government did us no favors. We pay taxes for these officials, and even Jordanian students look at us as a disgrace. It can spark big problems." She murmured, "I should walk the streets wearing a map of Palestine."

Once, when a Jaffa dance troupe played a student party at Hala's university, the *mukhabarat* (secret police) seized the party organizers' passports the next day and posted warnings against repeating the offense. Jordan is a monarchy, and Palestinian parties are essentially prevented from organizing there. Hala found "something real to fight for" in her community's struggle for civil and national rights. Since 2000, she had worked in a research and advocacy post dealing with refugee issues, democracy, and reform. The center had relations with all Palestinian groups, but Hala's heroes spanned an improbable gamut that included Gamal Abdul Nasser, Shaykh Ahmad Yassin, and King Faisal of Saudi Arabia. "I like Golda Meir and Yitzhak Shamir," she ventured bravely. "From the moment they were born they were fighting for their country." My translator balked at this, but Hala would not be deterred.

"They're still my enemies because it's my country too. But look at our leaders! Fatah and Hamas work for their own personal benefit, not the nation's.

Fatah is corrupt, and Hamas is Fundamentalist. You know the book *A Place under the Sun* by Netanyahu?" She giggled nervously. "These people work for the idea." Hala believed that Jews had a right to live in Palestine as equals in one secular state. Few Palestinians would talk openly of this in Amman.

"They're afraid because families warn their sons, 'Don't talk politics, or you could go to jail,'" she explained. Could an Intifada ever happen in Jordan? Hala was unsure. "Palestinians might follow if the Jordanians started it," she said hesitantly, "but it could also be dangerous. There are a lot of problems between Palestinian and Jordanian students. In a way it's a confrontation between the Muslim Brotherhood and the government." Hala told me she would choose life in a secular Jordan over an Islamic Palestine. With her yellow headscarf, painted nails, sunglasses, and bangles, she might not fit easily into Gaza's cultural landscape. Class affiliation seemed to have shaped her sense of the world as much as gender issues.

"Most Palestinians in Jordan are middle class or rich," she said off-handedly. "There are problems in the camps, but most of us live a good life. We're not hungry. We can educate our children. Most of Jordan's business sector is made up of refugees, and they're very dynamic. They didn't wait for European countries because they knew no one would help them. Palestinians don't need money. We need to continue to help ourselves and take care of our families."

Although she still dreamed of return, Hala had only been to Palestine once, when she was six. If she could, though, she would go back tomorrow. "Most people would because they feel so oppressed," she told me. "They are denied so many rights, and Jordanians talk to you as if you just arrived from Mars. It's not our country."

Almost imperceptibly she had spun 180 degrees back to her advocate's role. "There is no water, no good food. Why would they prefer to stay here? Sometimes I ask my mother why she chose to come to Jordan." The agony of Hala's "why didn't you stay?" question precisely dovetailed Omar's "why did they leave?" problem. The answer, of course, is that her choices were always limited and I think Hala understood that. But it is difficult to gainsay her one advantage—the option of remaining in a dangerous Palestine—from a place where that birthright has been denied.

Sayed Kashua, 33

*Journalist, Author,
Scriptwriter*

WEST JERUSALEM, ISRAEL

Zelig The waiter in Jaffa's famed Hinawi-Abu Nassar restaurant told me that he had just graduated in journalism. The problem was that, as an Arab, he would never be able to work in Israel. Before I could stop myself, I said, "But what about Sayed Kashua?" He looked at me, downcast. "For every Sayed Kashua, there are a thousand waiters like me," he muttered.

Sayed is an Israeli author, columnist, and TV scriptwriter in the unenviable position for an Arab of owing his career to Jewish racism and, to some extent, antiracism. The devil is in the percentages. While the blowback of Zionism keeps his voice in demand—as a conscience or novelty—it also frames the context in which it is heard and the meanings that are imputed from it. Humor is not just a coping strategy or a means of disarming critics in such circumstances, it is also a professional survival strategy, and Sayed is very good at it.

"Are you serious?" was his first response when I asked him how he thought of himself when he was alone at night. "That sounds like the Shabbak way of questioning people. I think I'm an Israeli Arab. I know you should say 'a Palestinian citizen of Israel,' but Israel—or we, with our own hands—created a nation with a different history and wishes. Of course, I also belong to the Palestinian nation and the Arab world. But I find it difficult to say I'm Palestinian—not because I don't want to be; the opposite is true. But I'm enjoying life as an Israeli citizen, and Palestinians aren't. I don't deserve to be called Palestinian yet."

Being an Israeli Arab "is not heaven but it's less of a hell than in the West Bank or Gaza," he said. In Sayed's purgatory, belonging was the struggle.

"Sometimes I feel that I'm saying things that I'm not really convinced of just to keep this national feeling. I'm blamed as an Arab and Muslim, so that's probably what I am. I'm carrying Israeli citizenship, so I'm also an Israeli citizen." Do you sometimes feel like a chameleon? "A Zelig?" he raised an eyebrow. "Yes, maybe, but I have no illusions that trying to fit into Israel's idea of us will help Israeli Arabs. My future is exactly the same as the people of Tira. I don't want any other."

For Sayed's family in Tira the Nakba was "hell," "a nightmare." It was still a source of fear. "The feeling that 1948 can happen again is a big part of my identity," he explained. "My grandmother lost everything. Her husband—my grandfather—was killed when my father was one year old. One of my uncles was killed a week before that." Prior to 1948 his grandmother had been a wealthy landowner, but during the war she became an itinerant worker, traveling through mountains and fields to try to protect her children.

Her son became a Communist. His participation in demonstrations scared the young Sayed. He still remembered the house preparations before protests. But after Oslo, "maybe half of Tira was voting for Zionist parties," he said. "My family environment was like, 'You will be a minister or a pilot in the Palestinian air force because the PLO is the best thing in the Arab world.' That was true for me until we met the PLO people in Ramallah and discovered that they were just Arabs."

If a Jew said this about Israel, they would be called self-hating. But Sayed did not see much mirroring between Jews and Arabs. "No, in what sense, are you a poet?" he asked. "I see a lot of similarities in one way, but we don't have enough money. And our mentality is different. I guess that after being kicked for hundreds of years, the Jewish people have good reason to be paranoid. But we were raised differently. We were strong and part of something really huge. We always won. We never lose. And then you see the news and you're losing all the time. Maybe we'll need decades to be . . . " His voice petered out. Sayed had a journalist's habit of not finishing quotable sentences.

As a child, he won a place at an elite Jewish school before going on to study sociology, but he struggled to be accepted. An incident in his novel, *Dancing Arabs,* where the teenage Arab narrator is spat at on a school bus was autobiographical. "These kids were singing songs and laughing at me and I cried," he riffed. "I got off the bus and tried not to take buses after that. I was very scared. Maybe I still am."

The book's narrator feels ashamed of his father's powerlessness and his community's lack of sophistication. Like him, Sayed is light-skinned and could pass as a Jew. Do you also feel proud when people think that you are

Jewish? I asked. "Yes," he said frankly. "Not in the sense of being Jewish, but not to be pointed at as an Arab. It was very important for me to fit in. I don't like to be stopped at checkpoints, but I'm doing my best not to be an 'undercover Arab.'" Sayed saw his family at a Tulkarem refugee camp less often these days. "I carry this feeling that they'll look at me as a collaborator," he said.

Life was easier at *Kol Ha'ir*, a small, well-respected Jerusalem magazine that offered a springboard for young left-wing journalists before the Second Intifada. Sayed began covering the West Bank for them "by mistake," as he put it. "Yusuf Cohen, the editor, said, 'We need an Arab yuppie to write about other Arab yuppies,' and they sent me to interview Hanan Ashrawi's daughter. But she didn't agree. I called Hanan Ashrawi, and she said '*Kol Ha'ir*? You wrote that I sold my land to the Jews! Shame on you!' and hung up." Without the support of Cohen and another *Kol Ha'ir* stalwart, Daphna Baram, Sayed believed he would have been fired when the Second Intifada started.

"The manager didn't like what I was writing. He blamed me for losing their audience. I'd been a star of the newspaper, and then suddenly I wasn't welcome anymore." Sayed was eventually sacked anyway without explanation. More setbacks followed. Israel's biggest newspaper, *Yediot Ahronot*, offered him a job—and then withdrew it "for political reasons," he said. "Even *Haaretz* never called me. I had to keep calling them." But perseverance paid off and Sayed eventually got a column at *Haaretz*, becoming a double-edged symbol of Israel's meritocracy to boot. "They only need one of me," he noted wryly. "If another young [Arab] writes books in Hebrew, I'll have no job anymore." It was time for another joke. "I'm the only one enjoying racism in this country," he cracked. "I'm making money out of it."

At *Haaretz*, Sayed found that the audience reaction was either "we love you or we want to kill you," with little in between. "But during the 2006 Lebanon War everyone was against me. My editor very gently told me that people were canceling their subscriptions after I wrote that Israeli air force pilots could rest easy because Arabs actually hate their kids. Of course, I would kill my son just to show it on the news! It was when they bombed tens of kids in a Lebanese basement and the Israeli media said Hezbollah faked it. Pilots are the most holy thing in Israel."

Sayed actually wrote the column in tears after attending a funeral for his friend David Grossman's son. But was there a broader danger of the "tears of a clown" syndrome? I wondered. "Maybe everybody hides behind humor," Sayed said. "But it comes naturally; nothing is planned that much." You don't have an "impostor complex," where you morph yourself into what others seem to want? "Sociologists will tell you that 'me' is what I think people think I am, no?" He scanned me for approval. "I think it's true everywhere." Minorities do put a premium on the ability to move in different worlds, and that can blur boundaries. Some Arab Israeli men say they feel less masculine or authentically Arab in the company of Palestinians from the occupied territories. On the other hand, some East Jerusalemites want to live in Israel because of the higher standard of living, according to Sayed. But their status is not always so different.

Sayed remembered reporting from a funeral in Umm al-Fahem at which three people were shot dead during the October days. "I was there the next day with the demonstrators—not the media—and two more people were killed. The mood was angry, like, 'Please don't let the peace die.' It brought me down to the street. They thought that they were Palestinian citizens after Oslo. Asmi Bishara was in the Knesset. It's okay, we're part of the Jewish state finally." The message of the killings, Sayed thought, was, "Don't think that you belong. If we need to teach you that you don't, then we will."

As a journalist, Arab, and Zelig, he felt torn. "I had my first weekly column about my wife being pregnant," he explained, "and it was a huge success. But we received death threats, so we moved from Jerusalem to Tira. Me and my brothers really were planning where to hide the baby. Should we start digging under the floor? This was the feeling. I was very scared of being attacked. Forget about my wedding day, the Second Intifada was the worst period of my life."

Such stress seemed a long way from the stylish if smoky office space in Jerusalem where he now worked on his acclaimed TV sitcom *Arab Labor*. It is a brilliant satire about an Israeli Arab journalist who's "a bit of a nebekh," Sayed enthused. "He really wants to fit into the Jewish society elite, but in every episode he fails. Like they tell him that the Subaru is a Jewish car, or he makes a Haggadah for Eid al-Adhar. In the end, he goes to a shrink who tells him, 'You have an illness called "Israeli Arab."'"

Sayed was encouraging a mostly Jewish audience to laugh at Israeli Arabs, or, more accurately, himself. But because he presented himself sympathetically, he could still exclaim, "I don't know why the Arabs are so mad about it!" He ridiculed one Arab critic who condemned him for writing for "a Zionist paper" the day before, repeating his criticisms in the equally Zionist *Ma'ariv*. It was exactly the kind of self-righteous and hypocritical indignation that Sayed's work fed off. But most Arab journalists have few choices who they worked for, as Sayed knew. The joke was ultimately on both of them.

By appearing to dismiss *asabiya* in favor of plaudits from Jews, suspicions about Sayed's loyalties were inevitable. This went doubly because he had prospered under Zionism while other Arabs had not. If there were a third Intifada, he said, "I'd be on the Arab side, as a left-wing Israeli. I'd support them from my flat in New York." And if it ended with one Palestinian state without Jews, would you stay? Sayed seemed genuinely taken aback by the question. "We won the war?" he repeated in disbelief. "If the Jews said, 'We're really sorry, we followed this crazy guy, and it was a huge mistake,' then I'll join this nation. I'll say I'm Jewish and do my best to belong. No, it depends on how they leave," he corrected himself. "If the Jews left after a war, I'd probably have already left because I'd never count on Arabs to win. But if we won and used the law to stop Jews living here, then I would not want to live in this country either." Although it was unfair, I left his office wondering if perhaps Israel had vicariously accepted him in a way that "Palestine" never could.

Tawfiq Jabharin, 40

Lawyer

UMM AL-FAHEM, ISRAEL

An apartheid state "Israel is an apartheid state," Tawfiq Jabharin said. "I see it every day. I feel it every minute. Ten years ago, Israelis were ashamed when Israel was called an apartheid state. Today they don't care. Once the Israeli High Court tried to defend Arab rights, but today they can't and they don't even seem to try."

Some anti-Zionists like the renowned Israeli Marxist Moshe Machover prefer comparisons to states such as America and Australia in their early phases—when they were still dispossessing indigenous peoples of their land.

Tawfiq, though, believed that a "race-based" statute such as Israel's Law of Return—which grants full citizenship to any Diaspora Jew while denying it to Palestinians expelled from their homeland—is a fingerprint of legal apartheid. He spoke with the meticulous, slightly monotonous tone of a case lawyer, worn down by years treading the Israeli court circuit. "It starts with the land issue," he said.

Tawfiq had built the house that we were sitting in. "Like about 70 percent of the buildings in Umm al-Fahem, it's illegal," he told me, his eyebrows sinking into the bridge of his nose. The Haifa district planning committee had refused the Jabharins a permit to build in what they classified as an agricultural area, and after thirty years, a proposed municipal council area redefinition was still being dealt with in committee. "They want to keep Umm al-Fahem small, and far away from the Mei Ami settlement to the south," Tawfiq said. There were several personal dimensions to these dry details.

In 1948 Tawfiq's family arrived in Umm al-Fahem from al-Lajjun, a nearby village that fought in the 1936 Revolt. The Arab Liberation Army, a pan-Arab force of volunteers that tried to defend it during the Nakba, was defeated, and Lajjun was cleared of Palestinians and most of its buildings. As the village had been built on the Mount of Megiddo ("Armageddon" in the New Testament), it was rebuilt as Kibbutz Megiddo. In 2002 a refugee from Umm al-Fahem blew himself up on a bus there, killing seventeen Israelis.

Tawfiq's forebears lost about 80 dunams (19.76 acres) of land in Lajjun and, like most of the village's residents, ended up in Umm al-Fahem. Some 34,000 dunams (8,401 acres) of Lajjun's land were confiscated without compensation under the Land Acquisition Law. Jewish apartments were built there, a Jewish forest was planted, and the surviving village mosque—which was briefly used as a Jewish carpentry workshop—was blocked off with mounds of earth. "I always remind my children that we have land in Lajjun," Tawfiq said. He had breathed new life into a tradition of visiting it that began with his grandfather.

In 1994 he became the first Palestinian to apply for housing in a Jewish settlement, the nearby *moshav* of Katzir. Katzir was partly built on Arab land acquired by another racialized law, the 1950 Absentee Property Act, which requisitioned the property of Palestinian refugees who fled during the Nakba. He said he was refused, according to a Jewish Agency representative on the acceptance committee, because he was not a Jew. Tawfiq published the story and threatened to go to the High Court. A few months later he was offered a home in Katzir and lived there during the Oslo years, from 1995 until 2000.

"But I didn't want to live in a Jewish area!" he protested. "I just felt that I had to, after the Israeli housing ministry declared that they were building in Wadi Ara to Judaize the area. We didn't want a better residence or quality of life, just to put the issue before public opinion." Katzir was a quasi-military part of Ariel Sharon's "seven stars" program, which aimed to increase the percentage of Jews living in northern Israel—and provide a buffer zone separating it from the West Bank.

Curiously, Tawfiq never felt that he was living among Jews there. "But I didn't go there to be part of the community," he added. "Katzir is a lonely settlement between Arab populations, and I always felt I was still in Umm al-Fahem." While Katzir's Russian immigrants were "a little different" as neighbors, Tawfiq did not suffer any racial discrimination from them. "Some of them even became my clients," he laughed. Others in the community saw him as "a fanatical Arab nationalist who was their enemy. They aggressively told me that they didn't like Arabs and didn't want me there."

When Tawfiq returned to Umm al-Fahem in late 1999, the Katzir house lay empty for a year. "When the Intifada burst a fanatical Jewish man from Katzir got into the garden, broke a stone plaque off the wall, and took it to his house," Tawfiq said. "I read about it in *Haaretz*. I'd written '*Jabal al-Aws*'— Katzir's original name—and 'the Jabharin family' in English and Arabic on the plaque." The story carried a picture of the man with the plaque in his house. But the police took no action, Tawfiq said. A stream of insults against him and "Death to the Arabs" graffiti were then scrawled on the walls of Katzir's post office. "This was during the Intifada, and a lot of people became very hostile to Palestinians," Tawfiq explained. "The Arab who moved in after me was harassed by the security police."

Interestingly, though, as well as extending his apartheid analysis, living with Israelis taught Tawfiq "not to hate Jews," he said. He began instructing his children to ignore other people's racial backgrounds. He sent his eight-year-old son, Ahmed, to Kfar Qara, Israel's only mixed Jewish-Arab school in an Arab town. "But now Ahmed tells me, 'I hate Jews.' He has no Jewish friends there, even though half his class are Jews," he said. Tawfiq was trying to change his son's views. But although he would accept his sons marrying Jewish women, "the girls cannot marry non-Muslims," he stated unequivocally. "It would be a big problem. I am not a religious man, but I respect Islam, and I will do exactly as my religion says."

Tawfiq and others had now applied to live in another nearby Jewish settlement, Mei Ami. Its residents told journalists that they would not accept Arab neighbors—"because we have a different mentality, culture, and language,"

Tawfiq scoffed. "The chairman of their settlement's administrative commission also said this," he added tidily. Tawfiq seemed to live and breathe such cases. He talked fondly of the famous Jiftlik campaign in the early 1990s, when he helped Bedouin villagers in the Jordan Valley beat back attempts to confiscate their land and demolish their houses.

Much of his work was focused on the Jewish National Fund (JNF), which owns 13 percent of Israel's lands. The JNF was established in 1901 to purchase land solely for Jewish settlement. Before 1948 Jews owned about 7 percent of Palestine's land (much of it acquired dubiously, Palestinians say). Today the situation has been reversed, with the state of Israel owning about 93 percent of the country's land (and occupying around 70 percent of the West Bank's). The JNF was a primary mechanism for the land acquisition. In 1960 it was incorporated into the Israel Lands Administration (ILA), a government land agency. But the JNF retained the right to nominate ten of its twenty-two directors. While the ILA leases land to Jews and Muslims alike for up to ninety-nine years, ownership ultimately rests with the Jewish state.

"The ILA cannot itself discriminate between Jews and Arabs," Tawfiq said, "but it can and does transfer leasing powers to 'acceptance committees' in settlements like Katzir or Mei Ami that can choose who they'll accept. The ILA has given hundreds of leases to committees like this in the Galilee, but it's never given one to a committee with an Arab majority." According to Tawfiq, while the ILA had granted permission for five or six new Palestinian towns in Israel, "all of them were established in the Negev desert for the Bedouins, in order to clear them off their surrounding lands." By contrast, activists point out that around a thousand Jewish communities have been created in Israel since 1948.

Sometimes the JNF and the ILA swap southern Negev lands for equal tracts in northern Israel, Tawfiq said. In the south, the ILA then displaces nomadic Bedouins into small but "recognized" desert slum towns while their land is turned into exclusively Jewish settlements. In the north, the JNF also uses its land to build exclusively Jewish settlements. The system is more complicated than in apartheid-era South Africa, but it was easy to see why Tawfiq pointed to land as the starting point in making the comparison.

Beyond this, some argue that hiring criteria—such as participation in national service—augments a systemic pattern of racism. "In the private sector," Tawfiq argued, "many nonmilitary high-tech jobs—even for accountants—are conditioned on military service. They'll say, 'It's because we're dealing with government and security projects.' But substantively, there's no connection." Many state mortgages also depend on military service, and, until recently, so did child welfare payments. "It's social, institutional, and national discrimination," Tawfiq averred.

The apartheid argument is clearer still in the occupied territories, where blue and green ID cards check a Palestinian's free movement. The mutable blue residency ID for East Jerusalemites allows greater access than does the green ID card given to other West Bankers. But Palestinians may have to relinquish either card if they leave the region for too long. "At least my Israeli citizenship gives me a right to work and vote and some security, and not to be threatened with transfer from my land," he said.

Talk about "transfer"—the forced displacement of Palestinians—has intensified within mainstream Israeli society in recent years. "People are frightened, but they won't accept it," Tawfiq said. "Some say that it'd be okay if the Israelis gave us all of our Lajjun lands back first. But they're just talking about drawing a line around our houses and transferring Umm al-Fahem to the West Bank." Tawfiq's analysis was that Jewish Israel had pushed many Arabs in Israel to consider themselves Palestinians. "You won't find any who will accept Israel as a Jewish state." Surprisingly, his father did, though, when Nasser's forces were defeated. "He became another man after 1967," Tawfiq said sadly. "He became convinced that we could not change the definition of the Jewish state, only fight for more rights—not even equal rights—within it."

Such ideas are anathema to many young Arabs in Israel today, even if many of them also speak Hebrew slang and enjoy Hebrew pop music, films, and friends. Are they becoming more Israeli, culturally? I asked. "No," Tawfiq replied frostily. "My child Ahmed became more extreme the closer he got to the Jews. He hates them and doesn't want to be their friend."

It was a persuasive argument, but a young worker in Tawfiq's office who gave me a lift to the bus station enthusiastically told me, "Maybe more educated people speak Arabic and call themselves Palestinians, but everyone speaks some Hebrew, even grannies. Whether they call themselves Israelis or Palestinians depends on who they're talking to." This was probably true, but it hinged first on the issue of consciousness rather than fact. Tawfiq would probably have noted that the man was only giving me a lift in the first place because Umm al-Fahem's transport system was so creaky. Israel's largest Arab city, Nazareth (metropolitan population 185,000), at least received two public buses a day from Jerusalem, but the illegal West Bank Jewish settlement of Efrat (pop. 7,500) received sixty-three.

Consciousness is a fickle flame. One Jaffan woman I interviewed, Nafisa Jimmi, was fighting attempts by the local council to prevent her from building a staircase in her home. This sort of petty discrimination had been systematically applied to Arabs in Jaffa's Ajami quarter to force them out of their neighborhood. Yet Nafisa told me, "When we tell people in Ramallah that we're from Jaffa, they get very excited and say, 'You're so lucky, Jaffa is a kind of paradise!'" As Nafisa knew, such views were insanely rosy. But many Gazans too—because of their unbearable conditions—wish for nothing more than to form part of a segregated and exploited labor force, as they did in the 1970s. The architects of South African apartheid would have dreamed of such a situation. Israelis of almost all hues simply dreamed of a land without other ethnic groups.

Despite Tawfiq's best efforts, in March 2011, an "Acceptance to Communities Law" passed its final reading in the Knesset, formalizing the right of communities like Katzir's to exclude Arabs.

Fuad al-Hofesh, 33

Psychologist

MARDAH, WEST BANK

The captain or me Fuad was introduced to me through the Palestinian Treatment and Rehabilitation Center for the Victims of Torture (TRC), a Ramallah-based group that, unusually, took up violations by Israeli and PA security forces alike. Until September 1999, torture was routine for detained Palestinians. An Israeli High Court ruling nominally barred the practice then—except in the cases of "ticking bombs" likely to commit attacks. But a survey by the Israeli human rights group B'tselem in May 2007 found that torture continued regardless.

In the West Bank too "torture and beatings have become a part of our culture," Hassan, an official at the TRC told me before adding the inevitable rider, "because of the occupation." Some victims of ill treatment by the PA didn't even consider it torture, he said. "They think it's normal to get hit by security officers because they have the authority and right to do so." Fuad never had that idea.

Born in Kuwait where his father, a steelworker, had moved to find work, every summer Fuad's family holidayed in the West Bank. In 1990 they found themselves marooned there when Iraq invaded the Gulf emirate. "We'd been very happy," Fuad told me, as he opened and flapped his leather jacket, an apparent habit. "My father had a high salary, and life was good. But during the war, we lost our house and all our life savings." Palestinians were seen by the Kuwaiti regime as a fifth column that had aided the Iraqi invasion, and after the war a campaign of killings, beatings, arrests, and harassment reduced the community's size from 400,000 to around 30,000.

In Fuad's case, the loss was double-edged as he had anyway wanted to return to participate in the Intifada. "We'd watched it on TV and seen how Palestinian bones were being broken," he said. "I felt that I had a responsibility to protect Palestine. The mood then was of a general revolution by all sections of society—women, kids, workers—and I wanted to be a part of it." He promptly got involved in the protests and was nearly shot during one demonstration.

Many Palestinians born in the Gulf States have a religious orientation, and Fuad was inspired by the new Islamic resistance growing in Palestine. "Hamas appeared at the same time as the Intifada," he said, "and each strengthened the other. They brought a new formula that combined political resistance with Islamic thought. It was a new social style." He quickly became a Hamas student activist. When he was arrested in June 1992 his family was devastated. His parents had expected Fuad, their eldest son, to get an education and then support them through their hardship. Instead, he was sentenced to two years in Tulkarem prison, which was known then as "the slaughterhouse."

The first two months were the toughest. From memory, he estimated that his isolation cell measured about 180 by 120 centimeters. It had no toilet and was called "the grave." The staple meal at that time, beans, was known as "concrete," and Fuad had to eat it with his hands. "I was isolated from the other Palestinian prisoners for sixty days of questioning," he recalled, "and every day they beat me all over my body. They kicked me and hit me with their M-16 guns wherever it hurt and could make a difference." The beatings often took place on the way from Fuad's cell to the interrogation room and were accompanied with sexual threats directed at his mother and sister. "They knew exactly what would hurt the feelings of Palestinians," he said.

From his position of powerlessness—he had never even been arrested before—Fuad saw the abuse as psychologically structured. "They know how strong you are," he said, "how you're likely to react, and exactly when to question you. They would tie my hands up behind my back and put a hood over my head so I couldn't see anything. Then they'd make me sit outdoors in July and August. There was no cover from the sun, so it was very hot." After this, he would be brought in for a good cop/bad cop interrogation. "The first soldier would ask a question, the second would beat me and threaten my family, and the third one was friendly. He'd say, 'You don't have to be hit, we could give you things. It's better to cooperate and get out of here.'"

The interrogator who made the strongest impression on Fuad was an Israeli captain. "He always said, 'I'm a psychologist, and I can tell you that because of your activities you'll never be educated at university. You're going to spend all your life as a worker in Israel.' I always replied, 'No, I'm going to be a better psychologist than you when I leave.'" When Fuad got out of jail in 1994, he went to An-Najah University to study psychology. In 1999, though, after helping a Hamas leader on the run, he was arrested again and reunited with the Israeli captain behind bars. "I told him that nothing he did now would make a difference," Fuad said, "as I was returning to prison with a master's degree in psychology. He responded by threatening me, 'This time you're not going to be leaving prison, or if you do, you won't be walking.'"

The questioning this time was completely different. When Fuad refused to cooperate, instead of using violence, the soldiers would bring in former friends who implicated Fuad in their activities. Up to sixteen Israelis sat in on these interrogations, he said, and CIA agents sometimes joined them. "The Israeli interrogators seemed to understand exactly what Hamas was doing," he said. "They knew what to ask and how to treat us. The CIA agents just sat in the room, trying to understand Hamas from how the prisoners spoke."

Fuad was taken to a tiny isolation cell through two doors separated by a space to heighten the sense of quarantine. Inside it, a weak yellow light was left on twenty-four hours a day. "Sometimes they took me down a long corridor to a space with other prisoners," he recounted, playing with some worry beads. "They would tie me up there on a chair without a back—so I had to completely bend over—and sometimes they put black spectacles with spirals drawn on them over my eyes for days on end." At night, the soldiers "put headphones on us and played noisy rock music to prevent us from sleeping. It also prevented us from communicating, but when the music stopped we would tell each other, 'You are good. You have to stand up. Don't say anything.'" This torture lasted for twenty-eight days.

In an odd way, Fuad's sanity seems to have hinged on a form of competition with the captain who returned to question him. "I told him that I had justice on my side, and right is always stronger than force," Fuad said. "Psychologically I was always thinking about who was going to win—the captain or me? I had this conflict in my head." It was resolved in practice. "I moved more toward Hamas," he said. "Israel was trying to create a psychological graveyard for us, but we changed the prisons into schools and universities."

The detainees taught each other languages, studied literature, wrote novels, and held parties whenever someone was released. "Every night prisoners from the different movements would give powerful presentations and debate the situation outside. It helped the younger prisoners to understand Palestinian history and gain confidence to express themselves," Fuad said. "If a resistance cell was caught, they'd start to debate what happened—what were your mistakes, why did it happen like that, and how can we develop it?"

There are only so many ways that a nonviolent activist can keep himself from being arrested. Between 1992 and 2006 Fuad was detained five times. On August 13, 2007, his sixth arrest came at the hands of the Palestinian Authority, in the clampdown that followed the June fighting. By this time, though, he was working as Hamas's general director for prisoners' affairs in the West Bank. He was severely mistreated in the PA's Beitunia jail.

"I was beaten several times in the beginning," he said, "and then tied up for hours on end. The people who questioned me had experience [of torture] because they were also arrested and questioned by the Israelis." How do you know that? I asked. "Because they were arrested with me, and we spent time together in different jails in Israel," he replied. "Some of the interrogators were with me in jail. I recognized them by face because I'd actually met them before. One of them was an old colleague from An-Najah University. He told me, 'This is my job, I have to do it.'"

How similar was their treatment to that of the Israeli officers? "The difference was that the Israeli way was very organized and scientific," Fuad said. "There's a way they make you sit, called 'the banana.' They turn the chair upside down and tie you around it so your back bends around the chair. The Israelis were prohibited from torturing you in this way for more than an hour, but in Beitunia, they tied you up like that for the whole night."

"There's another position where they tie your hands around a pole behind you and raise them until you're standing on the tips of your toes. In Israel you shouldn't be held for more than two hours in this position, but with the PA, it was two days. In the Israeli prisons, they prevented you from sleeping for forty-eight hours, but then they'd let you sleep for two hours. In the Palestinian prison, they kept you from sleeping for one week. When you're tied on the pole and you start to fall asleep your body relaxes, but as you start to slide down it pulls your hands up, so you can't sleep."

Over two weeks, Fuad slept less than forty-eight hours. "When I was allowed a meal, I used to sleep for ten minutes instead just because I needed to," he said. "They knew they were dealing with a strong man who'd served many years in prison without confessing, so they used tough torture routines." The questions were focused on Hamas's plans in the West Bank. The officers' abuse, though, was directed at him, with no threats against his mother or sisters.

Eyad Sarraj, the Gazan psychiatrist, told me that when he was jailed by Yasser Arafat, he once heard an interrogation taking place in a neighboring cell. "Gradually," he said, "the officer raised his voice until he was screaming—in Hebrew! I was shocked. I inquired and found that this officer had been in an Israeli jail for ten years. But at that moment, he adopted the role of the Israeli torturer. It took him over. He expressed it toward another Palestinian and was very proud of it. He was talking about this man, who was from Islamic Jihad, as a collaborator and traitor. He said, 'They're going to drive our country back 2,000 years. They should learn to be decent!' Part of dehumanization is a process called identification with the aggressor." In fairness, Hamas has also been condemned by human rights groups for similar rights violations in Gaza. "If that happened," Fuad told me, "it was wrong."

Despite his measured tone and uncreased face, Fuad was still experiencing raw pain. "What's changed in me is that before I never hated anyone," he said. "Now I've started to feel bitterness and hatred toward the people who tortured me. That doesn't mean I'm going to take revenge. I hate the Israelis too, but I don't have the motivation to kill them." He said he only sought legal redress.

The wider lesson Fuad had taken was that "every Palestinian must pay a tax to stay here, and this is the price I have had to pay." Does torture work? I asked. "Sometimes it gives them accurate information," he replied casually. I told him I found this strange, because it had not worked with him. "That's because I didn't have any real accurate information in the first place," he said.

So what advice would you give someone going into an Israeli or PA prison? "Victory is one hour of being patient under pressure," Fuad replied. "It's like two people putting their fingers in each other's mouths. The first one to open his mouth will lose. You understand the idea?" I think so, I said. But it seemed a strange way to finish the conversation.

Samer Azmi al-Zugayyar, 32

Policeman

RAMALLAH, WEST BANK

Awlad al-Sumud　Samer sat in the Blue Bar, but, unusually, he was not drinking. I knew him as a raucous fixture on Ramallah's party scene where Palestinians and internationals mixed almost freely. Every international seemed to have a story about Samer, and the photos on the bar's wall proved many of them. He was the life of the party; gregarious, kind, and eager to please. But not everyone knew about the family tragedy that followed him like a sad pet.

In June 1982 Samer's father, Azmi, was the commander of the PLO's forces in Tyre, and during Israel's invasion of Lebanon, he disappeared in action, presumed dead. The *Time* magazine correspondent Roger Rosenblatt mentioned Azmi and Samer in a journalism master class titled "Beirut: Seven Days in a Small War." Azmi, he wrote, was "a first-class haranguer. . . . He had the eyes for it and the fists."

Rosenblatt described a scene in which the six-year-old Samer entered his father's office and was called to attention. "'Who is Sadat?' [the colonel] asked the boy. 'Sadat sold Palestine to Israel.' 'Who is Jimmy Carter?' 'Carter supported Israel.' 'Who are you?' The colonel regarded Samer with mock intensity. 'I am from Palestine,' fired back his son. 'From Hebron!' Then the visitor asked Samer what he would like to be when he grew up. Samer said that he would like 'to marry.' The soldiers roared. The boy, not realizing that he had said something funny, froze in bewilderment. In answer to another question, Samer said that he would like to live in a world without soldiers. . . . After the boy left the room his father swore. 'If I am killed, my son will carry my gun.'"

Twenty-six years later, in June 2008, the still unmarried Samer was carrying a gun for the PA's security police, but he had maintained his earlier ideals. "I believe that as human beings, we should be friends with everyone," he said. "Israeli or Jewish, we're all human. I want peace so we can all lead normal lives." He paused and then began cautiously, "I'll tell you something. My father was killed by the Israeli army . . . "

Azmi al-Zughayar is a legend. Born in Hebron in 1937, he left for Jordan in 1966 and fought at Karameh, an epic battle in which the PLO inflicted heavy losses on the Israeli army. After Black September, he escaped to Lebanon with Yasser Arafat. Samer had several stories about the times Azmi cheated certain death. He was a man of integrity; smart, brave, generous, merciful even to spies, serious and yet witty, when the occasion allowed. His presumed death was shrouded in mystery. One fable had it that he was betrayed by a Lebanese newspaper vendor and killed in a gunfight at a friend's coastal villa. But the body recovered there was badly burned and remained formally unidentified. Soon afterward, the Israeli army set up its headquarters in Azmi's old office.

The family refused—and still refuse—to believe that Azmi was dead. They sought refuge in a church near Tyre for forty days and then escaped to Syria. In 1986 they relocated to Jordan. Samer became one of the *Awlad al-Sumud* (Children of Steadfastness), a select group of orphans whom Yasser Arafat semiadopted. Indeed, Samer said that Arafat became "like a father" to him. "He was everywhere. He made me the person I am today. We never called him 'Mr. President' just Amu [Uncle] Abu Amar. He gave us a home, money for a private school and for hotels in Tunis. Every year we went to see him there during our school vacations. He'd been a very close friend to my father, so he felt responsible for us."

To Samer, Arafat was simultaneously "brilliant, humble, and very proud." "If you met him just once," Samer said, "he made you feel as though you'd known him for years." Samer had fond memories of eating breakfast with Uncle Abu Amar in his pajamas. "He stayed with us and loved us," he said. When he died, though, Samer did not weep. "I'm not a man of tears," he explained.

In 1996, at the age of twenty, Samer joined the Tunis generation that was returning to Palestine after Oslo. "A lot of people say the *al-awdeen* [returnees] brought corruption with them, but it's not true," he declaimed. "I wasn't expecting to find heaven here—and we're not angels—but there's corruption everywhere." Samer joined the police academy in Jericho and immediately transferred to the Special Forces.

In some ways it was a career path foretold. Between the ages of nine and eleven, Arafat had sent him to military courses in Yemen and Algeria. "If my father was still alive he'd be proud of me," Samer said. "We work against the armed gangs by day and with the Presidential Guard protecting visiting diplomats by night. I love my job and feel very close to the people I work with. We're like a family, and everyone looks at me as a leader, a first lieutenant." Samer was then being paid around 3,000 shekels (US$800) a month, roughly twice his estimate of the local average.

I asked him whether it was true that PA policemen were given only three bullets in their training sessions. He gave me a toothy laugh. "That's funny," he said. "It's ten. They just teach you the technique of how to shoot." What about bullet-proof vests? I asked. "Israel refused," he batted back. "They said we might turn against them, so they had to be able to shoot us. They also refused to give us tear gas rifles in case we used them to fire real bombs at them. We just have normal equipment—sticks, shields, the Kalashnikov, and our uniform."

At the start of the Second Intifada, Samer's unit was assigned to protect two Israeli soldiers, but they were killed by a mob inside Ramallah's police station. The TV pictures of children waving bloodied hands from a compound window stunned Israel. "It was a big mistake," Samer said. "They should have moved them to the Muqata. I hate what happened. It's not our way. But the Israeli army kills Palestinians every day, and the men came here in their uniforms so it was a normal reaction. We tried our best to help those people. We failed because all of Ramallah—thousands of people—attacked us, so how could we protect them?"

His most difficult experiences involved telling grieving families when his friends had been killed. "If you let the anger control you, you'd be a failed person," he said. "I respect *shahids*—my father was one—but it really hurts to see your friends on wall posters." Most of the officers in Samer's unit voted Fatah or PFLP, but not Hamas. "Anyone who jumps off the rope doesn't deserve to work with the rope," he said. It is a Fatah line that Islamists see as "born to rule" pomposity. "Hamas is murdering people in Gaza," he continued. "They want to control everything, and they don't give a shit about the Palestinian people." He rejected Fuad's torture claims outright.

When I said that I had seen the PA police use violence to stem protests in Ramallah, his response again veered toward Israeli-style denial. "That happens everywhere," he said. "In England they use horses and sticks. Why does everyone talk about the police here? Why does every journalist take pictures when a policeman starts hitting?" I told him that at a Hamas demonstration in Ramallah against Israeli attacks in Gaza, I once tried to photograph PA officers who were truncheoning women who had been entirely peaceful. The officers wrestled me to the ground with boots and fists and tried to grab my camera. I was not released until I deleted the single photo I had taken.

"I'm totally against that," Samer replied, changing horses twice in midstream. "But you must remember that Hamas kills people demonstrating in Gaza. I think the police handled the demonstration here well. I didn't see any mistakes." Blanket denials are common to police forces the world over—Samer also denied that there was any Al Qaida presence on the West Bank—but he did not convince me about the veracity of Fuad's story, and I think he sensed this.

He went on to tack left, arguing that Israel should leave Hamas charities in Nablus alone because "it's an internal thing, and they don't have a right to stick their nose into our business." The collapse of trust with Israelis that accompanied the Second Intifada had made it difficult to imagine peace, he said.

During the revolt, Samer himself was arrested and held for twelve days. He denied using arms against Israel but defended those who did. "Because the Israelis came to us," he explained. "We didn't go to them. We have the right to fight back, but we don't have the equipment so we should fight politically." Before his return, Samer had wanted to fight very badly. But he believed "Oslo is a very good agreement." "We should put the spirit back into it." Do you like Mohammed Dahlan? I prodded. "No comment," he laughed.

The sun was falling over Ramallah's nearby Clock Square, but before we went our separate ways Samer told me warmly that he had more than a hundred international friends and was proud to be part of their lives. He stonewalled a question about door policy at Ramallah bars refusing entry to Palestinians unaccompanied by women or internationals. "Palestinians can go everywhere," he reassured me. "It's okay."

A few weeks later we met up again in Beirut but in very different circumstances. I was interviewing refugees; Samer had traveled there with his family, expecting Israel to release his father's body as part of a prisoner swap with Hezbollah. In the end, the bodies of two Israeli soldiers, Ehud Goldwasser and Eldad Regev, were traded for the incarcerated Palestinian Liberation Front member Samir Quntar, four Hezbollah militants, and the remains of about two hundred Lebanese and Palestinians. Azmi's body was not among them.

Samer and his older brother, Abdel, a computer programmer, invited me to their glamorous but strangely nondescript 1970s retro hotel room in Beirut's exclusive Hamra district. A two-liter bottle of whiskey numbed some of the brothers' pain but not their sense of injustice. As Samer slid into introspection, Abdel—who was "90 percent sure" that Azmi was dead—became increasingly animated.

During the past few days there had been "a lot of confusion, a lot of pressure," he said, his voice taut as a wire. The family had arrived in a Beirut bedecked in Fatah flags and posters of Azmi, for a reception in his honor that never took place. "The media led us to believe that the Israelis were going to hand over my father's body," he said. "Instead we've just been disappointed again. He was the highest-ranking name on the list, and we don't know why he wasn't included. The Israelis released all the bodies from one of their four 'numbers cemeteries' [in which each grave is numerically marked], but he wasn't in it." Abdel believed that the cemetery was chosen so that land around Kibbutz Amiad, which was built after 1948 on the ruins of the Palestinian village Jib Yusuf, could be cleared for a "settlement expansion."

Israel's retention of Azmi's body was experienced by the brothers as a form of collective punishment against the family—and all Palestinians—because he had fought. Abdel sympathized with Israeli families in similar positions. "A human life is a human life, and Goldwasser and Regev were at the start of theirs," he said. "Keeping bodies is a disgrace to humanity." Until Azmi was buried, Abdel added, "he will never rest peacefully."

"They were never going to return my father's body for nothing," Samer pitched in. According to one Hezbollah official, Israel had kept high-profile bodies back to pressure the group for more information about its missing air force pilot, Ron Arad. But Abdel did not have much faith in Hezbollah. "They don't like us or my father very much," he said. "They have their own agenda, but we don't really understand politics here."

"Every Palestinian lives between optimism and pessimism," he continued, in a reference to Emile Habibi's epic Palestinian novel, *The Pessoptimist*. "We can never be optimistic about anything, and we can never be distanced from anything either. We live in the middle ground. It's nothing new. Even in my father's time, there was always some [diplomatic intrigue] going on. They'd say, 'We'll give you an agreement—everything now, it'll all be fixed'—and then when you're deceived, you find that it was something you knew would go wrong all along."

But you've thrown in your cards first? I suggested. "Of course," Abdel said. "It's the game, and the Israelis play it very well. But even if they keep my father's body, I will not weep and be crushed. We will focus. It was important to our people that today we went and comforted the other families who received their bodies. We didn't show them our disappointment or weep." Samer nodded, looking down at the hotel bed with glassy eyes. The children of *sumud* did not mourn. Israel would not let them.

The
First Intifada
Generation

The final proof of how far the Palestinian psyche had recovered from the Nakba paradoxically involved the inflicting of new wounds. The First Intifada was mostly fought by a generation that had no direct memory of 1948 and little access or inclination to use military hardware. Strikes, demonstrations, tax boycotts, and grassroots mobilizations characterized the uprising. Tires burned on rubble-strewn streets in the West Bank and Gaza as masked youths hurled stones, often with slingshots. Suspected collaborators were routinely executed. The Israeli army responded with an "iron fist" policy that employed an array of riot control machinery—rubber bullets, tear gas, live ammunition—as well as curfews, mass arrests, administrative detentions, and directives to break stone-throwers' limbs. There could be no more pretense that the occupation of the West Bank and Gaza was accepted by the occupied.

The Intifada began when an Israeli tank transporter drove into a crowd of Palestinians in Gaza's Jabalia camp, killing four people. But frustration had been growing for many years because of arrests, rising unemployment, the creep of settlement expansion, and restrictions imposed on Palestinian housing and movement. Islamic Jihad activists set the pace on the streets in the revolt's first days. The group had been formed by Fathi Shiqaqi with Iranian support when he split from the Muslim Brotherhood in the 1980s, arguing for an immediate challenge to Zionism. The Brotherhood's focus then was on changing Arab regimes, educating the population, and building institutions. Within days of the Intifada's onset, though, they had abandoned this strategy to reconstitute themselves as Hamas and prevent Islamic Jihad from outflanking them. The mosque would play a crucial organizational role in the revolt.

But while the factions responded to the popular mood, they did not create it. Like the Land Day movement in Israel a decade before, the Intifada was a popular explosion with local democratic control. It was, however, more militant, sustained, deeply rooted, and able to take the initiative in a flexible and immediate way. Women quickly came to the uprising's fore as lessons learned about unity in action during the *thawra* were internalized by Palestinians. Miriam Zaqout, director and cofounder of the Culture and Free Thought Association in Khan Younis, was one of five women who established the Palestinian Women's Union in 1988. "It brought all the secular parties together to support the uprising," she told me. "All my work and thoughts were about how to move women into the streets and the community. We raised awareness and demonstrated peacefully, but the Israelis shot at our protests and people were sometimes killed." Political parties formed student wings, women's groups, and workers' sections.

In keeping with past Palestinian rebellions, the revolt was fought by the poorest segments of Palestinian society. According to Abla Masroujeh, a trade union leader in Nablus, "The rich were only affected by having to send their children abroad to avoid school closures and mass arrests." They thus avoided the trauma that the fighting created. Abla worked in a pharmacy on the old city's border. "We were at the center of the clashes, so all the injured people who couldn't go to hospital were brought there," she told me. "They mostly had broken bones and wounds from rubber bullets or live ammunition. Once I was asked to give first aid to a young man lying on the street who wasn't breathing. I tried to resuscitate him, but then I realized he was dead. I had a fever for three days afterward, and I couldn't eat because the dead were here," she said, pointing at her mouth. You had death on your breath, I said, guessing. "Exactly!" she replied. "Under such conditions, you mature."

The revolt marked a generational changing of the guards in terms of Palestinian self-image. No more was the public face of Palestine an urban guerrilla in a foreign airport. It was now the David and Goliath picture of a street child throwing stones at a tank. This vividly illustrated Palestine's struggle to be born. An estimated 120,000 Palestinians were arrested during the uprising, and 1,409 were killed by Israeli forces—compared to 271 Israelis killed by Palestinians. Many more suffered injuries, house demolitions, crop destructions, and deportations. One report by Save the Children estimated that between 23,600 and 29,900 children required medical treatment for injuries caused by beating during the Intifada's first two years. One-third of them were under ten years old. Some would no doubt later fight in the Second Intifada.

The struggle electrified the mood in the Palestinian Diaspora. Rakan

Mahmoud, mayor of al-Hussein camp in northern Jordan, had to watch it on TV but was still uplifted by the experience. "This Intifada came after a long period of disappointment," he told me. "The Palestinian resistance had achieved nothing so people felt depressed, and then the First Intifada came as an act of God. All the emotions of the refugees outside Palestine lit up and became like a fire." Rakan was elected to a support committee in Irbid and proceeded to organize Intifada solidarity demonstrations. His earliest memories had been of lacking shoes and shelter in a tent city surrounded by Jordanian tanks during Black September.

The political factions, exiled and exhausted by years of internecine disputes and military defeats, played an auxiliary role in the fighting. Still, the PLO's historic Declaration of Independence in 1988 recognized Israel on 78 percent of mandate Palestine, in return for a Palestinian homeland on the West Bank and Gaza. It was followed by a formal renunciation of violence and the development of a dialogue with the United States that would reach a high point with the signing of the Oslo Accords in 1993. At the same time, Jordan and Egypt cut legal and administrative ties to the West Bank and Gaza. This and the Intifada's concentration in the occupied territories placed a Palestinian people with a distinct identity and geographic area on the world's map for the first time since 1936.

It also created an activist generation, seriously engaged in politics, that had confidence its cause would win. Some became embittered, and many were burned out by a combination of factors: the rigors of life under occupation, the chinks in previously iron-clad principles one must strike to survive, the limited gains accruing from their many sacrifices, the way these were squandered by the revolt's beneficiaries, and the wrenching divisions in Palestinian society this caused, as well as the more general demise of a struggle over which they had felt they had ownership.

"Abu Ahmed"

Hamas Activist and Teacher

WEST BANK

Recover Hamas may be famous for its commitment to resistance, but it is also a party that seeks to negotiate and govern. It has created networks of schools, hospitals, youth clubs, mosques, and day care centers and convinced many Palestinians that an Islamic way of organizing society is possible and desirable. "Abu Ahmed" was a teacher in one such Hamas school. It was more than a job to him.

He was a party man, with a short haircut and a bushy moustache. He was born and lived in a refugee camp. When we met he was dressed neatly but plainly in beige trousers and an open-collar striped shirt. Polite and unassuming, he was every inch the family man, happily married and surprisingly well educated; he had been to the university twice and to prison five times—"probably," he said.

His grandparents lived in the Jaffa region, and his father was shot several times while fighting in 1948. The young Abu Ahmed was made aware of the scars on his body. "Of course, this caused us to hate Israelis," he said. "I can never coexist with them. They are the cause of what we are living in this life." "You lose a lot of things [as a refugee]," he noted. "I always wanted to go back to recover them."

Abu Ahmed spoke gently, with a considered style that invited discussion. His father and nine brothers had been jailed when he was a child, and he had never felt protected by them. "There was always shooting and bombing, and our house was at risk of being demolished," he said. "How could I feel safe with that?" When he was twelve, armed settlers and soldiers abducted him, seeking information about his brother who had "been active in the resistance during the First Intifada." But he would not talk. "Eventually they threw me into a patch of cactus trees," he said.

Such experiences in a conservative family world centered on Islam fed his later activism. "You have to practice the political side of the religion. I feel secure when I pray. I know that Islam is the solution in this life, and in the second life it is infinite peace," he said. As a teenager, Abu Ahmed had been locked up in a cell for organizing a mosque protest against the Madrid treaty. "I went to prison because there were spies around me," he said.

"The Israelis humiliated me," he added, reeling off a familiar screed of misery. "They used to beat us. When it was freezing they'd throw water over us. They made us go and sit on the ice. When it was hot, they gave us hot water to drink. We couldn't sleep, and they gave us no food. They put us in small cupboards for days . . . " The worst thing he remembered was having his head smashed into a wall almost fifty times. "The investigator was wearing a ring and hitting me on my side," he said. It caused him eye problems, and he now wore glasses. "I forgot them today," he added.

Abu Ahmed became active in street politics during the First Intifada, but he was coy about any involvement with the military resistance. "The words are too big to give a specific answer to," he said, smiling. "I was more into resistance when I was younger. I wasn't very involved with guns. Now I'm more involved with politics, talking to the youth. You know, when a Palestinian is born it is already taught what party they'll be in. There's no negotiation about it. This kid is Fatah, that kid is Hamas." Thus are lives decided in Palestine—"usually," he qualified. "What's special about Hamas is that they can see how kids will grow up, and they help them to shine. If a kid has a logical mind, maybe he could get somewhere in politics?"

Abu Ahmed's school may be the place to spot such young stars. It was run "by people around Hamas," he said, "but not by Hamas as an organization. There are many Fatah people in our school." All he would say about his other Hamas activities was, "Everyone has his specialism and his job. I work on activities like demonstrations. We are paid one month, and then not paid for four weeks." He was happy to put his own money into the organization. As he talked over cups of thick coffee brought by members of his family, Abu Ahmed stroked a string of worry beads. It was traditional. Hamas members often saw themselves as a humble but victimized constituency, righteous men in trying times. To outsiders they could appear fearsome, but in conversation they often seemed to me like ardent journeymen in a peasant army.

Abu Ahmed mentioned an incident when PA soldiers started shooting at worshipers inside a nearby Hamas mosque. "I went out and attacked one of the soldiers," he said, puffing out his chest. "I shouted, 'You are Israelis! You're not Palestinians!' Predictably, the soldiers beat and hospitalized him. Unlike Fatah, Hamas's leaders did not support a two-state solution, he said. "They think we can temporarily get to the 1967 borders and then reconsider what happens next. There is no such thing as Israeli land. It's ours." Some Jews could remain in his free Palestine, under Arab control.

Of course, rocket attacks on Israel were effective, and when Israelis were killed Abu Ahmed felt happy. "It's a really good thing," he said. "We don't like to kill them, but if they're afraid they should go back to wherever they've come from." Israel's slaying of several times more Palestinians in raids that followed were, he argued, an unrelated demonstration of how "the Israelis love killing." And yet in the depressed Ramallah winter of 2008, a rare suicide bombing in Dimona was also about the only event that demonstrably lifted Palestinian spirits. Shopkeepers near me cut prices the next day or waived payment altogether. Such attacks can seem the only way to salvage pride from humiliation.

Wouldn't blowing up the hated West Bank wall be a more effective form of resistance? I suggested. "No," Abu Ahmed replied firmly, "Why should anyone blow up the wall? So you can let someone in so he can blow himself up? In Gaza they blew up the wall to get to Arabs on the other side who supported you and would help you out. Here it's different." He accepted that "a lot of martyrs come from within Israel" and pointed to the thirteen killed in October 2000. But what about those who call themselves Israeli Arabs? I asked. "They don't really affect anyone," he said lightly. "You can just call them the garbage of society. They're nothing. You don't have to care about them. You just have to keep going."

It was easy to imagine how Abu Ahmed could be frightened of what he might find on the other side of the wall. "*Insha'allah,* we know that one day it will fall anyway," he declared, "because it says so in the Qur'an." He did not seem keen to meet non-Muslims who lived there. "The Druze just follow the strong," he said. "This is where a lot of people are at. You also have Dahlan who drank wine with Mofaz when there were massacres in Gaza." What would you ask Mohammed Dahlan if you met him? I nudged. Abu Ahmed mimed shooting him in the head. "I won't ask him anything," he said and laughed.

He did not see a need for making regional alliances. "Since I was a kid in the mosque, Hamas and the Muslim Brotherhood in Egypt were all one family, so we don't need to sit and negotiate with them," he said. "We're all the same." Do you support their fight for democracy in Egypt? I asked. "We don't really care about what they call democracy or whatever. We totally support them, but we won the elections, and we never got our right to rule. When Mubarak thought the Muslim Brotherhood was going to win the elections, he just changed everything. They call it democracy, but it isn't really."

His bottom-line confidence stemmed from the fact that Hamas was then growing. Political debate was thus reduced to a question of means and ends. In his view, "The most stable way to get to a Palestinian state is resistance. Events proved that the other, political way—to get into the Palestinian Authority—was a mistake." A third Intifada was on the way, he told me cheerfully, and if Israel invaded Gaza they would surely regret it and "lose a lot." This was in February 2008.

When we met sixteen months later, Abu Ahmed was more pensive and preoccupied with local events. A Hamas supporter had recently been shot dead by a soldier, and camp tensions were high. "Fatah told our people that if we raised our flags or said this kid was from Hamas, they would jail us, kidnap us, or shoot us in the legs," he said. "It's possible there could be a big fight. They're following us all the time. They kidnapped two Hamas people in the camp and broke their fingers and legs, and that created a lot of bad feelings." The biggest problem, though, was when a Hamas leader was released from prison and immediately rearrested by Israeli soldiers. "That puts Fatah and Israel on the same side," Abu Ahmed grimaced. "You'll find the information you give them in front of you in the Jews' office."

The Fatah clampdown was also affecting Abu Ahmed's work life. "Five people from my school have been arrested, and the PA stopped their salaries," he growled softly. "They said the school was a Hamas organization. The PA and Fatah people came with their guns and kicked out Hamas and everyone close to the group." At the same time, "the Jews were attacking our organization and staff. They were on the same side," he said. An even thornier problem was that Israeli and American pressure was preventing "clean and good" Fatah people from rising to prominence.

"There will be a fight not between Fatah and Hamas but between the Palestinian people and the PA [if the pressure continues]," he said, shifting in his seat. "The PA's behavior is anti-Palestinian." Still he sloughed off suggestions that Hamas was planning a West Bank takeover. "If Hamas fought the PA with guns now it would lead to a massacre," he said. But Hamas would defend themselves if attacked. "We can win a fight because we have power and respect, but we will not join a fight. It will not be open war. Change will come in another way, without guns. We will just defend ourselves."

How would you react if the Hamas leadership asked for a long-term ceasefire to pursue a political strategy of negotiations from a position of strength, I asked. "I think it's impossible," he said dismissively. "It will take years of discussions to start relations with the Jews. But if that happened, people would respect the leaders' decision. You have to respect the Shora [Muslim council]." And if Hamas were attacked, would you fight? "Sure," he said, raising his head proudly. "We're patient because we don't want to arrive at deaths. But if they did that, at least we would not allow anybody to delete us or ignore us."

Hamas was suffering from a political repression that seemed unrelated to any military threat they posed to anyone in the camp. But in both interviews it also sounded to me as though Fatah and Israel had melded in Abu Ahmed's mind. His words later brought to my mind a poem by the late Mahmoud Darwish, "We Have the Right to Love Autumn."

"Does the dream, like the dreamers themselves, sicken?" Darwish asked. "Can a people be born on a guillotine? We have the right to die any way we wish. May the earth hide itself away in a blade of wheat."

Naima Abdul Razek, 47, Rania al-Dabak, 23, and Shaykha Mahmud, 52

Villagers

AL-AQABA, WEST BANK

This land is our land Not all Palestinians experienced the First Intifada as a fiery challenge to the existing order. In many isolated villages the daily struggle continued to revolve around simply holding on to your land. Al-Aqaba perches on the fertile northern lip of the Jordan Valley. In 1967 around two thousand people lived in the village, but by May 2008 only some three hundred were left, and they were facing intense pressure to move. Demolition orders had been issued against thirty-nine of Aqaba's remaining forty-five homes and other buildings, including the kindergarten, health clinic, women's center, and one of the only two twin-turreted mosques in the world.

Forty years ago the people of this extraordinarily beautiful town owned 30,000 dunams of its land. Since then, Israel had whittled their ownership writ down to just twenty dunams in the town center. It classified this as "Area A"—the 17 percent of the West Bank assigned to Palestinian control under the Oslo agreement—but most of the buildings within it had been issued with demolition notices anyway. The rest was "Area C" territory—some 57 percent of the West Bank—within which any Palestinian building is considered illegal without a permit. Between 2000 and September 2007, the Israeli group Peace Now found that 94 percent of Palestinian building permit applications in Area C across the West Bank were refused.

Of course, the outside world nominally considers Israel's occupation itself illegal, but it is Israeli military bases and checkpoints that you see dotted to the south and east of the town, not U.N. ones. They cut off access to the Jordan Valley—which Israel covets as its eastern border—and prevent economic or human activity that could help the villagers survive. Eight kilometers to Aqaba's east, it is the Israeli settlement of Maskiot that is expanding while this sleepy, green-valleyed village contracts.

Under a huge carob tree that canopies Aqaba's open-air council meetings from the fierce sun, *al-Haj* Sami Sadeq, Aqaba's mayor, was holding court. He told me that successive Israeli officials tried to convince the villagers to move to nearby towns such as Taysir and Tubas. In 1999, when the townspeople refused, "Israeli bulldozers came and destroyed the village's electricity and telephone networks, Aqaba's only water reservoir, and several homes." Water now had to be brought in by tanker, and electricity was illegally siphoned from telegraph poles.

Sami was something of a hero in Aqaba. He had been confined to a wheelchair since 1971, when he was sixteen. "I'd gone to help my family cultivate our farmland when I was shot three times across my body from left to right," he said. "The army said sorry afterward, that it had been an accident, but the truth is they shot directly at me."

For years the army used Aqaba and its environs as a training ground because of its topographic resemblance to southern Lebanon. Between 1967 and 2008 eight villagers were killed in military "accidents" while working their land and scores of others were injured. But still the villagers had not left.

A short stroll from Aqaba's carob tree, Rania Ali-Dabak lived with her husband and three children in a tin shack. Her mother, Shaykha, and aunt

Naima walked me to her place. Naima, wearing an American baseball cap, initially bristled with confidence but deflated when challenged by her older, bulkier, and more dominant sister. All three of their homes had been issued with demolition orders, but Rania's house hardly seemed worth defending. The roof was made of corrugated iron plates held down by stones, the windows were little more than holes punched in the wall. The furniture consisted of three worn-down mattresses strewn across the floor.

Shaykha and Naima grew up in Aqaba, as did their parents before them. Both lost their husbands to cancer and now lived alone. But whereas Shaykha had ten children, Naima had none, and she often ceded to her older sister's wisdom. Naima left Aqaba when she married but returned and bought a dunam of land from Shaykha to build a house when her husband died. "A year later, the Jews gave me a demolition order," she sighed. "I asked a Jewish attorney to defend me, but it was useless. At every hearing I had to pay them 500 shekels and there were no results.'

"I have a huge amount of land," said Shaykha, who became restless when her sister spoke, "but the Jews prevent us from farming or even visiting it because it's next to a military base, so I've had to sell my goats and sheep. I only get a small widow's pension, and when my son turns eighteen in the next few months I'll lose that too. I don't know what I'll do then. One of my sons was a soldier for the PA, but he got sick and had to quit. Another son has seven children. You can't take care of a family that big and help your parents."

Shaykha needed help as she struggled to raise her children without a father. "I didn't want them to feel deprived, so I tried to be a father and mother to them. If they asked me for my eyes or heart, I would give it to them," she said. "Thanks to Allah, I did everything I had to do, and my children are now married and safe." Underage marriage is an oppressive tradition but also an economic fact on the West Bank, sustained in part by the underdevelopment that accompanies occupation.

Rania, who was born in 1985, married a cousin in 1999, but they came back to build her house in 2001. Her older sister had married at thirteen. "Because I married at an early age I couldn't really experience discos or parties," she told me. "Of course, I've been deprived of many things. I had to marry because I couldn't travel to a school far away in Tubas. Then I couldn't live in one small room with two children so I came back to the town where I was born. We didn't have anywhere else to go, and we want to save this land."

"This land is my land, and it is all of our lands!" Shaykha exulted. "It belongs to us, not the Jews. We would have a better way of life if it wasn't for them. Even if the Jews demolish our houses, we will rebuild them again and again. We will never give up."

"This land was always family land," Naima echoed her older sister. "If they demolish the house, I will stay even if I have to live in a tent!" But Naima spent the last of her money on the house. Her only income now came from selling soft cloth in a local supermarket. She could go hungry. "Demolition orders affected my health too," Shaykha pitched in competitively. "I've spent all my money on this house, and even thinking about it makes me sick." How much *sumud* can one family take? I asked, articulating a recurring thought. "We will stay here and struggle against them forever," Shaykha replied in the time-honored fashion. "We don't have other lands to go to."

With three children between the ages of one and six, Rania's economic situation was the most precarious of the three women. She earned between 200 and 300 shekels a month from odd sewing and cleaning jobs. "My children want 3 or 4 shekels. You know kids, it's nothing, but I'm getting nothing," she said. "My husband is under pressure because he can't find work. The Jews refused him a permit to work in Israel or even travel in the West Bank so he has nothing to do. He can't plant on his land, because the Jews prevent him, so he just sits at home feeling frustrated and hopeless."

Rania's husband made a little money from buying and selling goats but far less than he got for working in the Jewish settlements. "At the end of the month, 2,000 shekels is better than nothing," Rania said stoically. "There's competition to work on settlements, and he wasn't the only one working there! He didn't finish his education, and it was the only work he could get. On the other hand, as a Palestinian, you want to save your land, and they're stealing it." Shaykha's son also worked in a settlement, farming melons, but when I asked Rania if she would do the same, she recoiled in horror. "Absolutely not!" she shrieked. "Women are not allowed to work and serve Jews. I would never think for one minute of supporting them."

The economic necessity for male Palestinians to work on settlements underlined how the West Bank had been "deindustrialized." Local industries could not move goods freely around the West Bank—still less outside it—and employees could not travel from one village to another. None of Rania's family were free to descend into the Jordan Valley below because of Israeli checkpoints. Naima said she had never been there because she lacked a permit. Shaykha did not feel safe there. "We might meet Jews," she intoned.

The family also felt more at home in Aqaba than in cities like Jenin or Tubas. "Here," Rania explained, "when I feel at my deepest, I can go out and walk in this huge space around me. It's not safe, but my neighbors are relatives and I feel free. The people are different in the big cities." Naima also liked to walk the valley hills in spring to pick *zatar* (thyme) and *akub* (artichokes). "I lived in Tubas, and you can't visit people there without an appointment. It would be rude. I lived in Amman too, so I know about these things. Everything is available there, but it tastes different. The food is much better here. I cook by hand, and the secret is not about recipes or spices but something related to the homeland. I belong to this food, so it tastes better for me," she said.

And yet the land was tainted—with blighted opportunity, pollution, and repression. Rania's children were terrified of soldiers, and her eldest son screamed from fear of death or eviction whenever he saw one. "They arrested one of my sons for sleepwalking. He was held for six months," Shaykah complained. "No one can help us except Allah. We're living a miserable life."

When Rania was a child she wanted to be a teacher or a nurse. Today she just hoped that her children would finish their education and, *insha'allah,* have a better life than hers. "In the past, girls would get married without feeling anything," she said poker-faced, "but education is much more important now because guys have started to look for educated women." Unlike some of the men in the factions nearby, Rania did not say that she would give her life to save her hometown, but in a way she did not need to. In a way she already had.

Taghred Joma, 37

NGO Manager

GAZA CITY

First losers Safe in her office behind a Compax laptop, cocooned amid reams of policy papers and just one personal effect—a Mappa Mundi medieval globe—Taghred smiled broadly. Words rushed out of her mouth in a torrent, as though they had been dammed in for too long. She seemed pleased with the prospect of having them amplified to a world-outside-Gaza that was already becoming fuzzy. By May 2008 few outsiders were reaching the shores of Gaza, and very few Gazans could leave.

Taghred had come of age as Gaza's women were striving to become masters of their destiny. Two decades later she was married with three children and working as the manager of an NGO, the Civic Forum Institute, which accepted funding from groups such as USAID. But the struggle continued. "Many times I have to wear a hair covering because of my work," she said. "It's easier in terms of people's reactions. When I visit the Islamic university, I have to wear a jalbab and head covering. Even an international woman can't enter without Islamic dress."

Taghred said that before 1967 women in Gaza dressed as they wished and wore short skirts. "They had the freedom to go out and come back at whatever time they wanted. But after '67, fear spread that the Israeli army would sexually assault women, and men started asking them to dress up." The problem got worse after 1987, "when Hamas sent messages to girls like, 'If you don't dress, we will . . .'" She steadied herself for a second. "They threw burning acid at girls who weren't wearing headscarves or who wore Western clothes, and this frightened them into wearing Islamic clothing."

Taghred believed the preponderance of Islamic dress codes in Gaza was primarily "the Jews' responsibility." In the 1970s and 1980s Israel "supported what Hamas did because they wanted to destroy the PLO and they couldn't do it from outside." For my book *Occupied Minds,* I interviewed a senior Israeli intelligence officer who confirmed that Israel had for a time backed the Muslim Brotherhood. But Taghred was most angry that soldiers singled out secular left-wing women for arrest. "This is a patriarchal society, and if you kidnap women, people start to ask questions. They dirtied the image of these women," she said. Some have even said that the women who were arrested were seen as "damaged goods" and had difficulty finding marital suitors afterward.

Taghred was born in Rafah camp, to a trader father who sold oranges on the Israeli side of the border. He was an educated and enlightened man, with a musician's voice. Before the Nakba he was a village mukhtar in a small town near Majdal. He fought against the invading Haganah, but lacking weapons the family fled to Gaza in 1948. Taghred remembered him for his compulsive discussions with visitors about life before and after the Nakba. "People used to kid him by asking, 'Can't we talk about something else?'" she said. "He wasn't like the people here. He supported women. He was a special case."

Like her three sisters, Taghred went to the university in Hebron, with her father's blessing, to study psychology. In another place, at another time, hers might have been a familiar tale of female entry into the world's marketplace, but in Palestine, it was also a story about occupation. "My family were already members of the PFLP," Taghred said, patting the newspaper on her desk, "and in high school, when I was sixteen, I started to work with the PFLP students' committees, preparing for the First Intifada." In December 1987 she found herself in Hebron when the revolt erupted. After returning to see what was happening, she was refused permission to finish her studies outside Gaza.

"These four years from 1988 to 1992 were the most active times of my life," she remembered. "I joined the women's committee here and worked voluntarily, visiting families who'd had members killed, giving food and psychological support to the relatives of prisoners, and organizing demonstrations against the army when they entered the camp." Because Israel clamped down with closures and curfews, Taghred said, "women played the biggest role in the Intifada. We had to move weapons between houses and food to the fighters. The Israelians knew we were an Arabic society and didn't want to cause clashes, so they stayed away from us. It was an amazing feeling. When we crossed the checkpoints, we laughed so much at the Jews because they could not search us!" A ripple of delight spread across her face. At the committee's peak, as many as ten thousand women were involved.

Even so, the Intifada was not a romantic experience. Many of Taghred's friends were killed, and both her brother and her husband were imprisoned for several years. "We suffered a lot, and it tested our love," she said. Her family's house was situated on a street between the fighters and the Israeli barracks, so soldiers would regularly force her to scrub graffiti off its walls. "They used to come to the house three or four times a day and enter forcefully. They'd bring burning tires from the street outside and throw them into our house," she told me. "They just hated people." Taghred recalled there being no party the day her brother got married because soldiers came the night before and smashed all the windows. The night before that, the family had visited a local commander to plead for a day's respite from the harassment.

Inevitably, the feeling on the streets then was of "real resistance," she said. "All the people—women, men, and children—were fighters, not just the military groups. Everyone was a resister in work or at home, and all our houses were open to youths who fought the Israelians, not like now." The Second Intifada "was totally different," she argued, "a completely military Intifada that separated the fighters from the true resistance. Before, women were much more important. Now, our popular volunteer work is done by official organizations and ministries."

A militarized Intifada weakened women, Taghred argued, because "the men go outside to fight and the women are killed inside with their children. Very few women have carried out operations against the Israeli army, but they still have a big responsibility because after the army kills the fighters, they have to provide food for their families on their own." Many Palestinians feel that something was lost in the move away from popular Intifada, but activists like Taghred talked about it as something akin to a counterrevolution.

She blamed the loyalty of grassroots activists to PLO factions that never returned the favor. "The committees' work tailed off after Oslo," she explained. "The new government made volunteering more difficult. At first the women's, workers', and youth committees became connected to the parties, then they just supported those parties' activities." Today, she went on, Hamas was "occupying" the Women's Committee. But when Fatah controlled Gaza, the committee simply followed orders from Ramallah. On all sides, the once-autonomous movement became "just a picture organization," she said. But her animus seemed directed primarily at Hamas.

"Hamas uses women only when it needs their support. It sent them to demonstrate at the border—to show the world that we were all under pressure from the siege—and it stood women candidates in the election when it needed women's votes. But the other parties were little different. The PFLP men wouldn't vote for female candidates in their elections because of our culture," she said. With the distinct and independent voices of the grassroots committees silenced, there were few interventions by women's groups during the Fatah-Hamas fighting in 2007.

"Hamas wants to transform us into a completely Islamic society, and the first losers in those societies are women because Islam never gave women their rights," she said. "There are many misogynistic practices here, like polygamy and forbidding women from shaking hands with men or choosing their husband. If Hamas succeeds, women will play no role outside the home, and only those who follow Islamic codes will progress." Hamas even argued with teachers to change the name of Mother's Day because it was an "un-Islamic" holiday, she said.

Ultimately, though, Taghred's liberation story was a narrative of multiple betrayals. During the First Intifada, Palestinian society as a whole also used women "because they were the only ones who could do what was needed. That's the only reason they allowed women to go out in the middle of the night," she said. "After that time and need, they stopped respecting us, and our given role was inside the home again." I heard this story over and again, and I believed Taghred. Still I could not help noticing that a large number of the civil society photographs on the board behind her depicted Palestinian men in suits.

Huda Naim, 40

Hamas MP

AL-BUREIJ CAMP, GAZA

Keep the faith It was Gazi Hamad, the pragmatic and fiercely intelligent Hamas media liaison, who referred me to Huda Naim. I had wanted to meet a woman involved in Hamas's resistance activities, but if such people existed Hamas was not advertising them. The group was then under fire from feminists, and Gazi's recommendation seemed an implicit suggestion that Huda was a part of the group's "modernizing" wing. Other Gazans I knew thought her an artless beneficiary of nepotism, but I was intrigued by the fact that she had been an advice columnist for a local magazine.

As she breezed into her office in Gaza's parliament, Huda was brisk but friendly, thanking me for my visit. "I hope the step you're taking will help to make Palestine a state," she said pointedly. The hard-line interior minister, Fathi Hamad, had told me the same thing the day before, but he had seemed more interested in persuading me to become a Muslim than in answering my questions.

Unlike him, Huda came across as sincere, though unbearably gauche and bright, if intellectually dependent. She also appeared rushed for time but, as a mother of four, was clearly used to multitasking. By way of introduction, she mentioned that her family in Beit Hanun had briefly become refugees in 1956 during Israel's Suez invasion. It seemed an unnecessary pitch for street credibility.

Although her parents were illiterate, like Taghred Joma, Huda followed her sisters to the university and graduated with a degree in social services. "At first we were a moderate family like any other," she said. "But we started to get more religious when my second oldest brother did." Bassam Naim went on to serve as the Hamas minister for Youth and Sport. His own son, a fighter in the Izzedine al-Qassam Brigades, was killed in action in May 2003. "We keep the faith," she added tidily.

Huda said that she had been one of the most prominent members of the Hamas women's movement in Gaza before the group took power. She became "responsible" for it soon afterward. Although some labeled her a "Hamas feminist," she insisted that she was "just like a woman in any other faction." She continued, "In eastern society, it's known that men have the final say, but I became different. Hamas opened the doors for me to get more involved. My success in parliament makes them proud of me and happy." According to Huda's Islamic feminism, men and women should be servants to one another. "Here's proof!" she trilled. "My husband is a Hamas leader, but I'm surprised when I go home because he's the one who prepares the food and gets the kids ready for sleep." Is that typical? I asked. "It's becoming more typical because of religion," she answered. "The Prophet Mohammed— blessed be his name—helped his wife at home too."

Huda's interview style was light in those days. The main problem facing women in Gaza was the siege, she said. "Women might be finding all the pressure on them if their husbands are unemployed, like they're the ones who have to prepare everything." She believed that honor killings were more of a problem in the West Bank. "Here's an example!" she chirped. "Traditionally, if you knew your sister was having an affair, you'd kill her or something. But now, you can talk to her about it. If she really went further—like becoming a prostitute or something—then she would, you know, be killed. But only some families do this."

The U.N. Office for the Coordination of Humanitarian Affairs estimated that there had been fifty-one honor killings in the occupied territories over the previous three years, but only twelve men had been imprisoned in the previous thirty years, sometimes for just six months. Despite this, Huda saw grounds for optimism. "Traditionally, the man of the house was responsible for honor issues," she explained, "but when my neighbor had a baby ille- gally—she wasn't married to the guy—the baby's father was imprisoned and forced to marry her. Afterward, he ran away with the baby, and her uncle killed her for that. But notice that her dad and her brothers were open- minded about the issue. They tried to move her from house to house so that people wouldn't know about it. It was her uncle who made the decision."

This hardly seemed like great progress to me. In fact, I suggested, it seemed like an argument for stricter law enforcement. "Because of our laws, the uncle said that one of his kids was the murderer," Huda replied. Statute books in

Gaza and the West Bank reflect the legal systems of Egypt and Jordan, which administered the territories before 1967. Under these, minors often receive sentences of just a few months for honor killings. Hamas has not changed these laws.

On the question of rape within marriage, Huda's feminism seemed worryingly close to blaming the victim. "If a husband did that," she declared, "there must have been something going wrong in the relationship for a long time. We can open offices for women to talk about their husbands' violence, but we must ensure they understand why their husbands are acting like that." According to a 2006 survey, 23 percent of women in the occupied territories have experienced domestic violence, I started to say. "I think that in the Western world the figures are worse," Huda interrupted, increasingly agitated. "Normally a man—or any creature that experiences power—would commit violent acts, with just its conscience or God to observe. As Islamists, our role is to increase this observation."

But only one percent of Palestinian women report domestic violence, I protested. Doesn't that suggest a social problem as well? "Traditional close families solve their problems internally, so it's normal," Huda reacted. "In my mind, anything is better than marital separation. It's common in the West, but here we don't want it because it destroys the family. That's why a woman prefers to take all the violence and keep it in the house. If she is patient and tries to solve the problems, things will improve. We can't have legal cures. It's better to make people aware that it's wrong."

Correspondingly, Huda thought that it was "better and more correct" for men to retain the final say on divorce too. "A family should have just one head," she said, "like a corporation. A woman is more emotional than rational, so she will always jump to conclusions. A man would think about something before doing it." And at that she got up to leave. The adversarial nature of my questions had irked her, and the longer we talked, the more upset she had become. I had not walked a mile in her shoes, but Huda's feminism did not seem to run deep, and I wondered if she even talked to male MPs about these issues. I blurted out the question, and she stopped to give me one last piece of her mind.

"Western women are selfish," she said. "They want the right of divorce, the right to rule, all these rights. But it's different for us because we think about the good of the whole family. Our religion came from God, so we can't just follow one part and leave the others. If God says divorce is for men, why should we oppose it? You can raise your voice against Iran but in the 'Great West,' personality leads everything." She went on to say that parental control increased security while free choice just increased teenage pregnancies. "If you want to study the whole Islamic image, you can't just look at specific issues," she summed up. There seemed to be a lot that she did not want to look at.

When I returned a year later, in May 2009, Huda no longer had a whole office to herself, and Gaza no longer had a whole parliament. The building was partially destroyed in Israel's military offensive. Huda now sat at a makeshift desk in a colleague's room, looking tired and vulnerable. As we talked, she doodled a segmented rectangle onto a pad of red paper with diagonal lines coursing through it, like a Union Jack. She seemed sadder and wearier this time. When I asked her about her past as an "agony aunt" columnist, an experience I thought might humanize her for a Western audience, she answered a completely different question.

"People have suffered immensely in the war, and we have to concentrate on helping them," she said. Her family had suffered too. "My nephew was killed in the war. He was not a fighter, not a Hamas or a Fatah. Hinas was just an ambulance officer. He was going to Tel al-Hawa to help people who were besieged by soldiers when he was hit by two Israeli missiles. I heard the news of his martyrdom from the media." Some Hamas leaders had brothers who were killed during the war, she noted. "They suffered like the people." Huda wanted her children to be safe—and she took security precautions such as not driving a car. She also hosted friends and neighbors in her house during the bombing.

"I believed that we would defeat the Israeli forces," she said. "We will defeat them! Israel failed to achieve its goals of ending smuggling through the Rafah tunnels and stopping our rockets." This was only half true, as was Huda's assertion that Hamas "was prepared" for the conflict. "But Israel used heavy missiles and weaponry against us, and it was very sudden." As she spoke, Huda arranged her staple gun, Post-it notes, and cellotape into a barrier between us on the table. I told her that I found it difficult to conceptualize the 1,400 Palestinian lives lost as a victory.

"All peoples in the world fighting to liberate themselves have more victims to pave the way for liberation," she said piercingly. "Even European countries gave victims in wars to liberate their lands, and some of their cities were annihilated. I love my children. I don't want to lose any of them. But we must fight to achieve our human rights." Is the annihilation of Gaza's towns a price that Palestine can afford to pay? I asked. "What's happening here is already an extermination," Huda replied.

Gazi Hamad argued in a milestone essay, "It is we who give others the right to take our rights away when we sacrifice our people like donations to a blood bank." Huda would not discuss internal Hamas debates, but at least she would say that she respected the *sumud* of all factions, including Fatah. That out of the way, the PA was to blame for persuading Egypt to keep the Rafah crossing closed.

Huda differentiated between the Egyptian then-regime and its people. "The stance of the Egyptian people is with the Palestinian resistance. But the Egyptian government is with the world's international policy," she said. So should Hamas try to mobilize the Egyptian people rather than talk with its government? I queried. "It's not our business to mobilize against anyone," she said. "We are not against the Egyptian government. We want their financial help. We are defensive, not offensive. We understand what's happening in the world political arena."

I asked one last time about her magazine columns, but she would not be diverted. "Salaam Fayyad has good international relations with the West and Israel," she said, "yet the West Bank's suffering is very great so we are not encouraged to make reconciliation." I repeated the question. "Europe has made a great mistake, because boycotting Hamas and punishing the Palestinian people has just increased Hamas's status and extremism," she retorted. "Do you want us to be like the Taliban and Al Qaida? We represent moderate Islam. We renounce violence. We are for dialogue." Slightly flustered, she was nonetheless gathering herself up for a coup de grâce. "My question to all the Europeans is, Why have I had no visa to visit the European countries?"

Amal Masri, 39

Businesswoman

RAMALLAH, WEST BANK

Safe corners The cement and scaffolding that were slowly transforming Amal Masri's office building could have framed a story about boom time in Ramallah. With yearly predictions of the West Bank's economic growth running at 7 percent and internal migrants fighting each other for apartments, even the city's myriad half-finished construction projects seemed to be inching toward completion. Yet Amal told me that in just the past nine months, cement prices had soared and the cost of iron had doubled. "You can't even make a business plan because your yearly income is up and down every month," she grumbled. Her business was "in crisis and debt." She owed one contractor $60,000, and the wider economy was "deteriorating, dependent, strangled," she said. But she was one of its success stories.

In addition to managing her own media company, Ougarit, Amal was the founder of the Palestinian Businesswomen's Forum and, along with her husband, Khalid al-Masri, the owner of a printing firm. Her roots were in Nablus and a nearby village, al-Lubban ash-Sharqiya, where more than half the population was unemployed. Amal's family, though, "had a very good status"—both her parents were school principals—and her husband came from a Nablus family so prominent that it counted among its number the PA's economics minister, a former prime minister of Jordan, and the chairman of the Padico investment company, which is worth some $250 million.

Sitting behind her long wooden office desk in an early morning fug, Amal was waiting for coffee. Her kids were in school, and her phone practically buzzed itself off the table during our interview. She did not seem to mind; she was keen to project a casual business-like insouciance. It was not always this way. During the First Intifada, shortly after her family moved from Nablus to Lubban, Israeli soldiers occupied the top part of their house. "We saw soldiers every day," she said. "They dirtied the stairs and screamed so loudly. They believed they had the right to do anything. They shot some people from the roof, arrested others, and once they took some young men outside the house and cut their hands and legs with razors or knives. For two hours we heard them screaming! We were in a corner of our house. We couldn't even look out of the window."

Soldiers were always searching the house for young men, she said. "In '89, they came to our house and my three-year-old brother hid under the bed. The soldiers were searching everywhere, laughing, and when they found him, they dragged him out of the bed by his bare foot like a rat." Her brother, now twenty-two, still had traumatic reactions when he saw soldiers. But while most soldiers were rude, Amal remembered one French soldier who "used to find a corner downstairs and cry. I asked him why he was crying once. He said, 'What am I doing in this damn country?' He just wanted to see his family. He hated it." He was the first French person she remembered meeting.

In January 1989 the army closed An-Najah University—where Amal was studying biology—and she developed an interest in the French language. Over the long weeks of curfew she crammed, and three months later she passed a French Consulate exam and won a scholarship to study in France. And so she escaped "this doomed situation," she said. Amal graduated with a diploma in economics from the Sorbonne. By the time she returned in 1993, military permits were needed to travel anywhere in the West Bank. "It was shocking for me because we thought we were going to have a better life," she noted. Amal tried teaching at the French Cultural Center in Nablus but found that the First Intifada had "mutilated" the local identity. "People suffered so much in the struggle that they became increasingly conservative and afraid of each other," she said.

As a child, Amal had rejected the traditional Nabulsi gender stereotypes—as much as she had a Communist grandfather whom she saw as an "extremist." Her favorite song was Chris De Burgh's "Lady in Red," and, along with her sisters, she eschewed wearing a headscarf. "When people feel hopeless with no vision of the future, they look backward to religion for some kind of refuge," she said. "It's a safe corner." Amal's take was that women donned headscarves again during the First Intifada only because "the pressure of the occupation squeezes people into their sick corners and beliefs." The difference between safe and sick corners is moot.

Amal and her husband moved to Ramallah shortly after their marriage in 1995. "It's a hard, traditional mentality [in Nablus]," she said by way of explanation. "They gossip a lot and have less of a business approach." Her husband's relatives also viewed her as "a *fellah* from a village," she said. Amal found the new Ramallah—a cultural and political center for the returning Fatah movement—"bigger, more cosmopolitan, and more open to change." So she worked for the PA's Culture Ministry and then headed up the French Consulate's international relations section.

From there, she went into business, and in 2006 she launched the Palestinian Businesswomen's Forum with several other women. "We went to conferences together and suffered the same problems of finding good employees, ensuring their monthly payments, lacking movement for us and our goods, and being unable to expand our businesses or open new branches," she said. Only 2 percent of Palestinian companies were run by women, and the West Bank had few day care facilities. "When I had my last child," Amal informed me, "for eight months I went to work with my baby in one hand and my briefcase in the other."

At first the Forum was self-financing, but in 2008 it received funding from donors that included the U.S. Consulate. Such groups had some policy input, but Amal underlined, "We don't take any USAID funds because we don't think it's the right time to sign any Anti-Terrorism Certificates." The ATCs, which many international organizations demand from Palestinian aid recipients, are supposed to ensure that moneys are not used to fund "terrorism." But some are phrased in ways that forbid any Palestinian NGO from employing a relative of any member of any Palestinian military faction—including Fatah's Al Aqsa Martyrs Brigade. In Hebron, I saw one such document sent out by the Canada Fund. Its recipient told me that given the size of Palestinian families, no NGO in Hebron could make such a guarantee in good faith. He had, nonetheless, signed the ATC.

"It's a survival thing," Amal sighed. "It's like twisting arms. If you don't sign, you don't have the money. I've heard many people say, 'We're against terror, but we might support resistance.' They convince themselves that they're talking about the same 'terrorism.' They don't like to talk about it afterward, but it shows because all USAID programs come with ATCs attached." The ATCs are in any case "so long that you need an international lawyer to understand them," she said. "We're against terrorism all the way along, but I don't know if we agree on the same terms." Signing an ATC could leave a group in "the dark zone," she added. "So many hopes have been attached to this Forum, so many women see us as role models. It's a big responsibility."

Did the U.S. Consulate make you sign an ATC? I asked. "It's different regulations. Their terms are different from USAID," she answered hurriedly. When I asked how the terms were different, though, Amal paused for a long time before replying, "I don't remember." This corner felt less safe. "It's actually against Palestinian law to sign such an [ATC]," she said, "and at some point I think it undermines our loyalty to our country. Why would I sign papers for another country's government?" The U.S. government had the right to know where they were putting their money, she agreed, "and we can say no as well." But many NGOs say yes.

The cumulative effect of the aid bonanza had been to create what Amal called "a fake economy" in Ramallah. "It's so artificial," she said. "It depends on foreign aid, and we've seen what happens when it stops. The government employees go without salaries." Amal admired Salaam Fayyad and wanted his government to offer Palestinian businesses more protection from Israeli and settlement products. "But they can't do it because this would end the Palestinian government. How can you liberalize markets in a prison?" she asked. "The Palestinian economy is a completely captive market."

Even so, Amal saw Palestinian society as fundamentally business-friendly. "I would brand Palestinians for their smiles, hospitality, and generosity," she told me. "Good people ready to negotiate on a basis of dignity, entrepreneurial survivors who make something out of nothing." However Palestine was branded, though, she emphasized, "We don't own power. I could market Palestinians as people with red headscarves across the world if we had the right communications channels, but we own nothing." How optimistic are you? I asked. "I'm optimistic," she said quietly. "It's nature. We'll find a hope. We're digging for one. I have very big hopes for business. If we are led by businesspeople, we'll make a good country."

Fawsi Barhoum, 47

Hamas Spokesman

GAZA CITY

If the bullet does not hit its target   One of Fawsi's earliest memories was of the day in 1970 that Israeli bulldozers came to demolish his home in Rafah. "They warned us to evacuate our house in the morning," he said. "They told my father the demolition was happening because his son was in Fatah's military faction in Lebanon. My father had built a nice concrete house, and when he refused to evacuate it, this occupation—the captain—slapped him and pushed him down. He gave an order and the bulldozer destroyed the house without an evacuation." Fawsi spoke airily with a metronomic lilt.

The Barhoums, a religious family, had been displaced to a refugee camp in 1948, where they lived first in a tent and then in a tin shack. The experience "taught my family to see the occupation as our enemy," Fawsi said. "They destroyed my father and our house, and we were now on the streets; no building, no furniture, everything destroyed. We shared a tap and two toilets with about two hundred other houses. It was difficult even to go to school because you had to wait in a long line to wash your face or go to the toilet." These memories were still fresh. "They are the backbeat for an enemy movement to protect Palestine," he said, "to liberate our land, to protect my father and my family." Against this rhythm, Fawsi started attending a local mosque when he turned fifteen, as tradition requires. Soon he was praying five times a day. "You are a man," his parents told him, "and our God will punish you if you refuse to pray." Fawsi joined Hamas four years later.

"I had seen them [members of Hamas] at the mosque and been to their lectures," he explained. "I'd been searching for someone to guide me, and a friend at the mosque convinced me that Hamas could best define Palestine."

Fatah did not convince Fawsi because Yasser Arafat talked to Israelis and Americans and wanted to separate Islam from politics. "I heard about Fatah guys smoking and drinking, and I was afraid that in Fatah I would lose my sense of being a Muslim," Fawsi said.

His first priority in 1980 was to earn money to help his father, an agricultural worker. He dropped out of school to work in a market and then enrolled in the Islamic University's nursing college. After graduating, he took a job as a medic and began helping to pay for a new family house. At the same time he started speaking for Hamas at demonstrations and in mosques. He was in the Khan Younis hospital when the First Intifada began, but as it dragged on he routinely traveled during curfews, making house calls on the injured.

In Rafah itself, Fawsi organized meetings with Hamas leaders and helped to build a skeleton organization that could "guide our audience to throw stones against the occupation, write on walls, and protect people." At the mosque, worshipers "compared the quiet religious men of Hamas with those of Fatah who had big cars and big buildings," and they became convinced, he said.

Fawsi was arrested in 1992. "Fatah was preparing to implement Oslo so they had to repress Hamas," he narrated. "Their militia kicked their way into my house several times trying to shoot me." Fawsi resigned his job as the conflict escalated. But two months later he was arrested by Israeli Special Forces and deported to Lebanon with 450 other mostly Hamas leaders and activists. The event was to prove pivotal to Hamas's development.

"I was handcuffed, blindfolded, and put in chains," he recounted. "Because there were no more buses, they flew us to Lebanon on a Chinook [helicopter]. Everyone was made to lie on his back with hands chained behind a chair. They kept tightening the handcuffs. When we arrived, the Chinook started hovering, and my friend said, 'I'm afraid they want to throw us into the air.'" Fawsi chuckled. "I said, 'Don't worry, maybe we're being deported.'"

After the Chinook landed, the men were driven in trucks to a no-man's-land between the Israeli and Lebanese borders. "At the first checkpoint the Lebanese soldiers turned us back. We said, 'Khallas, we're Muslims like you!' They said, 'We have orders not to let you through because we have enough refugees already.'" The deportees were forced to drive back to the Israeli checkpoint, where they were shooed at gunpoint back to the Lebanese border. "When we got there, there were about a hundred Lebanese soldiers with metal bars in a line," Fawsi said. "They began hitting us with the bars and firing bullets so we walked back about three kilometers and ended up in no-man's-land for protection." Their appeals for support from the army of a secular pro-Western Arab government had not worked.

The men tried to sleep in the heavy rain and icy cold but failed. "Someone had plastic covering, and some of us hid in a cave," Fawsi said. "The next morning, a Red Crescent helicopter found us in the mountains and gave us food and tents, and we lived there for a year." Life in Marj al-Zuhour was harsh, with winter temperatures reaching –20 degrees, but for the first time the world wanted to know about it. "CNN, Reuters, all of them came to hear about our experience," he said. "We always talked about how we could use this to scandalize the occupation." More poignantly: "We always debated between ourselves whether to die there or return."

Different committees took care of the tents, food stores, and medical relief. But Hamas leaders including Mahmoud al-Zahar, Abdel al-Rantissi, and Aziz Dwaik ran a media committee that held daily press conferences in Arabic and English. Fawsi was its secretary. "Dealing with the world and journalists changed our mentality," he said. "In Palestine you only had to resist. Here you also had to market your message. This made us increasingly pragmatic." So less violence and more media, I summarized. "No, no, no," Fawsi corrected me. "More resistance and more media, to convince the world that this was our legitimate right. Because the occupation decided to use every shade of punishment to destroy Hamas—collective punishment, mass deportations, arrests, and killings—we need resistance to force it to stop."

The camp provided a forum for discussing how Hamas could "change the shape" of the resistance. Meanwhile, Palestinians in the occupied territories "increasingly rose up, using all shapes of resistance," Fawsi said. The most violent involved suicide bombing, a tactic that had been used in Lebanon in the 1980s but did not reach Israel until April 1993. After the fourth suicide bombing in Tel Aviv in October 1994, the anonymous caller who claimed responsibility for Hamas reportedly said, "Thank you to Mr. Rabin for sending us to Lebanon where we learned about sabotage."

According to Fawsi, the Hamas deportees in Marj al-Zuhour met with Hezbollah "all the time" because the region was "Hezbollah land, Shi'a land." He said, "Hezbollah soldiers always came in a group at night. They were fighting the occupation with missiles and giving us more and more assistance—aid, food, clothes, and goods—to help our return to Palestine. There was sharing between Hamas and Hezbollah, even with resistance. They respected us and helped us to be patient and conscious. But we were ordered not to speak about Shi'a and Sunni issues, just the resistance."

What methods of resistance did you talk about? I asked. Fawsi let the question float for a second. "We were afraid to be in direct contact with Hezbollah about anything military," he finally said. Hamas was afraid to even talk to Hezbollah about resistance, I exclaimed. "Yes," Fawsi replied urbanely. "Our leaders ordered us not to talk to Hezbollah about how to fight and not to take part in training camps because we wanted to return to resist, not go straight back to jail."

So you talked to Hezbollah about everything except how to fight? "Yes," Fawsi said. "Just how to fight, not to train because this accusation would put us in jail for seven years." From such talks, he said, Hamas constructed a decision-making hierarchy. It had never accepted military help from Hezbollah. He explained, "Because we already have engineers and can advance our resistance, there's no need for Hezbollah." A few months after the interview, Hezbollah's leader, Shaykh Hassan Nasrallah, admitted that his group had provided Hamas with military aid after at least one Hezbollah operative was arrested in Egypt. Predictably perhaps, Fawsi—officious, charming, and professional as he was—denied that Hamas had ever received Iranian military help.

Most deportees finally returned in 1994. The majority of them were rearrested and jailed again a year later, this time by the PA. "The remaining Hamas leaders went into hiding in 2001," Fawsi said. "Anyone who even talked about Hamas then would be arrested or detained, so the Hamas leaders wanted to be masked." Within days of a mass jailbreak that took place during a popular protest, "Hamas had made a skeletal structure to guide this Intifada," he said, "as in the First Intifada." As Israel assassinated Hamas leaders such as Shaykh Ahmed Yassin and Abdel al-Rantissi, the organization "adapted directly and became stronger," he added.

"Hamas's leaders believe in moving experience to others before they are killed. I've heard stories from these Hamas posters [martyrs]. I received experience from Abdel al-Rantissi before his killing. Now I'm a spokesman for Hamas. I have seven people prepared to take my place if I am killed." How do you deal with the knowledge that you could be killed at any time? I asked. "Yes maybe now!" he said, feigning alarm. "Yes, and I could die with you," I said. "Be afraid," he joked. But how do you deal with that? I repeated. "I'm the Hamas spokesman, and I must deal with all media situations," he said. "Maybe Hamas's bombers think about precautions and other leaders take extensive measures, but my mission is to deal with the media so I must talk to them. I've taken some precautionary measures by walking and not using

Jawal or other mobile phones. I believe there will be an assassination attempt, but this is my mission, and if they kill me others will take my place because I have given them my experience."

Fawsi told me he had only been out of Palestine once, to Lebanon. He could not imagine having Jewish friends: "They're our enemy; they came here to occupy my land, destroy my house, and kill people." When I mentioned Alla's statement that he might have Jewish friends after the occupation, he was outraged. "But I am in Hamas!" he exclaimed. "Fawsi Barhoum refuses to be friends with Jews—maybe with Americans but not Jews—because they always think about new ways of killing us. How can this guy in Islamic Jihad believe that the conflict will finish?" In England and America, some Jews support the Palestinians, I told him. "They support the Palestinians for their benefit, not ours," he said. Maybe it could benefit both, I suggested. "I don't know," he said.

As Fawsi showed me out, I asked him why Hamas persisted with rocket attacks that caused so little military damage in Israel and took such a heavy civilian toll in Gaza. He patted me on the back and shared a Hamas motto with me. "If the rocket does not hit its target," he grinned, "at least it makes some noise." He told me we could talk again and gave me his business card with contact phone numbers on it. Later I tried to call him to ask about his family's business interests and Asmaa's and Abu Adel's stories, but he could not be reached. His Jawal phone consistently rang unanswered.

"Haidar"

Taxi Driver

GAZA

The heart is black "Haidar" exuded the granite confidence of the self-made and self-interested. He pegged his sails close to the wind but was every inch the survivor—every inch the guide too—and if you treated him well, he would do the same for you, albeit from a position of strength. While driving in his taxi once, he shouted enthusiastically for me to look to the right. I swiveled my head to catch sight of a man in Pashtun-style clothing and immediately slid into my seat. "He's a Dagmush," Haidar cackled, eyes fixed on the road ahead. "Like the Taliban."

It was May 2008, ten months after the Dagmush—a notorious criminal-cum-Salafist clan—had released Alan Johnson, a former BBC colleague and friend. During his four-month kidnap ordeal, the Dagmush had forced Alan to wear an explosive belt. Haidar wrinkled his nose when describing them, as though toxins were in the air. They were "a bad family" that ran extortion rackets and fought gun battles on the streets, he said. Three months before my arrival, they had threatened to again kidnap any foreigners staying at my hotel. I sensed that Haidar was streetwise enough not to put me in danger.

Born in a refugee camp, Haidar dropped out of school early to help his family by working in Israel. His father had been an agricultural laborer there, he told me over coffee. "When I was fifteen I used to wait for him at the taxi station because sometimes he brought zucchini or potatoes with him. I'd help carry them the three kilometers back on foot. One day I asked if I could work with him. He said, 'It's better that you study so you have a future.'" Haidar decided to work in Israel that summer anyway, and he moved to Tel Aviv soon after.

Living out of a one-room bed-sit, he learned Hebrew and worked at an Israeli market for fifteen years, sending money back to his father. While some Israelis would swear at him, most were convivial. "I had Jewish friends. We sometimes went swimming or to the cinema together, and I even slept over at my boss's house. His wife would give me lunch, and we drank lots of whiskey. She'd put a bottle on the table and 'L'chaim!' We drank like this." Haidar still had contact with "a lot of Jews," he said, but he felt that Arab Israelis "have a nice life in Israel and have forgotten that they're Palestinians."

When Haidar was a young man, his father and grandfather had dreamed of retrieving their land and horses in Israel, but Haidar thought this foolish. Eventually his father "said *khallas* Palestinians! Ma salaama [Enough, Palestinians! Good-bye]," Haidar explained. "He slowly started to forget. I forgot too, and my son is too young to remember. I told him that we will never return as Palestinians."

Israel's policy of border closures eventually forced Haidar to seek a new career. He bought a taxi but still harbored impossible dreams of returning to Israel—as a guest worker. "I love Tel Aviv more than Gaza," he said. "I'd rather stay there. Life is shit here. It's like Guantanamo Bay—just war, prison, and siege. In Tel Aviv, when you finish work at night you listen to music and dance with girls. Here there are no places to be happy." Haidar said that he did not know who blew up Gaza's last bar, the UNRWA beach club, in 2006. "And I don't know who drank beer there either. Hamas cut their legs off."

He was a card-carrying member of Fatah. Not that he pinned his disagreements with Hamas to his collar, not in Arabic anyway. "If somebody said, 'Haidar worked with Israeli intelligence,' they'd cut me up and throw me in the garbage dump," he said. "In the First Intifada, they did that to a good guy I knew, a wrestler like Hulk Hogan. He was fixing a house when someone called out from behind his back and rat-a-tat-tat they shot him. An hour later, he was in the garbage. Then the family washed him and took him to the cemetery."

"If someone killed my brother," he continued, "I wouldn't forget him—even after a hundred years. If I didn't kill him, my son would. If he didn't kill him, his son would. Palestinians hate Palestinians now. The heart is black. When I was a kid, we were very close. All the neighbors came round and spoke good words with my father over tea. I felt their love. One love. Now it is one hate." Even Palestinians in the West Bank "really hate Gaza," Haidar said. "They think we're stupid, crazy farmers. They have a better life because they can go to the checkpoint and the soldiers close their eyes. They have international passports, so they can move to Israel or America and start another life. Here, I just have my ID card. Life is the border—and they are all closed. The sea is closed too, and so is the sky."

Within such a claustrophobic landscape, Haidar said that Hamas had stolen a list of staples: "the cooking gas, diesel, Kalashnikovs, military locations, cars, buses, even Abu Mazen's new black jeeps!" As someone not taking a salary from the PA or Hamas, he was struggling. "If I'm working, I have food. If not, I'll die from hunger," he said. "A lot of people like me don't even have a shekel to buy a cigarette." Haidar himself did not smoke—unless the cigarettes were from Israel or the West. Without UNRWA aid, "it would be like Somalia here," he told me. "Hamas ruined everything. Some of my family voted for them as a protest, but they don't support them. I've heard people say, 'If I'd known Hamas would get us into this situation, I would have cut off my finger in the election booth.'"

Even so, when I asked who he hated more—Hamas or Israel—his indignation surprised me. "I don't hate Israel!" he boomed. "I hate Hamas! If the IDF does a big operation here, some people say, 'I am ready to tell the soldiers: This is a Hamas house. This house has al-Qassams. This house has Hamas Special Forces.' I am waiting for the IDF to come in a big operation and kill all of Hamas, starting with al-Zahar, Haniye, and Said Siam, their leaders, to kill them and explode their apartments." Haidar had gone too far. He looked down and then around the empty café before murmuring a plea that I not use his real name.

His words stayed with me a long time, and not just because Siam actually was assassinated in January 2009. I did not think that Haidar was an Israeli spy—he was far too incautious for that—and I did not think that he was offering his services as a potential foreign agent either. But equally, few journalists were visiting Gaza then, and he must have known that this is what I could have been. I decided that in Gaza's febrile atmosphere Haidar had simply overheated. Nevertheless, seven months later when Israel began its bombing campaign, I called him for an update of the situation—and to make sure that he was okay. Of course he was.

"People are afraid," his voice pierced the ambient static of Gaza's wilting phone lines. "There are explosions everywhere. People don't support Hamas like before. They blame them for the fighting." Fatah was "happy," he said. "They want to make celebrations, but they can't. They hate Hamas because they took everything from them. A coup happened in June, remember?" I asked if the Fatah people would support an Israeli invasion. "Sure, sure, sure," he replied hurriedly. "They are waiting for that."

I was reluctant to question him further, but I asked if the Fatah people would tell the Israelis where the Hamas fighters and Qassams were. "I think so," he said excitedly three times. "Why not?" I suggested maybe that was how Israel got its intelligence for these bombings. "Yes, yes, yes," he replied again. "The Fatah people are waiting for the situation to change to help Abu Mazen and Fatah take the locations back." I wondered if Haidar was just telling me what he thought I wanted to hear.

In summer 2009 Gaza's mood music had slowed considerably. A semblance of normality had returned. Hamas checkpoints were either nonexistent or visibly more relaxed. Internationals—and life's basics—were somehow finding a way in, and Hamas's rule was unchallenged. In Jabalia camp I visited one Fatah family whose son, Shadi Ahmed, was facing execution on apparently trumped up charges of kidnap, murder, and terrorism. The family said that Hamas activists were following them, had tried to burn down their house, and had shot Shadi's sister. They complained that Fatah had done nothing to help them, and civic action seemed impossible. "Hamas is controlling the people's minds with religion now," Iyab Ahmed told me. "It is the opiate of the masses." Israel's bombardment of the Strip had not had the declared effect.

Haidar had come through the bombings unscathed, despite the windows in his taxicab having been blown out in an explosion that killed several nearby civilians. "Thanks to God I'm safe and my children and home are safe," he recited the words rhythmically, like a prayer. "It was too dangerous to move outside during the war. We ran out of food, and my children went hungry. I used a stove until I ran out of diesel, but the fridge was empty. Every morning I got bread for my children—but it was too hard to eat." To make matters worse, his children were continually crying and screaming during the explosions. "There was shooting from tanks, Apaches, drones, missiles, bullets, explosions," he said. "I never saw an operation like this before. It was the first time I've really felt afraid." He seemed to be suffering from post-traumatic stress.

"I don't understand what happened to the Israeli army," he said. His bewilderment was obvious. "Really, they went crazy. We are under siege, and we don't have any Apaches or F-16s, just Hamas guns." Some of his apolitical neighbors had died in the bombardment. The Israelis claimed they wanted to punish Hamas, he observed. "They destroyed all their institutions, but after that Hamas went into hiding underground and the Israelis started killing anyone in the street. Hamas were still okay, and after the war they were 100 percent in control everywhere."

When I suggested that Israel might have gotten unreliable information from Fatah informants with scores to settle, the scale of the psychic turn-around in Gaza became evident. "Fatah would never tell them that!" Haidar exclaimed in mock outrage before hushing his voice conspiratorially. "Look," he said, emphasizing each word. "Hamas is the power now. No more Fatah. Fatah is very weak. People are under more pressure than ever because they've lost everything. If anybody is planning a demonstration against Hamas, they won't show any mercy. Hamas has opened its eyes like the tiger. Hamas people are crazy. Anyone thinking of a coup is crazy. Hamas will kill them."

Haidar's own perspective on Hamas had changed accordingly. "The last two years of the PA were really bad," he said, curling his lip to indicate his disdain. "There was no security. The PA was very weak. We couldn't move in the streets because it was so dangerous with families shooting each other. We needed somebody to be strong, take control, and be a power in Gaza. Really, I agree with the Hamas security system. They stopped the family fighting and the wedding shootings. I am with Hamas on this. Their control is very nice. If you're driving in Gaza now, and there's a red traffic light, everybody respects it—and the police too. Before, with the PA, nobody did." The block-ade was spiraling prices and Hamas was still not business-friendly enough for Haidar's liking, but "their tunnels are supplying gas slowly, slowly," he said. "Hamas has really done good things."

My mind turned back to Haidar's suggestion the last times we had talked—that Fatah people he knew would give, maybe did give, the Israelis information about potential targets. I tried to imagine how they must have felt afterward. Haidar and I finished our nonalcoholic drinks and briefly discussed Barack Obama, who Haidar felt was too young to inspire hope, and then we called it a day.

The *Thawra* Generation

A *thawra* is a revolution, and if 1936 marked Palestine's first, its second was announced to the world by plane hijackings and Black September in 1970. More than ten thousand Palestinians may have died in the autumnal fighting that Jordan's King Hussein launched against Palestinian guerrilla groups in his realm, but perhaps it is willful to call the peers of this time a generation. There was no clear cutoff point from the Palestinians who came of age just a few years before. The PLO had only been founded in 1964 after all. But in practice, financial, military, and diplomatic support from Arab regimes all limited its—and Yasser Arafat's—scope for movement.

As the 1970s rolled on, Palestinians increasingly struggled to control their own destiny. Several "Marxist-Leninist" groups rose up only to be cut down—or cut each other down. The *thawra* burned until the PLO was expelled from Lebanon in 1982. It did not have a defining moment. It was more of a process that touched all elements of Palestinian culture, involving the explosion and popularization of a new wave of Palestinian poetry, literature, music, and art. It was preoccupied with questions of identity, and its proponents were often secular martyrs.

In 1969 the PLO's original aim to eliminate Israel was transformed into the political goal of establishing a democratic secular state embracing the territory's Muslims, Christians, and Jews. But beyond politics, the theme of standing up and proudly declaring oneself a Palestinian ran like a coal seam through, for example, the short stories of Ghassan Kanafani. In his haunting *Men in the Sun,* a group of Palestinian refugees suffocate inside a fuel tanker on the Kuwaiti border without making a noise that could alert the world to their presence. Kanafani lived by his principles and became a spokesman for the PFLP in Beirut. In 1972 he fell victim to an Israeli car bomb assassination.

Street art began to carry political weight. The famous Hanthala cartoon first drawn by Naji al-Ali as a bare-footed, spiky-haired, and sullen-looking eleven-year-old boy appeared in Kuwait's *al-Siyasa* in 1969. Four years later, the figure turned his back, whether in rejection of outside solutions or as a symbol of abandonment. Naji al-Ali was himself eleven years old when his family left Palestine. He was forty-nine when he was assassinated in London. The British government expelled two Israeli diplomats in response. The Mossad was reported to have had prior knowledge of the hit.

The poetry of Mahmoud Darwish also began to receive critical acclaim in this period. Like Kanafani, Darwish was finely tuned to the channels of identity. In his poem "Identity Card," he famously wrote:

> Record! I am an Arab
> And my identity card is number fifty thousand
> I have eight children
> And the ninth is coming after a summer
> Will you be angry . . . ?
>
> Record! I am an Arab
> I have a name without a title
> Patient in a country
> Where people are enraged

Ever since the battle of Karameh in 1968, when Palestinian guerrillas in Jordan inflicted heavy casualties on the Israeli army, a newly assertive generation had been inspired by a worldwide revolutionary movement—and several sources of funding—to tip the apple cart of their parents' more quiescent posture. As Hassan al-Kashif, interviewed in chapter 7, described it to me: "When Karameh happened and we fought all day, turning the Israelis back, destroying some tanks, and killing some soldiers, the people learned that this was a new age. The age of running away and not fighting Israel was over. It was the age of the Palestinian revolution."

Throughout the 1970s Palestinian revolutionary militias made propaganda and waged a violent, sometimes indiscriminate national liberation struggle. The failures of the guerrillas in Jordan to make common cause with non-Palestinian sections of that society ultimately left them isolated when King Hussein turned against them. That in turn accelerated a retrenchment of leaders, fighters, and activists in Lebanon. There they were sucked into the vortex of Lebanon's civil war until Israel's invasion in 1982 exiled most of them to Tunis and the Maghreb.

Inside Israel, a growing confidence was typified by the Druze Initiative Committee, which formed in 1972 to oppose military service, support peace, and stop land confiscations. It was also marked by the first rebellion behind enemy lines since 1936, when a peaceful Arab general strike against land confiscations was met with bullets. Six Palestinians were killed and hundreds of others were injured or arrested in what became known as Land Day. A few weeks later, the Soweto uprising began in South Africa, inaugurating both apartheid comparisons in Palestine and the first stirrings of a worldwide solidarity consciousness.

The leaders and fighters of the *thawra* swam in a sea of secular and modern ideas. Links with intellectuals, entrepreneurs, and militants outside Palestine grew as a new and more numerous populace, many of whom had not experienced the Nakba, interacted with the West, the Eastern bloc, other Arab regimes, and European radical scenes. But as it ever had been, Palestinian honor was to be regained by daring and selfless acts of sacrifice for the wider good of land and nation. It would not be a huge jump to the fetishization of altruistic suicide as a political tactic when the Intifada that followed the *thawra* was stifled. In part this was because of other regional changes.

Leila Khaled dated the current centrality of religion to Palestinian identity to the Iranian revolution in 1979. "Religious influence began to increase after that," she told me. "In Palestine, the Muslim Brotherhood grew more after the First Intifada and the Oslo agreements because Oslo broke the national project. The religious groups filled a vacuum." Unlike many of the *thawra* generation, which she in many ways personified, Leila Khaled had firsthand experience of the Nakba.

But what she shared most strikingly with the young Palestinians of the 1970s was a sense of political project—and organizational purpose. Palestinian political and intellectual society lived through inspiring but horrifying times. It took responsibility for advancing national consciousness and grew more sophisticated, cynical, democratic, enlightened, and kamikaze. Along the way, it lit the fuse for the First Intifada. But the dominant political movements of this time—Fatah in particular—were beset by existential decisions taken in lives that were spent mostly on the run, fighting desperate rearguard battles. They won political jewels—including the EU's Venice Declaration recognizing Palestinians as a people entitled to self-determination—but left few institutional treasures to outlive them.

Dr. Nafez Rakfat
Abu Shabhan, 49

Plastic Surgeon

GAZA CITY

Walking on bodies Nafez was grasshopper thin, with slender fingers, and he moved quickly. His words were mostly precise, his demeanor competent, and his outlook conscientious beyond circumstances most could imagine. But he also looked fatigued and haunted. His sentences were perforated with grand inhalations of air and strange "hunnhhhh" exhalations that suggested a man under great emotional stress coming up for air. He was the head of the Burn Unit in Gaza's Al-Shifa hospital, and we met in his threadbare office.

A few months earlier Nafez had tried to get permits to visit Israel with his seventy-seven-year-old mother who was suffering from lung cancer. He made an appointment in Jerusalem because the blockade had mothballed Gaza's radiotherapy facilities. But the authorities refused to issue papers—three times—and the appointment passed. "In the end," Nafez said, "they called to say that the military wanted to interrogate me at Erez [checkpoint] and that if I didn't come, I'd never get the permits." Nafez had never been politically active, but his patients had told him stories of Israeli officers demanding information about "terrorists" before they would issue permits. Fearing internment if he refused to cooperate, he decided to apply for his sister to accompany his mother instead.

"For six weeks we didn't get the permit," Nafez said, "and my mother died without any radiotherapy treatment . . . " His words dwindled away. "If they have good intelligence, they know that I'm a physician. I have no intent to harm the Israeli state or endanger anyone. I have Israeli friends, doctors, who I used to meet at conferences abroad. But this act strengthened my feeling that there will never be peace with them. I think they should go back to their original countries and leave Palestine to its original owners."

Nafez's family name still commands great respect. His father, a Gaza native, was the head of the Strip's Waqf directorate, entrusted with preserving religious endowments over generations. The national cause was a constant in Nafez's life from the time he hid in a basement during the 1967 war. "We never felt safe," he said. "During the occupation, I remember the fear in my father's eyes when the Israelis entered our house." The conviction that a Nakba could happen again was always in his mind. "I thought about supporting Fatah, but my father told me a lot about their corruption," he said. "When they came to Gaza, they were even more corrupt than we'd thought."

Nafez wanted a "good job" more than a career in medicine, and after studying in Alexandria and Glasgow, he returned to the Strip. "I was working in Al-Shifa hospital then," he said, "and we had a lot of badly injured cases, not just broken arms but gunshot wounds too. One day the Israelis shot a teenager at the hospital entrance. The doctor tried to save him, but his brain was out of his skull. It was the first time I'd seen such scenes, so it was very shocking." As he spoke, Nafez tensed up, visibly back in that zone. "I was on duty in the emergency department," he almost croaked, "trying to put a tube into his trachea so that he could breathe, but unfortunately I failed. The child died a few minutes later." He released a breath.

Nafez had always liked plastic surgery, ever since an Egyptian professor showed his class before and after operation photos of children with cleft lips. "Just ninety minutes later, there was a completely different child," he said, his face brightening. "It's like a miracle." Patients sometimes saw the plastic surgeons as "angels who came from heaven and changed their lives," Nafez said, "especially older people. When I showed one man his face in the mirror after an operation, he started crying and kissing my hands. He'd been so ashamed. It was very rewarding."

In late 1993, Nafez joined Operation Smile, an American children's charity, and traveled to China, Honduras, and the Philippines before taking a fellowship in Virginia. For two and a half years he studied reconstructive surgery and cosmetic breast surgery. "But the main focus was on cranial-facial injuries, deformities, and cleft lip and palate," he said, and the lights suddenly went out. There was a whirring noise for a few uncomfortable seconds. Then a generator cranked them back up again. Outside a muezzin wailed down the ill-lit street.

Nafez returned to Al-Shifa hospital. By the time of the Second Intifada, "most of the injuries we were receiving came from bullets or explosives," he said. "We had a very busy operating schedule, and there were shortages of everything so we had to be flexible." Little help was on offer from Israeli hospitals, which became especially problematic when the Gaza War of 2008–9 began.

"From the first day we were receiving huge numbers of victims, sometimes more than two hundred emergency cases in less than twenty minutes," he said. "I was actually moving on bodies, most of them very seriously injured." Nafez's voice shook in pain as he described the scene. "I was trying to save someone who was injured. As soon as he died, I would go to the next one and try to save him. Then I'd see that the other one was dying. All the time I'm walking on bodies."

"In the operating room, I was trying to save one victim on the floor and shouting at the surgeon on the operating table, 'Do it quickly, this patient is dying. He's dying!'" Nafez cried these words almost in disbelief. "And he died," he relented. "I decided to open him up on the ground. I told everyone, 'Just leave the one on the table,' and I operated on him on the floor. It was a real nightmare. Many of these people could have been saved if they were not that huge number." The doctor let out more brittle air in a "haaaahhh"-sounding puncture. "I can say," he began again, "that it was a mass killing, a genocide, a Holocaust. It is a real Holocaust actually."

In Gaza, people use the word *Holocaust* more to describe their experience than to minimize the Nazi slaughter. After all, to do so would be to diminish their own ordeal, so defined. In addition to jockeying for victim status in the international PR battle, it is a way to undermine Israel's claim to legitimacy through suffering. The use of the adjective *real* before "Holocaust," though, can sometimes mean something else. Constantine Dabbagh, head of the Near East Council for Churches in Gaza, once began a conversation with me this way and ended up questioning whether six million really died in the Nazi genocide. The Catholic Church imported European anti-Semitic strains to the Middle East via Syria in the mid-nineteenth century, and they have had some uptake. But the best argument against such casual relativism is that Palestinian pain has been calamitous enough without having to measure up against that of the Jews. And unlike Jewish suffering, Palestinian oppression is ongoing.

During Israel's bombardment of Gaza, every conceivable injury was sustained. "Some people needed amputations of both limbs," Nafez said. "Some had brain injuries. Sometimes whole families were completely charred. A grandmother came to the hospital with massive burns after her husband and four of her children were burned to death by white phosphorus [WP] in front of her eyes. Whenever the nurses went to her room she begged them, 'Please help my children! They are burning to death!' Even our psychiatrist couldn't calm her down. In the end, he took her to the graveyard and showed her their graves. He told her, 'Your children are dead now. They are not burning anymore. They are here.' Then she calmed down."

WP is an incendiary chemical flare with added value. "When WP comes into contact with skin," Nafez explained, "it continues to burn until the phosphorus is consumed or deprived of oxygen. In some cases, it burns down to the bone. In many cases, it's fatal." WP injuries can only be treated by removing the WP particles or smothering the wound area. Other "exotic" weaponry such as dense inert metal explosives (DIME) severed flesh like a scythe. "These amputations were clean-cut, as if a hot knife had been used," Nafez said. "There was minimal bleeding and no lacerations or crushing, which you'd get with normal explosives. Most of these amputees had strange outcomes. After the amputation had been cleaned and closed and everything should have been okay, the conditions of many of these patients were deteriorating and they were dying. I didn't know why."

DIME weapons use experimental heavy metal tungsten alloys (HMTA) to create intense explosions of micro-shrapnel in limited areas. This shrapnel is untreatable as it is too small to be removed. It has been found to cause neoplastic transformations of human osteoblast cells. In one U.S. Army test, ninety-two rats injected with weapons grade HMTA all developed a rare cancer within five months. Through the media, Nafez appealed for weapons experts to be sent to help. When two Amnesty International experts arrived, Israeli border officials confiscated their equipment before allowing them to enter. "We felt like guinea pigs," Nafez said. But DIME was not the only postconflict hangover.

In October 2009 Chris Busby of the European Committee on Radiation Risk reported that he had found a high degree of enriched uranium in soil samples taken from bomb craters caused by Israeli munitions in Gaza. These are signatures of depleted uranium (DU) weapon use. DU can cause diseases, including cancers, and congenital deformities for generations. "I've stopped buying strawberries for my children because they're grown in the north, which was heavily bombarded," Nafez says. "I'm even worried about our water. Is it safe to drink? Have our vegetables been contaminated by radiation or toxic materials?"

The Israeli army maintains that its operations were aimed at Hamas fighters, yet it was civilians who suffered most. Nafez insisted that there were no weapons stored under his hospital and that over the twenty-three days of war, he treated only civilians. "I didn't see a single fighter in the hospital," he said. "Maybe they weren't wearing uniforms. But most of the Health Ministry was stationed in the hospital, including the minister himself and most of the senior administrators. They controlled all the other hospitals from Al-Shifa." Under Israel's self-declared rules of engagement, this could have made the hospital a target.

Indeed, on December 28 an adjoining mosque was bombed, and all the windows in the Burn Unit were blown out, injuring one of Nafez's doctors. At one point there were reports that the hospital itself was about to be targeted. "It was terrifying for everyone," Nafez said. "Most of the nurses and patients left the hospital. Should we go too? It was a very confusing and difficult decision, but in the end I told the remaining doctors and nurses that whoever wanted to could stay with me. Some left, but the majority stayed."

During that time the hospital staff barely slept. They were racked by shortages of everything, "even the cream we used for burn treatment," Nafez said. The shortages were still continuing due to what he called "the shame to humanity" that is the blockade. "We can only get medications that the Egyptians let in," he said, "and only when they and the Israelis decide it's okay. Sadly, there is no difference between them. We need so much more."

Looking back, Nafez reflected, "The war changed me because for the first time I felt that death was very near. Every time I went home at night, I felt that I might not be coming back. I could be killed on my way, or my house could be hit. Every night I slept under the stairs with my wife and children, presuming it might be safer than sleeping in our beds. Every time we heard a rocket or an explosion, we thought that we might be next. I was holding my children all the time."

What he took most from the experience was "a strong feeling that this Israeli state will not stay here for long because people who can commit such crimes are not human beings. The Western governments are supporting them now, but this will not be forever. In the past I felt that we might live in peace in one country or two states, but after this war I no longer think so because they are gangsters more than a government, terrorists that call themselves a state."

"These people are criminals," he said, licking his dry lips, "and you cannot live with criminals."

Fawaz Dawoud, 52

Chief of Police

NABLUS, WEST BANK

Police society In March 2008 the Nablus police station was staffed by the friendliest cops I had ever met. While I waited to talk to their boss, some officers insisted on sharing their breakfast humus and beans with me. As we ate, they joked and asked me about my work. One would never have guessed that a few weeks before, an Israeli military spokesperson, Noah Meir, had called their city "the capital of terror." But in the not-so-distant past, gangs had controlled Nablus's streets. When I first visited the city in 2006, I arrived slumped in the back of a taxi. Militias had just kidnapped two internationals and threatened to abduct any other foreigners in the town in protest at a Danish newspaper that had published cartoons depicting the Prophet Muhammad as a terrorist. The rattle of gunfire had punctuated that interview. I wondered if disorder outside the station and camaraderie within might be related.

Fawaz Dawoud had been appointed two weeks before as part of an EU- and U.S.-backed attempt to "restore order" in Nablus. He joined Fatah in 1975 and trained in Cuba before serving in the Palestinian army as the leader of a company battalion. After Fatah's withdrawal from Lebanon he moved to Algeria, returning in 1994 to deputize and then head the Palestinian District Coordination Offices in northern Gaza, Qalqilya, and Ramallah. This bureau coordinated security arrangements with Israeli forces. Fawaz went on to serve as deputy chief of the Hebron police and director of the Jericho police department before taking on the Nablus brief.

He was a career security man, and he was not enthusiastic about being interviewed. Still, he allowed me into his office on a bad day. "Sometimes we're informed that there is some military action [planned], so we have to remove all our police and security personnel and vehicles from the streets," he said. "Sometimes we are not. Sometimes we confront each other, and the Israelis tell us to go back to our [bases]. Just now, the Israelis launched an incursion. We were not informed. People just phoned our operation room saying that Israeli vehicles were entering Nablus from the eastern side." What can you do when this happens? I asked. "We withdraw all our policemen from that area," he shrugged.

In addition to arresting or killing suspects, these types of raids also allowed Israel to claim that the PA was not fulfilling its security obligations to clamp down on "terrorists" under George W. Bush's "road map." "They're trying to show that the PA can't take security control in Area A," Fawaz said. "If you have two forces working in the same area, there will be no security. It has a negative influence on our work in the street. You can imagine how embarrassing it is for a policeman who is standing at a road junction to run away to let the Israelis come in." As a Palestinian police commander, how does it make you feel? I asked. "That my efforts in this job will fail," he replied. "It weakens the Palestinian police in front of the people. All the time I have to start again from the beginning to build a relationship between the police and society."

Goodwill was needed, he said, because his force required time to assess the local situation. "We've accumulated cases from the period of chaos, and we're working on them right now. I don't want to talk politics, but I blame the occupation for the chaos because it destroyed all the PA's security infrastructure. They didn't give people the chance to move freely between cities, and that gave the militias a chance to grow."

The Nablus police department "doesn't take sides," Fawaz stressed. But equally, "there are no police officers supporting Hamas in this force," he boasted, "none at all. After the problems with Hamas and the collapse in the Gaza Strip, we did some security investigations into all our officers. If anyone belonged to that party, he was out of the police immediately." So, I asked, how can your force police Nablus fairly when a party that more than half the city voted for is not represented in it? "Look," Fawaz lowered his voice, "we are concerned with crime. We will try to stop lawbreakers, whichever party they're from. I'm just applying law and order to this society."

It was a partisan reply. There were no human rights violations in Fawaz's police station and the city was safe, he said. "If there were no Israeli incursions or killings against the people, the PA could guarantee full control," he went on, splaying his elbows imperiously on the table. Yet from midnight until 6:00 A.M. the Israeli security services had carte blanche on Nablus's streets. "They are above the law," he agreed, slipping his chin into crocheted fingers. "This makes our job difficult sometimes."

Fawaz said that he wanted to build "a police society," restoring discipline and standardizing uniforms. "This is Brigadier Firaz al-Ahmed. He's the deputy police commander," he suddenly announced. Security officials were arriving in the room as the Israeli invasion advanced. "I will try to build up the Nablus police force because it's considered somehow broken," Fawaz went on. He was clearly concluding our discussion. But if your force retreats from the street every time the Israelis invade, how can they exercise authority there? I asked. "You should ask the political leadership about this," Fawaz replied. "I just execute the orders given to me." And then he was back on the phone, negotiating a way out of Israel's latest incursion, his men standing uncomfortably by his side.

Mohammed Dahlan, 47

Fatah Leader

RAMALLAH, WEST BANK

You are weak To his critics Mohammed Dahlan was possibly the most destructive living figure in Palestinian politics. He was reviled for alleged corruption, human rights abuses, and, most seriously, collaboration with the United States and Israel. After they met in 2003, George W. Bush reportedly said of Dahlan, "He's our guy." A former Israeli minister told me three years later that Dahlan had been Tel Aviv's preferred choice for PA interior minister under Yasser Arafat. In April 2008 an article in *Vanity Fair* magazine by

David Rose went further. Rose reported that Dahlan had plotted with the Bush administration and covertly received U.S. weaponry to overthrow the Hamas government in Gaza.

Rose's narrative, which was reinforced by some U.S. State Department documentation, was disputed by Diana Buttu when I met her on the grounds that there was nothing covert about the plan. With political assassinations plaguing both camps in 2007, multiple news reports claimed that the United States and the United Kingdom were arming Fatah as a counterweight to Iran's arming of Hamas. "I think we watch too many movies," Buttu said. "People need bad guys in every conflict, and there just aren't any when it comes to Palestine." The brutal Fatah repression and Hamas takeover in Gaza had their own dynamic, she argued. Nonetheless, to many pro-Palestinian activists, Mohammed Dahlan still had the reputation of being what one U.S.-based blogger, Tony Karon, described as a "Palestinian Pinochet."

In person he was dapper, by turns diffident and outspoken—and tightly corralled by advisers. Some appeared to be political appointees who had spent time with him during his frequent visits to Egypt. Some were Fatah veterans. Others just appeared shifty. Although he was at the time a Fatah central committee member and we met in his glamorous suite in Ramallah's exclusive Jimzo apartment complex, Mohammed had humble beginnings. He was the youngest son of a poor refugee family in the Khan Younis refugee camp. As a child, his father was mostly absent, working in Saudi Arabia. When I asked what the most important lesson his dad taught him was, he said, "I've just learned suffering from my father. All my life experience I got from my mum." He studied briefly in Egypt before returning to help build the Fatah youth movement. But he was a child of Gaza's streets. "And we graduated under the occupation!" he further stacked the profile.

As a child, Mohammed remembered "seeing blood, just suffering," all around him. "Going to school, there'd be two guys killed by the Israelis on the street in a bad way." How did it feel to be powerless and unable to protect your loved ones or community? I asked. Mohammed was momentarily at a loss for words. "I can't explain it," he snorted, "but these things give you the feeling that you are weak. You are alone, and all the strong countries are against you. It made the camp feel that we should strengthen. There could be just one way: to unite in the PLO and defend ourselves."

Mohammed's narrative—as he told it—was that of a refugee rising above blood and occupation to lead his people against powerful foes. First his mother lost nine members of her family to the Israelis. Then he became involved in politics "by chance." Politics in those days was a byword for fighting the occupation. In his case, Mohammed says he was recruited by "someone who had good relations with Abu Jihad."

"I only said hello to him on the phone, and I considered myself part of the organization," he explained. He rose quickly through the ranks and in 1981 became a founding member of Fatah's *Shabiba* youth movement, focusing his work on Bir Zeit University near Ramallah.

Rather than a popular uprising, the First Intifida, according to Mohammed, was "the outcome of seven or eight years of preparation. Most people were originally organized by Fatah." And by Mohammed. "I was in charge," he said. "We had 15,000 people in the Gaza camps cleaning the streets and mosques—the same thing that Hamas later did. We invented such activities. If we wanted to demonstrate, we just collected them and informed them. It was strong."

In 1988 Mohammed was deported to Jordan, an event he described as "the worst thing you will face in your life." After that he was imprisoned and sent to Egypt. Eventually, he found himself in Tunis, from where he says he led the First Intifada, "managing it, giving money, sending weapons, all this stuff." After the Oslo agreement in 1994, he returned to Gaza to head the Preventive Security Force.

This was a hard sell for Mohammed. "I used to fight the Israelis," he said emphatically. "Suddenly I had to take care of their security instead. It means you have to change your way of thinking." But at least now you could protect yourself and your loved ones, I suggested. "No," he said. "I couldn't. And it's even worse than that. Thousands of people worked with me against the occupation for ten years. Now you had to prevent Palestinians from taking action against the Israelis. Psychologically, it was the worst time of my life." It sounded as though his life had had many lows. Leaked U.S. embassy cables would later suggest that Mohammed had suffered a nervous breakdown in September 2005, during a meeting with the Israeli negotiator Gilad Sher. I could imagine how cooperating with the Israelis might have stuck in his throat. "Negotiations are a little easier," he said, springing back on the sofa. "It's normal in history. They are the exit from one stage to another. At the end of a conflict either you lose, you have balance, or you win. But this way my people—our friends—were asking, 'What the hell is going on?'"

Many people outside Gaza asked the same question. But when I raised allegations of racketeering, embezzlement, and financial corruption, a ripple of unease coursed through Mohammed's entourage. "There are a lot of gossips," Mohammed said, trying to clear the air, "but I'm from a refugee camp, and I feel proud of that." An internal Palestinian Legislative Council inquiry had cleared his name, he said, and the accusations originated with Hamas and his Israeli negotiating partners. "The minute negotiations stop, you will find yourself accused in the Israeli media of charging money on the crossings," he said. That practice had "started when Salam Fayyad became finance minister. He was in charge of collecting money and giving people salaries." Mohammed's tax-collecting powers were simply delegated. When Hamas took over Gaza, they had told him that they expected to get "at least £1 million a day" from the crossing, he claimed. "I told them, 'Guys, you will invest $100,000 a month just as a running cost!'" But multiple sources suggest that Hamas's taxes on Gaza's tunnels have provided a major source of government revenue.

Mohammed was equally dismissive of reports by Amnesty International about political arrests, detentions without trial, prolonged solitary confinements, and the denial of access to families and lawyers in Gaza on his watch. "They complained against the Authority, not Preventive Security," Mohammed said. "No one was killed in my jails. I arrested people because of political decisions by Arafat. I faced psychological difficulties because I had to arrest my friends." Hamas members such as Mahmoud al-Zahar—"He's always lying," Mohammed confided—were arrested "because they destroyed the political agreement between us and the Israelis." One of his aides added that "the jail was just to protect the Hamas guys," presumably from Israeli assassinations. "We are not like the third world punishing the opposition," Mohammed reassured me. He had simply been a victim of security force "mistakes" and his own notoriety.

One "mistake" that he did admit to was supporting the Second Intifada "for a while" after it broke out. "I changed my mind directly after September 11," he said. "It should have ended then." When I asked why he changed his mind, Mohammed changed the subject, talking about the warnings that he had given the U.S. diplomat Dennis Ross and his Israeli counterparts that a revolt was on the way. "I am one of the people on the street," he said. "I'm wearing a nice tie, but I represent them. I feel them. I know exactly what's going on with the street. They were frustrated, explosive, and ready to blow." Were you trying to protect them? I asked. "Of course!" he blasted back.

Palestinian analysts typically see the First Intifada as spontaneous and the second as having been captured by factions. For Mohammed it was the other way around. The Second Intifada was "an automatic reaction" by ordinary people, he said. "Believe me, I was in charge, and they used their weapons as individuals, not because of a political decision." Still Mohammed tried to reach a ceasefire with Israel that he would enforce. He says he warned

Israel to stay back from the initial protests around the Al-Aqsa Mosque. But "[Shaul] Mofaz, the chief of staff, used firepower, killed twelve more people in Gaza, and then asked me for a meeting. I told them, 'No way. You continue your way, and we'll continue ours.' The fathers of this Intifada are Mofaz and Avi Dichter, not Arafat. They wanted it, 100 percent."

Two months after the Second Intifada started, one of Dahlan's officers killed two Israeli soldiers in the Kfar Darom settlement before himself being killed. Mohammed gave him a posthumous promotion. Israeli sources then claimed Dahlan was orchestrating the fighting and sent helicopter gunships to strafe his Gaza offices. Egypt responded by withdrawing its ambassador to Tel Aviv. Mohammed may not have been able to protect his own people, but powerful forces in the region have often protected him over the years.

The strafing "was a message from the Israelis," he said. "The assassination attempt was at the Erez checkpoint [six months later] when they shelled my cars. If you'd seen them, you wouldn't believe that I'd survived. There were 120 bullets in them!" Three of Mohammed's bodyguards were wounded in the attack, which occurred as he was returning from negotiations with Israeli officials. His convoy retreated to the PA's headquarters in Ramallah, which the Israeli army proceeded to shell for thirty-five minutes. "I contacted [Saudi] Prince Bandar, and he contacted Sharon's office. Everyone could hear the heavy shelling while we talked. They were crazy. It was the Americans who stopped them."

Yasser Arafat, Mohammed believed, "was murdered by the Israelis. There is no question, but how I don't know." In an indication of the depth of hatred against him, Farouk Kaddoumi, the Fatah chairman, would later accuse Dahlan and Mahmoud Abbas of conspiring with Israel to kill Arafat. "You know, each time we got close to a deal with the Israelis, they assassinated someone," Mohammed said. "This was the mechanism. The Israelis thought that they could conclude everything by force. Their slogan was, 'If this force does not stop the Intifada, the IDF must use more force.'"

Still, I said, your position dovetails very neatly with Israel's. You support a return to Oslo-style direct negotiations with Israel, an end to armed resistance, the unification of security forces under a single leader, working in close coordination with security services in Jordan, Israel, Saudi Arabia, Egypt, and America. "You know what?" Mohammed replied. "I don't care if my interest coincides with another country's. I don't hesitate even. If my interest is for independence and 1967 borders—and Israel takes the same positions— should I regret it? I was not representing the Israeli or American interest, but I cared about the ceasefire." His aides began to hover.

Street perceptions that he was too close to the Israelis had "sometimes" hurt him, Mohammed conceded, but he insisted that Palestinians liked his "strong position." I asked if he was planning a comeback. "A comeback from where?" he boomed, looking around for support from his aides behind him. "I'm here!" Would you like to be president one day? "No, no, no," he corrected me. "President of what? Since Arafat's time everyone has talked about me as president. I'm looking for independence first, because to be president of the occupied territories is meaningless. I saw how Arafat suffered for fifteen years, and now I see how Abu Mazen is suffering with Hamas and Arab public opinion against him. It's a complicated mission." By this point Mohammed's minders had begun whispering in his ear and motioning for me to leave.

Bill Clinton, he said, was "an abnormal man, determined and fair." Mohammed seemed to view the United States as mistakenly following Israeli interests, although his choice of words was open to interpretation. "The ones who made the strategy in our cause are the Israelis, not the Americans," he said. I managed to get out one last question—"Which Israeli and American figures are you still in contact with?"—but Mohammed did not answer. The interview ended with promises of a follow-up that were not honored, despite well over twenty unreturned phone calls to his aides.

In January 2011 Mohammed was expelled from Fatah after apparently insulting Mahmoud Abbas, president of the PA. Abbas had previously employed him as his internal security minister and national security adviser. Mohammed went to Cairo, where his supporters appeared afraid to defend him. He faced charges including bribery, corruption, collaboration, forming death squads, assassination, treason, and gun-running to Libya. Hamas even denied him permission to attend his mother's funeral in Gaza. One of the group's leaders, Mahmoud al-Zahar, warned that if he was "ever allowed back into Gaza, the families of his victims would not allow him to live long. . . . [He must] first pay the price for the blood he spilled."

Nabila Espanyoli, 53

NGO Director

NAZARETH, ISRAEL

The hand cannot go against the machine   Nabila Espanyoli was turning twenty when the Committee for the Defense of Land launched a fight against the confiscation of Palestinian land in Israel. Israel's Palestinian minority had just achieved a breakthrough in her hometown of Nazareth with the mayoral election of Tawfiq Ziad, a poet and Hadash (Communist Party) member. The honeymoon did not last long. On March 30, 1976—Land Day—six Palestinian citizens of Israel were killed by Israeli security forces while protesting land seizures and house demolitions. For a generation of Arabs in Israel, Land Day announced their presence to the world. Nabila, a psychologist, community spokesperson, and director of Al-Tufula Women and Children's Center in Nazareth, saw the process up close.

Her family, the Espanyolis, gave their name to the Catholic neighborhood she grew up in. "We've been here since before church records began in the sixteenth century," she told me. "Everyone in our neighborhood knew each other. Because of my grandparents, I didn't need to introduce myself. It was enough to say, 'I am Nabila Espanyoli,' and they'd know me better than I knew myself." Nabila went to school locally and became politically involved with Hadash after applying to study social work in Haifa.

Initially, she wasn't accepted into the program. "That was my first … ," she began, then punched her hand. "When the university's rejection letter arrived, I cried. But my older sister told me, 'Nabila, if you cry, you cry alone. Take your letter to the university and see why they're refusing you a place.' I went from one office to the other and received several answers. Once, I wasn't intelligent enough. Another time, my Hebrew wasn't good enough. Then, my

English was too poor. I knew these were lies, so I fought and eventually got my place." Then, as now, Arab students had to fight on many fronts.

"It was impossible for Arabs to find apartments in Haifa, and you couldn't get places in the student dorms because you didn't serve in the army. Jews were always the priority," she said. Aren't 20 percent of the students in Haifa University now Arabs? I asked. "Yes," Nabila replied, "but only because the Arab villages of the Galilee are nearby, so people can work while they study. The general percentage is around 0.4." The percentage of Arab professors in Haifa is similarly meager. "You don't meet at the same level, at eye level, and you rarely meet at all," she said. "When you work together, you are beneath Jewish managers. Segregation remains."

In 1975 Nabila went to the first Nazareth General Assembly as a student representative to debate the first Palestinian general strike since 1936. "We'd been witnessing one law after another seizing our land," she said, "and then Israel announced a major new confiscation around Sakhnin. Land was an existence issue for us." Nabila remembered, "We filled Nazareth's biggest hall from one side to the other. There were thousands there. I remember Tawfiq Ziad arguing that we had to strike, and the whole crowd jumped to their feet, clapping and cheering." Electric as the mood felt, the strike was tough to organize.

"I woke up at 4:00 A.M. on the strike day and stood on the street corner telling people not to go to work," Nabila recalled. "We gave flowers to the people who turned back." There was no Internet to connect workers in those days. "We didn't even have a strike committee!" Nabila said. "We made sure all the shops were closed by talking to people and convincing them. Most people cooperated. Some were afraid to support us openly because they were told that they'd lose their jobs if they struck." Even so, the strike shut 95 percent of Nazareth's businesses for the day. "The main street was closed, and so were the small shops," Nabila said proudly. "Everywhere was closed. The Israelis couldn't deal with it."

Despite a decision to keep the strike peaceful, the army declared curfews around the region, and six people were killed during protests in Sakhnin, Kfar Qana, and Taybe. "There were real clashes with the police there. One woman was shot going to school because she was afraid of losing her job," Nabila said. Despite this, the strike—and the struggles that followed it—forced the government to back down and stirred Palestinian consciousness. "It was a defining moment for me, a before-and-after moment," Nabila said. "Before, we were dealt with as segregated Muslims, Christians, and Druze. All of a sudden there was a collective reaction. We were behaving as a national minority."

"There'd been a need to regenerate leaders from within the community which remained in Israel. The traditional family leaders were all out, and that enabled a new left generation. That was the big difference from the West Bank and Gaza. Although we'd been under military rule until 1966, we'd begun to reorganize a leadership. They had similar developments in the First Intifada." After Yasser Arafat's return to the West Bank, though, that generational upsurge was contained by the reinstallation of traditional tribal and family leaderships. "Our struggle went backward here too," Nabila said, "with the rise of the Islamic Movement and others looking for family and tribal allies in the villages."

Nabila graduated and went to work for the Social Security Ministry in Jerusalem. She was sacked three months later. "I asked my boss why, and she said, 'I don't know, Nabila. The decision came from the security services, and I can't cover it.' In Israel, you have to pass a security test after a few months' work. Nowadays it's done openly, but back then it wasn't talked about. It decided the course of your life." Nabila believed she was sacked for her political activities.

"My boss appreciated my professionalism, but she had her orders," Nabila said. "She even asked if I could help find my successor because they needed an Arab social worker! My Arab and Jewish coworkers campaigned for me, saying I was being dismissed for economic reasons. But everyone knew that wasn't true." When they eventually asked her to return to work for three months, Nabila told them, "Sorry, I'm not a Ping-Pong ball." She had been brought up with proverbs like "Walk beside the wall and protect yourself," she said. "If you walk against the wall, you protect your back. Or they'll tell you, 'The hand cannot go against the machine.' You can't fight this machinery on your own."

In a town as divided as Nazareth, this was a salient lesson. Since 1948 most of the city's population had been Muslim refugees. "A quarter of Palestinians in Israel are refugees," Nabila clarified. "Many people in the Ein el-Hilwe camp in Lebanon come from Saful, near here. In Nazareth they built a whole neighborhood called Safuli. Almost overnight in 1948, Nazareth's population doubled." Always a mixed town, Nazareth saw traditions such as Sunday closing enduring even after Muslims became the majority.

"For years we never talked about being Christians or Muslims," Nabila said. "If people asked me, I'd say I was Palestinian. But that changed because of the influence of the Iranian revolution, Israel's attempts to divide and rule, and the growth of the Islamic Movement." This movement rhetorically opposed the Israeli government, Nabila said, while exploiting the relative poverty of Muslim refugees. Nazareth's municipal budget was limited by central government. Any available funds went to the Jewish settlement of Nazareth Illit, high above the city. "The people were dissatisfied," Nabila told me, "and that was fertile soil for the Islamic Movement to misrepresent the problem." Under attack, though, the community reacted collectively.

In October 2000 Jewish residents of Nazareth Illit attacked Arab Nazarenes in an event Nabila described as a pogrom. "I was part of the street," she said, "and when we called the police for protection, they came and started shooting at us. Two people were killed when they shot at our demonstration from the court building." For both sides, "it marked a cut," Nabila said, "a feeling of psychological war. The Intifada had just begun, and we were receiving news of the killing of our brothers and sisters in the West Bank and Gaza. We were hearing that in Umm al-Fahem people were being shot dead, and out of that, a day of strikes and protest was called."

The atmosphere in Israel, she says, "was one of surprise": Why are Palestinians demonstrating about the Intifada? "It was [Yom] Kippur day, and in Nazareth Illit people had gathered for prayers. Someone told them, 'Go change your shoes and come back,' and then they began their attack. There's just one street between Nazareth and Nazareth Illit, and hundreds of mostly young men crossed it and began throwing stones at Palestinian houses. I would love to think that they were right-wing, but you don't know. Not one of them was arrested, but hundreds of Palestinians were."

"The mayor, town council, and other leaders asked the police not to enter Nazareth and escalate tensions, but they wanted to stop our demonstration. They used tear gas and people ran away. Then they started firing rubber bullets. Even when people tried to hide between the houses and protect their young, the firing continued. The first guy to die was killed by a bullet shot at his heart." In the days that followed, there was a conscious attempt to distance the community from the Intifada raging across the Green Line. "It was just a day of protest," Nabila said. "We weren't interested in continuing the struggle." Neither could it ever be abandoned.

Muna Wakid, 47

DFLP Worker

NAHR EL-BARED, LEBANON

The alternative to the camp　For a few weeks in May 2007 Palestinian refugees in Lebanon became a hot story. A military conflict broke out between the Lebanese army and Fatah al-Islam, an apparently Al Qaida-affiliated sect that had taken control of the Nahr el-Bared refugee camp. The fighting was merciless, and commentators speculated about extremism taking root among Palestinians. Muna Wakid must have wept.

Muna was a refugee twice over. When her family was expelled from Amqa village in 1948, they moved north to Nahr el-Bared. In 2007, when her home was destroyed along with most others in the camp by the Lebanese army, she decamped again. A year on, she was still dividing her time between Beirut and a rented house in Nahr el-Bared when I met her. For the past twenty-five years she had been a political worker for the DFLP. She was unmarried and had no children.

Perched on a chair in a friend's office, Muna stretched out her legs with her feet pointing inward. Occasionally she would shoot a deadpan grin at her friend, my translator, who had set up the interview. When I asked her what stories her family told her about Amqa, she replied dryly, "There are a lot. The wedding celebrations lasted for a week there, with traditional songs and folklore told every day, a lot of meat and sheep. Neighbors, even Jewish neighbors, were friendlier than they are here now. They used to exchange food with each other." Her extended family of about one hundred worked in the fields. Today they mostly lived in the Ein el-Hilwe camp.

Muna was told as a child how around 1,500 people fled Amqa in 1948, many to Lebanon. "The Jews focused on our people's weakest point," she said. "They announced over a megaphone, 'We will rape your women.'" The Wakid family took refuge first in a tent village in Baqaa and then in Nahr el-Bared. In winter, "they were always afraid that the storms would blow their tents away," she said. Sometimes the refugees chose camps close to the Israeli border, like Bourj al-Barajne. Sometimes they just followed routes that other relatives had already taken. A few of Muna's family found sanctuary in villages within Israel, but she had never met them. The consensus view was that the refugees had made a terrible mistake by leaving.

When I queried what Nahr el-Bared had been like to grow up in, Muna lit a cigarette and quipped, "Oh, the feeling of nostalgia. In my childhood, there were fewer people and simpler homes made of stones, zinc, and soil. Women used to wash their dresses and kitchenware in the river and bring cooking wood from the forest nearby." Until the late 1990s the refugees kept their village-friendly traditions. Palestinian fathers sometimes refused Lebanese suitors for their daughters because they expected to return. Gradually, as camp life improved and acquired permanence, "we took some habits from the Lebanese," Muna said.

Nahr el-Bared was always "the best-off and best educated of the camps," with overachieving students and a population that swelled to 30,000. Job opportunities with UNRWA had existed since the 1960s, and conditions were buoyed by an influx of concrete development. "People from as far away as Tripolis used to visit our market because it was so cheap," Muna told me. But government restrictions forced political activists to work secretly. Muna saw Lebanon as an "apartheid" society, even worse than Israel's in some ways. "Animals in some Western countries are treated better," she said.

As Muna related the story, "People started to take control of their lives with the announcement of the PLO in the mid-sixties. It improved our education, awareness, and identity. I felt that the Palestinian revolution was like . . . " She scratched her head and slipped her feet out of her flip-flops. "In our religion, there is a mythological figure called the Mehdi who will come to answer the people after they've been expelled from their homeland. We thought that the *thawra* was the Mehdi that would take us to the safe place, the homeland."

"Refugees saved their money to buy guns and be like keepers to the sea, the river, and the homeland," she said, "feeling safe." An Israeli naval commando assault on Nahr el-Bared in 1972 strengthened the mood to arm, as did harassment from Lebanon's dissolving state. "The Lebanese police had a center at our camp entrance that humiliated and oppressed people. You could be arrested for any justification, and it was suffocating us, so when the *thawra* asserted itself the people attacked it," she elaborated.

In 1972 Muna joined the Palestinian union of students and got involved in the women's movement, giving food, water, and first aid to the Fedayeen. She started off "mobilizing the community," but "women were trained to use weapons and even fight hand to hand," she said. Muna was inspired by Leila Khaled and other, more anonymous women who defended the Sabra and Chatila camps during the siege of 1986. Were you ever tempted to pick up a gun yourself? I asked. "I trained with the Democratic Front," she answered, "but I never used one."

In those days Nahr el-Bared held to a simpler Islam that was passed down traditionally. It complemented family networks, parties, and militias until the 1990s. The *thawra* had given Palestinians the authority to organize and build new institutions, but after Oslo "the PLO seemed weaker and the Islamic movement became an alternative. As people became poorer, Islamic groups helped them with youth clubs, religious schools, kindergartens, scholarships, and militias." In Muna's view they were just cheating politicians. "They never said what they wanted, just that if you weren't good, angels would punish you and God would set you on fire when you died," she said, sitting on her hands.

But Fatah al-Islam was different. "It didn't develop in the camp and doesn't belong to the camp," Muna stressed. "They tried to attract youngsters by giving money and religious lessons, but only four or five kids joined them. They're from outside, of various nationalities, and if you want to know more you should ask the Lebanese state." Shi'ites, Palestinians, and leftists often accuse the Lebanese, Saudi, and U.S. governments of nurturing Fatah al-Islam as a counterweight to Hezbollah. Sunnis and supporters of the Cedar Revolution that expelled Syrian troops disagree.

"Don't involve me in Lebanese intrigues," Muna said gruffly when I canvassed her opinion. She proceeded to ask how Fatah al-Islam's guns were smuggled into the camp, how they defied the army's checkpoints to move freely, and whether the battle of Nahr el-Bared was a fait accompli to clear the camp for real estate purposes. Fatah al-Islam only had about 150 supporters, she said, "but other religious parties such as Hamas and Islamic Jihad sympathized with them and that made them difficult to deal with. The PLO groups tried to kick them out before the conflict, but the Islamic groups supported them so they stayed." Fatah al-Islam had arrived in Nahr el-Bared shortly after Israel's 2006 war on Hezbollah. "They mainly gathered outside the camp in uninhabited areas," Muna told me. "When the security forces besieged the camp—months before the conflict—shoppers stopped coming to the market. People hated them for that."

On May 19, 2007, Lebanese security forces laid siege to Fatah al-Islam's Tripolis office after a local bank robbery. A gun battle ensued. In Nahr el-Bared, Fatah al-Islam seized Lebanese army positions—and two armored personnel carriers—at the camp's entrance. The army responded by launching a fierce artillery bombardment. Over three and half months, more than four hundred people died in Lebanon's worst internal fighting since the 1975–90 Civil War. "For the first two days, the army was targeting Fatah al-Islam, so people sympathized with the army," Muna said, "but then they started bombing the camp. The firing didn't stop for a moment. Many civilians were killed because people didn't take precautions. There was no food, water, or electricity, no big hospitals in the camp or even much medicine in the clinics so people started suffering very quickly."

The PFLP and DFLP organized a camp demonstration. "One part of it went to the Fatah al-Islam areas," Muna said, unpacking another cigarette, "and the other went to the army's. But the bombardment increased and people were killed while they marched." The protest had called for a cease-fire and a negotiated exit for Fatah al-Islam. Instead, the army displaced the camp's residents.

"It wasn't only the bombardment," she added with a sweeping gesture. "People were injured or killed as they tried to get water when the UNRWA brought in supplies. Also Hamas and Fatah were telling people to leave. Hamas was trying to persuade Fatah al-Islam to go too. The Popular Front tried to save the camp, but when I saw that people hadn't been convinced, I left with them on the fourth day." Some refugees escaped during the cease-fire that day; others stayed put. Muna said, "Every two or three days, they'd briefly cease fire to let ambulances take out the wounded—and the Red Crescent bring in food and medicine. But sometimes the injured couldn't be moved. The bombing destroyed large residential areas of the camp."

Muna went to stay with friends in another camp until the bombardment ended. Watching the fighting on television was "a tension that can't be described," she said coolly. "We spent days and nights not sleeping." The only way she could relax was by campaigning against the fighting. "I found myself obliged to work with NGOs to relieve the displaced people's suffering," she said. Muna returned to Nahr el-Bared with the first group to reenter the camp after the war. The damage was on the scale of "something like a tsunami or an earthquake," she said. "When I arrived at my home I couldn't recognize it. It had been destroyed by bombs—and so had the other houses. Everything was different." She estimated that in the old part of the camp 90 percent of the houses were destroyed.

"I had a feeling of depression," she said, "of being absent, and at the same time feeling that we had to work hard to fix the camp and make it like it was before, and the people too. We've gotten used to a violent life, to rebuilding our lives from the ruins. I see the camp as an obligation before returning home. There is no alternative. The alternative to the camp is a camp, nothing else."

Which factions are most popular in the camp today? I asked. "The NGOs," she replied mischievously. "They've taken this role because the political groups are prevented from working. In the north the DFLP is the first political power because during the disaster they provided services through friendly NGOs. People lost everything, and the NGOs helped them rebuild their homes. They provided relief, schools, and rubbish removal." It almost sounded like an NGO version of Hamas's "welfare, protection, and resistance" formula, I said. "NGOs are the most popular factions," Muna repeated with a tired smile, "which takes you to the DFLP."

Ehsan, 21,
Nawal, 46, and
Iman Fareiji, 20

Shatila Camp Residents

BEIRUT, LEBANON

Just neighbors Iman worked in a ladies' hairdressing salon. "I know how to cut hair and make it better," she told me. Her younger sister, Ehsan, was still studying and hoped to become an accountant. They were born in Beirut's Shatila camp, but because their father left them when Iman was just five months old, neither had an ID card. In Lebanon's infernally sectarian bureaucracy, they did not officially exist.

The patchy electricity in their squashed home came from a battery-operated generator. The walls were strangely empty too, apart from pictures of the Al Aqsa Mosque and a young man surrounded by a halo-like glow. Every few minutes, their sick grandfather would groan from the other side of the half-partitioned salon.

"We are from al-Shawka," the girls' mother, Nawal, told me above his cries. "In 1948 the British soldiers said that if we left the village for a day, we'd be able to come back. For sixty years we haven't been able to. They didn't kill us, but they pressured us to leave and took our food so we don't differentiate between them and the Jewish fighters." All three women were born in Shatila. "Everyone used to know each other here and relationships were very strong," Nawal said. "But most of the camp left during the war, and new people came. It's completely changed. I miss the old social life when we visited each other and ate together. There are always problems now."

Emotions in the razor-thin alley outside fluctuate with political developments. "Our neighbors are Lebanese Shi'a, and we try to avoid each other," Nawal said. "It's not a good relationship. They're just neighbors. Hezbollah thinks that we should support them against the followers of [Prime Minister] al-Hariri, who are Sunni Muslims. But Hariri's followers think we should be with them because we're also Sunni. We're not with either of them. We are Palestinians, *yani*." European Jews often faced similar situations during the past millennium. Unable to leave ghettos, sometimes living in close proximity to villagers who hated them, they lacked defenders and were vulnerable to atrocities.

In 1982, the Sabra and Shatila camps became global bywords for something similar. When Christian Phalangists entered the Shatila camp during the Israeli invasion, Nawal was in her home. She recalled, "My neighbors started shouting at us from the street, 'Leave Shatila! They're killing people! It's a massacre!' One neighbor from up the road said the Phalange had entered this valley and killed two brothers-in-law in front of her. Our family all just ran in different directions. I escaped to a nearby bunker, but then we didn't feel safe there so we went to the Red Crescent's Gaza Hospital in Sabra." But as Israeli soldiers lit the area with flares that helped the Phalange identify their targets, the hospital was attacked too.

Nawal had already decided to leave when she heard a weapons store explode outside. "Later I heard that all the people who stayed in the hospital were killed by the murderers," she said in a reverent staccato. "Some people returned on the second day, but the massacre went on for three days." The worst thing Nawal remembered seeing was the rape of a pretty blonde woman on the road. "Afterward they killed her and threw her away," she said. "There were dead bodies on the street, and they booby-trapped them with bombs so when people came to remove them, they were also killed."

While she talked, Iman and Ehsan left the room and some laughing children walked in. They looked around for a minute. Then their smiles faded, and they left too. It reminded me of family scenes during discussions about the Holocaust when I was a child. Such tales never end until they are finished. Nawal said that when she returned to the camp one week on, the stench of death was unbearable. It smelled "like animals that have been killed and left outside for a long time," she said. "You couldn't even breathe. You had to cover your mouth and nose when you moved around." Between 800 and 3,000 Palestinians were killed.

The Palestinians' trauma lasted for years in Shatila, Nawal said, and the community never had a chance to recover because fighting broke out again in 1985, one year after a multinational U.N. force withdrew. Perhaps thousands died in the "camps war" as Sunni gunmen fought to settle scores and seize Palestinian territory. But Nawal met her husband during this time. "He was a fighter in the DFLP," she said, "and during the camps war he defended Shatila." What impressed you about him? I ventured. "He just asked me to marry him," she shrugged. "He visited my parents, and they agreed. We only met because I helped the families who were cooking for the fighters."

After the war, Nawal's husband asked her to go to Jordan with him to register their marriage and get ID cards for their daughters. "In 1991 he went on his own and disappeared," she said blankly. "We don't have any contact. His daughters don't know him, but I heard that he married again in Jordan." In addition to taking care of two children, Nawal had to look after a sick mother and a disabled father, so she relied on her brothers in the building trade for support. "The main problem was how to buy and bring [home] milk and diapers for the girls," she said. "Later it was difficult to send them to school because they didn't have papers." Nawal, who has a Lebanese ID card, finally enrolled them in an UNRWA school under her name. "Even though it's not legal, UNRWA sometimes accepts people because they sympathize, but when they finish school the girls still need IDs to continue their lives." She called them back into the room.

But Iman and Ehsan were not at ease talking about the massacre. "I don't ask my mum about what happened," Iman said. "I don't like to hear about wars. I don't want to know about things that make me sad." Because the girls had no ID, they could not marry, work legally, buy a house, or even leave the camp. "At school when you sit for a test you feel uncomfortable," Iman said. "I'm afraid that if I even walked past the camp checkpoint they'd take me to jail." She tried not to let it destroy her life. "People help me," she added.

Ehsan rarely left the camp either. "The last time was when I went to take exams two weeks ago, but I can't remember the time before that," she said. "It was long ago. I just go to school and come home. It's a big problem if I need to go to the hospital because the first thing they ask you for is an ID. If you don't have one, they won't treat you. When I had an operation on my nose, my mum had to register me for it on her ID."

The most common argument against providing all Palestinians in Lebanon with citizenship rights was that it would normalize and tacitly recognize their expulsion. "I don't want to be a Lebanese!" Ehsan protested. "At least if they gave me an ID card, I'd feel like other Palestinians here." Her sister agreed. "I don't feel Lebanese at all," she said. To Iman, Palestine meant "yourself and everyone who protects you. It's very good there. Here, the Lebanese have guns and the Palestinian people are afraid of them. You just feel sadness and pain." So being a Palestinian is about being protected, I said. Iman agreed. "It's better to be in your homeland," Ehsan said. The girls sometimes talked to their family there by phone.

Return for Iman meant "a new world where you have your rights and lots of happiness." "We will find many students in our villages, and learn how to live in the world," she said. Her mother chimed in: "I'd even prefer to go back and live in a tent. It would feel safer than here. Even if it was the West Bank, I'd die to go back. At least we would be in our homeland." What does homeland mean to you? I asked Iman. "When you have your ID and your personality," she said. What do you think you will find there? I asked Nawal. "The most important thing," she replied confidently, "is just to return." The sofa, which initially felt comfortable, had grown hard and unyielding. We wound down the interview, and Nawal told me that I could photograph the family outside. Then she considered her neighbors' reaction and insisted that the picture be taken inside the house instead. She pinned a poster of the Al Aqsa Mosque above the door and embraced her family stiffly.

Marwan Shehadeh, 45

Web Manager

AMMAN, JORDAN

Without a father The margins of any society mark the limits of the center's imagination. They can represent an "other" against which identity is formed, a frame in which society develops, and over time, ideas that gestate there can transform the center itself. Palestine's murkiest borderland since September 11 has been the province of Salafi Jihadists, most notoriously Al Qaida. Palestinians are loath to talk up such groups—and play into post–September 11 narratives that Israel has skillfully manipulated. Jihadist groups were also small in numbers when I was researching this book. But as hopes of liberation and statehood declined their specter increasingly rose, especially in Gaza and Lebanon. I wanted to talk to someone from such a group to get a better understanding of their story—and how it connected to the broader Palestinian experience.

I first asked "Ibrahim," a friend in a camp militia to make discreet inquiries among one Salafist community. For months nothing happened. Then one day "Abu Khalifa," a man with a deep voice, called Ibrahim. He knew intimate details about Ibrahim's life and financial situation. He seemed to be speaking from a serene and noiseless place. Ibrahim had a bad feeling about him. Abu Khalifa offered him financial assistance and repeatedly asked, "Why are you helping this occupation?" I had never been called that before.

Abu Khalifa said he would meet me but only if I traveled alone—with no mobile phone, recording equipment, or camera—to a mountainous location he would name at a time of his choosing. I told Ibrahim this was too dangerous. He asked me how I felt about guns. Whether out of honor or boredom, Ibrahim suggested going to the interview armed, with a group of his comrades. The story was not that important, I said.

In June 2008 I was put in touch with Marwan Shehadeh by "Sari," a Palestinian and former radical Islamist who had gone to Iraq in 2003 to fight the Americans. On his return Sari had been arrested and tortured by Jordanian security forces. He still had the cigarette burns and a map of Palestine that an officer had carved into his arm to prove it. Marwan was involved with Al Qaida, he said, but he was safe. When Jordanian extremists tried to kidnap and kill two *New York Times* reporters he had brought to an interview Marwan had successfully defended them as guests. In person, Marwan introduced himself to me as a journalist, web manager, and founder of an NGO called the Vision Research Institute.

Marwan's sparsely furnished office was located next to the Al-Afghani souvenir shop in Amman. He had a way with words and seemed convivial, interrogative, and highly strung. He also had a disconcerting need for continuous eye contact when talking, and his sentences often became bland if I looked away. His father had worked as a chef for the British army, and after his family was expelled from the village of Artuf in 1948 he had joined the Jordanian army. Marwan was born in Zarqa—the same hometown as Humam Khalil al-Balawi, an Al Qaida "double agent" who killed seven CIA officers in Afghanistan—but he grew up on the Wadi Seer military base.

He said, "I decided early on that the roots of our struggle were religious—not national—because Israel was supported by the U.S. and the whole world, including Arab countries. So you needed a wide front to oppose Political Judaism—which is the Zionists, okay? We fight the Jew because they occupied our country. It is a religious duty for all Muslims to fight—Arabs and non-Arabs—because our religious laws say this. You understand me?" I kept his gaze and nodded. Despite his Manichean outlook and racist language, he seemed rational. He had worked as a marketing manager for twelve years, was a computer expert, and had studied communications before dropping out to fight in the Lebanon War.

In 1982 Marwan joined the Egyptian Islamic Jihad (aka Al-Jihad) after an invitation from a relative, Mohammed Abd-al Salam Faraj. Faraj had been sentenced to death the year before for his part in the assassination of the Egyptian president Anwar Sadat, but he escaped. Ayman al-Zawahiri would later lead Al-Jihad before becoming Osama Bin Laden's Number 2 in Al Qaida. But in those days Al-Jihad fought with Fatah against Israel. Marwan arrived in Lebanon via Syria and began training on the PLO's military bases.

"At first I panicked on the battlefield because I was only nineteen, but I started to get used to seeing people killed or injured by bombs," he said. "War is not easy *yani,* but I prefer to fight with an Islamic ideology because in the other life, I will go to a nicer place. You understand me?" I wanted to. "What is taken unjustly by force will not be returned by negotiations or peace agreements," he said. Were you injured in Lebanon? I asked. "I saw others injured, but myself no," he laughed. "There is nothing wrong with my body."

What were the most important lessons you took from the experience? I asked, expecting a philosophical reply. "Actually," Marwan replied, "I became a professional in gang war. I can use any kind of weapons, explosives, mines. They gave you intensive military courses so that you could use guns, machine guns, anti-tank missiles, and anti-aircraft missiles. At that time, they only had Sam 7 and Sam 9 missiles from the Syrians. We used what we called the anti-craft network—two big machine guns that were 37mm and 23mm. One could be used by many people, the other gave cover." Marwan's face was expressionless as he reeled off the menacing list. "It was an adventure issue," he said. "Maybe I couldn't do it now because I'm forty-five years old."

But the idea of building one big pan-Arab Islamic caliphate was gaining popularity among younger Palestinians. "The national groups have been weakened by their failure to achieve anything," he explained. "They became resistance movements without the resistance. Their only call was for political activities and peace solutions. This led to disjointedness, weakness, and lies. Ask any Arab child, 'Do you trust the peace solution?' and they will tell you, 'No.' It is the Jew mentality to keep shifting from one point to another without closing any subject." What was his alternative strategy? "To continue with Islamic resistance," he said. "A Gaza faction called Jaish al-Umma has launched about forty-five military attacks against Israel this year, and the Army of Islam that kidnapped [BBC journalist] Alan Johnson has a pure Islamic ideology. They are very close to Al Qaida, but they aren't strong enough to join them yet."

"They are even debating these ideas inside Hamas," he claimed. "Hamas is a moderate Islamic group that accepts the political power game—negotiating with Israelians and the two-state solution—but its roots are with Sayed Qutb. So Hamas has an internal struggle between the Izzedine al-Qassam Brigades that are very close to Jihadist Salafism and the traditional political leadership." Marwan thought that "circumstances will influence people to rise up for Salafism in Gaza." His analysis was subsequently confirmed by an Al Qaida–style declaration of a caliphate in Rafah in 2009 that sparked fighting that left twenty-five people dead. As I was editing the book, a church bombing in Alexandria on New Year's Day 2011 killed twenty-three

Christian worshipers. The Egyptian government blamed the Army of Islam. Reports continued to suggest that between 2,500 and 3,000 Jaljalat armed Salafist fighters were operating inside and outside the Izzedine al-Qassam Brigades in Gaza. In April 2011, Vittorio Arrigori, an Italian solidarity activist, was hanged by self-styled Jihadists in Gaza.

According to Marwan, Al Qaida would "be happy if Hamas goes directly to a peace solution. Then the people will choose Al Qaida directly because their discourse is pure, stronger than Hamas's, and closer to the public." Marwan said he was not a member of Al Qaida, and I took his estimation in that spirit. Within Jordan, "many refugees" were being recruited by Osama Bin Laden's organization, he said. "Al Qaida is the only group implementing military actions, okay? And they target the regimes as well as Israel."

But how can radical Islam unite Palestinians when it doesn't even support a Palestinian state? I asked. "Salafi Jihadists don't care to kick the occupation out," Marwan replied. "Their main target is an Islamic state, a *khilafa* [caliphate]. That's why so many Palestinians were killed in Afghanistan. We'd like to return to an Arab world without visas and borders like in the European Community. We want a *khilafa* with moderation and development because it gives us strength."

Al Qaida is actually a fringe of a fringe, a violent outrider of the overwhelmingly peaceful Salafist (Sunni) religious current that aims for a renaissance of early Muslim thought. But Al Qaida's strategy proposes seven more or less violent stages along the way to a caliphate, from awakening to eye-opening, a moving-on period when there would be attacks, and an arising period characterized by conflict in countries such as Syria, Turkey, and Israel. When I asked Marwan how close he thought Al Qaida was to an "arising," he replied, "This is what we are optimistic will be executed on the ground, but you don't know. In Iraq, Al Qaida became weaker. The interesting thing is that it was the first time an Islamic group had developed a strategy, and many of their steps happened in reality, okay?"

Hezbollah was now more of a threat to Israel than Al Qaida—Marwan conceded that. But don't the vast majority of Palestinians also see Al Qaida as a threat to them? I asked. "It's not easy to destroy the ideology, forms, and factions of a national identity that led the resistance for thirty to forty years," he replied. "You need time, but this leadership will transform people toward Salafism." And what would that mean for Palestinian traditions such as dabke dancing? "This is nothing," Marwan said. "It's a folklore issue. One of Al Qaida's big mistakes in Iraq was to come to a Ba'athist environment and warn people not to wear glasses or watch satellite TV. This will not work. To change from being a revolutionary movement to a state, you need political transformations through religious fatwas that match the time, place, and people."

Marwan saw no conflict of interest between his views and his journalism. But I told him that his admiring descriptions of the late leader of Al Qaida in Iraq, Abu Musab al-Zarqawi, as "the master" and "the prince of terror" in one article made me uneasy. "We Arabs haven't had a clear identity or trusted leadership for the last hundred years," he responded. "We feel that we are without a father, without any identity to lead us, because the Arab world is divided. In our deep thoughts we respect strong leaders and people who sacrifice themselves to resist occupation. Even if I don't totally agree with Abu Musab's approach, I deal with him as a hero."

Al-Zarqawi's bombing of three Amman hotels—which killed sixty people—had been "a strategic mistake," he said. He cited a terse letter from Ayman al-Zawahiri to al-Zarqawi censuring Al Qaida in Iraq for its massacres of Shi'a Muslims to illustrate his point that within Al Qaida there was sometimes "a dispute between mentors and military leaders." "Abu Musab was a leader," he explained, "but Ayman al-Zawahiri has more wisdom. He knows that killing Shi'as restricts Al Qaida's progress in Iraq."

For Marwan, Jihad was legitimate, but it depended on the situation. He believed in democracy, non-violence, and elections too, but, he averred, "sometimes you need power to protect your achievements." The day before, Sir Hugh Orde, chief of the Northern Irish police, had suggested negotiations with Al Qaida. "About which issue?" Marwan held his palms out and laughed. The British government would not meet Al Qaida preconditions such as prisoner releases, he said. They had done so before with the IRA, I countered. "They are cleverer than the Americans in dealing with Al Qaida," he agreed.

The day was growing late. September 11 was "a terrible attack," Marwan went on. "I'm also against killing Jewish civilians, and this was one of Al Qaida's mistakes. Even if they wanted to pull America into an open war it was a terrible accident really. Even the train accident in London has not happened [before] in the whole of Islamic history." The "train accident" was in fact a series of suicide bombings on London's Underground and buses that killed fifty-six people. A burly, short-haired, and fresh-shaven man in a striped sweater entered the room and took a seat. Marwan introduced me, beaming. The man looked like a bouncer.

Did you fight again after 1982? I asked. "No," Marwan said. "We have a different, political struggle against the Jordanian regime. I have been arrested and tortured." There was a second knock at the door, and a trim, bespectacled, middle-aged man entered. He had wisps of black hair lacquered over his bald head. "They use sticks to hit you on your legs and the soles of your feet," Marwan continued, still smiling. "They tie you up with ropes by the knee and raise them as they hit you. This is normal in Jordan. But they only use torture for Al Qaida members."

The suited man sat beside me, fidgeting anxiously and perspiring under the air-conditioner. Marwan said he was the author of a forthcoming "encyclopedia about the Palestinian Holocaust." The man tried to grin but seemed distressed, like an accountant working for the mob. Marwan suggested an interview with him but cautioned that I would need a translator because he was "not good enough to express himself." It was an uncomfortable moment that I found difficult to read. "I can understand everything," the man said in English, "but I cannot express anything."

Sami Mahmoud Khader, 45

Zoo Curator

QALQILYA, WEST BANK

The memory of the animal   Palestine has a dearth of civic treasures outside Jerusalem. Few cultural institutions have outlived the generations that created them. But perhaps the most affecting individual modern landmark is the Qalqilya Zoo, a kitsch design riot of stuffed animals, dinosaur models, and space exhibits that vie with the bears, crocodiles, kangaroos, lions, leopards, and monkeys for attention. The zoo's animals have also been victims of Israeli invasions, and the park has become an offbeat symbol of pride and resilience. More than anything, it is Sami Khader's mindscape—absurd, macabre, exhilarating, and hewn from that most precious of national assets, the imagination.

You needed mental resourcefulness to survive in Qalqilya. The West Bank wall had separated the city from Israel—and Qalqilyans from their land. "It's complete cover," Sami said, "all the way around, full circle, the biggest jail in the world." But it was not always like this. In 2005 after Yasser Arafat's death and before the wall was built, Israel opened the city's gates for a year. Arab Israelis flocked to shop in a cheaper economy. "Big shopping malls opened at this time," Sami said. "They were destroyed when Israel closed the gate because they're so expensive and Palestinians don't like to buy from them." As things stood, Qalqilyans mostly bought cheap Israeli products that came off a special line renowned for its poor quality. The zoo was a "cage within a cage," and the bigger enclosure was subject to Israeli whims that prevented free movement outside. "This is bad psychology for the people," Sami said.

Sami's father, a pharmacist, fled to Qalqilya from Jaffa in 1948. He stayed for ten years and then moved to Saudi Arabia. Sami only knew Jaffa from black-and-white movie reels and, later, from fishing trips that lasted until dusk, before the Second Intifada. "Return is a big word," he said. "Streets, buildings, and everything there have changed now. My grandfather kept the key to his house as—what do you call it?" A memory, I said. "Just for memory, yeah," he continued, "because it cannot open any door there." Out of pain and shame, his grandfather's generation had rarely talked about 1948. "Most of them tried to forget," he said.

Unlike them, Sami grew up in a physical and cultural desert about a hundred miles from Dahran in Saudi Arabia. He had nothing to forget. Feeling Palestinian but unable to openly communicate any national affiliation, he went to small meetings where Palestinians remembered the old country. "When you cross the [King Hussein] bridge to Jordan, I don't want to say you forget what happens here, but you are made forgetful," he said. "The pace of life makes people run and work just to get money." One of Sami's sharpest memories was of finding a dying cat in the street when he was ten. "I like cats," he said "the small shape of them. They come close and ask you, 'Show me some love,' so you have to. I did my best to give this cat water and food, but it died in my arms. It was so sad." To "solve these problems," Sami said he eventually became a taxidermist and veterinarian in Saudi Arabia.

His journey to Palestine began with his wife. They met on one of Sami's visits to Palestine in 1988. The courtship lasted three days. "It was a very fast marriage," he laughed. "Love at first sight. Maybe we can record it in the Guinness record book?" Sami had never before met his wife—a cousin from his Qalqilya family—but she was keen for them to move to Qalqilya. In 1996, when Sami returned to facilitate his visa application, he bumped into the zoo's manager and offered to stuff some animals for the zoo. "He sent a lion's head to my cousin's house," Sami said. "I fixed it, and then they gave me a broken elephant's skull. It was too heavy to take to the house so I came to the zoo." Within three years he was working there.

Sami liked stuffing animals—"after they're dead," he cautioned. "When I repair them, I'm happy. You see, when any artist starts to paint or draw, they sleep at night dreaming about it. It's the same for me. The animal dies, and you want to stuff it. You have to imagine inside the shape of this bird, how it will come [out]. Sometimes you want it to be eating, drinking, sleeping, or hanging, so you use your imagination." Sami was then working with a crocodile—"a dangerous thing," he said. "I concentrate on the important parts, the teeth, mouth, and tail." Taxidermy was not about keeping the animal's appearance alive, he said. "It's about keeping the memory of the animal alive."

Ultimately, the most difficult but rewarding animal he had stuffed was a giraffe. "Its skin is thick, and the stitching is very difficult," he explained. "If you want to slaughter this animal to remove the skin and put it in the fridge, it's difficult. Everything is difficult with this animal . . . " The giraffe was too heavy to move easily—or bring into the open for chemical treatment—so Sami had to strip off its skin in layers. "Also difficult!" he shouted. It could not have been emotionally easy either. Brownie the giraffe had formerly been a live zoo attraction.

Sami opened the story like a familiar prison door: "In 2002, one night the Israelis entered the city from the south and started shooting loudly. The road they took goes behind the giraffes' area, and Brownie was always nervous. He got so afraid that he started running around in circles; he didn't know where he wanted to go. He hit his head on an iron bar in his cage and fell down."

Because of the high pressure giraffes need to maintain blood flow to the brain, Brownie suffered brain damage during his fall and died soon after. "His wife came in the morning and saw that he was lying close to his daughter," Sami said. "Then she cried. I saw her tears. She stopped eating and drinking, and we were afraid for her because she was thirteen months' pregnant and two months from delivery. We sent her to her room for ten days and covered the walls with plastic—to make her forget the male—but for nothing. When we opened the gate, I thought she'd forgotten, but no. From sadness she aborted, and we lost the baby too. Last year she died." In a dark twist, Sami decided to stuff both Brownie and the fetus.

"These animals need a quiet place," he continued. "Sometimes I tell visitors not to play or be so loud. They want a quiet time. You can imagine what it's like if people start shooting or firing flares on parachutes that come down slowly." Among Sami's extraordinary range of museum artifacts, you could easily miss the cabinet display of tear gas canisters and sound bombs. They killed three zebras. "When the Israelis enter Qalqilya, the young men start throwing stones and the Israelis reply with tear gas. But one day, we came in and found that tear gas had landed in the zebras' area," Sami said and rubbed his neck. "You know these zebras are very strong animals, but they're also sensitive, so something like that can kill them very easily." Giraffes and zebras are expensive animals to obtain, and Sami was unable to find replacements. "Brownie was a big loss for us," he said. But his memory lives on. One zebra was also stuffed.

Sami's affections were not reserved for dead animals. He took one baby baboon to live in his house after its mother stopped giving it milk. "I started to care for him, and now he's alive," he said. "He's like my son. When I come to his cage, he jumps around happily and waits for me to open it, so he can play with me. They're very close to humans, monkeys, not like the lions." During the closures of the Second Intifada, Sami once brought two monkeys from Nablus to the zoo by ambulance. "I went as a sick man," he said brightly. "The only way to go anywhere from Qalqilya is by ambulance. Sometimes the driver charged me 150 shekels to get there." He still went to work by ambulance during curfews.

"During the Second Intifada, they stationed tanks in front of the zoo," Sami recalled. "Sometimes I walked very close to one tank. I can't imagine what the man sat inside was thinking. Maybe he'd kill you in a minute, right? So I entered and left through the back door." Visitors mostly stayed away in this period, and the zoo lost money. Its revenues came largely from the municipality, and most of the animals—some, like the lions, castrated so they could not reproduce—came from an Israeli safari outfit in Ramat Gan. "They try to help us," Sami said. "My relations with the vets and managers are good. From time to time I visit them." Palestine being Palestine, Sami's statement was apocryphal.

According to local lore, the zoo was founded in 1986 as a quid pro quo for the "help" that the town's mayor had given Israel. "When I came here they said the mayor built the zoo because he had a good relationship with Israel," Sami said. "I don't know about these relations, but imagine the city without a zoo! Who would come here? There's nothing here except the zoo, so this man did something very great. They say, 'Ah, he worked with the Israeli military command.' But he also built our stadium. They can't remember the good things he did for the city. They don't care for him now because he's finished." Is he dead? I asked. "No, I believe he lives in Israel," Sami replied.

The mayor gave Sami his break in Qalqilya in 1996 when, taken with his work on the lion's head and the elephant's skull, he asked him to build and design a museum for the zoo. Now it had three cavernous museums, themed around dinosaurs and space (replete with flashing red lights and wild noises), insect and plant life, and stuffed animal kitsch. Other features included massive animal skeletons that visitors must walk through, walls made of bones and skulls, huge models of scorpions and bees, and gruesome jars of animal organs. But there was also a Palestinian well in one hall and a space shuttle bedecked in the Palestinian flag in another. "This is a message," he said. "We are Palestinian, but we can do anything. Maybe in the future we'll go to space."

Sami designed and built all the exhibits. He changed the zoo's plan, removed old buildings, and built new ones. He brought in exotic animals, information signs, and new attractions. Crucially, he helped Palestinian children to see something of the world's wonders. "Maybe they've seen the zebra in pictures, but they won't forget seeing it in real life," he said. His priority was finding animals native to Palestine. "A man caught a hyena with a trap and brought it here," Sami said. "His paw was broken. It was a big, old injury, so I had to operate and remove part of this hyena's paw. He's alive now, living in the zoo."

Memory is a funny thing. Sami walked me to his house to show me the canaries he kept on the roof, but my recollections faded with time. Now I remember best a show of warm splendor from the peacocks on the zoo's walkways as we passed, a rash of bullet holes that had polka-dotted the concrete walls and metal lampposts around the zoo's entrance, dusty roads, sweet mint tea in Sami's living room, a bird cage with raggedy-looking tropical birds on the roof, and Sami gesturing forlornly toward his family's land on the wrong side of the wall, which they now could not reach. Most vividly I remember watching the crazed hyena that Sami saved as it compulsively ran in circles around its cage. With its furious eyes pegged open and gnashing teeth, it looked as if it was already anticipating an earthly afterlife.

The 1967 (Naksa) Generation

A *naksa* is a failure, and the Arab world's inability to defeat Israel in the Six Day War of 1967 changed the course of Palestinian history. The march to war was triggered by Egypt's unilateral closure of the Straits of Tiran, which separate the Red Sea from the Gulf of Aqaba, an Arab fact on the ocean that Israel's military could not countenance. The conflict ended with Israel in control of the Sinai Peninsula, the Golan Heights, the West Bank, and Gaza. But the commander of Israel's forces, Yitzhak Rabin, later traced the conflict's roots to the January 1964 Cairo conference of the Arab League. At this conference the "liquidation" of Israel was threatened if it continued to divert water from Jordan and Syria. More significantly, the Palestinian Liberation Organization was formed there under the auspices of the Arab League. Fatah had already been established in 1958, but the most determined Palestinian nationalists had then dispersed to the various Arab countries with a mission, patronage, and funding.

The abject defeat of Arab forces in June 1967 finally dispelled any illusions among Palestinians that Gamal Abdul Nasser's pan-Arabism—or any initiative from the wider Arab world—would liberate their homeland. The war led to another wave of Palestinian refugees reaching Jordan, but some of those who remained in the West Bank and Gaza paradoxically welcomed the direct Israeli occupation. For the first time since 1948, refugees could visit homes, cities, and fields in Israel that they had been expelled from. The PFLP fighter Aisha Odeh told me, "[The outcome of the war] was very difficult because Nasser was our ideal, and I had believed that he was so strong. When everything collapsed, we said, 'Now the Israelis have come to us. It is our chance to fight them.'"

If one wanted to apply the Kubler-Ross five stages model of recovery from grief—denial, anger, bargaining, depression, and acceptance—then 1967 may have ended Palestinian denial about the nature of the Nakba and presaged a storm of anger. Palestinian existence before 1967 had been obscured to the outside world and tarnished by defeat internally. But a new meaning now evolved, typified by the oft-photographed graffiti on a section of the West Bank Wall near Qalqilya: "To exist is to resist." Fedayeen training camps spread across Jordan. George Habash's Arab National Movement (ANM) reconstituted itself as a resistance organization, the Popular Front for the Liberation of Palestine, and a new leader/protector arose.

As Eyad al-Sarraj put it to me, "People were not sure what a 'pure' Palestinian identity was until Yasser Arafat took over the PLO. He actually embodied our national identity." Arafat charismatically strode the international stage as a guerrilla colossus and national father figure. It was no accident that many Palestinians felt orphaned when he died. The 1967 period, though, was one of despair followed by hope, unity, and growing confidence. The PLO's embrace of armed resistance slowly percolated into Palestinian civil society, augmented by the relevant passages of international law. Women entered academia for the first time, the economy improved, and after the Battle of Karameh in 1968 refugees walked a little bit taller.

Within the now-occupied territories of the West Bank and Gaza, there was shock when Israel emerged victorious after six days, as Egyptian radio had been broadcasting tub-thumping triumphalist propaganda for months. In Israel there was a different kind of astonishment, as newspapers there had stirred a sense of imminent catastrophe. On both sides of the Green Line, national religious movements were able to explain events more convincingly than politicians. Occupation brought Judaism to the forefront of Israeli politics and allowed Islam to open up new political possibilities in Palestine, for the *naksa* belonged first to the secular forces of Nasser in Egypt. Palestinians now had a new responsibility.

Israel's conquest of Jerusalem, the third most holy city in Islam, offered an affront—and a challenge—to Palestinians and to the Arab world as a whole. For centuries, Jerusalem had been central to the character of the Arabs of Palestine as a trading center, pilgrimage site, spiritual and cultural hub, and national capital. It united the Bedouin of the Negev with the fishermen of Jaffa. Protecting it was and is to some extent a matter of national honor. With Jerusalem had come custodianship of a place, an idea—the birthplace of the three monotheistic religions—and, after 1967, the last bastion of pan-Arab resistance to the West, as well as Palestine's most vital connection to the outside world. Symbolically and actually—because of Jerusalem's status in the Muslim world—the restrictions Israel gradually imposed on worshipers at the Al Aqsa Mosque were felt as something much greater. Religious Jews had already established a presence in East Jerusalem before the first settlements in the West Bank had begun to bloom.

Hamid Bitawi, a Hamas religious leader and MP who returned from religious studies in Jordan during the 1970s, complained to me, "I used to make speeches as an imam in Al Aqsa that lasted an hour, but now I can't reach it. I was arrested the last time I visited the Al Aqsa compound five months ago. I was one of the guys who were trying to make peace in Al Aqsa after Sharon's visit [in September 1999, which sparked the Second Intifada]. I was seen on television shouting at people not to throw stones. Although I am from Hamas, I don't want violence. We are not going to destroy Israel and Zionism, but we will defend ourselves."

The 1967 generation was highly motivated and entrusted with a calling—and place in the world—that still resonates in coffee shops and casbahs. It made several breakthroughs and achievements—most significantly, the PLO—without achieving liberation. The West Bank and Gaza had been relatively homogeneous societies, with few social or factional divisions, when they were conquered. Political currents and movements were concentrated among émigré communities in Arab countries. Until 1967, organizing openly had not felt safe for West Bankers, Gazans, or for Arabs in Israel, who lived under a state of emergency until 1966. It would take time for Palestinians to come to terms with the new regime—its oppressions and occasional freedoms to travel and work—before an authentic national response could be formulated. The *thawra* had already begun by the time of the 1967 war, but it would not reach critical mass until the 1970s.

Leila Khaled, 64

PFLP Fighter

AMMAN, JORDAN

Be friends Few people could wear her mystique with such an air of reluctant grace. A fearsome terrorist to Israelis, Leila Khaled is also an outlaw icon and inspiration to generations of Palestinian women the world over, partly because of the success of her autobiography. Leila hijacked two planes without killing anybody. She blazed a fighting path for women—embodying modernity as she went—and more than anything, she announced Palestine to a world in flux. She lived in an affluent but anonymous suburb of Amman.

Leila's father moved to Haifa from Lebanon during World War I, and she remembered him allowing Fedayeen messages to be passed in his café in 1948. As the fighting of the Nakba intensified, Leila's mother decided to take the children to stay with her family in Tyre in southern Lebanon until the war subsided. Leila, who had just turned four years old, dug in her heels. "One of the neighbors found me in the kitchen, hiding behind a big basket of dates that my father had bought," she said. "When they asked me why, I said, 'I'm afraid the Jews will take the dates.'" Much of their eventual journey to Lebanon was spent crying. "All the way," Leila said, "we saw refugees walking."

Leila's Lebanese childhood was unhappy and deprived. "My mother planted the idea in us that we must return to live better," she said. "So the Jews took our land. Our houses are still waiting for us." Their home and café had in fact been seized by Jewish forces after the family left Haifa—and Leila's father was arrested. He suffered a heart attack after being deported to what Leila called "a concentration camp" in Egypt. Seven months later he returned to Lebanon by boat in disguise. He was never granted Lebanese citizenship and died a broken man.

The Khaleds did not feel at home in Tyre. "We kept our Palestinian accents and were pointed at as refugees. The children, our neighbors, everyone was waiting to return," Leila said. When her older brother joined the Arab National Movement, Leila and her sisters followed suit, despite her mother's fears about their working so closely with men. Leila had wanted to be an engineer, but in 1967 she dropped out of an agricultural studies course to help her family financially by teaching in Kuwait. The next year, she joined the newly formed PFLP.

At that time, according to Leila, "the whole atmosphere was with the revolution. You saw different classes—engineers, doctors, workers, and farmers—in the PFLP, but we were focused on the camps because class differences diminished there." The party instructed her to organize in Kuwait, and she recruited new members there until 1969, when she left for a Jordanian training camp. "I learned how to use guns, pistols, hand grenades, and I think some tactics," Leila said. "It lasted about twenty days." The camp was segregated by gender to help more women from the occupied territories feel comfortable. "We were about 20 out of 150 or 200 people," she said. "We trained as women together."

In 1969 Leila was ordered back to Lebanon. At a meeting with the PFLP leader, Wadi Haddad, she was asked whether she was ready to die or be jailed. She answered yes to both. "Then Wadi said, 'Are you ready to hijack a plane?'" Leila recalled. "I started laughing because 'hijacking' was new terminology. I thought [he meant] that I would have a plane on my shoulder, and everyone would be [chasing after me]. I said, 'Yes, I'm ready for anything.'" About three thousand Palestinians were in Israeli jails then. "I'd read about their torture and would have done anything to help release them," she said. The second goal was "to ring a bell for the world, to ask the question, 'Who are the Palestinians?'" "I told Wadi the world knew about us," she continued. "He said, 'No, we are dealt with only as refugees who need humanitarian aid. They don't know we have a political cause.'"

During Leila's preparations for the hijacking of TWA flight 840 from Rome to Athens, she was strictly instructed not to injure any passengers or staff. "It should be clean," she said. "I met my comrade who went to Rome to hijack the plane because Yitzhak Rabin was expected to be on board. I was just told that an Israeli VIP we could do an exchange with would be on the plane. So we went." In her intensely focused state, two human encounters on the bus to the plane forced her to examine the morality of what she was about to do.

"There was a girl with a T-shirt with very small writing on it that said, 'Be friends.' I wanted to tell her, 'I would like to be your friend too.' I looked at her and remembered when I was a child how we were treated in the camps. In just one second, a scene came into my mind like a film in front of my eyes. It was summer in a tent school, and one of the children was sick. He was vomiting blood because he had been walking in the rain. I wanted to tell her that we lived a very miserable life but that we'd like to be friends. I couldn't say it of course."

"A man sat beside me," Leila continued. "He asked, 'Where are you from?' At that moment I couldn't think. I said, 'Guess.' He said, 'Cyprus? Spain? Israel?' I said, 'Where are you from?' He told me he was Greek and was living in Chicago. He was coming to visit his mother after fifteen years. I remembered my father. In 1963 he had been given permission to meet his mother at the Mendelbaum Gate in Jerusalem. He waited for three days and nights with presents for her, but she didn't show up because the Israelis didn't tell her he was there." He never saw her again before she died. "This man began to speak again. He said, 'Are you from Bolivia?' I said, 'Yes! How did you know?' He said, 'From the book you're reading.' I had a book about Che Guevara. So we got on the plane. He went to his place, and I went to mine." In Palestine there is a saying, "Good morning dear neighbor, you are in your house and I am in mine." It means "Mind your business."

Leila described the hijacking itself in functional terms. "It wasn't difficult to take over because if you hold a hand grenade over the head of a pilot—and my comrade had a pistol—he would accept it. We were sitting in first class, and it was easy to get up and walk to the cockpit. When we arrived, I asked the pilot, 'Do you know what this is?' He said, 'Yes, it's a hand grenade.' I said, 'Yes, it's a hand grenade,' and I pulled the pin out. I told him, 'Take it as a souvenir.' He didn't accept, of course, and I said, 'You and the passengers will be safe if you listen to us. We're not going to harm you.' They were only concerned with the safety of the plane and the people on board it."

Much of Leila's role involved explaining over a loudspeaker who the hijackers were and why they had taken over the plane. She told the passengers to go to economy class, where the stewards would give them food and water. "At the same time I had to speak to the control towers along the way," she said. "But when we reached Palestine, at about ten thousand feet, I told the pilot to turn around and fly over Haifa so we could see it. We were visiting our land, and Salim, my comrade, was also from Haifa. We told the crew that we didn't know this city we were born in. So we turned three times over Tel Aviv, looking at it. My father was dead, but at that moment I saw him smiling, as if he was content that it was the right way. Then I gave the pilot a map showing the route to Damascus. He asked if there was an airport there. 'Of course,' I said, 'but it is a new one.' We were the first plane to land there."

Leila felt no regret about her action. "I felt that I was doing what I'd been asked to, the way we were taught, and it was successful. We didn't hurt anyone. Of course, there was panic among the passengers. We knew that would happen. They had nothing to do with the conflict, and we apologized on behalf of our people when we landed. The Syrians gave them food, and they left the next day. Of course, Israel refused to negotiate with the PFLP. They would only negotiate with a country—Syria—through the Red Cross. There were six Israelis on the plane, four women and two men. We didn't know which ones they were. They released the women directly, and after forty-five days the Israelis released thirteen prisoners, including two Syrian pilots, for those four men."

If your lives had been threatened, or the operation's success had been jeopardized, could you have killed somebody? I asked. "No," Leila answered definitively. "We were sure that nobody was going to attack us. There were no security men on the plane. But we also had very strict instructions not to hurt anyone, even though we had pistols. I didn't use mine because I had to carry a microphone in one hand and the grenade in the other." Yet she still pulled out the grenade's pin.

After the hijacking, Leila's face quickly became iconic around the world as a symbol of the Palestinian revolution. She had plastic surgery—"to change some of my facial features"—and went through six months of transformation. "At first it didn't work, so I had to repeat it and make major changes," she said. "I just told the doctor that I wanted to marry my fiancé who lived in Europe, and I couldn't see him because I was wanted by Interpol. He accepted that and made some changes here." She motions to her chin, nose, and forehead. "He said, 'I'm a doctor who beautifies people; I don't make them uglier.' I said, 'Never mind.' Maybe he realized afterward that I wasn't getting married, but he was involved and he was afraid, so he did it. I came out looking as if I'd had an accident, with bruises. I changed a lot. Only people who knew me by face recognized me." How did she feel when she looked in the mirror afterward? "I was just happy to do it," Leila said. "When George Habash saw me he was furious because [my next job] was supposed to be in Palestine. I said, 'If one is to die [it is better] not to be known.'"

By the second attempted hijacking of El Al flight 219 from Amsterdam to New York a year later, in September 1970, airport security measures had tightened—and so had the risks to the PFLP. "We knew the Israelis had armed security on the plane," Leila said. "That's why there were supposed to be four of us there." But two of the hijackers were not able to board. Still, she and a Nicaraguan revolutionary, Patrick Arguelo, proceeded according to their plan—as a married Honduran couple.

On the plane, "the minute we stood up there was shooting from the security men behind us," Leila remembered. "Patrick told me, 'Go ahead, I'll protect your back.' I ran for the cockpit door, but it was closed. Somebody had looked through the magic eye. I was telling a hostess that I had unpinned grenades, but they would not open the doors. So I threatened very loudly—because of the engines—'If you do not open the door, I will blow up the plane.' I didn't get an answer. People were screaming. I was hit on the head from behind, and I fell down. I thought that we were being thrown out in the air, but when I opened my eyes I found people just hitting and kicking me. I was trying to protect my hand, and I don't know what happened." She was still holding the grenade. For the first time, Leila's voice cracked as she related the experience.

"Suddenly the pilot landed, and I was tied up," she said. "I thought, 'Where are the hand grenades?' I saw Patrick lying there, bleeding. He'd been shot, but he wasn't dead. Then a man came with a pistol, put his foot on top of him, and shot four bullets into his back. Another man came with a bottle and smashed it over his head. I thought they would shoot me too. There was nothing I could do. I was tied up, and these two men put their feet over my body." But they did not shoot. It was reported that Arguello was shot after he had himself shot and wounded an air steward, Shlomo Vider.

After landing, "I was fainting," Leila said, "because I could feel my ribs cracking and breaking. Somebody said, 'Catch her!' and threw me from the plane. I was put in a car. Patrick was there with an oxygen mask on his face. I was just thinking, you know, 'What happened?' The policewoman said he passed away and took the mask. I was crying and screaming at them until they untied me. I was saying in Arabic, 'Why did you die? I should have died! I'm the Palestinian.' Then I remembered that he didn't understand Arabic, so I said the same words to him in English. Before we'd got on the plane, I'd told him, 'I am Leila Khaled. I have experience here,' because the other two had not come. It was a very sad moment for me."

In the days that followed Leila was held in a British jail cell while negotiations took place to resolve what became known as the Dawson's Field hijacking. She developed an intriguing relationship with the detective from Scotland Yard who had been assigned to interrogate her, which could one day form the basis of a fascinating play. Two seized planes landed on that

Jordanian airstrip the day Leila was captured. A third—commandeered by the PFLP hijackers who had been prevented from boarding the El Al flight—eventually landed in Cairo, while a fourth plane hijacked three days after Leila's capture also landed at Dawson's Field. Most of the 310 passengers were freed on September 11. The next day, the PFLP blew up the planes in pictures that were beamed around the world. Four days later King Hussein declared martial law, and Black September began. At the end of the month, Nasser died in Egypt. Leila was freed two days after that.

Looking back, she saw the *thawra* period as an inevitable outcome of the *naksa*. "It was a unique situation when this revolution broke from outside—not inside—Palestine," she said. "People had waited a long time since 1948 for Palestine to be liberated—especially by Nasser's regime in Egypt—and instead, after 1967, they found that it was all occupied. The defeat was the responsibility of the Arab regimes. We expected their support. We didn't have any choices." The initial convergence of fighters in Jordan happened, she said, because "it was our right to use Arab lands to fight in Palestine. Most of the refugees had come to Jordan, and at 650 kilometers, the borders between Jordan and Israel were also the longest."

"We needed some Arab country that could protect the revolution. But the revolution also had to defend itself—from Israel and Arab regimes like Jordan." Fighters thus had to be armed. "Not all Arabs accepted the revolution," she admitted. "The DFLP wanted to overthrow the regime, and that was not the PLO's goal. Unfortunately, some armed fighters walked around Amman in their uniforms, which was a threat to the regime. They used the hijackings as an excuse."

Leila remained convinced that democratic revolutions in countries such as Jordan, Egypt, and Saudi Arabia would help the Palestinian struggle. "Those regimes weakened the Palestinian revolution," she said. When I mentioned that Hamas would not call for such revolts, she chuckled to herself, "Of course, they don't criticize the regimes," and lit a cigarette.

Leila was still active in the PFLP and sat on the Palestinian National Council, the PLO's legislative body. The divisions in Gaza had been "disastrous," she said. "Throughout history, even if factions had different positions, we were taught that arms were only for use against the enemy." Without unity in action, revolution would only re-create autocratic regimes in the worst regional traditions, she argued. Leila abhorred Oslo as a dead end that legitimized Israeli colonization. But the one-state solution she fought for "will take generations" now, she felt, because "Israel is not ready for any kind of coexistence." Thus she supported an interim 1967 borders Palestinian state.

But the world around Leila had changed, and it would be strange if she had not changed with it. She balked when I asked her opinion of the September 11 attacks. "In all our hijackings over three years we didn't hurt anyone," she insisted. "You can't compare what we were doing with what happened in New York. We declared who we were, what our intentions were and why. To this day, nobody knows for sure who those people were, or why they did it. It was a terrorist act." She took a long drag from her cigarette. "We didn't hurt anybody," she said again. "We did it cleanly."

The atmosphere as we talked on Leila's beige sofa had been calm, almost pacific. Looking around, there seemed little in her salon to distinguish it as hers. No pictures of her sons. Apart from her little dog, I noted two African dolls, a ceremonial sheesha pipe, photographs of George Habash in front of a red Palestine, one tile from her family's house in Haifa, and a "God Bless This Home" sign hanging over the front door. That too felt like a station on her journey.

Abu Adel, 64

Sulha *Committee Judge*

EAST JERUSALEM,
WEST BANK

Lost Abu Adel lived in Casa el-Badria, one of Jerusalem's "seven palaces." It was a grand old Oriental building with decorative arches. His family's butcher shop was next door. Abu Adel left school when he was sixteen to help his father run it. During World War I his father had been blinded by a bullet to his brow. "He died in 1980, and my mother was so very sad that she died fifteen minutes later," he said.

Abu Adel did not want East Jerusalem to be given over to a Palestinian government. "I say, 'No, no, no!'" he shouted, his hands shaking. "And I ask God not to let it happen. Palestinians don't have a constitution, law, or any rights. I have a friend in Gaza I know from my butcher shop. When Israel left I called to ask how it was with the PA in control. He told me, 'Don't throw rocks at the Israeli jeeps. Throw flowers! And if the Israelis want to leave Jerusalem one day, hold onto them by their legs!' Much as he hated the West Bank Wall for stifling his business, Abu Adel could not live on the other side of it. "God forbid," he said. "Even if I had to live on bread and onions I would stay here. I don't want to live with the Palestinians."

Abu Adel had four brothers and was neither the eldest nor the youngest. It is said that the middle child is a negotiator, and Abu Adel always had what he called "a hobby of making peace between people." In Palestinian society, family disputes were traditionally resolved by tribal *sulha* courts, and in 1988 he decided to form one in Jerusalem. "I was the judge," he said. "It was the beginning of the First Intifada, and our community wanted to avoid using Israeli courts."

A *sulha* judge needs to be a well-mannered believer in God, Abu Adel informed me. "I was not paid profits or commissions," he said. "I made peace for God's sake. Whenever I saw fire, I turned it down. That was my interest. I inherited it from my father. He was always at peace with people around him." The committee heard cases ranging from killings to family, marital, and neighborly disputes. "For example," he almost yelled, "if a girl was caught in an unmarried relationship, I would find the guy and help make them marry officially." He dealt with ninety-four such cases. "In all of them the girls were married obligatorily," he said. They were either pregnant or from conservative families that were unaware of their relationships. If he had not intervened they would have been killed, he asserted.

The *sulha* formula was straightforward: "We mediate between the families. The government deals with the criminal side. But as tribes, we talk with the families to prevent more murders and make *hudnas* [truces]." "When I bring happiness to families," he said, "when I see a mother going back to her family, when I intervene and stop a fight involving four hundred people, I feel that I'm fighting evil." This sounded grandiose, but Abu Adel was not above feelings of self-importance. "I hold the highest position in the Supreme Court of Jerusalem!" he bragged at one point. The *sulha* judge, like the *mukhtar,* is a respected leader in traditional Arab societies, and one that successive waves of Jewish settlers—and Palestinian autocrats—have used as a middleman, salesman, or buttress. But *sulha* judges should never challenge the legislature. When some Israeli Jews began using his court, Israel's security services were alerted, and in 1996 Abu Adel's house was searched after rumors circulated that he had been appointed by the PLO. The authorities' attitude changed when they learned that his committee was actually competing with a PLO court run by his brother. "The Israeli police in Jerusalem gave me this certificate because I made their workload lighter," Abu Adel said proudly, proffering a signed paper with a still-shaking hand. "It's a letter of gratitude for my cooperation from the chief of the Jerusalem police." They even started to send work his way, he said.

Abu Adel also had letters of thanks from the (Jewish) mayor of Jerusalem, municipal offices, and an Israeli TV company. "And I have been nominated for the $3,000 Teddy Kolleck prize for the most dedicated members of the public!" he added. Have you ever been called a collaborator? I asked. "Yes," he answered plainly, "many times. My response is always the same: 'Show me proof that I caused harm to any person.'" While he admitted to being "a bit respected or well known in the Israeli security world," he flatly denied working with the police "to prevent violence."

"I don't feel that there is any danger in this position, because I am true with people," he said. But in the 1990s he was kidnapped twice by his elder brother, who was also a judge. "He was paid for it," Abu Adel said, "and this means that he was not clean. It was like business. People trusted me, and they didn't trust him, so he was jealous. He threatened me, 'If you don't stop this work you will find trouble.' He had a friend in Palestinian intelligence who told him that I was working with the Israeli police because they'd visited my house to get my signature as a witness in honor cases." As a result, Abu Adel was arrested in Ramallah, drugged, blindfolded, and interrogated for six days.

Soon after his release, he was seized again in Hebron "for the same reason," he said. This time, though, "they threw me down a well and left me there. It was frightening because they tied my hands and took my clothes off, so I was naked. I was very cold." Abu Adel compared his story to that of Joseph in the Bible. He was saved, he told me, when some local goatherders found him. "I think my brother behaved like Joseph's brother because he blamed me for his lack of income," he said.

But there was also a political dimension. "My brother was involved with the PA and the PLO," Abu Adel backed into the story again. "They hire people in East Jerusalem who sometimes make problems by taking control of everything." Still he was loath to condemn them. "My father taught me to 'hold your tongue on countries,'" he said. It sounded almost Hasidic. "I'm not involved in the PLO or PA," he continued. "I would rather have a confederation with Jordan because Hamas and Fatah are always fighting each other." With Jordan, Israel, and the Palestinians sharing Jerusalem, "the country will be like Switzerland and the people will be happy," he believed.

The question of how he defined himself seemed odd to Abu Adel. "I am lost," he replied loftily. "Not Jewish, or Palestinian, or Israeli. I can't get an Israeli passport and the Jordanian *laissez passé* I have is unhelpful." He said that "a huge percentage of people here wish for Israeli passports"—and so did he: "I would be treated better and could travel more easily."

When I asked about his family's experience during the Nakba, he asked, "What Nakba?" before rebalancing himself. "You mean in 1948? I was only four years old and my father was blind, so I didn't have any special . . . " He lost his thread. Did your family ever talk about it? I asked. "No," he said. "No one in my family resisted or faced anything. They were poor." What about 1967? Abu Adel sighed, "We were forced in 1967 to get into this [country], so as someone would say in Arabic, 'He who took my mother is my uncle.'" He looked very sad. "One camel left and another camel took its place," I said, repeating an old Bedouin saw. Abu Adel nodded and belly-laughed softly to himself.

Mustafa al-Kurd, 63

Musician

EAST JERUSALEM,
WEST BANK

A stone, an onion, and a bucket of water   "I wanted to get to the heart of the music and live in it," said Mustafa with a flourish. As a young man, his dream had been to play a musical instrument like the oud. With his black beret, beard, red scarf, and fine wooden oud, Mustafa now looked like a man whose dream had come true. He could have been a troubadour at a sixties benefit gig. His ever-present wife, Helga, a left-wing East Berliner, was just the red star on the cake. But Mustafa did not look contented. He had traveled a long way in life and returned to where he began. You could call him a reverse refugee.

When Israel invaded East Jerusalem at the start of the 1967 war, he immediately left Nablus where he had been working as a blacksmith to return to his hometown. "I came in a service taxi, but the driver would only take us as far as Jalazun, north of Ramallah," he said, looking up to the skies as though expecting a thunderbolt. "I wanted to get to the Old City where my mother, sisters, and one brother were living so we walked to Shu'fat. There was fighting, and it was impossible to take a straight route."

When the travelers tried to tack east of the city, the Jordanian army warned them it was too dangerous. "There were already soldiers up on Mount Scopus shooting down," Mustafa said, "so we had to take the direct route past the Ambassador Hotel and then by Salah-a-Din Street. Somehow I managed to get through between 6:00 and 7:00 P.M." Israeli soldiers had passed through the same street one hour before.

A narrative of Arab cowardice and collapse has congealed around the defense of the Old City, but "there was some resistance," Mustafa insisted. "Many individual soldiers put up a brave fight. They didn't withdraw immediately when the orders came." As the occupation began, when the Israeli army gathered people together at the Al Aqsa Mosque, "the *mukhtar* went up on the highest house and started to shoot his gun," Mustafa said. "Jordanian soldiers were still stationed in the Muslim quarter where we lived, and they were also shooting."

At the Old City gate near the spa, "fighting between the Jordanians and the Israelis was still continuing," he recalled. Israeli warplanes were being used to attack Arab positions. "One whole family—seven people—died in a napalm bomb," he said with a wave of his hand. "We were painfully aware that we were incapable of putting up any resistance. We couldn't stand up against an invading army and a developing occupation, so we stood there passively, incapable of reacting."

The al-Kurds had lived in Jerusalem for several generations. When Mustafa was born, his father owned a small sweets and nuts shop in "a neighborhood that was like a family." Now those social bonds and traditions had strained. "People have been thrown back on themselves," he said. Mustafa's earliest memories were of the Nakba. In 1948 his family had just built a house in Baka, West Jerusalem. It was lost, as was the family's shop, because the Jaffa Gate, which was close by, had "been turned into a dead end."

As Jordan took over East Jerusalem and the West Bank, it became dangerous for Palestinians to talk about the Nakba. "Even when we listened to a
Cairo radio station—the Voice of the Arabs—we had to put a kid on the
street outside to watch for passing soldiers or *mukhabarat*," Mustafa said.
"People only talked about their personal memories of cities, houses, the sea,
and their families." But Mustafa learned that his uncle fought in 1948 and
was wounded in the battle of Notre Dame.

Music, not politics, captured his imagination as a child, and he became
increasingly enchanted by the sounds of Jerusalem. "You had Muslim religious music," he said, "the shaykh and the muezzin. My family came from
the Sufi tradition so, as the eldest son, I was taken along to Sufi meetings in
houses all over the city. My father liked to sing classical traditional songs with
his friends, and he had a beautiful voice." He died when Mustafa was just
eleven. "I think it was asthma-related," Mustafa said, his head slipping into
his shoulders, "poverty-related. He didn't have the right medicine."

While he was still in Nablus, Mustafa wrote his first nationalist songs.
One was called, "The Road of Honor Is in the Hands of the People." But it
was not until 1967 that he began playing live concerts and recordings of his
music started circulating in small listeners' groups. "Most of the time, people
would learn the songs through the concerts," he said. "One fan from Ramallah used to record at every single concert with these big cassette recording
spools." Acclaim spread by word of mouth. Some of the tapes went abroad,
and people began to order recordings. In 1973 his first record *Il-ard* (The
Land) was finally released. The buzz around him by this point was becoming
deafening.

"People realized that I was doing something totally different from the
dominant Egyptian, Lebanese, or Syrian songs," he said. "I was taking up
their daily experience of suffering and struggle." In the 1967–70 period no
other artist was writing "direct struggle songs," as Mustafa called them. In
Lebanon, he argued, "Fairuz was doing nostalgic songs about Jerusalem, and
when Marcel Khalife sang about Palestine he just put Mahmoud Darwish's
more emotional love poems to music. In Egypt, Shaykh Imam started at
about the same time, but we didn't know about each other. At first he
sang about Egypt, Marcel Khalife sang about Lebanon, and I sang about
Palestine."

Egyptian state radio shows padded the space between the romance of pre-
1948 Palestine and the catastrophe of the Nakba with official Arab paeans to
Nasser or the Nile dam. By contrast, Mustafa described his early tracks like
"Beit Iskariya"—about the first settlements—as "a poetic newspaper, a direct

call to the peasants: Don't leave your land! Stick to it, or it will be gone. At the time no one could write that in the papers."

Although Mustafa saw himself as "more leftist than nationalist," his musical milieu quickly became the haunt of nationalist groups. "Once the PLO and others were driven out of Jordan," he said, "they realized how important music, theatre, and painting were. Through them they could reach out to the street." Fatah, the DFLP, and the Communist Party were the most supportive factions of what by now was a new Palestinian artistic community. Inevitably, the authorities clamped down.

"If I announced a concert, they'd put border police or security services around the entrance," he said. "Some concertgoers would see them and not come in. Others would have to show their ID cards and answer questions. Very often I would be called in to the secret services and asked why I was writing these songs. Whenever I wrote a new one, it would be published in one of the [Israeli] leftist newspapers—*Iftihad, Eljadeed, Alhaq*—to pass their censorship test." Words already published in Israel were legal in the occupied territories by default.

In 1975 Mustafa was arrested for participating in a violent protest while he was working as an actor in a play, *When We Became Crazy,* about the link between the occupation and mental illness. He was beaten so badly by Israeli officers that he was unable to continue performing. "I was held in a stress position by two people, and someone pulled my sweater over my head so I was hooded," he said. "Then they beat me on my balls from below and behind with a stick that I think was electrified because it gave me a shock."

In 1976 Mustafa was rearrested again and held in Jerusalem's Muskovia prison, where he was interrogated day and night. After four weeks of beatings, he was put in administrative detention. Several months later, he was offered a deal. "It wasn't a written agreement," he clarified. "They just said, 'Listen, you'd better get out of here,' so I left, for Jordan." And then the music stopped. "There was this void because I didn't make new songs and neither did anyone else," Mustafa said. He went first to Beirut and then to Berlin. He branched out, writing film scores and universal songs of exile and performing on the international left music scene. At one festival, he played on the same bill as Mikis Theodorakis, Mercedes Sosa, and Pete Seeger.

In the 1980s he began picking up urgent messages on the grapevine that he was needed in Palestine. He called his Israeli lawyer, Leah Tzimmer. In 1985, when he and his wife, Helga, returned, "there was a lot of tension in the atmosphere," Mustafa remembered, "a lot of clashes across the West Bank." Culturally too, Mustafa found it a frustrating and oppressive time. But he wrote a cassette full of songs in December 1987, the month the Intifada began.

"I felt that something important was happening," he said. "I performed the songs for some friends on New Year's Eve 1987, and they were very well received." Helga, who had been sitting with us, suddenly held up her hand. "If I may interject," she said delicately, "I remember that people would sometimes use Mustafa's words in political discussions; his emphasis that there should be national unity. All the movements quoted from his songs, and walking on Salah-a-Din Street, they would play them if Mustafa passed by." She still seemed very proud of Mustafa. He did not seem to notice.

In 1988 Israeli officers seized a carton of Mustafa's Intifada cassettes as he was unloading them. "The secret service guy saw the cover—a picture of a boy with a stone—and he took me to the Muskovia [prison]," Mustafa said. "They translated the lyrics—which were printed in a booklet inside—to present a case against me for incitement. But I'd made sure that the texts had already been published in *Iftihad*."

Perhaps Mustafa's greatest contribution to Palestinian culture was the song "A Stone, an Onion, and a Bucket of Water," a reference to Intifada resistance and a tear gas antidote. "Blessed be your hand that throws the stone," it begins, then continues: "Don't ask me which organization, don't ask me which party, I'm a Palestinian from this land." The song explains how Palestinians buried the fear that oppressed them with their own hands. "People were afraid of armed soldiers," Mustafa said. "The history had built up since 1948. The crimes at Kfar Qassem let fear dominate our society, and in the Intifada these kids who stood in front of the tanks with a stone and an onion broke it." Despite the Intifada's failures, this fear had not reemerged, he said, "just a bitter sense of defeat." Do you feel defeated? I asked. "Yes," he said.

In the period between the two Intifadas, the PA began to consciously try to shift Palestine's musical culture away from resistance and toward Arab celebrity pop. "They gave up all the songs of struggle for their interpretation that 'We're living here with neighbors; they recognize us, we recognize them . . . ,'" Mustafa said. He was less involved in the Second Intifada. "They should have found a different name for it," he chided, curling up in his chair. "It wasn't an uprising like the first one. That was a mass reaction of a whole society that felt alone. The 'Second Intifada' was on a political level with a political agenda."

This may be one reason why few young Palestinians seemed to have heard of Mustafa. One older academic who was never a fan told me, "He was significant in a certain period. His music had some national content, but today that genre has lost its edge. People prefer Trans-Arab pop." Mustafa seemed like someone whose time in the spotlight passed while he was too active to explore all its possibilities. "Art belongs to the individual first and above all," he said at one point. "It goes beyond the fetters of nationality." Even so, the PA did not do enough to support it, in his view.

Hanan Ashrawi, 62

Civil Society Leader

RAMALLAH, WEST BANK

Agent of change   Hanan Ashrawi sat on the PLO's executive committee and was a Palestinian whom Westerners could relate to. Eloquent, cultured, and highly secular, she was a leader during the First Intifada and a national spokesperson during peace talks afterward. When the Second Intifada arrived, she was already the world media's Palestinian pundit of choice. Her passion for the national struggle was not a media turn. But her background would not automatically scream "activist" either. "My mother comes from a wealthy Victorian family," Hanan told me over biscuits in her office, "very prim and proper. Her mother was taken up with issues of decorum. My father, a physician for the British army, was from the clans of Ramallah. Every two years he was stationed in a different city, and in every city they had a baby girl. I was the youngest, born in Nablus: child number five. We came to the family home in Ramallah when I was two or three."

If the British had ever created a postcolonial governing class in Palestine, Hanan's family might well have been part of it. "If they were looking for an educated elite and people who had a sense of belonging and community then, yes," she told me. But as things were, her father distanced himself from the mandate powers. "He was proud of his identity and aware that it was being suppressed," Hanan said. "He ensured we knew who we were. I found out later that he'd taken food and medicine to the fighters in the mountains using his medical officer's pass." Hanan's family actually fled to Amman during the 1948 fighting, but her father ensured that she imbibed the lesson of "not being a victim but an agent of change."

Palestinian consciousness for Hanan involved "a special organic relationship with the land" that extended to the use of its cities as stations for pilgrims. Ashrawi was herself the daughter of an Anglican and a "Christian atheist," with Catholic nuns, Baptists, and Greek Orthodox among her relatives. Even so, her first experience of religion was "absolutely negative." She shuddered when she said this. A more potent influence was the 1967 war. "I was a student at the American University of Beirut, feeling helpless, and that's when my father's prediction came to me," she said. "I wanted to go back and fight. I joined Fatah—not the PLO—and I think I was the first women's delegate in the General Union of Palestinian Students in '68 or '69."

"Palestinians put a very strong emphasis on education as a source of security, a way of getting ahead, or social prestige," she elaborated. "I came from an educated family, and we took it for granted that I'd go as far as I could with my studies." In practice, this took her to the University of Virginia— until Israel issued her a permit to return to a West Bank they now controlled. Hanan had discovered the women's movement in Virginia, and she initiated consciousness-raising discussion groups in (illegal) feminist meetings back in Ramallah. She found that Palestinian women were facing a matrix of oppression that ran from the occupation down to traditional codes of honor and shame.

"Of course, men in power try to define you, limit you, exclude you, or put you down in the traditional modes. 'Ah Hanan, you look good.'" She adopted a slimy tone of voice for a second, then burst into laughter. "'Thank you, you look good too.' Usually it's fine for women to sacrifice—even the revolutionaries—but ultimately you have to be nice, demure, stay in the kitchen and conform to the mode. We were always told, 'Now we face the national conflict, you don't introduce women's rights. It's not a pressing issue.' We had to fight those attitudes."

Palestine was not lacking fights in the 1970s. Hanan was appointed dean of Bir Zeit University just as the *thawra* was reaching its peak. Campus demonstrations were violently suppressed, and on one occasion she had to cradle a dying student's head, an incident that still haunts her. For Hanan, the

Intifada that followed was "a period of crystallization of the power inherent in the oppressed. They closed down schools. We set up secret popular neighborhood schools. They closed the university. We taught in our homes. They placed us under curfew. We defied curfew. They told people to open their shops. We told them to close them. This daily confrontation transformed victimization into a sense of power. Young women became guards or, like my niece, were elected heads of neighborhood committees. We changed social behavior around honor and shame, and it was really popular."

As her political stock rose, so did her career. After a bravura performance on ABC's *Nightline* news program in 1988—she had dated the show's anchor, Peter Jennings, in Beirut—Hanan was nominated by Fatah's underground leadership to head the Palestinian delegation at peace talks. "They asked me to go to America to talk to people in the State Department," she recalled. "Their dialogue with the Tunis PLO had been very stilted. That's when I first met Dennis Ross." Ross was a notoriously pro-Israel career diplomat who served as a Middle East envoy under the Clinton and Obama administrations.

"When James Baker [President George H. W. Bush's chief of staff] arrived, he was very sharp, very smart. He didn't know enough about us, so I'd tell people, 'We're educating Baker.' But you could engage with him. If he made us angry we told him. If he got angry, he raised his voice and we answered him. It was a real dialogue. It wasn't diplomatese. Every time he came, they'd build a new settlement and say, 'This is a gift for Baker.' It bothered him. Eventually we told him, 'Please stop coming! Every time we lose more land.' But he saw firsthand." In March 2010 so did the current U.S. vice president, Joe Biden, when he was greeted on arrival in Israel by the announcement of new settlement construction in East Jerusalem.

In the Madrid talks themselves, "we had to meet outside the negotiating room because the Israelis didn't want Palestinians from Jerusalem there," Hanan said. "[Yitzhak] Shamir's government was dragged kicking and screaming to the talks. He later said he wanted to prolong them for ten years until he'd filled the West Bank with settlers. He was a repulsive character—extremely right-wing, immoral, and restrictive. But we were confident we could fight the power narrative. We wrote the peace initiative, the world was with us, and I was sure that we were going to present our case and end the occupation. Once people knew what was happening, no one would condone the Israelis. To us it was simple."

Her team soon found itself squaring up against Israeli power games. "They wanted us to be part of the Jordanian delegation. They'd search us when we crossed the bridge, decide who could enter, and confiscate our papers. Several times the delegation went back in protest. Once, [Eliyahu] Rubinstein repeated Golda Meir's words, 'We shall never forgive you for making us kill your children.' So I told the delegation, 'We walk out; don't let him ever use this language!'"

In Tunis, though, the Fatah leadership was ambivalent. "Arafat was afraid," Hanan said. "People were lying to him that we were an alternative leadership—which at the time was treason. They'd say, 'Look, they're being treated like heads of state! They're taking over the Palestinians inside.' I told Arafat, 'If we wanted to sell you out we would have done it when there was a price.' The PLO was a sacred sign of legitimacy, belonging, and identity. We were constantly in touch, telling Arafat what was happening, and he was always hesitant. He worried that [the talks] would diminish the PLO and empower Palestinians here, so he'd send PLO people to follow up everything. He was more comfortable at Oslo, even though it took place in secret and had the opposite components of our process."

"We started with the core issues—settlements, Jerusalem, human rights—they took the American approach and started with the easy issues. Not only did they not solve these, but they did all the things that weakened Palestinians and maintained Israeli control." This also allowed Arafat to maintain control of the PLO. "That's how they sold it to him," Hanan said. "'We're opening the door for you to come home. What else do you need?' Oslo came to save individuals and institutions, not the cause. There was gradualism, a separation of people from the land, no guarantees. Even the language was shoddy. The agreement was so amorphous. It could lead to statehood or disaster. I hoped we could make the most of it because we couldn't flush it down the toilet."

The Camp David negotiations in 1997 were also handled badly, Hanan believed. "If the talks haven't reached the stage where you can conclude an agreement, don't go," she said. "But they were unable to say say no. I was there when Clinton and Albright told Arafat, 'Try your best. We're not going to blame you if things don't work out.' He asked for more time and preparatory talks—they didn't give it to him—and of course he didn't sign because there was nothing to sign, frankly. Camp David was a big hoax, an attempt by [Ehud] Barak to rescue his failing coalition. He'd already lost public confidence and wanted to rescue his career. Clinton was trying to rescue his presidency. These two points of self-interest met at the expense of the Palestinians and peace."

"The Israelis tried to separate the issues and discuss each separately. You cannot. You have to take an integrated approach in negotiations because it's part of a whole picture. It has to have a binding, credible result. Things kept moving, positions changed, and the best example is Taba." Barak's generous offer? "There was no offer at all," Hanan replied. "There were exploratory talks to find out what worked, and toward the end Barak, I understand, became a recluse. He went to his room and refused to see anybody. I think he panicked because he wasn't committed to a deal at all. I think he thought he could get the end of the conflict done quickly, no further claims, and the Palestinians would cave under pressure. When he saw that even his exploratory positions were provoking reactions in Israel and when he felt he couldn't deliver, he came out with this ridiculous argument that 'I exposed Arafat' as if it was the purpose of the whole exercise."

"He'd had polls taken that showed that even an agreement wouldn't help his reelection chances, just give ammunition to the opposition. By the end, he just wanted a sort of 'We're making progress; elect me and we'll conclude an agreement.' Of course it backfired." The red line issues for Hanan in any final status deal included the right to return for refugees, East Jerusalem as capital, 1967 borders, and removal of all settlements, including Ariel and Ma'ale Adumim. "They'd have to go," she told me. "If you believe in the Geneva Convention, then it applies to all settlements."

"Now if you want arrangements and discussions on specific areas," she went on cagily, "present your proposal, we'll look at it. But you do not start by saying, 'We're going to annex all these territories' or 'We have a swap idea and let's start there.' No."

The United States was "never an honest broker," as Hanan saw it. "They brought a broad strategic alliance with Israel to bear on the talks. Dennis Ross even told me openly, 'Israel is our special ally. You think we're going to in any way hold them accountable or criticize them in public?' The modus operandi was (1) the U.S. never surprises Israel; (2) the U.S. never criticizes Israel in public; (3) the U.S. never uses sanctions against Israel; (4) the U.S. never allows the U.N. to vote against Israel in the Security Council; (5) the U.S. never presents a document without clearing it first with Israel. The American documents were primarily Israeli with just a few cosmetic changes, and sometimes they were more protective of Israel than the Israelis themselves." Hanan blames the Israel lobby for this. "It is effective and can make or break political careers," she said. But she also noted "the collective guilt of the West, the fear of the anti-Semitism charge, and the sense of Judeo-Christian [traditions] versus the rest of the world" as causal factors. Ultimately, she argued that the Israeli tail was wagging the U.S. dog.

Hanan was associated with Oslo and its legacy, but she was scathing about what she saw as its "built-in flaws." These delegitimized the PA, she told me, "because people began to feel that this whole approach to peace was a sham. Israel was buying time while creating facts on the ground." And there was also corruption, which she linked to "a sense of entitlement, partly overcompensation, I guess—power, they hadn't had that—the examples of the countries they were exiled in where it was acceptable, and I think it was also plain greed. We have a saying, 'It's apricot season.' They felt they had to gather their apricots while they could."

In common with other civil society advocates, Hanan did not call the Al Aqsa uprising an intifada. "The First Intifada really was the popular will," she explained. "We were more dragged into the second uprising when Israel took the initiative and forced our hand. Many of us adopted Israeli methods. I didn't believe that Palestinians should target civilians. That arena is not authentic, not ours, and it adopts the tactics of occupation. I don't think that you can defeat Israel militarily, and we shouldn't. Once you lose the moral high ground, the integrity of your cause is in question. The Second Intifada fragmented the national cohesion that was augmented in the first one. It excluded women and civil society and turned this into a military conflict that lent itself to exploitation by Israel, painting us as terrorists."

The faction's move to armed engagement was partly "bravado," she said. "There were weapons, and it was more a show of 'We have our pride, dignity, and the ability to protect our women and children.'" There seems to be a Palestinian crisis over its inability to protect itself, I said. "The one way to protect ourselves is to expose the limits of power," Hanan retorted. "That should have been our strategy. We tried. We had the women's march, and we were shot at. We had the artists' march, the academics' march, and we were shot at. Then Hamas took over and redefined the term *resistance* in a very negative way."

Isn't it more of a generational challenge? I asked. "The secular nationalist movements failed to deliver good governance, freedom, or independence," Hanan sighed. "They failed to stand up to Israel or provide any kind of human security, and the United States and Israel had a lot to do with that. We fell into a trap when we became a typical Arab country polarized between a corrupt regime and a religious alternative. Democratic forces were easily silenced." Of course, "democratic forces" can easily end up as code for America or Israel, I noted. "People try to delegitimize nationalists by saying that," she said, "because of the failure of the left. The PFLP used to be the second largest faction. It's now down to three MPs. It couldn't compete with Hamas on the armed issue or Fatah on the nationalist issue, and it compromised its ideology by going to bed with the extreme right. You cannot defend Hamas because ideologically you're supposed to be defending women's rights, human rights, pluralism, and tolerance."

The Second Intifada, Hanan argued, ended long before the Gaza infighting. "People paid lip service, but everyone knew," she said. "It backfired and distorted our standing in the world, our domestic realities and relationships." She blamed Hamas for the bloodshed in Gaza: "Dahlan and the security forces were always corrupt and abusive of power. That's nothing new. You don't fight them by doing worse." Hamas argues that Fatah was being paid by the Americans to destroy the Palestinian unity government, I said. "It sounds like the 'preemptive strike' argument that Israel uses," she countered, tongue-in-cheek. "Frankly, if Dahlan was doing all these things, Fatah would have succeeded at least in defending themselves," she laughed. "They collapsed immediately! Dahlan's strong point was not military strength or preparedness." What was it? I asked. "Money, probably," she said. "Let's say some security forces were allowed to raise funds at crossing points for protection money and became warlords. Some used mafia tactics. Some smuggled. The Palestinians knew. We were against this. When Hamas took over, they quickly became intoxicated by power, and when they wanted to reconcile, they asked for their share of the spoils."

Do you think you could you make a case for Israel unconsciously trying to construct Palestinian identity in its own shadow image? I asked. An educated people without a land, forced into exile and diaspora, where they are demonized as oriental extremists, living behind ghetto walls at home, boxed into an increasingly religious, militarized aid economy? "Subconsciously!" Hanan exclaimed ironically. "You could. As an outcome of these policies, that's what's going to happen. You're also creating a society regressing in education, cohesion, and the rule of law that's driven by a very artificial dynamic through Israeli intervention."

Hanan did not dispute the thesis that during the Second Intifada, Palestinians discovered the lengths they could go to, to make the other side recognize their pain. "But it's scary when your pain is your motive, means, and message," she said. "Suffering should not be an excuse to inflict whatever pain you can on others. We tainted our own struggle. It was misrepresented. Pain is not a positive motive. Revenge is not a positive motive. And when you lose control of your rational faculties you become a victim of circumstance because others can always call the shots by pushing your buttons. We always thought we deserved better, and I think we shortchanged ourselves."

Within the PA, she pointed to "a resurgence of violations, the curbing of free speech, and targeting of people because of their political affiliations." These, she said, were "extremely alarming patterns, but it's not a weakness of the state system because we really don't have one. We have a sort of government structure under occupation without sovereignty or freedom and with internal rifts. That has given some people the excuse to say we are in a state of emergency."

Hanan's analysis was that Fatah became a victim of untrammeled power and greed while Hamas was quickly tainted by the trimmings of office—"the red carpets and official seats"—without any real power. "Instead of holding Fatah accountable, they started hiring their own people for the civil service and cleansing appointments for political patronage," she said. Hanan was especially alarmed by the targeting of Christians in Gaza: "Hamas says they didn't do it, but they also tell Israel, 'We are the security address.'" At least they have improved security for their constituency there, I said. Abu Mazen doesn't even have a political base in Gaza. "Except blackmail," Hanan shot back, then paused. "Abbas has been used by Fatah in many ways," she said. "They blackmail him. They use pressure on him [to preserve] their privilege, self-interest, and different centers of power. He entered this arena, which is really difficult. Most people are angry with the factions, but if we have elections, you're going to see a repeat performance. Hamas will win in spite of itself, not because of what it did but what Fatah failed to do. I've decided that I will not run in the next elections. My generation's job now is to support the rise of a new leadership and give it some buffer zone protection."

Would that help create a partner for peace in Israel? I suggested. "It's unfortunate that we're always asked to take responsibility for Israel," Hanan said. "'Why don't you understand why they don't trust you, why they're afraid of you?' I mean, fine, let's have a dialogue. But we have our own fears. We're under the boot. I feel let down by the [Israeli] peace camp. With very few exceptions, they abandoned the peace agenda and lost their voice when it came to standing up to power. We had a jubilant and genuine dialogue with activists in the seventies. But most were easily co-opted by power. They changed their agenda very easily and gave themselves the right to shape the 'peace outcome' unilaterally. So we lost this partnership."

Compared to the Israeli activists she worked with in the 1970s, the ones she met today were "much more jaded, much more political. They have more of an agenda. They fall within the establishment. Before it was a kind of defiant 'We're all together against the occupation.' This is the dialogue of activists that I really liked. We would go out and demonstrate together with people like Leah Tzimmer—even if it was illegal. We'd get beaten up, and they wouldn't. At one point, many of them got imprisoned and we went to visit them as Ramallans. It was solidarity and a shared vision, not this conscious sort of political self-interest, the language of compromise and cynicism. 'You're on your side and I'm on my side and we'll see what can be done.' It was an age of innocence for us."

I tried one last question for the road: Do you think you'll see a Palestinian state in your lifetime? "I used to think it was inevitable, but now I find it difficult to envisage because Israel is systematically dismantling its foundations," Hanan answered me. Couldn't they be put back together under a one-state banner? "That's one option, yes. Even if by some miracle you end up with a statelet in the West Bank and Gaza, it will have to come to terms with larger regional realities. Maybe we can start rethinking the whole region, and that will be an impetus for change. Look, the U.S. sucks up all the oil, and its friends in the Arab world protect its oil interests. Israel's functional role has gone, with Arab regimes playing the American game. But other issues will come into play if the Arab world reawakens and there is genuine democracy." She paused one last time, smiling naughtily. "Regime change can go either way."

Raleb Majadele, 56

Former Minister of Science and Technology

JERUSALEM

An Arab in the government   Raleb was the first Arab Muslim to have given orders in an Israeli ministry. As I waited to meet him, his office's yarmulke-wearing security guard was taking a close interest in me. He asked to see my camera and then demanded that I open it. "Take a photo," he said. I raised the camera. "Not of me!" he warned. Then he looked at the digital viewfinder to make sure a picture had been taken. He wanted to see my press card, then my phone, and then my voice recorder. I had to record something and play it back for him. Israeli security is often like this, nowhere more so than in government buildings. I wondered what would have happened to me there if I were Palestinian.

Thirty minutes late, I was led in to see the minister by another security officer and someone who may have been a civil servant. They sat in on the interview. Raleb was fluttering about his office, taking phone calls, folding his arms, receiving a visitor here, walking off midsentence to receive an aide there. He was clearly enjoying the trappings of power. Unusually, he had Jewish and Arab aides—helpful and conscientious, they mostly kept their heads down—but the office lingua franca was Hebrew. As we sat around the governmental biscuit table, Raleb asked me whether my book would be about Palestinians or Israeli Arabs. Both, I told him. He said that he saw himself as "an Arab of Palestinian origin and a citizen of the state of Israel." Then his phone rang, and I was told to stop recording.

Raleb came from Baqa al-Garabiya, a town in Israel's north famous for the concrete wall that cut across the middle of one road, shutting out the West Bank. "It's like the Berlin Wall," he lamented, "and one day it will be torn down." Raleb grew up in a poor agricultural family with fourteen brothers and sisters. Two died when he was a child. When the 1967 war broke out, he was selling newspapers to raise money for his family, and as a teenager he joined the "left Zionist" Histadrut youth movement Hanovar Ha'oved. Before 1948 the Histadrut played a key role in building the nascent Israeli state. It increased Jewish ownership of land and Jewish control of employment and production. Its first secretary-general, David Ben-Gurion, went on to become the country's first prime minister. But after 1956 it also admitted Arabs. "It helped to integrate local young workers into the job market," Raleb said. When I asked if he ever felt pressure within it to hide his Arabness, he talked blandly about the Histadrut's history instead. He had a politician's habit of looking away when he talked to you.

"Nobody in the Labor Party can be a racist," he said slowly. I suggested that settlements began and grew fastest under Labor. "The party made some mistakes," he said, staring confrontationally at me for a second. "But that doesn't mean they're racist. You need to satisfy a lot of forces when you're in power. Our leader Ehud Barak said that all illegal settlements must be removed. The problem is that there are a lot of them." In 1999 Barak also described Israel as "a villa in the jungle," I responded. Raleb said he had not heard of this.

Many Israeli Palestinians believe that he was given his ministerial job by the then-Labor Party leader Amir Peretz as a sop to get out the Arab vote in party primaries. Raleb, however, put his rise down to "good luck" and his insistence on representing, or perhaps protecting, his Arab constituency. "I always talked about how I needed to take care of them," he said. "I spoke the truth clearly and loudly." More generally, his philosophy was that "you must compromise in the middle; you need to do everything very gently." So if Israel felt insecure, there would be no peace. Likewise, peace with the Palestinians would require a compensation package. It was all about trade-offs.

"It's always on the table that the Israeli state is fighting my people, the Palestinians," he said. "I have to deal with it all the time. The government discriminates against Arabs. The Jews don't hug you on the streets. They don't even hug their own leaders. There's a separation from the Arab community, and each side is moving farther away from agreement in the center. The extremists are growing stronger and more aggressive." To succeed in such circumstances "you should be very strong and never forget the people who sent you," he said, circling his arms expansively as though shaping the world. A new arrival joined our biscuit table.

Raleb walked a difficult line in government. He refused to sing Israel's national anthem "Ha Tikva" but stood in respect when it was played. "It's not so easy for me," he said. "I'm an Arab nationalist. Everything that represents me, my culture, and past comes from that side. The national anthem has a Jewish and Zionist narrative. It's not talking to my people." If it is ever changed to include reference to Arabs, though, he "will sing it loud and proud," he said. "Not everything Israeli hurts my culture and nationality." But one thing that did was the Absentee Property Act. "Of course, it needs to be canceled," Raleb said. "It takes land from Arab communities all over Israel, which is a big problem because there's no land for Arab cities to grow. Any state land not in use should be given back." He observed that regional Jewish councils like the Misgav were founded with 183,000 dunams for only 7,000 residents, while Arab cities such as Sakhnin had 9,800 dunams for more than 40,000 people.

Would you prefer a Jewish state or a state for all its citizens? I nudged. "I'm dealing with reality," he jostled back. "If Israeli Jews want to live together with Arabs, we want an equal share of what the country has to offer, to live as equal citizens in peace. There's no other way. When my neighbor is hungry, my plate is in danger. Would you like a photo behind the desk?" Raleb left the biscuit table, sat in front of an Israeli flag, and smiled.

When we met a year later in a Histadrut café in Tel Aviv, he was dressed less formally, in an open-necked shirt. It was summer 2009, Benjamin Netanyahu was in power, and Raleb had lost his office and security guards. But he still checked his watch—as though quartering every minute—and spoke into the middle distance as though reading from a script in his head. A diligent former aide told me he was taking time off "to advise Israeli institutions on Arab issues." The experience of government had not been kind to him. Raleb was not reelected because he was placed fifteenth on a party list that privileged Jewish sectors representing smaller sections of the Labor Party and, indeed, Israel. Raleb talked about his time in office absently, with one finger over his mouth.

It was hard to be part of a government bombing Gaza, he said. "Civilians were hurt, not just military targets. Armies should fight against armies, not civilians. Israel was in the right because of the Qassam rockets, but the response was too much like, 'I hit you. You kill me.' So Israel lost an argument to act against the Palestinians." Raleb voted against the war and skipped one cabinet meeting in protest. But he did not consider resigning. "The right wing of Israel's public never wanted an Arab minister," he explained. "They were just waiting for me to go home. It would have played into their hands and served another agenda." He looked ill at ease when I suggested that he had been used. Many Palestinians prefer Likud governments for the honest face of Zionism they arguably present to the world.

Resigning would have expressed his constituents' anger "for a short time," Raleb said, but "the war was only for a few weeks, and you need to have an Arab in the government. If we go home every time they break the rules, it will never work. For Netanyahu and Likud it was a big issue: How can you give the space industry, the science industry, to an Arab? In the end, Arab citizens said they appreciated it. Now there is no Arab minister, they can say they're not using anyone because no one in the government takes care of their needs. In opposition you can only shout. We did that for forty years. Government gives you the power to do things." In his short time in power, Raleb's office said that he channeled millions of shekels into funding Arab cultural and sport institutions.

But now a new party was in office. Of foreign minister Avigdor Lieberman's proposal to make citizens swear a loyalty oath to a Jewish state, Raleb said, "If the state wants my loyalty it first needs to be loyal to me, to Arab citizens, by giving us equal rights." Another proposal before the Knesset to make commemorating the Nakba illegal was "a big free speech issue," he said. "You can't ignore the fact that Israel's establishment in 1948 also created a very hard reality for Arabs. You can't legislate to ban their feelings."

But Raleb would not defend Asmi Bishara, the Israeli Palestinian architect of the "state for all its citizens" idea who, in Arab eyes, was punished for it with exile in Jordan. Raleb was pursuing a strategy that he imagined would win fewer plaudits but more tangible change. "I don't shout," he said. "Shouting in public will never get results. You need to change the system from the inside, legally. People can say what they want about the Nakba. Actually they want their houses back. I want to be a part of making a solution not just shouting "Nakba, Nakba, Nakba!" His voice had risen as he had gone on. He would permit me one last question, he said.

Almost randomly, I asked if he supported the Law of Return that allows any Jew Israeli citizenship. "It should be open for everybody," he replied. "I'm against every law that discriminates, and this law discriminates against Arabs in favor of Jews." Israel should provide dignity for all, he said. "If the state neglects its citizens' rights, she will be hurt back." He looked again at his watch. "I am leaving," he said. I thanked him for his time and wished him good luck in Arabic. He reciprocated in Hebrew. It was a mechanical farewell.

Ahmad Yousef, 59

Deputy Foreign Minister

RAFAH CAMP, GAZA

Face your fate Ahmad Yousef strolled into Gaza's luxurious Al-Dire Hotel a few minutes late and proceeded to chat to the concierge in a steady and familiar tone. Dressed simply, he was accompanied by a beefy bodyguard. In spring 2008 the hotel was already protected by several armed checkpoints and Hamas militiamen smoking cigarettes on the rocks beneath its terrace.

Three months before, a small bomb had exploded on the beach outside. The threat of Israeli air strikes and incursions was constant, even if food shortages and power cuts were sharper concerns. Hamas was one year into a blockade imposed by Israel and the world community after it deposed Fatah in fighting that claimed more than one hundred lives. Hamas took power in Gaza weakened by public perceptions that it had crossed a red line when it killed other Palestinians.

In the hotel foyer, Ahmad sat with me at a coffee table beneath clinking chandeliers, his bodyguard at a 90-degree angle to us. He was then speechwriting for Prime Minister Ismail Haniyeh and working as his aide. Ahmad was associated with the "political strategy," or moderate camp, in Hamas, which had less clout than the Izzedine al-Qassam Brigade or hard-line leadership in Damascus. He was adamant that his party was a broad enough mosque to contain both streams. For much of his life, Ahmad had lived in the United States, writing books and speaking in interfaith panels with Christian and Jews. He had lost half of the fourth finger on his left hand during an assassination attempt on his boss, Ismail Haniyeh. He carried authority dutifully, exuding bonhomie, steadfastness, and a hangdog, droll air. He clearly enjoyed debate. Just back from "Europe" and down with a flu, he was still generous with his time.

In December 1950 Ahmad was born into a large family in Rafah. His roots were with "the first generation of activists who grew up in camps after '67," he said. His father was a wealthy man who had worked for the U.N. and the British. But he lost all his possessions in 1948 when his family was funneled from its hometown of Fallujah into Gaza. They were reduced to aid dependency in a tent shared with four other families. "The Israelis tricked us," Ahmad said. The lesson he drew was unequivocal: "Stay where you are, face your fate, and accept the challenge." When the 1967 war started, "my father said, 'I will die here in my house,'" Ahmad intoned, "and he insisted that we stay. Leaving had been a disaster for them in 1948, and they weren't going to repeat it. My father was a great man. He never fled from the Jews." He was also irreligious. "No one in my family except my grandmother prayed, and neither did I until I was fifteen," he said. "Few young people attended the mosque, just the older people who were seeking a one-way redemption."

Ahmad was an Arab nationalist in those days, but after the shock of Israel's victory in 1967 Islam offered new hope. "The soldiers who were supposed to face Israel took off their uniforms and guns and hid or else pretended to be civilians," he said. "We saw our people humiliated. I became obsessed with how Islam could be the alternative. When you're prepared as a Muslim you will not run away. We heard about the Muslim Brotherhood's struggle against Nasser's oppression, and I started reading Sayed Qutb and attending a neighbor's meetings with Shaykh Ahmed Yassin."

To "deal with the pressure," Ahmad used to write poetry. "I can't remember it now," he said. "Politics kills all the skill of memorizing poems. We became so obsessed with this harsh life with sanctions, but I was inspired by the resistance and trying to uplift my soul. There's a funny story about my poems actually. When I returned from Egypt I found that, during a curfew, my family had looked for fuel to cook with and all they found was my library. They thought it was risky to keep it because the soldiers might search us, so they cooked my handwriting and half of my library too." Ahmad's poems went up in flames. "My father wasn't an educated man," he said.

At Cairo's Al-Azhar University Ahmad joined the Muslim Brotherhood in 1973, just as President Anwar Sadat was releasing its activists from prison to fight against Communist street protestors. When the left was destroyed, the Islamists began to mobilize against the Arab regimes. They picked up some bad habits along the way, and the Hamas charter of 1987 mixed Islamism, national liberation prose, and anti-Semitism borrowed from the infamously fraudulent Protocols of the Elders of Zion. But Ahmad did not believe it should be amended.

"The Jews have problems everywhere, *yani*," he drawled. "This affected their mentality to see everybody as an enemy. They don't trust anyone. They should have learned not to turn people against them, [but instead] they became obsessed with security. Our fathers had a good life with them, but they treat Palestinians the same way they were treated by the Nazis and sometimes they actually practice the Holocaust on us." He saw no parallels with his own people's experience. "As Palestinians, we've never been exposed to the ghetto mentality," he said. "Wherever we are, we never isolate ourselves in our own communities observing rituals together—the Qur'an talks about this—so we are different."

When I spoke to the Hamas spiritual leader and MP Hamid Bitawi in Nablus—shortly before Israel arrested him in a dragnet that jailed thirty-five other Hamas MPs and a third of the government—he told me that the Protocols could certainly be removed from the Hamas charter. "Of course, we can change it because it's not in the Qur'an," he said. "If ordinary people wrote it, there's no obligation to follow it. There is the example of when Sharon said, 'We will never withdraw from any place in Israel,' and then he pulled out from Gaza. Everything can be exchanged." When I suggested to Ahmad that Hamas was keeping the Protocols as a bargaining chip, he replied that Hamas would not make concessions ahead of talks. "We learned a lot from the failed experience of Fatah's negotiations with the Israelis," he said.

His olive branch was that a negotiated *hudna* with Israel "could be twenty years, it could last to infinity. For a *hudna* of five to ten years, we've said that Israel has to withdraw to pre-1967 [borders] and release prisoners." In the meantime, Hamas would confront the world's fourth biggest military with tin-shed rockets that claimed more Palestinian lives in reprisals than they did Israeli ones in wrath. "The Qassam is not a lethal weapon," Ahmad admitted. "It's not really very effective, but five years ago we fought with stones, bare hands, and Kalashnikovs. Now we have homemade projectiles. Tomorrow it might make the Israelis feel the same pain that we feel [today]." In five or ten years' time, "we might have submarines," Ahmad said, "we might have drones. It sounds very sophisticated. We can do it." As he talked, piped strains of Ray Conniff's "If You Leave Me Now" wafted across the foyer.

"We quit suicide bombing because the world community said it was a crime against humanity. You kill Israelis, its terrorism. So we listened to the world, hoping they would reward us. We didn't even receive praise. If the world's conscience won't hear Palestinian tears, we have other means at our disposal." Gazans grew up in camps and could cope with poverty, blood, and tears, he said. "They can take it, it doesn't matter how painful the struggle. Dignity and homeland are the most important things." His own relative affluence "doesn't mean anything, believe me," he cajoled. He gave a passable impression of someone who had been forced into a mine and would blow it up before surrendering.

Interestingly, Ahmad named one of his daughters Shiraz, after a women's demonstration during the Iranian revolution. Others in his party's Damascus leadership—and its military wing in Gaza—favored creating a crisis to shore up street support and break the siege. "That's what the Chinese, the wisest people on earth, have said," Ahmad affirmed, holding rank. "Crisis always creates opportunities. We are suffering and we have nothing left to lose anymore. We have to break the silence and shake the world's conscience." How might you do that? I asked. "You might think about something inconceivable even," he replied. "Gaza is the land of surprises."

One surprise for international solidarity activists has sometimes been Hamas's "cultural" position on gender issues. Ahmad claimed that the hijab was a matter of personal choice. "We leave it to the families. They're dominated by the Islamic culture," he said. "I might tell a woman, 'Please, a headscarf makes you look more beautiful,' but this is not being imposed."

Asmaa's experience suggested otherwise. Gay rights were also "not a problem in our country," Ahmad said. "Forget religion, this kind of behavior is just not accepted by the Muslim culture. There is a normal way to have male and female [sex]. It's against our society's values, but I don't think it's punishable."

So a militia execution of a gay man would be wrong, I said. "Of course," he replied. "You can't take the law into your own hands. You can charge those people with violating the culture or something." But why shouldn't gay people be free to enjoy their sexuality? "Even in the West, gays always have some restrictions on their freedom and they accept that," he said. "You never have a free hand, *yani*. Nobody is talking about this or feels proud that they're gay here. You know, in the West when someone commits adultery you put them away for life in jail . . . " For rape, maybe, I interrupted. "To us this is a very harsh sentence," he continued. "Somebody who has taken—raped— a woman will spend his life in jail. This shouldn't be in a democratic country." In private, one senior Hamas MP in Ahmad's camp expressed support to me for liberalizing Hamas's attitude toward homosexuality, but he has not said so publicly. The man was an avid reader of Keats, Shelley, and Wordsworth.

Hamas's own democratic credentials have been questioned because of its repression of free media. "Most of the journalists here used to work for Fatah and were bribed to report in their favor," said Ahmad. "They twist the facts all the time, whenever there is a clash with the police. Some of them misuse their cameras, and some have been arrested, but they were all released." Yet Hamas had shut down at least nine media outlets since the July 2007 fighting. They also stood accused of grave crimes against Fatah members—including torture and summary execution. Ahmad said that Hamas could talk to Fatah figures such as Jibril Rajoub and Marwan Barghouti. "Marwan's a good guy. He sends us letters and we respond positively," he said. "If Abu Mazen gets closer to us, the Americans and Israelis will end their support, so he's very weak."

"We tried to play politics the way they should be [played]. We formed the unity government and gave Abu Mazen the go-ahead—'You are the most moderate the Israelis have seen,' *yani*. More than a single hug, we didn't see one [positive] fact on the ground. Mr. Bush said he would give the Palestinian state in 2005. Then he said maybe in 2008. Then we are talking about a state that is like a drawing on paper, and if Israel changes politically, everything will crumble. It's garbage. The Israelis just bought more time and tried to satisfy Abu Mazen with money from the European donors. The Palestinian cause is becoming like an investment project."

Of course, Fatah says that you are just taking Iranian money and guns,

I responded. "They don't have proof," Ahmad snorted. "For a long time we rejected taking a penny from Iran, but now when everybody tries to isolate us and makes our people suffer and somebody offers us a hand, we have to accept. But we've never tried to make a religious state. Nothing has changed here. The people are enjoying the summer. They dance and sing, and we don't interfere. See Gaza! It is much safer and more secure than in the fifteen years under the PA. I was amazed on the way here that you don't see any guns. I'm the prime minister's political adviser, and I feel secure even to walk to my house."

Hamas had certainly astroturfed a semblance of order over Gaza, but the earth beneath it was cracking. That evening, as I walked around Gaza City with a Palestinian friend, we saw a large wedding party opposite a Hamas police station with men—only men—dancing to a Fatah dabke song called "Raise Your Scarf." "They're going to fuck them," my friend said. We nervously walked on but could not have been more than ten minutes down the road when we heard a loud explosion—fireworks? a gun?—and then the music stopped.

A year later the streets were quieter. I met Ahmad at his office in the Foreign Ministry's new think tank, the House of Wisdom, and at his impressive villa in the Rafah camp to which he drove me from Gaza City. From his balcony, he pointed out the children playing "Fatah versus Hamas" war games with plastic AK-47s in the streets below. Beautiful trees had been ferried to his garden from the Gush Khatif settlement after it was abandoned. Ahmad was friendlier this time, with an open-hearted thirst for new ideas. He was also less defensive and clearly straining at the leash to enter negotiations. But his preferred Israeli partners—Uri Avnery and David Grossman—were a long way from office.

Ahmad's faction in Hamas was then openly lauding Nelson Mandela, Gerry Adams, and even Winston Churchill for offering political ways forward out of conflict. The war of 2008–9 had been a disaster for Hamas. Their Qassam rockets, which were supposed to end the siege, were staunched without any concessions in return. The political strategy faction now claimed the support of Ismail Haniyeh and some 40 percent of Hamas members, Ahmad said. But at the leadership level, it seemed to be becoming progressively marginalized.

Contacts with the Obama administration were spasmodic but ongoing. "There are a lot of restrictions in the Congress regarding contact with Hamas as a 'terrorist organization,'" he said. "We have one way or another sent letters, signals. We said that we had the leverage to bridge the gap between the East and West. We spoke the language of interests, not just the moral approach." Did you receive any replies? I asked. "Not yet," Ahmad said, "but we heard from a certain group that things will come. We will keep whatever talks or letters we have had [secret] until the administration discloses something." He was optimistic then that the White House was willing to deal with Hamas, "but they don't have the key because it involves changing some legislation." It would also involve redrafting the Quartet's preconditions that Hamas abandon resistance, recognize Israel, and accept the Oslo agreements.

"If Hamas recognized Israel," Ahmad told me, "the people who did that would be killed. I would be killed. Recognition happens at the end of a process on a state-to-state basis, *yani*. It showed they were not serious by demanding we do it up front." If Hamas were included in a political process, a formal ceasefire might not be impossible, he said. Recognition of Israel as a "Jewish state," though, was. "I don't think there can be peace with Israel as a Jewish state," he confirmed. "America is not always going to be a milk cow of money, weapons, and support to the Zionists. Time is on our side. It's much better for them to forget about a Jewish supremacist state. An independent Palestine would give them a new birth in the region."

Ahmad did not strategize around pan-Arabism but seemed happy to use it as a bogeyman. "People stand with the underdog," he said. "When Arabs saw Palestinians dying under phosphorus bombs, they responded with demonstrations. Of course, if the street got mad, this could even have risked Western interests in the region. Some Arab regimes were scared during these demonstrations." Hamas was "not agitating for people to target American interests," Ahmad insisted, but if the war had gone on, he believed this would have happened anyway.

He expressed surprise that "after all these protests, no Arab countries withdrew their ambassadors or cut relations [with Israel]. This was a shameful signal that some countries were complicit with the Israelis." He would not be drawn on which ones. "Everybody knows what was in people's minds at that time," he coughed. "Everyone saw people throw stones at some Arab embassies. The people understand. The Arabs were part of that aggression against us, or they tolerated it."

Even so, he would not countenance a strategy of supporting democratic revolutions against the region's dictators. "We will not repeat the mistakes of Fatah and Abu Amar [Yasser Arafat] to be involved everywhere in internal politics, always being used as a card in any conflict in the Arab region, and end up having big bloody clashes with other countries like Jordan or

Lebanon," he said. "We're not going to intervene in any internal situations or Arab problems. We just need people to give us a hand with our struggle. Yes, we are from the Muslim Brotherhood, but for now we are focused on our ultimate goal: how to end the occupation and liberate our land." So you don't take a position on what's happening in Egypt, I cajoled? "At all," Ahmad stressed. "At all, *yani*."

But if the Egyptian government reflected the will of the people, I said, wouldn't you have more leverage to create a Palestinian state? "We'd like support from all Arabs and Muslims," Ahmad replied sagely, "so we're not going to take sides or encourage Islamic movements. Internal conflicts will weaken these countries for Israel's benefit." So you believe that Mubarak has democratic legitimacy, I summarized. "This is for the Egyptian people to decide," Ahmad parried. Even if the Egyptian regime facilitates war in Gaza? I pushed. He would not budge.

"This is for the history books to say. The legacy of Mr. Mubarak will be how the people of the region look at him. We weren't happy when we were under attack and the Arabs were sending medical relief and humanitarian supplies and there were thousands of injured people who needed medical treatment and they closed the Egyptian border. Yeah, this is not going to please any Palestinian. But it's much better for us to have a strategic relationship with Egypt and not turn them into an enemy because we are so connected historically and geographically. We are like a family. This is our big brother. We have a strong affinity and respect, so I don't feel that they were in any way unfair to us. We understand that Egypt's internal politics make the regime suspicious of us because we are Islamists, from the Muslim Brotherhood. But we are not following the steps of any Islamic movement. We are independent. We do not want polarization."

You don't feel that supporting democracy could help you seize the banner of modernity as a political strategy? "We would prefer to have political pluralism in Gaza and Ramallah," Ahmad granted. "This benefits the Palestinian people. We really endorse democratization and are willing to, *yani,* participate in power-sharing." In essence, though, Hamas was a conservative movement, and this had some advantages, for some Hamas members, at some times.

Returning the discussion to 2008–9, Ahmad said he was tipped off about the war's timing. He planned to evacuate his office the morning it began. But "strange signals, a sense of things made me not leave Rafah," he said. "Then we heard all these explosions because we have an al-Qassam barracks near our home. We saw bombs dropped on the tunnels." Despite the electricity and phone shutdowns Ahmad kept himself busy dealing with the media. At night, he visited the border "to see our monitors, help with the humanitarian supplies, and show moral support. As someone in a high-ranking position, I should be close to the people so they don't feel alone." Earlier, he had driven me to a border post, where he inspected the Hamas troops and looked as happy as I ever saw him. The troops appeared starstruck.

"Day after day people suggested that we should leave the house because the Israelis might target it. Two of my daughters had come with their families, and I asked them if they thought we should divide up, to prevent the whole family from being killed in one place. We had relatives we could stay with. My daughters told me, 'We either live together or die together,' *yani*." In the end he stayed. "I knew my neighbors were watching, and if I left my house, they would evacuate theirs. I went up on the roof every day so that they'd see me and know I was there. If we had left, one-third of Rafah would have evacuated, and that would have been terrible, like we were defeated and surrendering." Whether the Izzedine al-Qassam Brigades could say the same was a moot point.

"There was a sense that the Israeli tanks really should not have reached Tel al-Hawa," Ahmad said. "The resistance should have stood and defended Gaza, but it was a puzzle for us. How could they move into that area so fast? Where is the resistance? We knew the resistance might have a plan to drag them into the residential areas where they'd be easier targets for the anti-tank missiles or hand-held weapons." So why weren't these fired? I asked. "The weapons were not capable of handling these huge tanks and the F-16s and Apaches," Ahmad replied. "Maybe the Israeli tanks moved into an area outside our defense strategy. Maybe they surprised us by going into that vacant area with that huge number of tanks, which made defense very difficult. Maybe the people were prepared for something else. Their expectation was different from what actually happened. That is the situation."

Hamas moderates had also expected the international political game to play out differently. The world's blanket support for Israel strengthened their party's hardliners. "We understand that we don't have Hezbollah's deterrent capability," Ahmad said. "They have more advanced weapons and missiles that can hit anywhere in Israel, but this also made people ask why we don't have these weapons. If we are challenging the Israelis, we should. Everybody believes that we should arm ourselves with lethal weapons because the political attempts have failed and this is the only way we can deter the Israelis. Strength and good military equipment are the only language they understand. The Israeli mentality is like, born to kill."

It was dark, and as we had been talking, the crickets and sporadic gunfire from Hamas fighters training in nearby bases had grown increasingly noisy. Ahmad asked me an oddly direct question. Did I think the Israelis would strike Iran without American support? I told him no. Ahmad thought the Americans would be "stupid" to start such a conflict themselves. "Iran has sleeper cells everywhere and can attack U.S. interests in Kuwait and Saudi Arabia," he said. Even here? I asked. "They might," he replied. I told him that people in Gaza City said his faction had become less powerful since the war. "We will stay influential," he said grimly. "We will keep trying. We don't have strong voices to mobilize people, but we are the real thinkers and ideologues for the movement, the driving force of the future."

In another Arab country, Ahmad might have been a famous spin doctor. His repeated slogan, "We are Erdogan [the moderate Turkish Islamist prime minister], not Taliban," was adroitly phony enough. In a Western country he might have been attacked as an Islamo-fascist or jailed. But here, he could not even arrange meetings with his government's militia, which seemed to pay no heed to his faction. Perhaps the political strategy was a snare to entrap naive Westerners or a desperate last throw of the dice by beleaguered Islamists. One member of Ahmad's camp cautioned me, "If the Israelis don't want peace, behind the curtain there is always suicide bombing." It would certainly be an upset if the reformers were yet to become Hamas's public face. Ahmad actually lost his governmental positions in the period after our interview. But then, as he himself so wryly noted, Gaza is the land of surprises.

The Nakba
Generation

All roads in Palestinian history lead back to the Nakba. During the war to establish a Jewish state in 1948, many thousands of Palestinians were killed, upwards of 750,000 were expelled from their land, and between 369 and 531 villages were destroyed. Ninety-six percent of villages in the Bisan valley were demolished—the same proportion as in Jaffa—and this was not unusual. The Israeli historian Ilan Pappe noted that both areas fell to the Palmach before the state's founding declaration in May 1948. Israeli forces thus had more time to complete their operations there.

The first Arab Jerusalemites were displaced in November 1947, and by February 1948 waves of Palestinian refugees were fleeing their homes in land assigned by the U.N. to the new Israeli state. Haifa was all but deserted after its fall in late April 1948. Yet on the eve of war, Jews had owned just 7 percent of the land in mandate Palestine and, despite huge population growth in the 1930s, still constituted little more than 30 percent of the population. The U.N.'s partition plan had given their proposed state 55 percent of Palestine's territory, including the most fertile land, and the slenderest of demographic majorities within that. Without the forced removal of Arabs—and the seizure of their properties—it is fair to question whether a viable state for Jews could have been created in Palestine at all.

In 1961 the Palestinian historian Walid Khalidi revealed the existence of an Israeli army document that appeared under the aegis of Plan Daled to give official approval to the ethnic cleansing of Palestinians in 1948. It recommended dealing with "enemy population centres" by destroying villages, planting mines in the debris, and expelling the population. Some Israeli historians contend that the expulsions were solely a response to resistance. But David Ben-Gurion wrote extensively in support of the compulsory transfer of Arabs with no mention of military security long before 1948.

After the fighting for Lyd and Ramle during the Nakba, the Israeli historian Benny Morris described how, "arriving at the scene, David Ben-Gurion, Israel's first prime minister, was asked by General Allon, 'What shall we do with the Arabs?'" Ben-Gurion, wrote Morris, "made a dismissive, energetic gesture with his hand and said, 'Expel them.'"

Fifty thousand Palestinians were sent on a ten- to fifteen-mile "death march" toward Ramallah in which hundreds died from exhaustion, dehydration, and disease. But atrocities were committed on both sides, and Palestinians were not always deliberately forced out of their homes at the barrel of a gun. Fighting in villages—or the fear of it—also impelled many to flee, and a series of atrocities, most notoriously a massacre at Deir Yassin, spread a pall of dread. As Menachem Begin, a contemporary Irgun leader and future Israeli prime minister put it:

> Arabs throughout the country, induced to believe wild tales of "Irgun butchery," were seized with limitless panic and started to flee for their lives. This mass flight soon developed into a maddened uncontrollable stampede. The political and economic significance of this development can hardly be overestimated.

None of the refugees were allowed to return. Eventually, most of the destroyed villages were either rebuilt as Jewish homesteads or planted over, often with non-native European pine trees bought by the Jewish National Fund. A mental hospital was built over the ruins of Deir Yassin, and the Yad Vashem Holocaust Museum was erected 1,400 meters away. The Nakba affected almost every Palestinian family, dislodging about three quarters of them from homes in which their families had often lived for centuries. While the dispersal of the Palestinian people to the four winds cleared the land for the new Israeli state, it also shattered the Palestinian nation in a way that continues to reverberate down the generations.

Within Israel, to be a Palestinian was to be in pain. Until 1966 a state of emergency prevented Arab Israelis from moving freely outside their hometowns and villages. The Nakba was often a source of shame. In Gaza, where refugees found themselves in unsanitary and miserable tent cities, lacking even basic rudiments of modern life, the response was despair—and anger. The Fedayeen began intermittent cross-border actions within Israel that at least symbolically maintained a spirit of defiance. But during the Suez War in 1956, hundreds of innocent Palestinian men were killed in Rafah and Khan Younis in a shocking collective retribution that Joe Sacco investigated in his 2009 book, *Footnotes in Gaza*. To this day about 70 percent of Gazans are refugees or their descendants.

In Lebanon, Palestinians were for the most part isolated, disenfranchised, and ghettoized in refugee camps, separated from the country as a whole. In the West Bank and Jordan, the feeling was more of having fused with a bigger Arab nation, in which Palestinians were now a disempowered majority. The social upheaval caused by a mass refugee influx permanently altered the structure of both regions. However, in all cases, Palestinians were discriminated against by host countries that used the pretext of not wanting to normalize their dispossessed status to deny them equal rights. Ultimately, they were seen as a dangerous source of instability. Any relief refugees may have felt at escaping the existential terror in Israel was undercut by their inability to return and a sense of betrayal at the hands of the international community and the Arab regimes they now lived under.

The common denominators they shared were major trauma at a national uprooting, disorientation after a global abandonment, separation from kith and kin, fragmentation—as various Palestinian communities evolved in different directions—and some feelings of shame and even meaningless sacrifice. Just twelve years before, Palestinian nationalists had roared like lions at the British Empire. Now Israeli collective punishments such as the massacres of Kfar Qassem and Qibya seemed to boast to the world that to be Palestinian was to be nothing more than weak, powerless, or even nonexistent. Palestine itself was meanwhile reconstructed among refugee communities as something between a fallen temple and a paradise lost. The Palestinian people were in need of time to heal.

Gabi Baramki, 78

Former University President

RAMALLAH, WEST BANK

Stolen property At the entrance to Jerusalem's Museum on the Seam, a sign reads, "Olive trees will be our borders." It looks like pacifist agitprop beside the ugly highway that spans the Green Line dividing Israel from the West Bank. Inside, ambient whale sounds comfort the mostly liberal tourists perusing the lightly political works on display. Outside, the eye is drawn upward to a beautiful old stone balcony that looks as though it has had a bite taken out of it. A small English-language information poster on a ground floor pillar mentions that the house was built by the "Arab Christian architect Anton Baramki." Gabi, his son, does not visit.

"It's stolen property," he told me. "I feel very angry about it because my father built it and inside they have put up half-truths that mask the whole truth." Most of the museum's wall notices cover the building's post-Nakba existence as an Israeli compound. "The idea of turning a military outpost into a site for peace and tolerance led to the opening of the Museum on the Seam for dialogue, understanding, and coexistence in June 1999," one reads. When I mentioned to Gabi that travel guides recommended it for an alternative history of both sides' experiences, he sniffed, "How nice! An alternative history of the thief and the person whose property was stolen." He had not visited the building since 2000. "I'd never come even if they invited me," he said.

As 1948 began, the Baramki family was renting a property opposite this grand house. When the year ended Gabi's parents were in Gaza, where they had fled after a stray bullet narrowly missed his mother while she sat in her living room. Gabi himself was marooned in Beirut, where he had gone to study at the American University. When the family reunited in 1949, Gabi discovered that all their possessions had been left in Jerusalem. Israel subsequently refused to allow the Baramki family to return to their property—which is now the Museum on the Seam—under the Absentee Property Act, even though Gabi's father held the relevant deeds, he said. In 1952 his parents came to Beirut; the next year they all moved to al-Bire, a suburb of Ramallah.

Gabi comes from what he describes as a "well-to-do" Greek Orthodox family that can trace its lineage in Jerusalem back several hundred years. He is one of Palestine's most celebrated academics, the holder of an officer-rank Medal Palme Academique, and an impeccable résumé. For nineteen years he was acting president of Bir Zeit, Palestine's first university, for twelve years an adviser to the PA's Education Ministry, and he founded several pioneering educational institutions and programs.

His first taste of the national struggle came in Beirut when he took part in demonstrations against the gathering Nakba. "Some people wanted to go to support the Palestinian army here," he said, "but they didn't. It wasn't easy. I was just getting a letter from my parents through the Red Cross every now and then. I felt cut off." Gabi was an untrained nineteen-year-old and had never considered a career in academia, but when he was offered an assistant instructor post at the American University, he jumped at the chance. In 1953 he returned to teach chemistry and biology at Bir Zeit.

On June 5, the day the 1967 war broke out, Gabi's wife was nine months' pregnant and Bir Zeit was beginning a week of exams. "They'd already advised the U.N. to leave and people were very tense," he recalled. "The Jordanian army was small, and they told us that as far as they were concerned the West Bank was not defendable. It was more or less demilitarized and Jordan's army was a poorly trained farce. They had antiquated weapons and five bullets each." Gabi's school was evacuated because of the Israeli army's bombing. "But when our schoolbus tried to take the Jerusalem students home the army sent them back," Gabi said. "So we had a kind of refuge room in our house, which neighbors also used. We were in the basement listening to Jordanian radio. They said that if you can't beat them, you can 'fight them with your teeth and nails.'" He looked genuinely appalled.

The Jordanian army left al-Bire on June 6. The Israeli army arrived the next day. Gabi's Gaza-born wife had told him stories of the massacres on the Strip in 1956, and when the army finally knocked on their door, he said, "the pictures I had in my mind were of Israeli soldiers shooting Gaza's men in front of them." The soldiers first evacuated the family from their house. "Then they went inside and stole my mother's jewelry, some binoculars, and beer from the fridge," Gabi said. "They left in our first car, a Peugeot 404, which was just one month old. Everybody was crying." The Peugeot at least was eventually returned after Gabi explained his wife's condition to an Israeli commander.

Under Israeli rule, schools in the West Bank and Gaza initially carried on using Jordanian and Egyptian models. The Palestinian reputation for educational excellence continued. "But of course things started changing," Gabi said. "Gone were the references to national emblems, courage, even territory that encouraged people to sacrifice. In one Arabic grammar course, the phrase 'the president came back home tired' was substituted for 'the army returned victorious.' Wherever the word *Palestine* appeared, it was crossed out and replaced with 'Israel.'" Textbooks now talked of "when the crusaders left Israel in the eleventh century. It was ridiculous."

Throughout the 1970s Bir Zeit's status as a female-friendly engine room of national aspiration grew. "No one got any education in Palestine except through Bir Zeit," Gabi said. "We were the leading part of the national movement." In 1973 the university suffered the first of fifteen military closures that would shut the college for months at a time. "It was a collective punishment that opened our eyes," he said. "People looked to see how we behaved, and they followed us. We never gave in."

"The PLO was our sole representative, and we worked very closely with them. But I never identified with people who put themselves in a straitjacket and repeated slogans like 'Long Live the Soviet Union!' I hated the idea of my party right or wrong, and I tried to transmit this spirit in the university." Invariably, there were clashes with the army. "Young men were angry, but they expressed themselves by demonstrating peacefully. When the army came, they would hide and the army would shoot and the students would throw stones. Eventually they closed the university."

The Oslo Accords eventually gave the PA control over its education portfolio. Gabi worked on a Palestinian syllabus for West Bank and Gazan students with colleagues at the Education Ministry. "Only in 2007 did we have the same exam," he stated. The new syllabus reflected a national agenda, but students also had to take twelve years of religious studies courses. "I felt this was out of proportion," Gabi said. The more serious flaw in the curriculum was that it "was constructed on the idea of a Palestinian state living next to Israel," he continued. "I was just an adviser." Under the circumstances, though, he thinks the committee did a good job. Some Palestinians argue that the curriculum played down national struggle in favor of a bland narrative of coexistence, I suggested. "Maybe," Gabi responded. "But they have to be careful. What about issues like suicide bombings?"

In the late 1990s pro-Israel lobbyists advanced a claim that Palestinian textbooks taught hate and demonized Jews. "It was totally unfounded," Gabi said. "We didn't incite hatred, but we did incite against occupation." By 2006 Hillary Clinton was condemning "violence" and "dehumanizing rhetoric" in Palestinian textbooks. Gabi wrote the official responses. The criticisms were "total lies," he says. "Our rebuttal was sufficient for the European Union, which said that these criticisms were unfounded and that our syllabus was free from incitement."

But what is wrong with teaching an Israeli perspective on the Holocaust and Nakba? I asked. "We're not going to teach our students lies," he answered, stone-faced. "The 'War of Independence' is the core of our Nakba. We're not going to tell them that Israelis did not commit any crimes just because they say that to their own people." One problem with that, I said, is that it leaves students unable to dispute arguments that Zionism was a national liberation movement—because they have never studied them. "We know the Zionist narrative," Gabi slammed back reflexively. "It is that we do not exist. We are not going to teach that."

Academic boycott was the way forward. "This is one form of resisting occupation," he said. "We learned the hard way. We wanted to talk and gave the impression that there was peace while the Israelis created more facts on the ground, the opposite of what peace needs." He dismissed the idea that a boycott would hurt academic links with Israel. "We never had any," he said indignantly. "They look down at you or try to be philanthropic by giving you crumbs. How many Israeli academics condemn the occupation or the university closures? They have to realize that they're occupying us." Israeli schools, he noted, do not teach about the Nakba or even the Green Line.

They also promote hatred, he argued. In 1966, a survey of more than a thousand Israeli schoolchildren by George Tamarin rated their approval of the biblical story of Joshua and the battle of Jericho, which involves divine sanction for theft, arson, and genocide. Sixty percent of the group gave "total approval" to the passage. When the same story was re-presented to them with Chinese names and places replacing the Jewish ones, only 7 percent approved. "The children said Joshua was right because he was following God's orders," Gabi explained. "Some students approved it because they didn't want to mix with the goyim, and if they spared their lives, they would intermarry. Others said, 'At least they could have spared the oxen and sheep so we could have used them.'" A more recent poll of Israeli schoolchildren found that around half opposed giving Arabs equal rights with Jews.

During the Second Intifada, the most important struggle at Bir Zeit was fought over the question of violent resistance to occupation. "You don't attack civilians," Gabi asserted. "If you want to attack you should target the army or do sabotage." But he had a grassroots understanding of the militia's appeal. "If students get through a checkpoint to college," he explained, "they are mad at how they were treated. There are school closures and military occupations and constant Israeli pressure—demolishing homes, hitting civilians, terrorizing people." In such circumstances, "you don't feel what happens to Jewish families. Maybe they are feeling a small fraction of what they've made you feel."

After the Palestinian election in 2005, Hamas took over the PA's Education Ministry. "There was an unhealthy move to control," Gabi told me. "We were unhappy about it. Their politicization of Islam came as a reaction to the politicization of Judaism. They saw the Jews doing the same thing—using religious arguments that they had always dreamed of Jerusalem—and Israel encouraged them." Hamas mismanaged the Education Ministry, and "increasingly we were left out," he went on. "They changed job descriptions and the ministry's whole structure." Ultimately, his place on the PA's certification committee was stolen too, he felt.

Every so often, Gabi used to pass the Museum on the Seam on the twenty-minute ride to see his brother and sister in Jerusalem. Nowadays, lacking a permit, his visits have become rarer. "I'd been sneaking into Jerusalem with friends," he said, "or going with a special permit that I got during feasts. But I can't remember the last time I visited them. They come here." Even so, Gabi's memories of what was lost were gouged in stone. On the roof terrace of the museum his father built, you could still see bullet holes in the walls, although some had been cemented in. Nearby there was an affecting metal sculpture of a crow pecking at a man's stomach. He had one arm raised for help. Man and crow were joined by iron and crimson sand. Beside it, there was also a small container of hot red sand. It felt soft and earthy when you dipped your hands in. But it stained them red for hours afterward.

Nuri al-Ukbi, 66

Bedouin Activist

AL-ARAQUIB, ISRAEL

They said no one lived here Nuri had been evicted from this land more than twenty-five times in the past three years, but on each occasion he had returned. He was born here, in al-Araquib, a lonely expanse of ocher desert between Rahat and Be'ersheva. His family was wrenched from this vast tract of earth when he was nine years old. At the time of our interview, he had hitched his black tarpaulin tent to its rockface and was clinging on for dear life.

With his sun-drizzled good looks, baggy shirt, and dapper belt buckle, Nuri could have passed for a tired film star. But his life in the Negev desert was spent frugally, squatting over tea heated on a portable stove, sleeping on a mattress in a spartan tent held down by stones. A desert wind peeled at its tarpaulin flaps as we talked, and Nuri had to excuse himself to secure them. He decided to live this way in April 2006, after the central court in Be'ersheva ruled that his tribe had no rights to their land.

"I just put a roof over my head and some concrete on the floor, and then the Green Patrol came," he said. The Green Patrol is a paramilitary police force Ariel Sharon established in 1979 to combat the "infiltration" of state lands by Bedouin shepherds. "They even kill the farmers' sheep and goats," Nuri said. Four days after the patrol's visit, Nuri was awakened at 6:00 A.M. "I heard noise and so many police jeeps and bulldozers. An officer told me he had 250 men there. I asked him if he had a court order. He said, 'We don't need papers,' and two of his men arrested me. The bulldozer demolished my tent."

During one demolition in April 2007, he was attacked by a policeman who yanked at his thumb. "It was badly hurt, with internal and external bleeding. It didn't heal properly, and I'm still being treated for it," Nuri said. A monument he built from local stones, with the words "No to racism" inscribed on it in Arabic had also been demolished. "I built it three times and the bulldozers destroyed it three times," he told me. "Each time I rebuilt it."

The story of Nuri's protest is rooted in the aftermath of the Nakba, during which around two-thirds of the one thousand al-Ukbi clan members fled or were expelled from the Negev to Gaza and Jordan. When I asked him about it, Nuri looked to the sky and pleaded, "God give me patience to face the state of Israel." This was no rhetorical flourish. "Israel came to our house on November 13, 1951," he said. "They expelled us for the state's security—so the army could exercise here—and said that we would be allowed to return after six months. They were liars. We were forced to leave. Trucks came and took all our tents and possessions."

When Nuri's father returned after the six months had passed, he was immediately arrested and expelled again. Al-Araquib was registered as Israeli state land—as was around 85 percent of the Negev—and in the years that followed its twelve Bedouin tribes were corralled into an enclosed zone that made up approximately 10 percent of the desert. Nuri's father was stripped of his tribal authority by Israel's Interior Ministry, which was now anointing shaykhs. "They said he had been causing problems," he explained.

Nuri has maps and tithes to the land that stretch back to mandate and Turkish rule. He unrolled them in front of me with gnarled hands as though they marked buried treasure. But although the British and Ottomans accepted the Negev Bedouins' rights to this land—which they had lived on and farmed since the eighteenth century—the Israeli state's position was that the land had been empty. Some of Nuri's 19,000 dunams of land were recently given over to the gated Jewish settlement of Givaot Bar. "They built it overnight," Nuri said. "It was planned for another area, but they just moved it here. It makes me sad that I'm not allowed to walk on my land while they bring other people to live there."

Nuri's clan had always been respected—his grandfather was a shaykh under the Ottomans—and was known for dealing with women's issues in the tribal courts. "If a woman in the field was sexually harassed by a stranger or there were problems between married couples a few shaykhs would decide how to solve it," he said. The last court hearing was in 1950.

Shortly afterward, twenty-year-old Nuri decided to move north to Lyd to work as a mechanic. "The Bedouins didn't have it so good in Lyd," he reflected. "They suffered from poverty, crime, and drugs." In 1963 the agriculture minister and former Israeli army chief Moshe Dayan told Israel's *Haaretz* newspaper that he planned a proletarianizing "revolution" in which the Bedouin would disappear within two generations. Every Bedouin farmer would become "an urban person who comes home in the afternoon and puts his slippers on," Dayan said. But the fear of Bedouin terrorists so close to Ben Gurion Airport helped to stymie the plan. Instead, seven "recognized" towns were created in the Negev that today house around half of the area's Bedouins.

"They have access to water and electricity," Nuri told me, "but they suffer from poverty, unemployment, and crime. The Bedouin social system there has been changed. People don't help, support, or even contact each other as Bedouins used to do. Each Bedouin became an egoist, thinking only of what is best for themselves, not their tribe." Life may be harder for the Bedouins who live in unrecognized villages using illegal water and electricity siphons, without roads, education, or health care, but at least "people have kept more traditions and they're closer to each other," Nuri reasoned. To his mind, the Israeli state had practiced a form of "cultural genocide" on the Bedouin, its forced displacements destroying a people with a different culture and traditions.

He pinpointed what he called "an existential problem facing the Negev": pollution from Israel's biggest toxic waste dump in Ramat Hovav, next to the unrecognized village of Wadi Na'am. "It has caused many diseases," he said, "cancers, asthma, women lost their children. The death rate was going up, but the government didn't do anything for the people in the village besides moving them to areas around Arad and Dimona, which are also affected. People demonstrated, but their voices were not heard." Nuri blamed radiation for an increase in cancers and other diseases around Israel's nuclear weapons complex in Dimona. "Some people in my tribe have been affected by these," he said, "and no one is sure why."

The land, air, and water of al-Araquib are hugely important to Nuri. When I asked him why, he read to me from a poem he had written. "I had a grandfather," he began. "He had a house and a tree. They destroyed the house and took the tree. It happened. It really happened. They stole the crane. They stole the hill. They took also the goats, also the sheep. It happened. It really happened. I was left without milk, without grain, without a house too. They said no one lived here. Nothing was here. In my hand there was a green leaf, olivelike. I asked loudly, 'Why did they do this? Why did they destroy the house and take the tree down?' I cried. They laughed. They laughed and laughed and laughed. For how long will I cry and they laugh?"

But the importance of the land lies not just in establishing historical truth. Land also means survival. "It is my society, my culture, my generation," Nuri proclaimed. "It is my grandson's generation. This is where I want my children to live, eat cream, and drink my cow's milk. Regardless of the fact that my land was taken, I want to live here. In a TV interview, they asked a woman in Givaot Bar why she wanted to live there. She said 'clean air and also a bit of Zionism.' It made me angry. They're taking my land just for a bit of Zionism and clean air?"

But Nuri immediately cautioned, "Not all Jews are like this. Many of my friends were fooled by Zionist propaganda and didn't realize that this would be at another people's expense." Still there was clearly a difference in indigenous and Western attitudes toward land—and water. "The Israelis who came here were immediately connected to water by technology and never took it from a well," Nuri said. "They will not appreciate it because they get it easily from a tap, and they waste it. A Bedouin cares more about it because for us, it is a source of life."

We started to talk about Mokhorot, the state water company, which will not provide water to unrecognized villages. Nuri told me they simply declared themselves owners of all the Negev's water when the state was established. "They never asked," he protested. "Therefore I always say: 'Recognize first that this land is mine, and then we will talk about the other properties.' I wonder why you are laughing?" I hadn't noticed that I was. I thought about it for a minute and decided that I was laughing because the precondition would render any further talks unnecessary. But then I reflected and wondered whether this was not exactly what Israel has asked of Nuri, all Arabs, and indeed the world when it demands recognition of the legitimacy of the Jewish state—and its founding. "I think you're right," I told him. Both peoples' sense of who they are is determined by their relationship to the land. Why should Nuri compromise the truth of who he is—his connection to the land—so that Israelis may have a lie of who they are reinforced? The only answer I could think of was power.

In March 2010 Nuri was sent to prison, facing forty charges of trespass. Later that year, hundreds of riot police invaded and destroyed the nearby al-Araquib village that housed between 200 and 300 Bedouins, for the fifth time. As has become the custom, the villagers vowed to rebuild it.

Nuri was eventually freed on condition that, as "a serial invader of state lands," he never set foot in al-Araquib again. So he returned to Lyd, where he was promptly charged with operating his garage business without a permit and sentenced to another seven months in jail. The judge, Zacharia Yemini, said that he was treating Nuri with exemplary harshness "to send a message to the Bedouins that they must obey the law." On his way back to prison, Nuri collapsed and was hospitalized, under heavy security guard.

Jamal Freij, 71

*Former Well
Maintenance Worker*

KFAR QASSEM, ISRAEL

No feelings Jamal had few memories of the Nakba. "Nothing much happened here," he muttered as we sat in his long, dark living room. "There were no feelings. The houses were open to the streets. We just saw the soldiers passing through in their tanks. We survived. People's lives even improved. They went to work for the Jews in the olive groves and in the quarry, cutting stones. We were treated well." Jamal's town, Kfar Qassem, sits on the rim of the West Bank, just inside Israel. Under military administration, it was Druze soldiers that strictly controlled the village, Jamal said, not the Jews. But it was Jewish soldiers who committed a terrible atrocity here on the day the Suez War began. As usual, on October 29, 1956, Jamal was at work maintaining the village well in a nearby field.

"People were very scared because the army came and surrounded the village, leaving the eastern side open so people could flee to Jordan," he said. The villagers felt "unsafe and insecure," he added, but no one left. That afternoon, two village children came to tell Jamal to return to the town because a curfew had been declared for 5:00 P.M. "I gathered everyone," he said. "There were twenty-five workers between seventeen and twenty-three years old, and we all drove back in the lorry. When we arrived at the village entrance at 5:30 P.M., three ugly soldiers with weapons at their sides signaled for the driver to stop. They first asked us to get out and then said, 'Where were you?' We answered that we'd been at work. The soldier walked back three steps and said, 'Harvest them!' in Arabic."

The soldiers looked "normal," Jamal said, but "they started to fire on us, shooting everyone. We were all on the ground outside the car. I could run away, so I got up and ran. I hid between the olive trees. When I got back, I saw everyone shouting, struggling, and dying. I hid behind a spare tire under the car. The same soldier shouted, 'Put a bullet in each one's head.' Whether they were alive or dead, they shot everyone." How did the soldiers miss you? I asked. "Allah," he replied, motioning upward with his eyes. "There is a God. If they had seen me, they would have killed me." As Jamal lay under the car, he recited verses from the Qur'an, praising God and asking for his mercy. He also considered trying to escape to Jordan.

Soon, a car arrived filled with women who had been working in the nearby Petach Tikva olive groves. One was pregnant. "The soldiers signaled for the car to stop," Jamal said, "but when the driver saw the dead bodies, he didn't. So they started firing. They shot the window of the car out from 150 meters away. Then the car stopped. The driver came out and put his hands up. He said, 'We're dying, girls. Oh, we're dying, girls,' as though their destiny was over. The soldiers told all the girls to get out, but they didn't. So they shot them all. I tried to get out from under the car, but because of the fear I couldn't do it. The soldiers were leaning back on the car now so I could see their legs. I could have grabbed them and done something, but I didn't. I wouldn't have scared them. They shot everyone who came back to the village on their bikes."

Eventually, at around 9:00 or 9:30 that night, "a jeep came, and someone asked the soldiers, 'How many of them have you shot?' They replied, 'We don't know the number, but we're carrying on.' The people in the jeep told them, 'Keep going. Continue.' At 10:00 the last car came to the village. They stopped the driver—who was delivering food to soldiers—and followed him back in their jeep. When they returned, they saw me. They saw me! Someone said, 'There is one under the car. Pull him out.' They thought I was dead. The soldier kneeled down and tried poking me with his Uzi. I jumped out on him and clasped his arms. I was shaking him, screaming and crying, 'Please, please, what did I do to you?' The soldier didn't speak a word, he was so scared."

"The officer ordered, 'Take him and kill him right away,' and the other two soldiers came to free the soldier I was holding. While they tried to do that, I saw a light from a vehicle coming toward the village." It was an Israeli army truck carrying about thirty soldiers. When it arrived, the soldiers at the village entrance backed off. "Come," an officer from the truck said to Jamal. "Hold me."

"In imperfect Arabic, he said, 'I will take you home,'" Jamal remembered. "I wasn't convinced. He asked an Arab soldier to come to me. The soldier said, 'I'm an Arab like you,' and then he started to cry hard. He also said, 'Come and hold me.' So I released the Israeli soldier and hugged the Bedouin. Then he took me to sit twenty meters away from where the soldiers were."

By this point, some forty-eight dead bodies were scattered around the town's entrance. Jamal remembered how the soldiers started to collect and stack them in his lorry and one of theirs. "I was sitting on a stone in the same place where the mosque is now," he said. "I saw the dead bodies of two uncles." In those days Kfar Qassem was "a small farming village of only 1,000 or 2,000 weak and poor people," Jamal said. Were there any attempts at resistance against the three soldiers? I asked. "No," he said. "We were workers. We didn't have any weapons. They had rifles. There was no way to fight them. If anyone in the village had left their house, they would have been shot." Perhaps the Israeli soldiers would have understood such a dynamic better in other contexts.

Afterward the bodies were sent to the neighboring Jewish town of Rosh Ha'ayin. "They wanted people to identify the bodies," Jamal said. "Then they asked fifty people from the village of Jaljuli to bury them. A soldier stood next to each body. We were not allowed to leave our houses for four days until the soldiers left town. Later the government initiated a *sulha,* and the mayor of Petach Tikva came, but no villagers attended. People from other villages came."

Because Kfar Qassem was such a small village "everyone lost some relatives," Jamal said. "I knew many of the dead, may they rest in peace. They died as *shahids*. I wish I had died." Jamal seemed to have his emotions under very tight control, but when I queried how he thought the event had changed him, he snapped, "Don't ask me. It was very harsh, and for years I couldn't sleep at night whenever I thought about it. I always thanked God that I survived. But each year in October, I can never sleep. On the twenty-ninth, I remember all the fear." Another townsperson later told me that her father—who lost his mother in the massacre—also had difficulties in October. Jamal did not think such an incident could happen again, "but they practice the same horror in Gaza and the West Bank."

Curiously, perhaps, he sounded proud when he told me that the month before our interview the interior minister had visited the now 20,000-strong locale and declared it a city. "We are living happily," he said. "I get my insurance and pension, and my sons get their insurance. We wouldn't get this money in the Arab countries." Even so, he saw himself as "an Arab Palestinian."

"What a question! I heard on the news today that some Israeli authorities want to transfer Arabs to the West Bank and bring settler Jews from the West Bank to live here," he said. Just as anti-Semitism once framed Jewish identity, so now does Jewish racism often frame Palestinian identity, especially among Arabs in Israel. Perhaps it is no surprise that Israel's Islamic Movement was born in this town.

After the media blackout ended and the truth of October 29 was established in an Israeli court, many Israeli Jews wished that the survivors of Kfar Qassem would move on. But the most salient gestures toward reconciliation after the massacre remain these: The two soldiers found guilty of murder—Shmuel Malinki and Gabriel Dahan—served just one year in prison before being promoted; Dahan was appointed head of Arab affairs in the nearby city of Ramle, and Malinki was later made a security chief at the Dimona nuclear plant; Yisca Shadmi, the officer in charge, was found guilty of exceeding his authority and fined one grush (approximately 10 Israeli cents today). Shadmi was pardoned in 1958 and went on to become a high-ranking government official managing Israel's relations with its Palestinian minority.

When I asked Jamal what conclusions he drew from the promotion of the soldiers that perpetrated the killing, he said, "Nothing is in my hands. I can't do anything about the Israeli state." Ilan Pappe wrote that the Shadmi case revealed two long-standing features of Israeli policy: "The first is that people indicted for crimes against Arabs are likely to remain in positions in which they continue to affect the lives of Palestinians, and secondly, that they will never be brought to justice."

Aisha Odeh, 63

Women's Center Founder

DEIR JARIR, WEST BANK

A ghost "I remember the Nakba very well," Aisha said. "My aunt is from Deir Yassin." Every Palestinian knows about the massacre at Deir Yassin. On April 9, 1948, an estimated 120 Palestinians were killed there—96 of them civilians. Whole families were riddled with bullets or shrapnel from grenades that were bowled into their houses. Survivors were spat on, cursed, and beaten with rifles as they were loaded onto trucks that paraded them as trophies around West Jerusalem. The atrocity turned the flight of refugees from Palestine into a stampede. Aisha lost one of her relatives in the village's killing fields. In 1967, a month after the borders were reopened, she returned to Deir Yassin but could not bring herself to enter the village. Two years later, she was jailed for bombing a Jerusalem supermarket and killing two people.

Aisha's English sometimes faltered, but her choice of words was still evocative for a native speaker. She dusted off her story of Deir Yassin for me like a frightful bedtime story. "My aunt escaped with her family to my mother's village near here," she said. "My mother went to see her, and because I was four years old I ran after her all the time then. I remember how the women were weeping when we entered that place. My aunt's daughter Zeinab was sixteen or seventeen, and she used to get up in the morning to bake dough in the oven [at the village bakery]. She was maybe the first person to [arrive]. Then she heard the militias with guns enter and kill a man and a woman who were working there. She was afraid and hid under some wood. Then she fell unconscious."

Zeinab's panic-stricken family had fled their home, barefoot and in their pajamas, before they realized Zeinab was missing. When they returned, "they found the people who were killed in the oven, but they didn't see Zeinab. They thought that the women had been taken as prisoners so they went to the Red Cross, but they couldn't find her name. They became crazy. A relative of theirs died there."

Two days later, when they returned to the village bakery, the family found Zeinab crying out softly from her hiding place. She had been left mute by her ordeal. Aisha recalled her mother's constant weeping and the story of another Deir Yassin mother whose husband worked cutting stones. "They had a good Jewish friend who brought them coffee the night before," she said. "In the morning, he came to the house dressed as a soldier. He killed her husband and tried to kill the baby. The woman said, 'Please leave my baby, and I will give you everything.' She gave him all her money."

"Our family was very close," Aisha continued. "We saw how our aunt's family was crying and dreaming of returning to their village. We felt it very much, especially when we saw the refugees walking. I was loved by my aunt's family. They had children like me, and I remembered their house. It was so nice. I compared it with my own. I loved them so very much that I wanted them to return. How could I help them? This affected me to struggle."

In 1967 the Odeh family was the first in the area to contact the Fedayeen and organize. "All of us worked for the struggle," she said. "The Israeli army destroyed my uncle's house in '68 and my family's house in '69, when they captured me." Aisha's brother went on the run while a sister's husband was jailed twice and deported. Several cousins faced similar hardships. After the *Naksa*, Aisha enthusiastically joined the newly minted PFLP.

Initially, she organized petitions, demonstrations, and strikes and provided shelters and food to refugees from three villages west of Ramallah that were destroyed during the 1967 war. But military resistance was an imperative. "The Israelis took the land with weapons," she said, "not demonstrations and love. You can try to be an angel, to pray and write poems, but the world will not give us our rights like this. We lose a lot. In our minds as Arabs, you must be brave and fight against your enemy." Aisha began transporting weapons from the Jordanian border—"And I used them!" she stressed. How did it feel when you first fired a gun? I asked. "You feel empowered," she replied. "You're making your future, and it's a great feeling." Her own military action, though, was not.

"I think the operation was very silly," she understated the case. "It wasn't my idea. I'd always wanted to fire weapons, and when a friend asked me if I wanted to take part I said, 'Yes!' So they prepared everything. I had to put the bomb in a Supersol supermarket in Jerusalem that they decided on. There was a big debate about whether it was a civilian target. They said most of the people who went there were soldiers and older people. No children. So I said that we should first place a bomb that makes a loud noise—so the soldiers and detectives would go there—and then put a second one that explodes five minutes later among these people."

In fact, the first bomb did not make a loud noise and the second was found before it went off. Even so, two people were killed in the first explosion and several injured. One of the dead was a soldier. "He was a big one!" Aisha exclaimed. "The second person I don't know about." She did not apologize for this, but afterward, she admitted, "something inside me was not okay. I felt nothing, and I wouldn't do it again. I wanted to see the soldiers as I fought them, like you read in novels. You wait on the street until the military comes and then"—she made a machine gun gesture, sweeping her sights round the living room—"ra-ta-ta-ta! I'd like to have done that. I never did."

After the attack, Aisha sat with her mother on their veranda in Deir Jarir. "I put my head on her leg in the sun and we listened to the radio," she recounted. "My mother said, 'Hear what is going with the Fedayeen! They came from Jordan and jumped a three-meter-high wall with bombs. Then they returned, and no one caught them.' But I really didn't feel happy."

Did you feel guilty? I asked. "Not at all," she said stoutly. "To fight against your enemy is not a cause for guilt." But you killed a civilian, I said. "They also killed people who were not soldiers when they entered Deir Yassin," she scolded, "women and children—and they continue to kill. Why do they have the right to kill when we mustn't?" Because they are the occupiers fighting a colonial war and a liberation struggle is fought differently, I suggested. "Now we can say it," she exhaled, and her anger ebbed slightly. "At the time, the most important thing was to fight."

Aisha was arrested at her house on March 1, 1969. "We were young beginners in our work, and we made a lot of mistakes," she said. "When they arrested a person who prepared—and gave us—the bombs, they tortured him, and he said, 'I saw this one.'" She shuddered at the memory. The trial lasted nearly a year and ended with Aisha sentenced to two life terms plus ten years. "We didn't think we would spend all our lives in prison," she said. "We always believed that we would be freed in a prisoner exchange. We didn't allow ourselves to feel weak in front of the Israelian soldiers. At first they would say, 'You are killers,' but after two years they came to respect us."

Aisha learned Hebrew in jail, but relations with Israeli prisoners were tense. "Most of them were from the underclass," she said. "Some were killers, some with hashish; just criminals. They were so nervous and aggressive. For the first two years we lived in the same building, and they tried to beat or kill us. We had to be strong to face them. We told the Red Cross: We must be alone." Eventually, the Palestinian female prisoners were moved to another building. There, Aisha joined the DFLP, because it was the first group to support a two-state solution, she said. "For me, it was an aim we could fulfill."

More mundanely, the guards' strategy was "to divide us and get everyone thinking only about herself. You weren't allowed to use the word *we,* and sometimes they forbade books and family visits. If I asked why, they'd punish me with a week in solitary confinement. Once they locked us in our cells, so we started banging on our doors. Then they sprayed tear gas in our faces. It was like fire. We felt that we were finished. We couldn't take any more air into our lungs."

While sexual threats from guards in prison were a fact of life, assaults were uncommon. "But it happened with me and Rasmieh Odeh," Aisha said. "They tried to rape us in a very bad situation. They tried to rape me with a stick, and really they did. I reached the point of death, and they succeeded. I fell unconscious." Aisha was unable to say any more about the incident, which she wrote about in an Arabic-language memoir. "I don't like to speak," she said. "Please don't ask me to. It's not easy for me to talk about this again and again." She offered coffee, and I watched as she stirred it silently but relentlessly over a small gas stove for fifteen minutes. She showed me a set of pictures she had made out of cut flowers for an exhibition in 1999. Then we returned to her story.

"I got out in the first prison exchange between the PLO and the Israelis in '79," she said. "Seventy-six prisoners were released in return for an Israeli soldier in Lebanon captured by the PFLP." She was taken to the Geneva airport and then Libya for a week before traveling on to Damascus, where she chose to live in Jordan. One sister and a brother already lived there, and Aisha's mother could visit easily. Exile was difficult. "But in the end I was free," she said. "You discover that you were in prison when you get out. While you're in prison, you're fighting in another world. When you get out and find that life has moved on so far, you discover that you were in hell. During your ten years in prison, you built a world for yourself from books. They were the most important things for us. We saw our enemy in front of us. Outside, you don't know what you want to do. Other people's ways of thinking are strange. Everything is strange. Just living is difficult. Then you discover that the prison is inside you. The first year was the most difficult. I was a stranger."

Aisha was elected to the Palestine National Council in 1981 and worked for a PLO prisoners' association. Watching the Intifada from afar was hard, but Aisha also felt personally and politically marginalized in post–Black September Jordan. "There was no democracy, and I was under the spotlight," she said. "I wasn't even allowed to travel freely." After the Oslo Accords, she decided to return to the West Bank. "It was great for me," she said, smiling. "I was in my homeland under occupation, divided and destroyed, but it was my land and I was in it. I wasn't a ghost." On the day she returned, "it was very cold," she remembered, "but they welcomed me like a queen. The people of Taybe and my village stood on the roofs waving Palestinian flags. The streets were full with hundreds of people buzzing and the women were 'Woo-loo-loo!'" she said, ululating.

Aisha still faced bureaucratic wrangling with the authorities over a permit and was briefly forced to abscond to Gaza. But she now lived in a modern chalet-style cottage home, working with other women in the Deir Jarir Women's Society for Development, which produced beautiful handcrafts. Most important, she had returned to the land where her family grew olives, wheat, figs, and grapes. Oddly, she was unaware that land adjoining Deir Yassin had been used to create the world-famous Yad Vashem Holocaust Museum. When asked if it might have been done unconsciously to bury the Palestinian tragedy beneath a bigger Jewish tragedy, she replied, "It's very important for the Jews to remember what happened to them. What happened to others, they have to forget."

Victimhood can confer moral, political, and diplomatic advantage, but it can also perpetuate trauma. "We never wanted to throw the Jews into the sea," Aisha had told me. "But is it fair for Jews from America to come to Palestine, dismiss me from my land, and live as kings? Palestinians have to speak about this, like they drink water. They have to remember. They don't have the luxury of forgetting because the reminders are everywhere—the refugee camps, the soldiers, the wall, the settlers. It's not something you can be finished with. It lives within you." But, I asked, doesn't that mean there is also a pain inside that you can never let go of? "Yes," she replied insouciantly, "sure."

Eyad al-Sarraj, 66

Psychiatrist

GAZA CITY

Dealing with it   Around the time that Eyad was born, his father was advised to buy land in the family's original Gaza homestead and build a house. His supervisor in the British mandate police had told him, "The time will come when you will all move there." Eyad spoke slowly. "My father told me that the plan was there," he said.

We were seated in the bountiful gardens of the house that Eyad's father began building all those years ago. The villa was now four stories high and beautifully decorated. The walls surrounding it shut out the street on the other side. Eyad also had expensive cars and a catamaran. His lifestyle, the siege notwithstanding, was haut bourgeois. He was also suffering from acute leukemia and, on the days we met, a side pain that cramped his style and energy but not his insight. His tone was professorial.

Shortly before the Nakba, Eyad remembered, "one of my uncles came to the house with a big machine gun. My parents took us away, and he started shooting at a wall. I thought it was a game, but apparently it was military training. Another uncle arrived on a motorbike, completely masked. He was in hiding and unable to fight. We took him into the house."

Eyad remembered many things about the journey to Gaza: his father sitting in the back of the lorry while his mother cried, the sewing machine that she had been forced to leave behind, and the way she wept in Gaza whenever she had to sew anything after that. "I just wondered what we were doing and where we were going," he said. "I wasn't alarmed, just puzzled and sad that my mother was crying. She was sitting and holding my hand, and my head was resting on her chest."

In Gaza, the Sarrajes were lucky not to have ended up in a refugee camp. "There was discrimination," Eyad said, "almost racism between refugees and nonrefugees. Refugees were looked down on. Originally, some of them had been nobles and landowners, but because of the uprooting they were destitute. The Gaza high classes wouldn't let their children marry them." Eyad, though, had schoolfriends in the camps. He was always an exception. His decisions to study psychiatry in Egypt, to specialize in the human rights of mental patients, and then to move to Cornwall, England, all cut against the local grain.

When he returned to Gaza in the early 1980s, he met "the worst extreme-right Likudniks," he said, "like Moshe Arens—who was Netanyahu's teacher—and I liked him! I met him because I wanted to establish a clinic in Gaza. Other Palestinian doctors were opposing me. I explained my story to him, but I didn't complain about people who weren't there. He said, 'Are you sure you're an Arab? Everyone comes here to complain about the others behind their backs.' I said that I just wanted to finish this business by dealing with it. He said, 'I like this attitude,' and we became friends."

Arens would test Eyad again when there was an outbreak of fainting among schoolgirls who lived near settlements. "It started in the West Bank," Eyad said. "The news spread that settlers were poisoning the schools with gas. I was appointed head of a medical committee, and I examined the cases myself. My decision was that the girls should be turned away from hospitals and sent back home. A doctor said, 'You can't do that. The PLO will shoot you!' I said, 'I'm a doctor, not a politician.'" Eyad's diagnosis of mass hysteria so pleased Arens that he was appointed to investigate all medical negligence cases in Gaza. He had to be tough because many doctors came from the big Palestinian clans. So Eyad threatened to publish the malfeasances of negligent doctors unless they resigned. But the influence of clans was weakening among affluent Palestinians.

"Traditionally, people relied on the family and the tribe against the state, which was alien and foreign," Eyad explained. "This and *sumud* were the main frames of security and support. You can talk about the Palestinian struggle in terms of families. You can talk about political parties representing or replacing families. But tribalism was a way of life as well as a state of mind over the centuries. It helped people to sustain their culture. Now, with modernization and competition, the family and tribe are less cohesive, particularly if you're educated or middle-class. I haven't seen many of my close relatives for years. Twenty years ago, we met regularly."

The decline of the tribes was something Eyad saw as double-edged. "If you can only substitute militant groups, you encourage violence because these groups need a war to stay strong and keep their momentum," he said. "Some people will rely on them, be guided by them, and be hostages to them. It's very dangerous. You see signs that people are giving up with apathy, indifference, and feelings of failure and despair. But then the defiance and resilience kick in."

Throughout the 1990s and 2000s, Eyad's Gaza Community Mental Health Program attracted the ire of Fatah and Hamas alike for its human rights defense of all segments of Gaza's community. Eyad's status as a civil society figurehead grew. He wrote op-eds for the *New York Times* and teleconferenced with the likes of Javier Solana, Ban Ki-Moon, and Tony Blair. In summer 2009 he felt optimistic that Barack Obama could "understand the situation in a way that helps Israelis and Palestinians to ease their paranoia." For Eyad, steps to counter Paranoia, with a capital "P," were vital. "There's even room to talk to Netanyahu, who looks like the devil," he said.

"Israel has a tradition of paranoia. They have a history of centuries of persecution. Jews were hated everywhere, and then there was the trauma of the Holocaust. It now goes into the school curriculum. That must affect you. We also became paranoid. We think the world is conspiring against us. Political leaders on both sides feed it, consciously or unconsciously. They thrive on it. Israel's violence needs Palestinian violence to justify itself. The big Israeli peace camp was killed by our suicide bombing. When you start killing civilians in the country's heart, you reinforce a collective paranoia. Sadat was a Christ-like messiah because he treated that paranoia. He came from the strongest Arab country and laid down his sword in front of Israel.

Everyone cheered. Menachem Begin—not Netanyahu—was forced to sign a peace treaty because the Israeli people wanted it." Obama could do the same.

Playing the doctor prescribing yucky medicine, Eyad recommended immediate talks involving the Israelis and Hamas, along with a total cessation of hostilities and opening of borders. "Paranoia grows in the darkness," he said. "When you meet people, you start to see human beings. If you don't, you imagine that they're like beasts. They eat children. When I meet Jews, my God! They're so nice and beautiful, like us. Many Israelis are shocked that I come from Gaza and speak English. At parties, they admire the fact that I wear a tie."

The diagnosis seemed to be that paranoia was a primary symptom of the conflict that had to be disabled to allow awareness of its emotional core—dehumanization—to filter through. Eyad described dehumanization as "a part of victim psychology. It can be used as a weapon and a cultural defense mechanism. It makes you feel elevated and justifies your actions. When we dehumanize refugees, we project our guilt onto them as we blame them. To this day, people say they shouldn't have left. They should have died. In Deir Yassin, they shouldn't have come to Gaza. In the same way, the Israelis say, 'We didn't ask the refugees to leave. They left of their own accord.' Blaming the victim means you don't have to deal with your own guilt. I believe that the Israelis are basically victimized, but they haven't dealt with their trauma in a healthy way. They created a new victim and projected their inner feelings onto them. This is how Palestinians became dehumanized and the cycle of violence was created, from one nation to the other, from one humiliation to the other."

This mind-set spread within and without Palestinian society. "Gazan natives dehumanized the refugees," Eyad said. "The West Bank looked down its nose at Gaza and then the Palestinians at the Jordanians and the Gulf people. We went there claiming that we were sophisticated and they were stupid camel riders. We went to Lebanon and dehumanized them. Now we're hated in those countries. We became like the Jews of the Middle East. We haven't dealt with our own dehumanization. Part of the problem between Fatah and Hamas is dehumanization."

In tandem with this was a dependency culture. Eyad called it "a loss of the internal locus of control." "People who are victimized and dependent," he explained, "believe that the environment—country, state, or world—should solve the problem, and they're totally at its mercy. Many of them are unhappy with Hamas and Fatah and the siege, but they don't protest. Why? Part of the explanation is dependency. We feel inferior to the West. Self-accusation, mutilation, and deprecation are also part of this story. Because of a thousand years of defeats at the hands of the West, Arabs feel that we deserve what we get. Punishing ourselves is a common feature of our culture. One Arabic saying has it that, 'Nothing will work on us except beating.' People compare us with the Israelis as a subhuman to a Superman. They glorify the victimizer at the expense of appreciating themselves."

In this context, Eyad's analysis of Hamas's growth began with "our ongoing story of uprooting, destitution, denigration, and exile since the defeat in Andalusia." It continued through the world's inability to end the occupation and Fatah's failures in war, social rehabilitation, and institution building. Eyad actually spent time in jail with Hamas leaders during Arafat's reign. "They considered me a hero," he said. "Ismail Haniyeh, who I voted for, used to visit me frequently. I was very anti-Fatah because of their corruption and lawlessness, and I was happy when Hamas won the elections and took over militarily. I thought they would establish a better system of governance and assumed that they'd be exposed to the world and that an exchange of ideas would begin." Once they were isolated, though, they became more extreme. "They were never given the chance," Eyad said.

"Islam, like all religions, has a fatalistic belief," he said. "Everything is designed by God. That's why so few Palestinians commit suicide. And what is the way to God? The mosque. And who do you meet in the mosque? Hamas. Children met them there and started a journey of identification, to replace the father and increasingly the family. This is why Hamas has countered tribalism. A new identification with a symbol of power is created for you, and it's a barrier to the rest of the community. This also partly explains why Hamas thinks of Fatah as traitors and collaborators. 'We are the defiant ones who resist occupation! The others are working for Israel's security.' Part of this involved creating a cult of suicide bombers. At first, Hamas went through a rigorous process of selecting bombers because they believe so much in individual sacrifice for the group. It makes them stronger. Everyone serves, prays, kills, and dies for God, and whatever happens to you is God's will."

In the process, violence is normalized. "When I was a teenager a killing in Gaza was so evil that the whole Strip would mourn," Eyad said. "It was so rare and unacceptable. Today, violence is just a widespread part of life. Maybe there'll be a period of apathy now, but the next violence when it comes will be internal, external, and maybe worldwide. Hamas will be looked back on as a moderate force. It's very possible that a much more radical group will emerge from inside Hamas if this situation continues. The impact of the recent war will only be seen when the next generation grows up, gets married, and has to raise children. What kind of children will we have in the future?"

"All of Gaza was exposed in this war, but not everyone received help or could analyze their trauma themselves. A large group will have internalized the violence. We have poor education, lack of resources, poverty, cultural xenophobia, the Palestinian division, Islamic Fundamentalism, extreme Israeli attitudes, a continued Israeli and Egyptian siege that has turned Gaza into a prison, and, if Obama fails it will make the next generation much more militant. There will be serious outbreaks of violence, and in ten years' time people will be thinking about the question of chemical and nuclear warfare." Independently, the Israeli journalist Gideon Levy told me something very similar.

Eyad's panoramic grasp of the conflict's emotional and political roots did not inoculate him from trauma during Israel's Winter War. "There was an overwhelming sense of fear that I'd never seen before in my life," he said. "You saw it in people's eyes, particularly children's, and in their behavior on the street. When the war finished, my wife said, 'The next time I hear a plane going by, I'll drop dead.' For nearly a month, there was continuous panic."

"One night, twenty-six of our neighbors came to my house in a state of absolute fear because they were warned that their houses would be bombed in five minutes," Eyad said. Even the tactic of *sumud* seemed to be turned against Gaza. "Some people who stayed in their homes because of *sumud* were killed. A friend in the north called me about this question. He said, 'What should I do?' I said, 'Leave now, with one understanding: that you want to come back alive! But if you don't leave we will lose you.' It was agonizing for him because he'd started a movement in his neighborhood encouraging people to stay. He went only when he'd convinced the rest of them to leave."

Almost every night, people visited him to ask if they could sleep at his home, thinking it was a safe place. "I took so many dramatic phone calls," Eyad murmured. "One of my staff rang, saying, 'There's a wounded man in front of me. He's dying! Please send the Red Cross! I can't do anything!' And you hear people screaming around them. You have people calling about their children wetting the bed every night. Everyone was frightened; every class, every citizen. I was frightened." For a second Eyad seemed unsure of the emotional quality his delivery was conveying. The doctor quickly returned.

During the war, he said, the women in his house slept downstairs while he retired to the bedroom upstairs with his son Ali. "I was always frightened for him because any bomb would explode first through my bedroom window," he said. "Every night, after half an hour, I carried him out to sleep with his mother. Sometimes it was quiet, but then suddenly there'd be an explosion and the house would shake as if there'd been an earthquake. You felt the ground moving beneath you or heard sudden explosions from the sky above your head. The noise was unbelievable, and the children became frightened when women started screaming at two o'clock in the morning."

"One day, I smelled something burning in our garden. I went out to see what it was, and the burning sensation went into my nose. I called someone and they said, 'This is phosphorus. Be careful. Stay indoors and don't open the windows because it kills.' We have an asthmatic child here who needs a ventilator. Asthmatics become more asthmatic when they're anxious, and now with this burning dust raining down, I thought, 'My god, he's going to die.' I was so scared. And I live in one of the most protected houses in Gaza!" Looking around his serene and splendid grounds, it was difficult to imagine Gaza City outside, let alone phosphorus on the lawn. That changed for me a few days later.

In the hours after the attack mentioned in the introduction, Eyad, who seemed physically unable to close his door on a stranger in need, opened it for me too. His family had been my first port of call. Eyad's assistant, Yasser, had met me at the police station, stayed with me during the questioning, and driven me back to the house. As I sat in the garden with its groves, lamp posts, and bougainvillea, Eyad listened attentively as I recounted parts of my story, the perfect therapist and the kindest host. The sun slowly clambered down the sky, and he invited me in for a sumptuous dinner cooked by his staff.

As we ate, Eyad again briefly inquired about my episode and then held court to his other Western guests about the far more grievous symptoms of trauma in Gaza. I could not shake the dread that my near-victimization at the hands of a Palestinian was an unwelcome and potentially dangerous guest at the table. Was I projecting feelings of persecution onto my generous de facto protector? In Gaza's landscape of repressed trauma it was difficult to say. Instead I just sat mutely at the table and watched the sky bruise above the immaculate garden that Eyad's father had thankfully, and so presciently, built.

Hassan al-Kashif, about 64

Journalist

GAZA CITY

All the authority of the Palestinian resistance "I'm about sixty-four," Hassan purred in his deep baritone, "'about,' because I have no birth certificate. My parents lost it when they became refugees." They left Hassan's birth village of Beit Daras in a hurry after it succumbed to a fourth wave of attacks by Jewish militias trying to cut the road east. His memories were "like a vision," he said. They inspired him to become a PLO fighter in Jordan, then a reporter, and ultimately Palestine's most hard-hitting television anchor. His son became a journalist for BBC Arabic. The vision had been powerful. "Our village house was built from the mountains," Hassan said, "not from stones. I remember a small sweet shop in front of it, and part of our land where a calf was born." The journey to Gaza "was the first time I saw the sea," he continued. "We slept on blankets near the seashore and listened to the voice of the waves all night. It was windy in the early morning, very cold, and the blankets got wet somehow."

Hassan's father, a farmer with no land, struggled to find work. "He talked about the Nakba with anger and sadness," Hassan recalled. "He blamed the Arab governments and never trusted them again." Under Egyptian occupation, Communists and Islamists were suppressed while Cairo assumed control of Fedayeen raids into Israel that had been launched to reclaim meager items of property or sometimes to mount attacks. "They were Palestinian refugees who knew the land and village roads," Hassan said. "They were brave men without political minds. Nasser organized them and gave them salaries and weapons." Even so, they were too weak to resist the Israeli invasion of 1956. In Gaza City, Hassan remembered mass arrests and curfews. As soon as he was able, he left to study in Egypt.

In 1967, his last year at college, Israel again occupied Gaza. By the year's end, Hassan was training to fight in Jordan. "My family was waiting for me to finish my studies, work in the Gulf, and send them some money," he said, "but I wanted to fight to liberate my homeland. After the battle of Karameh, thousands of volunteers arrived and the guerrilla bases moved to the mountains and then the cities. We had many big dreams." Hassan was not well liked, but he had a reputation as a good fighter with a political mind. Because of his university education, he was made a commander. "But I always thought independently," he added.

"When I was in Karak before Black September, we wrote on the walls, 'All the authority of the Palestinian resistance.' It was a city in Jordan's south, and a Jordanian boy I knew asked me, 'What about us? We're not Palestinians.'" Hassan paused. "It was not for Palestinian camp refugees to write slogans like this. I told my superior, 'The Jordanian enemies of King Hussein refuse this slogan.' He said, 'Okay, all authority for Palestinian fighters, soldiers, and armed people.' So the battle was between Palestinians and Jordanians. It was a big problem." Black September was its fulcrum. "We had good relations with the Jordanians, but when the battles began in Amman, every Jordanian soldier sent [word] to his family in the south. It became difficult to stay while their sons were being killed," he said. Hassan's unit left for the Mujid valley, and their last battle in the mountains near Jerash was the worst he experienced. "We were completely surrounded with no support," he explained. He escaped to Syria, traveled on to Iraq, and in 1972 began a new life as a journalist.

Hassan interviewed the former Communist military leader and president Mengistu Haile Mariam in Ethiopia, covered the Iran-Iraq War, and was elected president of the Palestinian Writers and Journalists Union in Beirut. "I was a newspaper political writer and a radio reporter," he said carefully. To report well, "you must be independent-minded and have experience and vision," he expanded. "You must trust yourself and believe that you are as important as any minister. You must have a cultured mind because you speak to millions. People look to the journalist to be respectable and honest. They can't believe a dishonest man, even if he's the best writer in the world, especially in small societies like ours. When I walk in this city, everybody knows me." Hassan carried a natural authority. Hamas supporters might construe it as arrogance.

When he returned to Gaza in 1995, Hassan refused Yasser Arafat's request to head up the Ministry of Information in Ramallah. Instead, he presented a weekly TV news show, *Face to Face,* that was "like [BBC World's] *Hard Talk,*" he said. "They stopped the program three times." The first time was in 1997 when he interviewed the author of a report that claimed corruption had cost the PA around $329 million. "All the people [responsible for budgets] were corrupt," he said. "It was the first time many donors had heard this. They began to ask, 'Where's our money?' And they stopped paying." After Hassan spoke out about the fatal shooting of two protesters at the Islamic University by PA forces, the studio lights were again turned off. When Fatah fell in Gaza, they were dimmed permanently.

"Hamas asked me to change the program's name," Hassan said, "so I called it *Red Line.* I made a program with three businessmen as guests. They said that under Hamas all the factories were closed, no materials were coming, and they couldn't export or import. Hamas turned off the power and prevented the program from being broadcast."

Although he was critical of Fatah, Hamas had clearly gotten deeper under Hassan's skin. He took the litmus Fatah position that Hamas could not "be" the PA because it refused negotiations with Israel. Its rocket strategy had hurt Gaza most. "Maybe if they had a third of the parliament it would be good for them. But now they've made many problems with the world, Israel, and Fatah," he said. "Breaking the siege with a ceasefire would be easy, but Hamas is not ready for this."

The key for him was unity. "Arafat's genius was to create unity when we faced the [Lebanese] invasion of 1982 together as one people," he said. "The Israeli interest is for the Palestinians to be divided into the West Bank and Gaza because then how can we create a state?" People did not blame Israel for the "siege of hope," he said. "Come on, they're the enemy. I need electricity. You're the government in Gaza. I need access. I want therapy, treatment, a job, a future for my children. You're not going to make your Islamic state. You haven't been able to yet. Give me my daylight!"

"We're in the worst period in modern Palestinian history. We have maybe one more chance. The Palestinian people need an Orange Revolution now, or else we'll have to wait for another Nakba and then see many Al Qaidas among our people, with this pain." If ever it had appeared pan-Arabic, Palestinian identity after decades of betrayal was now a strictly national affair. "A Palestinian will stay a Palestinian until the end of history," Hassan said. 'No Palestinian will forget for one minute who he is because of the land and because he is a stranger wherever he goes. He has hope of a land that was taken from him by force." Being a Palestinian for him meant "that you have to return to Palestine." "You are not American or British," he said. "I saw many Palestinians who married Americans, but they were Palestinian. The map, the flag, nobody forgets his homeland."

Hassan's fatigue and despair were obvious when we talked on the phone during the 2008–9 war. Many people he knew had been killed. "Most were civilians," he said. "They died under their houses when Israel bombed the ministries and the university. Gaza City is very crowded, and fighters can't be separated from civilians. Places are very near to each other. If the Israelis bomb a Hamas security ministry, people in a nearby house die. Hamas is inside the people. They're not in the Sinai Desert. So if you talk about destroying Hamas, you're really talking about destroying Gaza's people." What would follow if they were ousted? I asked. "Nobody accepts Gaza becoming like Somalia," he said. Hassan's electricity and water had been cut off, and he was going to live in his son's flat. "There's some food there," he said. "Today we ate potato, eggs, and tomato. We're saving some cheese and tea and olives. But this is the worst situation I've seen in Gaza. We are human beings. We are like you. We want to live in peace. We like life. We hate killing. Please, we don't only need food or blankets. We need a life. Let us have a life."

I visited Hassan's affluent but sparsely furnished flat once more after the war. The same bullet holes from the pre-takeover clashes were sprinkled around the same neighboring buildings. But some had metamorphosed into rubble dumps, as though a giant Pythonesque foot had squashed them from the sky. A family member was watching a bootleg DVD of the film *Wolverine* next door. Hassan himself had recovered his composure, but his anger was still raw. "I was afraid during this fighting," he said gruffly, "everyone was, but nobody can be afraid all the time. They got used to the fear and overcame it. At first you searched for a safe place, but there were none. U.N. schools were bombed when people went there to shelter. After two weeks, queues appeared outside the bakeries. It was a great feeling to see a crowd around the bread in the ovens. It was survival."

The windows in Hassan's flat were blown out, and the balcony suffered structural damage. "Even the eggs in the refrigerator were broken!" he said. "Nobody can compensate me." For Hassan, the heroes of the war were medics, not militants. "There was more steadfastness among the Palestinian people. They couldn't even see the bombs falling because they wanted to protect themselves. There were huge fires. You don't see the face of your killer because he is sheltered from the air." Hassan's narrative was spinning from the south pole of *sumud* to the north pole of suffering. "We are victims," he said. "We are prisoners. During the war you couldn't go to a funeral. Sometimes you heard who was killed from the radio." Hamas had been weak and stupid to confront the Israelis in a war they could not win. "They exaggerated their reputation and lost this war," he said. "We have to reconcile now. We must wake people up. Both Fatah and Hamas are a dead end. They can't make a new strategy. The alternative strategy comes from the past, and the past can't be a new one. Maybe a small part of the past." He murmured quietly and lit a cigarette. The strategy always comes from the West, I said. "Peace can also come from the West," he responded.

Hassan's strategy involved making the Obama administration commit to guaranteeing the security of Israel and a Palestinian state. If negotiations did not create a state by a deadline, the U.N. Security Council's 1967 frontiers would be imposed. But every time Israel felt more secure it launched wars and occupations, I said. It only retreated—from Lebanon and the Sinai—after resistance and a war that it nearly lost. "We are talking about a Palestinian state!" he growled. "For Israel's peace we must live here in a cage now? I was born in my village before 1948. The Israelis have not let me visit the graves of my grandfathers for sixty-one years. Who gave them the right? I don't see them go to their graves. Should we be reasonable? No, we need justice to be more reasonable! We're not afraid of Israeli weapons. No military can kill all of us." He still had some fire in his belly.

But before Gulf War I we had Oslo, I continued, playing devil's advocate. Before Gulf War II, we had the road map. Before the Iran war, maybe we are getting the two-state solution? "Kissinger came and went," he said, "Warren Christopher, another, then another. Ten years after Oslo, here we are with more settlements, this wall in the West Bank, no Jerusalem, the siege. This made the Palestinian peace camp weak. It had no credibility." When I suggested that this might also result from the failures of the *thawra* to support democratic—and revolutionary—forces in the Arab world, Hassan became agitated. "Come on," he scoffed, "I refuse anyone who demands that I wait until the Arab world becomes a democracy. I have the right to live in a free country without occupation, poverty, siege, or an Israeli telling me that he is a better human being or a better writer than me." Was there a hint of malice in Hassan's eyes? Perhaps I had not earned the right to raise such questions.

"Let's be frank," he continued. "Do you think the Egyptian people care more about Palestine than about their food? In Gaza the food of the Egyptians is very important." But if there were real elections in Egypt, I began ... "The Muslim Brotherhood would win," Hassan finished my sentence for me. "Kifaya [the secular left coalition] would take nothing." So what would happen then, I asked? "More problems for us and Egypt and the Arab world." In Saudi Arabia, the people would elect Osama Bin Laden, he said without batting an eye.

But until you have Arab governments that are democratic—"Egypt is an authoritarian dictatorship," he interrupted again. "There are 1.2 million Palestinians who are Israeli citizens. Now a new law obliges them to say that they are in a Jewish state, so where is the democracy? Democracy means a good life for the Israeli and a bad one for the Palestinian." In his view, dictatorships such as Qatar and Saudi Arabia had provided their people with roads, hospitals, and universities.

"In 1948 I saw refugees carry their flags and tents," he continued, an unstoppable train. "In the recent war I saw people carry their children and a few blankets. They were not going to military castles to kill Israelis. They wanted places to protect them from death. Nobody can ask the Palestinian why he is angry, *yani*. And beside all this injustice, we should recognize the 'Jewish state' and what happened to the Jews during the second world war? Come on. Am I responsible for that? Am I thinking about that? I am thinking about what happened to me, not in the last war, but for the last sixty years, in many wars. Is this world going to recognize that?" It was a fine if misdirected display of bravura, and it seemed to take much out of Hassan. His righteous anger ebbed beneath jowls that now seemed to quiver with reproach, pride, pain, and fatigue.

Rajab al-Hise, 82

Fisherman

BEACH CAMP, GAZA

All this history "How was the fishing today?" I asked Rajab. "Like normal," he replied lackadaisically. It was a misleading answer. There was nothing normal about Gaza's fishing industry. At night, you could see—and hear— Israeli gunboats firing machine gun and red tracer bullets at trawlers off the coast. They were warning shots, mostly. Since the blockade of the Strip began in 2007, Israel had prevented any fishing activity farther out than six kilometers, and within that catchment area there were precious few fish left. The fishermen anyway had precious little fuel. Rajab al-Hise was the Strip's oldest angler. "The situation has never been as bad as it is now," he told me outside his shack in Gaza's shabby but atmospheric port. This can usually be said in Palestine. "Most people have been unemployed since the Second Intifada started," he added. In good times there were "about three thousand" fishermen in Gaza.

"We don't have any gasoline, and so we can't catch many fish," Rajab said. "I buy gas on the black market. But instead of 80 or 90 shekels a gallon, it's going for 350 or 400 shekels—black market prices. We're actually using cooking oil. Anything that burns will run the engine." What if it runs out? I asked. "We're not going to sit back and watch," he answered. "The next step will be to try other things." In the West people even made petroleum out of corn nowadays, he said. But the blockade was narrowing his world: "You come and see us thinking that if there's no gas, there's no fish. It is the Israeli policy. They don't want us to think about politics—or land—just gasoline." It had been that way "since the soldier [Gilad] Shalit was arrested," he said.

Rajab held the net he was sewing up to the light. "These kinds of nets catch tuna and catfish," he announced. "But we can't go far enough out to catch them. The first 19 kilometers of water are dead. After that, there are a lot of rocks, and after that, it's all good for 56 kilometers. But only Israelis and Egyptians go there now. The people of Gaza just catch sardines." Most of the time even these were elusive, and it was dangerous to look for them. "The Israelis open fire at ships even within the 6-kilometer limit," Rajab remarked. A friend of his, Abu Hani, was shot dead about 2 kilometers outside the limit eighteen months before. Another friend had to have his arm amputated after being shot in the hand.

Gaza's spicy fish cuisine is a treasure that could one day help put the Strip on the tourist map. It is typically grilled with chilis inside it and garnished with sauces such as tahini and tomato, before being dispatched commu- nally by hand. The experience is similar to eating Peri-peri (a spicy barbecue sauce), Ethiopian, or Lebanese fare. But like the sheesha cafés that visitors are routinely taken to, the price prohibits all but perhaps 5 percent of the Strip's population from enjoying it. "The restaurants don't get their fish from here," Rajab explained. "They import it from Israel. Three traders bring fish through the Kerem Shalom checkpoint every day." He dragged on a cigarette and coughed up black sputum. "If the siege continues there has to be an explosion," he said, "even if it means that a lot of people die. Things will go back to where they were."

Rajab started working as a fisherman in Jaffa in 1943. "I've seen the days of the English, the days of the Egyptians, all this history," he said. "During the English occupation, we could fish from Port Said to Jaffa, anywhere we wanted. It was all open. You went straight to wherever you heard there was fish. There were no limits." Before the Nakba, Rajab fondly remembered, "[there were] just small numbers of Jewish fishermen. They weren't even seen. We had a really good relationship, importing and exporting. We were just like a country together." Do you miss those days? I pried. Another fisherman sitting next to Rajab answered, "Yes, I used to sell things for whatever price I wanted," adding, "I would never forget my land no matter what." He was adorned in a white *dishdasha,* white skullcap, and white bushy moustache, resembling a cross between a guardian angel and a walrus.

Rajab motioned for me to look at his cigarette. "They used to sit like this," he said, flexing his arms demonstratively, "smoking. We were friends with them. When there was a marriage, we'd invite the Jews to sit with us." Do you think Jews and Palestinians could live together in one state now? I asked. "I don't think it's possible because of the hatred," he shook his head. "There's killing in it now. You killed my brother. I killed your people. You can't just get back to where it started."

Rajab had vague recollections of the 1936 revolt but seemed wary about talking about them to a stranger. "I remember seeing rebels attacking the British, killing them and hiding at night," he said. "The British took many of them to jail." His family, though, was not involved. "My father was a fisherman," he says. "He didn't have anything to do with the rebels." During World War II, "all we cared about was surviving the day," Rajab said. "We didn't really think about Palestine and land. In 1942 the Jews used to tell us, 'If the Germans win the war, you Arabs will beat us, but if the English win, we will beat you.'" Rajab insisted that he did not take sides.

Nonetheless, in 1948 he and his family, along with most of Jaffa's population, were pushed into the ocean by the advancing Jewish forces. "Everybody escaped by sea," Rajab said. "I took a boat from Jaffa to Herbia, and then I sailed on to Khan Younis." He did not fight. "I'm just a fisherman," he repeated, but he was clearly bitter about other Arab countries. "We lost because of betrayal and treason by the Arabs," he stated. "They collected our weapons and gave us guns with bullets that exploded inside the barrel before they were fired. We couldn't technically fight the Israelis, so when we heard that they were attacking, everybody started to run. People panicked. The Egyptians retreated. We ran back with them. The Iraqis left. The Saudis left. It was a mess. The Jews took over. But the main country responsible for our Nakba was Britain. They escorted the Jews into Palestine."

Rajab's attitude toward Israel was not unambiguous. He described the period after 1967 in glowing terms. "The Jews opened doors for a lot of money," he said. "Our pockets were full, so it was a good life. We never expected the Jews to actually leave. We wanted them to stay with us." Israel's capture of the Suez Canal also opened up new fishing grounds for Gaza's fishermen: "Every day we would catch sixty or seventy tons of sardines. There were five factories in Israel. I used to give them all the fish they needed." Good times, I said. "The best," Rajab agreed. "We forgot about all our sadness and started thinking there was a better way of life for us. We could go to Jordan. We could go inside Israel. It was easy to get permits at that time. You could just get in a car and drive to Tel Aviv."

But Jaffa had changed beyond recognition. "It was annihilated," Rajab said. "All the buildings were demolished or burned down." His own house had been reduced to rubble, and Jaffa's Arab population had been concentrated in one district, Ajami. "They moved people from their houses to relocation places and brought other people to live in their houses," he said.

Rajab bought himself half a dunam of land in Gaza's Beach camp and built a four-story house there, which he now lived in with seventy-five relatives. He had nine sons and eight daughters. All his sons were fishermen. Were their children fishermen? I queried. "Everybody is a fisherman!" Rajab shouted. "Fish is in the family. It becomes part of you." He had been caught at sea during storms and once had to swim several kilometers back to shore.

Return was also a part of his life. The question of whether Palestinians would ever go back to Jaffa was axiomatic. "Our minds say that we will come back," he declared. "If not us, it will be the next generation. If not them, the generation after. We teach our kids about this. We have papers that say we still own the land and houses in Jaffa, and when our kids—or their kids—read them, they will know that one day we will go back and get it."

The Fatah-Hamas split did not overly tax him. "In 1994 when Fatah came with Yasser Arafat, they took all the lands and the money," he said. "I see that Hamas is not taking any land. It's returning it to people who owned it." Aware that this was a tricky current, Rajab rowed back gently. "But we're not into all that politics business," he went on. "All we care about is if there's fish in the water or not." Are you a fisherman or a Palestinian first? I asked. "Palestinian," Rajab answered in a heartbeat. "I won't deny who I am. My homeland is Palestine. Even though I'm a fisherman and all I care about is fish, I'm still a Palestinian."

The angler in white next to him asked whether I would deny my father's name. I said no—although as it is Chaim, I might not always volunteer the information either. "Well, then," he said. "It's the same." Rajab noticed a British mandate–era coin that I was wearing as a necklace. "It's a Palestinian coin!" he cried, eyebrows raised. "When I saw it I knew it was Palestinian. It's ours! One Palestinian pound. It has Hebrew, Arabic, and English writing, yes?" I nodded. The interview had tapered into something more congenial for Rajab. "If there was someone here I'd make you tea, but no one is here," he said, and I turned my recorder off. Strangely and unexpectedly, I felt at home.

The 1936
Generation

The first stirrings of Palestinian national identity are sometimes said to have occurred in 1834, during an uprising in the cities of Jerusalem, Jaffa, Nablus, and Hebron against an Egyptian invasion led by Muhammad Ali Pasha. Ever since the Ottoman land reforms that followed that revolt, Palestinian *fellahin* had been reluctant to register their land for fear of taxes and conscription. Most land had been owned collectively, often registered in the name of just one villager—or else merchants and Ottoman administrators who had never lived on it. This became a legal problem for Palestinians in Israel today. But in the nineteenth century too, Zionist immigrants took advantage of this practice to acquire land from absentee landlords in the coastal plain. This aggravated local *fellahin,* and after one dispute in 1886 the Jewish settlement of Petach Tikva was ransacked.

But the European newcomers brought with them modern agricultural techniques, technology, and money, giving them advantages over the *fellahin,* who still farmed traditionally. As world markets encroached on Palestine via the coast, hill farmers increasingly had to migrate to cities as unskilled laborers. Very quickly, two ethnically delineated economies emerged. In one, new cities, railroads, and telegraph networks sprouted. In the other, class differentials widened while *fellahin* increasingly migrated from the mountains to the coast and back again.

By the end of the nineteenth century, just twenty-one Jewish settlements with fewer than 4,500 inhabitants had been established, compared to a Palestinian population more than one hundred times greater. But more Jewish immigrants were arriving all the time as a consequence of European anti-Semitism and the new Zionist movement. Ominously, the defeat of the Ottomans in World War I was followed by the arrival of the British, whose (anti-Semitic) foreign secretary, Arthur Balfour, had pledged British support for a Jewish homeland in Palestine in November 1917.

British rule and the Zionist project became inextricably linked in the Palestinian mind—and in Britain's constitutional proposals for the territory. In April 1920, as Britain obtained the mandate to govern Palestine, riots broke out in Jerusalem against Jewish immigration and the new mandate authorities, ending with the deaths of four Arabs and five Jews. In 1921 the riots spread to Jaffa and escalated, claiming forty-eight Jewish and forty-seven Arab lives. The British responded by creating a new position, Grand Mufti of Jerusalem, and appointing Hajj Amin al-Hussayni, a young, virulently anti-Semitic nationalist from one of Palestine's most powerful, feud-wracked, and notable families.

Al-Hussayni actually received the fewest votes of the four candidates who stood in the poll of Jerusalem's Islamic religious leaders. But after assuring Herbert Samuel, one of the architects of the Balfour Declaration, of his "earnest desire to cooperate with the government and his belief in the good intentions of the British government towards the Arabs," he was offered the job. Al-Hussayni's pitch, that "the influence of his family and himself would be devoted to maintaining tranquillity," proved persuasive.

More than 120,000 new Jewish émigrés arrived in Palestine in the 1920s, escalating discontent. Wealthy Palestinians could see their new country slipping away from them. The urban poor were largely excluded from the dynamic new Jewish economy, and *fellahin* were forced off their lands. British divide-and-rule tactics heightened religious tensions and sectarian hatreds alike.

In 1929 about sixty-seven Jews were killed during rioting in Hebron that Jews experienced as a Palestinian pogrom. Even so, Nazism helped turn the trickle of Jewish immigration into a flood. Correspondingly, Palestinian nationalist politics began to take on a populist and anti-imperial tone. The underground Black Hand organization led by the Syrian imam Shaykh Izz a-Din al-Qassam had recruited seven hundred supporters among the poor underclass in Haifa by 1935.

Baruch Kimmerling wrote that the shaykh would preach with gun or sword in hand, urging "the bootblack to exchange his shoe brush for a revolver and to shoot the Englishman rather than polish his shoes." In 1935 al-Qassam was killed in a gun battle with British soldiers who had followed him to a village near Jenin, from which he had hoped to spearhead an uprising. A few months later, in April 1936, two Jews were murdered, probably by one of al-Qassam's disciples. Two Arabs were swiftly dispatched in retaliation by a Jewish group. A few days later a general strike kicked off the Great Arab Revolt.

The mass protests that would characterize the uprising—often involving stone throwing at British soldiers—were unprecedented. The driving force behind the initial protests was the shebab of the Palestinian street and the secular Arabist Istiqlal party. Their demands for the first time placed British withdrawal before halting Jewish immigration, which they had come to see as an auxiliary to the British Empire. A British decision to distribute 587 rifles to Jewish settlements provoked particular ire. Sporadically, Palestinian activists organized guards to protect Jewish properties, even if communal violence remained the norm.

The traditional Palestinian leadership, which had depended on the British, increasingly found itself challenged by a younger, more impatient, and urban generation, in a pattern that has repeated itself throughout Palestinian history. The rebellion's demand was for a secular independent state, but the importance of the mosque to street mobilizations placed Islam at its forefront. It also forced the religious leadership to take a more prominent role.

Before the revolt, London's man, Hajj Amin al-Hussayni, had called for violence against Jews rather than the British. But as Britain's ties to the leaderships they had cultivated waned—and Istiqlal's accusations of collaboration hit home—al-Hussayni's rhetoric grew more militant. Behind the scenes, though, al-Hussayni's Higher Arab Committee (HAC), which formally led the revolt, negotiated with Britain to end it without any concessions. Many urban notable families quit Palestine for Lebanon, fearing the revolt's violence and the *shebabs'* demands that they leave their mandate jobs, start paying taxes to the revolution, and join the strike. Few of them participated in the revolt.

It mattered little. Banks and post offices across Palestine were shut down by the strike and rocked by constant raids afterward. The port of Jaffa was closed. Oil pipelines, railroads, and communications infrastructure were sabotaged. Large swaths of the country including Jaffa, Nablus, and even, for a few days, the Old City of Jerusalem fell to the rebels. But al-Hussayni called off the strike in October 1936 after the HAC persuaded monarchs in Iraq and Saudi Arabia to issue a text implicitly promising the fulfillment of Palestinian demands. Ahmad Shuqayri, who would go on to head the PLO when it was created in 1964, described this as a victory for the World War I generation of Palestinians that had put their faith in the Allies. The losers, he argued, were a younger generation that had been disillusioned by the British Empire's trickery and deceitfulness and had now become a victim of their elders' irresolution too.

The struggle continued at an uneven tempo until 1937 when the assassination of the acting British commissioner Lewis Andrews marked a turning point. Martial law was declared, and the rebel leadership was arrested en masse. Al-Hussayni fled to Nazi Germany via Lebanon, where he switched imperial allegiances.

The British tactics and economic shutdown somersaulted the revolt from the cities to the countryside as the urban poor migrated back to their villages and an anarchic guerrilla war developed. Bands of village fighters formed intelligence units and revolutionary courts. They were joined in battle by hundreds of *mujahidin* (guerrilla fighters) from other Arab countries. But unlike their contemporaries in Spain, Palestinian fighters later turned on some of these, fearing an attempt to stifle their autonomy.

For a time, a situation of "dual power" existed in Palestine, with many districts coming under a kind of autonomous peasant control. These areas experienced a period of social revolution. The revolt's leaders demanded that city Arabs stop wearing the fez and round tarbush hats (which were associated with the rich) and don the *fellah*'s black-and-white-checked *kaffiyeh* instead. This helped rebels to surreptitiously enter cities and cemented a reversal of the Palestinian self-image that remains to this day.

Equally, though, Muslim and Christian women in the cities were ordered to wear the veil, as also happened later in Algeria, and *fellah* hubris vis-à-vis the urban cultural centers took hold. The *fellahin* enforced a rent boycott against city landlords—and rural landowners—while demanding that they make greater national sacrifices and finance the uprising. Some urban landowners were banned from entering villages, while loan collectors were issued with death threats and many *mukhtars* were killed.

But the revolution was besieged by massive British repression, the indifference of neighboring Arab regimes, and a bloody campaign of reprisals against civilian targets by Jewish militias. Over twenty thousand British troops were deployed to crush the revolt, and between 1936 and 1939 more than 10 percent of the Palestinian adult male population were killed, wounded, imprisoned, or exiled.

Lacking a strategy to democratically unite the antimandate forces behind an assault on the nerve centers of British power or, alternatively, to create a centralized power base capable of at least keeping its leaders alive, the rebellion floundered organizationally and then decayed from within. Rebel bands began squabbling and using the dreaded "collaborator" epithet as a means of settling long-standing family feuds. Some degenerated into traditional bandit gangs. Communists and labor union leaders were assassinated; Druze and Christian communities were attacked. An exhausted and fragmented Palestinian public despaired of civil war.

In one village near Hebron, three thousand people demonstrated against the terror of the rebels and pledged to help the mandate authorities defeat them. The measures used by the British included house demolitions, collective punishment of rebel-supporting villages, hangings, mass arrests, and forcing prisoners to act as human mine sweepers. Zionist militias enthusiastically collaborated with—and learned from—their colonial tactic book.

By the time the revolt was finally crushed in 1939, the Jewish Yishuv had never been stronger and the British were able to turn their undivided attention to Germany. The Palestinians, by contrast, were shattered. Their leaders, like their best fighters, were either dead or in exile. A shell-shocked, defeated, and hungry Palestinian society was in no position to fight off a highly organized, well-equipped, and strongly motivated Jewish army. My last interviewee, Abdullah Rashid, lost a chunk of his leg to a British bullet in a shootout during the 1936 revolt. In 1948 he did not fight.

Jalil Sharqawi Fawadli, 79

Retired Teacher

ABUD, WEST BANK

A presence in this land   The towns of Abud and Bisan have lent their names to thousands of Palestinians over the years, and they still command attention. International visitors began visiting Abud in 2005 to protest the Israeli wall that was stealing the villagers' land. But streams of people and pilgrims had passed through the town since Jesus walked this route on his way to Nazareth, as local tradition has it. Abud's Church of St. Mary, built by Constantine, dates to the fourth century and boasts of miracles in the parish. Sometimes survival can be wonder enough. A fifth-century church in the beautiful village was accidentally destroyed by the Israeli army during Operation Defensive Shield in May 2002.

Unlike his father, Jalil was not born here. At the beginning of the twentieth century his father moved to Jaffa to work as a civil servant for the British mandate government. Jalil was born in Jaffa's Ajami district. We talked about it on his patio next to a small shrine to the Virgin Mary. A valley wind took the edge off the midsummer heat as members of his family drifted past, buffeting us with cup after cup of sweet mint tea as they went.

Jalil remembered 1936. "I was just a school student, but I used to go on demonstrations against the Jews and Britain," he said. "England was responsible for Jewish immigration here and for consolidating their presence after Balfour's declaration in 1917." This complaint is often voiced, especially by older Palestinians. "The demonstrations were very strong and angry," he said. "The demonstrators were of all ages—ladies and men, children, the elderly—all the people. We shouted slogans against a British high official called General [Sir John Greer] Dill, like, 'Why did you take part in belliger-ent acts of war?' It was a reference to Britain's role in the Sykes-Picot accord that divided the Middle East. Another slogan was 'Palestine is our land and the Jews have to leave.'"

The revolt of 1936 "was a revolution against the Jews because they were using weapons against us," Jalil said. Palestinians, by contrast, "had guns but no cannons or mortars. The Jews used to smuggle a lot of weapons in through Jaffa port by pretending they were for commercial use. Once, the port police became suspicious when one of the barrels broke. The British government was fully aware of what was happening, but they put any Palestinian found with a gun in jail." At the same time, "Yafa [Jaffa] was being attacked by Jews. It was surrounded by Jewish settlements—and their residents shot at the Yafa people."

National identity in those days was a clear-cut affair. "I equate the mean-ing of being a Palestinian with a presence in this land," Jalil said. "The Jews claimed that they had no homeland except Palestine, whereas the Arabs could settle in other Arab countries. So they expelled us by using intimida-tion." One such incident occurred in Jaffa on January 4, 1948, four months before Israel's declaration of independence.

"It was just before noon, and the Stern Gang left a car packed with explo-sives on the street between the headquarters of the Arab High Commission, the Ottoman Bank, and the police headquarters," Jalil recounted. "When the car exploded, it caused massive destruction to the High Commission and totally destroyed the bank. Its money was scattered in the street, and we collected it up. A bank worker from the Atitni family in Abud also collected it in a purse to return it to the bank." Another man from Abud called Abdul Rahman died in the attack. "My father was about to throw a banquet that Abdul Rahman had been invited to," Jalil said. "When we heard the noise we rushed to the site, and I saw wounded people, casualties, and bodies scat-tered all over the place. Abdul Rahman's body had been torn to pieces by the blast." In all, fourteen people were killed.

By April 1948 Jalil's father had lost his job and the violence was spread-ing. "The Jews used to invade Palestinian areas and shoot people dead in their homes," he said. "We felt under threat, so the Abud people decided to resettle. We lost our house in Yafa, and the furniture too. I remember how we left in the car. Only one exit, Nater, was kept open, and all Palestinians were checked by the Jews. They forbade Palestinians from taking their money out with them or even their furniture except in person. They stole all our money."

People who could not afford to travel were forced to stay in Jaffa. On May 15, the day following Israel's declaration of independence, they were rounded up behind barbed wire in Ajami.

"Yusef, we make more tea!" Jalil cried out. "The British love their tea." Staring straight ahead, he continued: "I'm still overwhelmed with vivid emotions, thoughts, and feelings for Yafa. I remember the position of my house, the school, the street, and the neighborhood. After 1967 I traveled there by bus once a week, but it was depressing. The Arab houses were in a bad way because the Palestinians weren't allowed to renovate them."

When the Fawadlis returned to Abud, Jalil continued his education with a view to helping his father, who had started working on his family's land there. "Abud was filled with around five thousand refugees who had fled Yafa and other places," he said. After months of waiting in vain to return, they eventually relocated to cities like Ramallah and Jenin. But Abud had an ancient folklore that enchanted Jalil. "It had been populated by Christians since the dawn of the religion," he said. "The pilgrims used to pass by on their way to Jerusalem." In the fourteenth century, a village Muslim named Banglas allegedly went to the church to pray to the Virgin Mary. Jalil described what happened: "He told her, 'Invaders are approaching so you must defend the city! If you don't, I will convert the church into a stable.' He heard a voice respond, 'I will defend the village, and in the afternoon victory will be achieved.' The Virgin Mary prevented the church from being demolished."

Abud is a simple farming village with few schools, but Jalil taught English, Arabic, and mathematics there and in neighboring towns. Of necessity, relations between the villages were close. When, in 1967, the Israeli army destroyed three villages near Latrun and emptied them of residents, "some of us from Abud visited the town of Aywas," Jalil remembered. "The Jews had demolished their homes and planted big trees where the houses had been to remove any evidence of the people who had lived there. They had even taken the stones of the houses." He shook his head and sipped from his cup.

After 1967, Palestinians from Abud took advantage of the opportunity to again work in the cities of what was now Israel. For twenty-five years, until the Oslo process began, their economic situation improved, but as they left their farms fallow, Israel began reclaiming them as state land. After Oslo, villagers were forbidden from cultivating large tracts of Area C territory around newly built settlements. Then came the wall. "I have about two dunams of land left," Jalil said bitterly. "Originally, I had around one hundred dunams. I used to grow wheat, barley, lentils, beans, and peas. I also grew olive, fig, and almond trees and grapevines—although these were uprooted in 1982.

The land was on the outskirts of the village and the confiscations took place in stages; first in 1967, then in 1982—when the settlement of Beit Aryeh was built—and recently a large portion of land was confiscated by the wall."

Jalil had refused compensation from the Israelis and wanted it from the international community instead. "I'm very sad I can't pass this land down to my children," he said. "We have nothing in our hands. We have lost everything. I no longer have crops and olive oil with which to make money and pay for our life expenses. My family has become dependent on food from the market." Ironically, many connoisseurs regard Palestinian olive oil as among the best in the world, due to the West Bank's tradition of picking olives by hand. Yet more than seven thousand olive trees around the village had been uprooted by "Jewish bulldozers," Jalil said. The Israeli army "did the same as Britain," he added. "They issued military orders and declared closed zones. It's very difficult now to reach our land, or even land inside the wall that is very close to it. Many people have been shot when they've tried. I used to pick olives from my trees near the Israeli colonies. The Jewish army would come and point their guns at us until we finished." The trees now belong to Beit Aryeh and another settlement appended to it in 2004, Ofarim.

But the villagers did not take the land confiscation by Israel's wall lying down. Inspired by the example of neighboring Bil'in, they began a campaign of weekly demonstrations with Israeli and international activists to stop the barrier's construction. Abud had experienced hand fights and skirmishes between Fatah and Hamas supporters that threatened to divide the town on religious lines, but "all the parties were united in their resistance to the wall," Jalil said. "All of Abud demonstrated against it. I went with my wife and children. But although the protests were peaceful, the Jewish soldiers attacked them with rubber bullets and tear gas. When people approached the wall, they would use live bullets to disperse them. I wasn't frightened because I was losing my land, so I had to be there. Suppose that people came to your house to drive you away, would you leave without resisting?"

In Bil'in tensions occasionally flared over female activists who came to protest dressed in short skirts and sleeveless tops. Some argued that young Palestinian men might be corrupted and that allowing Israelis to visit on non-protest days was an act of "normalization"—or acceptance of the occupation. Jalil said this did not happen in Abud. "The foreigners were invited by the Popular Committee," he explained. "There was no criticism of the internationals who came with miniskirts because we are all united in the same goal. *Yani,* they are welcome." Even so, the wall had almost been finished by 2009 and the demonstrations had petered out. "The Israeli military said such protests were useless because they were so stubborn and determined," Jalil said. "Those who have power can do whatever they want. There is no voice for justice." Maybe, I said, the problem is that Abud, Bil'in, Budrus, and Nil'in mostly fought—and were defeated—alone at the start of the anti-wall campaign. Should they have all fought together at the same time? "Even if there had been an arrangement between the villages, the situation wouldn't have been too different," he replied, "because Israel, backed by the United States, is intent on building the wall."

Jalil spoke solemnly but allowed himself the odd twinkle in the eye. What, I wondered, would he advise a child in Jenin who wanted nothing more than to be a *shahid?* "Muslims believe that it's their duty to defend their religion, and suicide bombing is one means of achieving this goal," he averred. "I can't change this belief, but as children they should try to be hopeful and keep their dreams for the future. The Palestinians' best weapon is education, and they should pursue their studies." What if they had seen their friends die, or nearly died themselves? I asked. "I would tell them that life goes on," he said indignantly. "I would draw on the example of Winston Churchill. When Hitler bombed Britain he made the victory sign and didn't give up hope." Jalil flashed two fingers, and there was a slight uptick in his moustache. "I trust and call on Christians in the U.K. to help alleviate our suffering," he said. "When Roman soldiers surrounded Jesus to arrest him and Peter cut off Malthus's ear, Jesus ordered him to put down his sword. He said that what is taken by force cannot be regained by force." The moustache wobbled again. "But I'm not sure," Jalil added.

Abdullah Rashid, 94

Retired Farmer

AL-HUSSEIN CAMP,
IRBID, JORDAN

Paradise Abdullah is a gentle and slow-moving war veteran, but his hands are still lithe and his worry beads are well worn. He has a kind but weathered face that wrinkles up like a sponge when he is struggling to hear or understand my questions. Then it sags as his brow tightens and he begins to answer. "Abu Suleiman" (as he is known) hails from the al-Sahne tribe, which is famous for its fighters and poets. He was born and brought up in the Bisan area, living in a tent like his father and grandfather before him. "We were Bedouin so we moved from one place to another," he said, "wherever there was grass and water. Most of our tribe were nomadic shepherds raising sheep, goats, and cows. Some also had camels and horses. It was a pure life."

It was not always peaceful, though. "We used to fight other people for land and water," Abdullah said, "the usual things that nomads fight about." The Sahne were also generous. "If they had a guest, no matter who he was or where he was from, our hospitality was something indescribable," he said. "Only those who have experienced it know about it." The tribe's many poets were also a cause for honor. "Each small tribe is made up of families, and if one had a poet, they would be very proud," Abdullah said. A local leader of the 1936 revolution, Shaykh Hussayn al-Ali, was memorialized in the Sahne's poems after he was killed by the British army.

Hussayn al-Ali "was a thin, very brave man, brownish skin, and very accurate in shooting," Abdullah said. "If he shot, he killed. Every Sunday some English soldiers used to swim in a spring in Bisan. They'd bring one man to protect them, and he'd sit there with a machine gun watching the area. One day during the uprising, our spies confirmed that these soldiers had come as usual. Hussayn al-Ali went there and hid. When they took their clothes off and started swimming, he shot the lookout and killed him instantly. Then the other rebels came and shot the rest. Just one English soldier survived. He escaped to a nearby settlement, Beit Ilathia."

The revolt had broken out because of a pervasive fear that "something was going on," Abdullah said. "People thought that there were plans to forcibly expel them from their homeland. The revolt was mainly against the British army. But each village and town fought by itself. There was no organization between us. The people of Bisan did not fight with any other village. We divided into sixty or seventy men in each area working together. There was a very high level of cooperation among the fighters. Once I went with two friends to Damascus to see people I had been told about. We got guns and uniforms and bullets from Syria and brought everything the fighters needed."

Abdullah described his role as that of a "fighter-adviser" in the 1936 revolution. He said, "My group was active in the Bisan area—the town, nearby villages, and colonial settlements. We were fighting the colonials [Jewish settlers]. There was a petrol and oil pipe. We went there, dug, and exploded it." The settlements in those days "were surrounded by wire fences, with controlling towers," Abdullah said.

Sabotage was a frequently used tactic, but there were direct engagements too. "Once, Dr. Abaya—a doctor with a gun—entered an English police station and killed four soldiers before he was shot and killed also," he said, sotto voce. "This was one of the best things I saw." Abdullah was arrested at the beginning of 1938. "By then the uprising was almost finished," he said. "I was with a group of my friends when we were suddenly surrounded by British soldiers in Wadi Shubash village. We started shooting, and they shot back. We killed four of them; they killed a number of us. Two men were caught and hanged in Akka. I was shot in the leg but managed to run away. I went to a nearby spring for water and then carried on."

Abdullah was eventually caught by another group of British soldiers. "They asked me how I got this injury. I lied to them that British soldiers had approached me when I'd been with my sheep and goats. I got frightened and ran away, and they shot me. I told them that I had been running to a police station to tell them what happened. 'As you're here now, you can take me with you,' I said. And they took me to a hospital and healed my injury. After that they sent me to the Akka jail."

Abdullah showed me the bullet scar on his upper leg, just a long lopsided crease now where flesh had been gouged. "One good thing about England," he said cheerfully, "when they caught a suspect, they didn't hit, harm, or hurt him. They just brought him in and investigated. If there were witnesses, they charged him. I liked that about England. I remember two British officers, called Fillebrooke and I think Fickens. I had to go to the English police station to sign a register every week, and we became friends. They used to deal with me kindly."

Before he was released, Abdullah was interned for a year in a large hangar that had been turned into a prison. "The British respected us," he reiterated, "and even offered us very good food. But by 1938 people felt that they'd been totally suppressed and were very sad. What killed the uprising was a lack of fundamentals like food, water, and money." The villagers confined themselves to their homes in the years that followed. "We didn't go outside, but if anyone attacked us we defended ourselves," Abdullah said. "People continued their ordinary lives. He who grew his land went back to growing his land. He who reared sheep and goats did this once again."

For Abdullah, being Palestinian was more about the land than its people. "For me, Palestine means paradise itself. All kinds of earth and fruits that come from the earth exist in this land. It was a very peaceful life—trees, farms, fields of corn—and Bisan was a large trading center for a lot of the tribes. I'm now separated from my homeland as a small baby that has been taken from its mother's womb."

A younger member of Abdullah's tribe, Rakan Mahmoud, who is now the elected president of the al-Hussein camp was raised on such stories by his family. "They used to tell me about Palestine as the green land," he said, "the land of the trees and green grass. It was just like a green carpet. In other words it was paradise." The al-Hussein camp he grew up in "was like a ghetto" by comparison. "It was completely closed. You couldn't contact anyone outside," he told me. "There was real suffering here—whole families would sleep in just one room—and it got unbearable in winter. My parents had no money to buy me shoes, and food wasn't available for us. There was no shelter to protect you, no warmth, no electricity, we didn't even get warm clothes, and there was no privacy either."

Similarly, when Abdullah talked of Palestine, it was of a lost idyll. "There were no borders, and we could go anywhere without passports," he said. "Just walk, and you will arrive at any place you want. We knew the area's mountains and valleys. We knew the river separated Palestine from Jordan and Syria. We knew that the Mediterranean and the Sinai Desert were our borders. Everyone knew which people were Jordanian, Syrian, or Lebanese. They were thought of as one nation. Visiting traders knew they were coming to Palestine."

In those days, "the Jews were shepherds," he coughed violently. "They were the very old Hasidic Beit Alpha who had always lived there [on the site of a sixth-century synagogue]. They came to visit us, and during the night we'd sit and have friendly chats together. Some of them even spoke Arabic. We used to call them the national Jews. They were born there and were just like Palestinians." Abdullah even had Jewish friends as a child, although they did not play together. In 1936, he stressed, "we were fighting against the new-comers that Britain brought here, not the old Jews. We hated England for bringing the Zionists."

"They started to make life harder for our people. We began suffering from poverty and hunger. People were forced to sell their land to the Jews for money to feed their families. That's why there were no contacts with the newcomers. We just fought them. When we were forced to leave, the old Jews asked us not to go. They said, 'It's our homeland. Don't leave it for these newcomers.' Even the newcomers' faces were different. The old ones looked like us. The new ones had yellow faces, white faces, red faces, something very strange for us. I will smoke hashish now."

Abdullah Rashid leaned forward, curled himself over, and began rolling a joint, using only crushed marijuana leaves and buds, in keeping with Bedouin tradition. "After Britain withdrew, the Zionists started arriving in huge numbers," he sped up his story. "People felt as if they were being strangled. The newcomers started competing with us on the land, in the small farms, the shops, even rearing sheep and cattle. They forced people to leave their land by shooting at them. We had a few guns but nothing compared to what they had. We tried to buy some guns, but they didn't work. Even the bullets were no good." If the British had not armed the newcomers with the most modern machine guns, the Palestinians would have won, he said. The local *mukhtars* fought with just five rifles each.

As Abdullah remembered it, the Nakba "started with gossip." "Because we were near the border, we saw people from other villages coming toward the border and heard that the Zionists were killing people and had raped girls. As Arabs and Bedouins, we thought a lot about this. We prepared to defend ourselves, but they arrived in very large numbers. I was working on the fruit trees with twelve people when they came and started shooting people with machine guns. After this, people in the area started to leave. Each tribe heard from other tribes what was happening. The fighting reached Bisan in April. Everyone pulled down their tents, collected their things, and left at once for areas far from the Jews. Hundreds of us moved in one group. We left our village for another one nearby, Ain el-Birde. But in 1967 the newcomers attacked us even there. They planted land mines, which killed people, and I saw the Haganah enter a house belonging to refugees from Bisan. They killed a woman there and shot three of her children. They forced us to leave for Jordan."

Abdullah's tribe traveled first to the Jordan Valley. "Then we came here and put up tents for the refugees," he said. "It was a catastrophic life in the camps. In winter, we used to sleep on mud between the tents and shelters. I spent most of my life in al-Ayma, the first camp they put us in. It's better here. There were no work opportunities at all there. We just lived on what they gave us, and the land was not good for rearing sheep or goats. There were just a few points for water. All the women of the camp would go to collect it. But there was no electricity, just candles and oil lamps."

Abdullah said that he had experienced no discrimination from the Jordanians. "[But] I feel completely Palestinian," he added, "and if I had a chance to go back, I'd return tomorrow without thinking, directly. The place you were born in is too precious. It's something you can't give up. After all this time, all that I wish for is just to stay one night in my village." Abdullah knew the soil there as the best in Palestine. "To the west of Bisan the earth was white, and to the east it was red," he said, then turned to face me. "You have asked me many questions. Now I have something to ask you. Could you bring me just one handful of that earth?" I told him I would try. Abdullah gave me a dignified but pained smile, and a Qur'an.

POSTSCRIPT:
IN YOUR EYES A SANDSTORM

The Number 90 bus to Beth She'an was air-conditioned, which was a good thing as the mercury outside read over 100 degrees Fahrenheit in the shade. A Mizrahi with a pitted face sat beside me, shouting impatiently into his cell phone. Across the aisle, Israeli soldiers slouched languidly. To our left the hills of the Jordan Valley scraped at the sun, while on the right the mountains of Jordan loomed over the Dead Sea like cutlasses.

Every few minutes, our Egged bus recklessly coiled around another hairpin turn, seemingly magnetized to the tarmac. Until recently, Palestinians could travel this road only at the risk of harassment or detention, but seated in Western-style comfort, behind bullet-proof windows, it was difficult to feel unsafe. The scenery could have been taken from a tourist brochure.

Strings of massive date plantations dotted the arid basin; dust spirals from tractors twirled gently into the China blue skies. Below, chartreuse grass sprouted from sour hills like a halfhearted hair transplant. But it was not all palm trees and sunshine. The farther north we went, the more Bedouin workers we saw trudging disconsolately, sometimes towing camels or riding donkeys. Their bowed heads were wrapped in kaffiyehs to protect them from the sun. We could not see their faces, and they did not look at ours.

In one particularly hazy stretch of orange desert, we approached a group of soldiers swarming around an overturned car ahead. They appeared to be pushing someone into an army jeep at gunpoint, but it was difficult to be certain. In a second we had passed them, and dust and heat haze obscured the view once more.

A sculpture resembling a rifle on a hillside raced by. It was followed by rusting tanks knotted in barbed wire—relics of the 1967 war—that remained dug into the sand facing Jordan. And then the settlement of Yafit (Beauty) rippled into view like a mirage. When the bus door opened to let us off at a nearby service station, it felt like the hatch to a stove had been opened.

The Jordan Valley is an inhospitable place to live, especially if you are an Arab. Israeli army regulations similar to those in effect between the Green Line and the West Bank wall forbid Palestinians from entering the valley, unless they have a residency permit or transit visa stamped by an army official. Farmers from outside the valley who own land there cannot access it, and couples including one partner born outside the valley must tiptoe around checkpoints and ghost through their lives.

At 120 kilometers long and 15 kilometers wide, the valley makes up a quarter of the West Bank's landmass. But Israel aspires to keep it as its eastern border. In negotiations with the Netanyahu government in 2010, Barack Obama's administration reportedly offered to guarantee a long-term Israeli security presence in the valley as part of a package of inducements in return for a one-off final three-month settlement freeze.

Because of the Dead Sea, the Jordan Valley is Israel's second biggest tourist attraction. Yet more than 50,000 Palestinians still live here, most in sleepy desert cities like Jericho, others in slums that spill higgledy-piggledy up the mountainsides. They share the land with around 9,500 Israelis who live in twenty-six West Bank settlements and seventeen kibbutzim. But it has not been apportioned equally.

Settlers and soldiers in five infantry encampments control the lion's share. Palestinians hold sway in just 4 percent, and within that, they need military permits to build anything at all. These are rarely forthcoming—home owners say they even need permission to grow geraniums in some areas—and ramshackle corrugated iron structures are mushrooming. Among the tin shack and tarpaulin villages, only a minority of residents have connected access to water and electricity. Fewer still enjoy schools, kindergartens, or health centers. While Palestinians often see their goods perish at checkpoints, settlers transport theirs to local markets within hours.

Bisan is first recorded in the fifteenth century B.C.E., as one of Thutmose III's conquests. But its history spans the Pharaonic, Hellenic, Roman, and Byzantine empires as well as the seventh-century Caliphate. Crusaders, Mamluks, Ottomans, and British all came and went, taking treasures and leaving behind buildings. Bisan was the capital of Rome's Decapolis. In legend, Dionysus, god of wine, is said to have buried his nurse, Nysa, under its soil. In recent history several scenes from the film *Jesus Christ Superstar* were shot in the town.

Bisan's multiethnic tapestry was famous. In 1923, when the second wave of

Jewish emigration to Palestine was peaking, a group of Arab shaykhs in the Bisan Valley wrote to the British High Commissioner, Herbert Samuel, in the oldest traditions of Arab hospitality, telling him:

> We have seen no evil from the Jews. We have sold the American *[sic]* Jewish Agency some of our lands, and with the help of the money we received we are developing and cultivating the large tracts that still remain ours. We are pleased with these Jews, and we are convinced that we will work together to improve our region and to pursue our common interests.

Nonetheless, when the Nakba began, Bisan was heavily bombarded by the Palmach. "The Beit She'an Valley is the gate for our state in the Galilee," wrote Joseph Weitz, director of the Jewish National Fund, in his diary on May 4, 1948. "Its clearing is the need of the hour." One week later and just three days before the state of Israel was declared, the Bisan local committee surrendered, worn down by a lack of food and military supplies. A minority of its roughly five thousand residents were expelled to towns such as Nazareth and Jenin, but most were driven across the nearby Jordan River into Jordan. Their homes were confiscated, and the newly proclaimed "Jewish state" began demolishing them the following month. The work was quickly stopped, however, to allow Ashkenazi Jews, many of them Holocaust survivors, to move in. A camp was opened nearby for Mizrahis, whose numbers swelled; today they are the majority in what has become a poor, nondescript development town. Few Arabs remain, if any.

The soldiers at Al Hamra Green Line checkpoint wore sunny yellow bibs over their olive uniforms, or else they were adorned in ersatz sunglasses, jeans, baseball caps, and Uzi submachine guns. To Israelis, such dress is reassuringly informal. To Palestinians, it often suggests death squad chic. The village of Al Hamra itself was destroyed in 1948 and its population expelled. Now it had been fenced off and turned into an Israeli cow pasture. Just two Arab houses built of bricks (but no mortar) still stood.

There were no Arabs on our bus, and we passed the checkpoint without incident, quickly reaching Beth She'an's central thoroughfare, Menachem Begin Boulevard. It was a land of drab prefabricated housing projects replete with laundry hanging from windows and sand blowing down the streets. The shopkeeper I asked for directions in a pizza café didn't understand why I wanted to go to the spring. "There's nothing there but water," he said, "water and good earth." I could not tell him why I was there without stoking security fears. And I doubt that he would have understood me if I had tried.

Many Israelis still believe that there was no significant, permanent Arab population in mandate Palestine before Jewish immigrants arrived. Many more argue that those who fled during the war forfeited their homes, land, and citizenship rights. Either way, a national consensus holds that they must not be allowed back, and befriending or visiting Arabs who once lived in the valley is viewed as suspect behavior.

At the gates to the spring, the park guards asked to see my passport and press card. They wanted to know where I was from, why I had come, and how long I planned to stay. I pointed out signs advertising entry to the public for twenty-nine shekels. Eventually they allowed me thirty minutes on the site. But they would keep my passport as a deposit. Inside, the park had been beautifully landscaped with conifer, pine, and palm trees. A large stone-bordered natural spring served as a swimming pool, and children played on a rubber tire attached to a pulley. It slid out into the middle of the spring, and then they fell in. One lone Palestinian family sitting on a slope told me that the spot was still popular with Palestinians and that parties were sometimes held here. But they looked nervous and unused to conversation with non-Arabs.

With its straw beach parasols and tree trunk railings, the only things linking this leisure complex to the Middle East seemed to be the exotic birds and flies that whizzed past like bullets. The grass really was greener there, and the lawns around the pool were freshly mown. In stark contrast to the cracked sod on the way, the earth around the spring was moist, sinewy, and obliging. Gently, I pushed a spoon into the ground and started to dig.

It was not so easy to move the earth back to Abdullah. The journey to Irbid in northern Jordan involved several taxis and buses and took most of the day. At the King Hussein Bridge border, I had to wait for hours in extreme heat before being fingerprinted and closely questioned by Jordanian officials. In Irbid, my contact did not turn up and I had to take a taxi to al-Hussein camp, asking passersby for directions as I went. My taxi driver, a Palestinian from Tulkarem dressed in a pink shirt and gold bracelet, did not like this. He said the refugees were bad people and their houses too close together. Nonplussed camp residents kept misdirecting us. Finally after perhaps two hours we arrived.

In his salon, Abdullah looked frailer this time and could not walk unaided. Several younger members of his tribe sat on plain cushions laying about the floor, waiting on the great man's utterances with hushed reverence. I handed him the cup of earth. He opened it, spilled its contents onto a silver tray, and examined the dirt within, sifting, smelling, and rubbing it between his fingers. Finally he looked up at me and said, "But why is this earth black like oil?" I did not know. "It's not the way I remember it," he said and shook his head. Ziad, a member of Abdullah's Sahne clan who served in the PLO's Badr Brigades implored me, "Mr. Arthur, it is sixty years since he has been there. He can't understand why the earth has changed color." A younger man, perhaps one of Abdullah's grandsons, sighed morosely, "They've changed everything, the earth, the people, the air, the water . . . ," and then he looked down at his sandals.

Later I talked to an Israeli parks engineer who noted that in older photographs the spring's earth looked white. He confirmed that darker topsoil might have been laid "to help the grass." Over the years European-looking brown soil, which was thought more fertile, was sometimes imported by the settlers, along with pine trees that were not native to the Middle East.

Later still, I discovered that the spring I visited was actually a few miles from Sahne, the place where Abdullah's tribe once lived. But when I traveled to the Sahne spring I found that there too the land was neither white nor red. It was rich and clearly defined, with topsoil the shade of a light brownstone building. I could not be sure whether it had changed since Abdullah left or whether his memory had simply weathered with time.

The Sahne park grounds were beautifully landscaped and neatly spaced but also unnervingly off-kilter. Its turquoise waters possessed a water temperature of 28 degrees year-round, according to the Israel Nature and Parks Authority. Visitors could swim and lounge there for hours without any reminders of the land's churning history, or the resistance it still gives birth to. But the park's Hebrew name, Gan Hashlosha, or Park of the Three, refers to three Jewish National Fund delegates who were killed there in 1938, when their car hit a land mine.

The park also includes a reconstruction of Tel Amal, which at the height of the Palestinian revolution in December 1936 was the first Jewish kibbutz to be built in the style of "the wall and tower." This was a pioneering method of creating "facts on the ground" that has, arguably, provided inspiration for today's Israeli settlements and security innovations such as the West Bank Wall. In my book *Occupied Minds*, an old kibbutznik called Dov Yirmiya, who lived behind one such structure in 1938, explained what this meant: "The area where [Jewish] groups planned to settle would be cleared of Arabs, and within twenty-four hours a wall of about half an acre would be built," he said. "It would have a [double] wooden frame filled with [cement] chips so that bullets couldn't penetrate it, and in the middle a ten-meter-high electrified tower would be erected with a [spotlight] projector lighting up the surroundings."

But it was difficult to imagine conflict there now. Despite all the blood spilled on its soil, Sahne remained an oasis so lush that *Time* magazine reportedly named it one of the twenty most beautiful national parks in the world. As I stood on its esplanade, I tried to imagine what Abdullah must have felt when he surveyed the landscape. After the violent sands of the Jordan Valley, it almost looked like paradise.

GLOSSARY

Abu Amar: the *kunya,* or honorific name, of Yasser Arafat. Such titles utilize the name of the bearer's firstborn son or daughter.

Abu Jihad: a legendary Palestinian military leader and founder of Fatah, assassinated in Tunis by Israel in 1988.

Abu Mazen: the *kunya* of Mahmoud Abbas.

Al Aqsa: the third holiest place in Islam and the holiest in Judaism. It is a compound containing a mosque with a foundation stone at its core that is believed by some religious figures to be the rock on which Adam, Cain, Abel, Noah, and Abraham offered sacrifices to God, and the center of the earth. Muslims believe that the Prophet Mohammed ascended to heaven from the mosque during the Night Journey.

Al Aqsa Martyrs Brigade: a Fatah militia created in 2002 that fought Israeli soldiers and was responsible for suicide bomb attacks in Israel during the Second Intifada.

Allenby Bridge (aka King Hussein Bridge): the border crossing between Jordan and Israel.

Areas A, B, C: three temporary administrative districts created by the Oslo Accords that are distributed according to population concentrations in the West Bank and Gaza; still in use today. The PA has full control of Area A—about 2.7 percent of the land area—including all Palestinian cities and surrounding areas without an Israeli presence. Area B—some 25 percent of the land area—is shared between Israeli military control and Palestinian civil control. Area C—72.2 percent of the land area—is under full Israeli control, except where Palestinian civilians are concerned. Area C includes all settlements, surrounding land, roadways connecting settlements, and "security zones."

asabiya: communal loyalty.

Ashkenazi: European Jew.

Battle of Karameh: an epic military confrontation between the Israeli army and the PLO and Jordanian forces in the Jordanian town of Karameh. Israel eventually took the town but not before suffering heavy casualties, including 33 dead and 161 wounded.

British mandate: mandate or administrative approval issued by the League of Nations under which the British ruled Palestine from 1917 to 1948.

Cedar Revolution: a wave of demonstrations in Lebanon in March 2005 following the assassination of then–Prime Minister Rafik Hariri. The movement ejected Syrian troops from the country and dislodged a pro-Syrian regime.

DFLP: Democratic Front for the Liberation of Palestine. A Marxist split-off from the PFLP with an emphasis on grassroots political work rather than military actions. It was also the only Palestinian militia that admitted Israeli Jewish members, most notably Udi Adiv in 1972.

dishdasha: an ankle-length robelike garment with long sleeves traditionally worn by Arab men.

dunam: a unit of land measurement established under the Ottoman Empire. One metric dunam is equivalent to 1,000 square meters.

Egyptian Islamic Jihad (al-Jihad): a radical Sunni Jihadist group in Egypt that aimed to overthrow the government and create an Islamic state. The group was outlawed after it assassinated Egyptian President Anwar Sadat in 1981. In June 2001 the group merged with Al Qaida.

Eid al-Adha: a major Muslim religious event known as the "Festival of Sacrifice" to commemorate Abraham's willingness to sacrifice his son to God.

Fatah: the largest faction within the PLO and sponsor of many of its militant groups.

Fatah al-Islam: a radical Sunni Jihadist organization in Lebanon that draws inspiration from Al Qaida.

Fedayeen: lit., "those who self-sacrifice"; used to denote Palestinian guerrilla or resistance fighters.

fellah (pl. fellahin): a peasant or small farmer with land to till. As Islam spread, the term was used to differentiate agricultural laborers from Bedouin or other nomadic populations.

Ghajar: Lebanese town on the border with Israel whose southern half is occupied by Israel.

Gush Dan: the Tel Aviv municipal area that stretches from Herzliyah to Rehovot.

habibi: "dear," a term of affection.

Hagada: a Jewish prayer book for the festival of Passover.

Haganah: the Jewish standing army under the British mandate and precursor of the Israeli Defense Forces.

Hamas: Palestine's largest national-religious movement, combining a political wing that has held sole power in Gaza since June 2007, with a militia that has engaged in attacks on Israel.

haram: "forbidden."

Hassan Nasrallah: the leader of Lebanon's Hezbollah movement.

Hezbollah: a Shi'a-based Lebanese political party and militia that was born as a resistance group under Israeli occupation and has fought Israel several times since.

Histadrut: Israeli Jewish trade union.

Hizme: a relatively liberal checkpoint near Jerusalem.

hudna: truce, armistice, or ceasefire.

IDF: Israeli Defense Forces; the Israeli army.

insha'allah: lit., "God willing"; used to indicate a hope or sometimes a noncommittal fatalism.

Islamic Jihad: national-religious militia and political party that split from the Muslim Brotherhood in the late 1970s.

Istiqlal: radical Palestinian Arab nationalist party established in 1932 that grew in tandem with a mood for mass resistance.

Izzedine al-Qassam Brigades: military wing of Hamas.

jalbab: a long, loose-fitting garment worn by some Muslim women. A modern jalbab covers the whole body except for the hands, face, and head.

Jibril Rajoub: former head of the Palestinian Authority's Preventive Security Force in the West Bank and a current member of Fatah's central committee.

kaffiyeh: a checked scarf traditionally worn by Bedouins that first became a symbol of resistance during the 1936 Revolt. Black and white kaffiyehs are associated with Fatah, red and white with the PFLP and the DFLP, green and white with Hamas and sometimes women.

Katyusha: a multiple rocket launcher first developed by Russia in World War II and used extensively by Hezbollah in its 2006 war with Israel. Katyushas can fire massive amounts of explosives but are difficult to aim accurately.

khallas: "enough."

khilafa: caliphate.

kibbutz (pl. kibbutzim): an Israeli agricultural commune widely used to settle land in the pre-state period.

L'chaim: lit., "To life!" A Jewish toast.

laissez passé: an identity document issued by a government or international treaty organization to facilitate the movement of individuals across international boundaries.

Likud: a right-wing Israeli political party founded in 1973 by Menachem Begin, a former leader of the far right Irgun militia, inspired by the revisionist Zionism of Ze'ev Jabotinsky, a fellow traveler of Mussolini.

Lyd: the original Arabic name for the Israeli town of Lod.

Ma salaama: "good-bye."

Majdal Shams: a large town in the Israeli-occupied Golan Heights.

Marwan Barghouthi: Fatah leader and founder of the Tanzim militia from the West Bank's "young guard." He was arrested by Israel in 2002 on charges of killing Israeli civilians and soldiers and sentenced to five life sentences, in what Palestinians regard as a show trial. He remains one of the most popular Fatah figures in Palestine.

Mizrahi: a Jew from an Arab country.

moshav: an Israeli agricultural unit similar to a kibbutz, without collective ownership.

mujahidin: fighters in a jihad; in modern usage, guerrilla insurgents.

mukhabarat: secret police.

mukhtar: lit., "chosen"; a village head elected or consensually appointed, often for purposes of negotiation with external forces.

Nakba: lit. "Catastrophe"; the name given to the war of 1948 and subsequent flight and exile of at least 750,000 Palestinian refugees.

nargila: water pipe, also known as a sheesha or hookah.

National Liberation Front (FLN): a former Algerian national liberation movement that became a governing party.

nebekh: Yiddish, meaning madman or crazy thing.

Negotiations Support Unit: a twenty-person-strong office of the PA's Negotiations Affairs Department providing legal, policy, technical, and communications advice to Palestinian negotiators concerning Permanent Status negotiations with Israel. It was originally set up and funded by the British government's Department for International Development but has since been financially supported by Denmark, the Netherlands, Norway, and Sweden.

October days or events: a series of protests by Arab citizens in Israel in support of the Intifada over the course of October 2000. Twelve Palestinian Israelis were shot dead by the Israeli army while demonstrating.

Operation Defensive Shield: a massive Israeli invasion and reoccupation of the West Bank that followed a suicide bombing in Netanya that killed 30 people. During the offensive, 500 Palestinians are thought to have been killed and 1,500 wounded.

Palestinian Authority or Palestinian National Authority (PA): a pregovernmental administrative body set up to govern the West Bank and Gaza under the Oslo Accords in 1994. It was supposed to be a five-year interim body to serve until final status negotiations were completed but is still in place today.

Palestinian Legislative Council (PLC): an elected legislature or parliament of the Palestinian Authority. At the time of writing it had not met since 2007.

Palestinian Liberation Organization (PLO): the political and military group founded in 1964 to represent secular national aspirations. It was subsequently recognized as "the sole legitimate representative of the Palestinian people," but since the 1980s Islamic movements such as Hamas have challenged this.

Palestinian National Council (PNC): legislative body of the PLO.

Palmach: the regular fighting force of the Haganah, Israel's 1948, pre-state army.

Popular Front for the Liberation of Palestine (PFLP): A Maoist militia that grew out of George Habash's Arab National Movement (ANM) in 1969. It was frequently more militant than Fatah and famed within Palestine for audacious plane hijackings and attacks such as the 2001 assassination of the Israeli government minister Rehavam Ze'evi. It is a faction within the PLO, although it remains opposed to the Oslo Accords.

ruwwad: pioneers.

Salafi: lit., "predecessor"; a religious strain that seeks to re-create a "pure" form of Islam based on an interpretation of the Muslim religion as it existed in the seventh century.

Sayed Quth: the leading Muslim Brotherhood intellectual in the 1950s and 1960s who was tortured and killed by the Egyptian state in 1966. He has been cited by many as an inspiration for Al Qaida.

Shabbak: an acronym for the Shin Bet, Israel's internal secret service.

shahada: martyrdom.

shahid: a Muslim who has died fulfilling a religious obligation or waging war for Islam; martyr.

shaykh: lit., "elder"; a revered wise man or scholar with communal authority.

shebab: street youths.

sheesha: a water pipe.

Shi'a, Shi'ite: the second largest branch of Islam and the majority religious current among Muslims in Lebanon.

Shura, Shora: a Muslim consultative council.

Stern Gang (or Lehi): a far-right Jewish militia that attacked Palestinian and British civilian and military targets under the British mandate.

sulha: a process of third-party mediation, compromise, and reconciliation leading to peace. The three letter root of the word *S-L-H* has the same root as the Hebrew word *sliha,* meaning "to forgive."

Sunni Islam: the largest branch of Islam and the majority denomination among Palestinians.

Tunis generation: the PLO and Fatah exiles who were expelled from Lebanon in 1982 and took up residence in the Maghreb. Tunis was their headquarters.

Yahud: Arabic term meaning "Jew."

yalla: "Come on!"

yani: "like," "you know," "sort of."

Yishuv: the pre-1948 Israeli Jewish parastate structure.

SELECTED BIBLIOGRAPHY
AND FURTHER READING

Achcar, Gilbert. *The Arabs and the Holocaust: The Arab-Israeli War of Narratives.* Metropolitan, 2010.

Armstrong, Karen. *Jerusalem: One City, Three Faiths.* Random House, 1996.

Ashrawi, Hanan. *This Side of Peace: A Personal Account.* Touchstone, 1996.

Busby, Chris. *Uranium and Health: The Health Effects of Exposure to Uranium and Uranium Weapons Fallout.* European Committee on Radiation Risk, No. 2. Brussels, 2010.

Caridi, Paola. *Hamas: From Resistance to Government?* Passia, 2010.

Chomsky, Noam. *The Fateful Triangle: Israel, the United States and the Palestinians.* Black Rose, 1984.

Cohen, Hillel. *Army of Shadows: Palestinian Collaboration with Zionism, 1917–1948.* University of California Press, 2009.

Darwish, Mahmoud. *Unfortunately, It Was Paradise: Selected Poems.* University of California Press, 2003.

Finkelstein, Norman. *Image and Reality of the Israel-Palestine Conflict.* Verso, 1995.

Gaza Community Mental Health Project. Coping with Stress and Siege in Palestinian Families in the Gaza Strip (Cohort study III). 2009.

———. "Trauma, Grief, and PTSD in Palestinian Children Victims of War on Gaza." 2009.

———. "War on Gaza Survey Study: Death Anxiety, PTSD, Trauma, Grief, and Mental Health of Palestinian Victims of War on Gaza." 2009.

Habiby, Emile. *The Secret Life of Saeed: The Pessoptimist.* Interlink World Fiction Series, 2001. 1st ed. 1974.

Hroub, Khaled. *Hamas: A Beginner's Guide.* Pluto, 2006.

Human Rights Watch. *Off the Map: Land and Housing Rights Violations in Israel's Unrecognized Bedouin Villages.* Human Rights Watch, 2008.

Humphries, Isabelle. "Highlighting 1948 Dispossession in Israeli Courts." *Al-Majdal Quarterly* (1997).

International Crisis Group. *Tipping Point? Palestinians and the Search for a New Strategy.* Middle East Report No. 95. 2010.

Kanafani, Ghassan. *Men in the Sun and Other Palestinian Stories.* Lynne Rienner, 1998.

———. *Palestine's Children: Returning to Haifa and Other Stories.* Lynne Rienner, 2000.

Khaled, Leila. *My People Shall Live: The Autobiography of a Revolutionary.* Hodder and Stoughton, 1973.

Khalidi, Rashid Khalidi. *Palestinian Identity: The Construction of Modern Palestinian Consciousness.* Columbia University Press, 1997.

———. *The Iron Cage: The Story of the Palestinian Struggle for Statehood.* Beacon, 2006.

Khalidi, Walid Khalidi. *All That Remains: The Palestinian Villages Occupied and Depopulated by Israel in 1948.* Institute for Palestinian Studies, 2003.

Kimmerling, Baruch. "Process of Formation of Palestinian Collective Identities: The Ottoman and Colonial Periods." *Middle Eastern Studies* 36, no. 2 (2000).

Kimmerling, Baruch, and Joel S. Migdal. *The Palestinian People: A History.* Harvard University Press, 2003.

Luyendijk, Joris. *Hello Everybody! One Journalist's Search for Truth in the Middle East.* Profile, 2010.

Masalha, Nur. *The Politics of Denial: Israel and the Palestinian Refugee Problem.* Pluto, 2003.

Matar, Dina. *What It Means to Be Palestinian: Stories of Palestinian Peoplehood.* I. B. Tauris, 2011.

Morris, Benny. *Righteous Victims.* Vintage, 2001.

Orwell, George. *Homage to Catalonia.* 15th ed. Mariner, 1980.

Palestinian Central Bureau of Statistics. "Palestinians in Diaspora and in Historic Palestine End Year 2005."

Pappe, Ilan. *The Ethnic Cleansing of Palestine.* Oneworld, 2007.

———. *The Making of the Arab-Israeli Conflict, 1947–1951.* I. B. Tauris, 1992.

PCHR Special Report. "Inter-Palestinian Human Rights Violations in the Gaza Strip." 2009.

Robinson, Glenn E. "Palestinian Tribes, Clans, and Notable Families." *Strategic Insights* 7, no. 4 (2008).

Rose, John. *The Myths of Zionism.* Pluto, 2004.

Roy, Sara. *Failing Peace: Gaza and the Palestinian-Israeli Struggle.* Pluto, 2007.

Sacco, Joe. *Footnotes from Gaza.* Metropolitan, 2010.

Said, Edward. *Orientalism.* Vintage, 1979.

———. *The Question of Palestine.* Vintage, 1992.

Sayigh, Yezid. *Hamas Rule in Gaza: Three Years On.* Brandeis University Middle East Brief. 2010.

Schulz, Helena Lindholm, and Juliane Hammer. *The Palestinian Diaspora: Formation of Identities and Politics of Homeland*. Taylor and Francis, 2003.

Segev, Tom. *One Palestine Complete*. Little, Brown, 1999.

Shahin, Mariam. *Palestine: A Guide*. Interlink, 2005.

Shlaim, Avi. *The Iron Wall: Israel and the Arab World*. Penguin, 2000.

Suleiman, Yasir, and Ibrahim Muhawi. *Literature and Nation in the Middle East*. Edinburgh University Press, 2006.

Terkel, Studs. *American Dreams: Lost and Found*. Pantheon, 1980.

———. *Hope Dies Last: Keeping the Faith in Troubled Times*. New Press, 2004.

———. *Race: How Blacks and Whites Think and Feel about the American Obsession*. New Press, 2005.

Tolan, Sandy. *The Lemon Tree: An Arab, a Jew, and the Heart of the Middle East*. Bloomsbury, 2007.

U.N. Human Rights Council. *Human Rights in Palestine and Other Occupied Arab Territories*. U.N. Human Rights Council, 2009.

U.N. OCHA. *Locked In: The Humanitarian Impact of Two Years of Blockade on the Gaza Strip*. United Nations, 2009.

White, Ben. *Israeli Apartheid: A Beginner's Guide*. Pluto, 2009.

WHO Mission to the Gaza Strip. "Extended Report." 2009.

Zaharna, R. S. "The Ontological Function of Interpersonal Communication: A Cross-Cultural Analysis of Palestinians and Americans." *Howard Journal of Communications* (1991).

PHOTO CAPTIONS

All photos were taken by the author.

Page 17. Bisan and Abud Abdul Khadr Fihad

Page 21. Sharif al-Basyuni

Page 24. Amira al-Hayb holding up a photo of herself in military uniform in front of Al Aqsa Mosque

Page 28. Niral Karantaji

Page 32. Doha Jabr in traditional dabke costume

Page 37. Abdul Rahman Katanani sitting on a car in a Shatila street

Page 41. A protester in the West Bank village of Na'alin. "Nabil" wished to remain anonymous.

Page 50. Firaz Turkman

Page 53. Alla Subharin

Page 55. Ayman Nahas and Hanna Shamas

Page 59. Asmaa al-Goule at Gaza City's beach

Page 63. Neriman al-Jabari with one of her children in her husband's old guest room

Page 66. The late Mohammed al-Jabari

Page 67. Tamer Nafar onstage in Ramallah

Page 72. Abu Abed working underground

Page 76. "Omar" smoking in his flat

Page 87. Diana Buttu outside a Ramallah café

Page 94. Haifa Dwaikat in a Nablus women's center

Page 97. Hala Salem

Page 101. Sayed Kashua in his office

Page 105. Tawfiq Jabharin above his family's old land

Page 110. Fuad al-Hofesh

Text: 11.25/13.5 Garamond
Display: Ultramagnetic
Compositor: BookMatters, Berkeley
Printer and Binder: Sheridan Books, Inc.